THE CHURCH OF STOP SHOPPING
AND RELIGIOUS ACTIVISM

NORTH AMERICAN RELIGIONS

Series Editors: Tracy Fessenden (Arizona State University), Laura Levitt (Temple University), and David Harrington Watt (Haverford College)

Since its inception, the North American Religions book series has steadily disseminated gracefully written, pathbreaking explorations of religion in North America. Books in the series move among the discourses of ethnographic, textual, and historical analysis and across a range of topics, including sound, story, food, nature, healing, crime, and pilgrimage. In so doing they bring religion into view as a style and form of belonging, a set of tools for living with and in relations of power, a mode of cultural production and reproduction, and a vast repertory of the imagination. Whatever their focus, books in the series remain attentive to the shifting and contingent ways in which religious phenomena are named, organized, and contested. They bring fluency in the best of contemporary theoretical and historical scholarship to bear on the study of religion in North America. The series focuses primarily, but not exclusively, on religion in the United States in the twentieth and twenty-first centuries.

Books in the series

Ava Chamberlain, *The Notorious Elizabeth Tuttle: Marriage, Murder, and Madness in the Family of Jonathan Edwards*

Terry Rey and Alex Stepick, *Crossing the Water and Keeping the Faith: Haitian Religion in Miami*

Isaac Weiner, *Religion Out Loud: Religious Sound, Public Space, and American Pluralism*

Hillary Kaell, *Walking Where Jesus Walked: American Christians and Holy Land Pilgrimage*

Brett Hendrickson, *Border Medicine: A Transcultural History of Mexican American Curanderismo*

Jodi Eichler-Levine, *Suffer the Little Children: Uses of the Past in Jewish and African American Children's Literature*

Annie Blazer, *Playing for God: Evangelical Women and the Unintended Consequences of Sports Ministry*

Elizabeth Pérez, *Religion in the Kitchen: Cooking, Talking, and the Making of Black Atlantic Traditions*

Kerry Mitchell, *Spirituality and the State: Managing Nature and Experience in America's National Parks*

Finbarr Curtis, *The Production of American Religious Freedom*

M. Cooper Harriss, *Ralph Ellison's Invisible Theology*

Ari Y. Kelman, *Shout to the Lord: Making Worship Music in Evangelical America*

Joshua Dubler and Isaac Weiner, *Religion, Law, USA*

Shari Rabin, *Jews on the Frontier: Religion and Mobility in Nineteenth-Century America*

Elizabeth Fenton, *Old Canaan in a New World: Native Americans and the Lost Tribes of Israel*

Alyssa Maldonado-Estrada, *Lifeblood of the Parish: Men and Catholic Devotion in Williamsburg, Brooklyn*

Caleb Iyer Elfenbein, *Fear in Our Hearts: What Islamophobia Tells Us about America*

Rachel B. Gross, *Beyond the Synagogue: Jewish Nostalgia as Religious Practice*

Jenna Supp-Montgomerie, *When the Medium Was the Mission: The Atlantic Telegraph and the Religious Origins of Network Culture*

Philippa Koch, *The Course of God's Providence: Religion, Health, and the Body in Early America*

Jennifer Scheper Hughes, *The Church of the Dead: The Epidemic of 1576 and the Birth of Christianity in the Americas*

Sylvester Johnson and Tisa Wenger, *Religion and US Empire: Critical New Histories*

Deborah Dash Moore, *Vernacular Religion: Collected Essays of Leonard Norman Primiano*

Laura Yares, *Jewish Sunday Schools: Teaching Religion in Nineteenth-Century America*

Katrina Daly Thompson, *Muslims on the Margins: Creating Queer Religious Community in North America*

Jonathan H. Ebel, *From Dust They Came: Government Camps and the Religion of Reform in New Deal California*

Gale L. Kenny, *Consecrating Empire: Race and the Cosmopolitan Practices of Protestant Women, 1900–1945*

George González, *The Church of Stop Shopping and Religious Activism: Combatting Consumerism and Climate Change through Performance*

# The Church of Stop Shopping and Religious Activism

*Combatting Consumerism and Climate Change through Performance*

George González

NEW YORK UNIVERSITY PRESS
New York

NEW YORK UNIVERSITY PRESS
New York
www.nyupress.org

© 2024 by New York University
All rights reserved

Please contact the Library of Congress for Cataloging-in-Publication data.

ISBN: 9781479817702 (hardback)
ISBN: 9781479817733 (paperback)
ISBN: 9781479817757 (library ebook)
ISBN: 9781479817740 (consumer ebook)

This book is printed on acid-free paper, and its binding materials are chosen for strength and durability. We strive to use environmentally responsible suppliers and materials to the greatest extent possible in publishing our books.

Manufactured in the United States of America

10 9 8 7 6 5 4 3 2 1

Also available as an ebook

*For the Stop Shopping Choir with gratitude for all the days spent standing and all the nights spent dreaming.*

All proceeds from the sales of this book will be donated to the Stop Shopping Church emergency fund.

CONTENTS

Introduction: Reverend Billy, the Stop Shopping Church,
and the Religion of Everyday Life ... 1

ACT I: SCHOLARS AT THE SHOPOCALYPSE

1. Ritualization in the Age of Starbucks: Scholars and Activists
   in a Brand-New World ... 33
2. Privatizing the Consumer Soul ... 63

INTERMEZZO: REVEREND BILLY AND THE STOP
SHOPPING CHURCH AT MILLENNIUM'S EDGE

3. Crucifying Mickey Mouse to Save the Earth: From the
   Critique of Fetish to New Animisms ... 95

ACT II: ACTIVISTS AT THE SHOPOCALYPSE

4. Becoming the Beloved Community of Musical Earth ... 129
5. Performing the Shopocalypse in the Age of
   Post-Secular Capitalism ... 173

Conclusion: Scholars and Activists at the End of the World ... 207

*Acknowledgments* ... 229
*Notes* ... 237
*Bibliography* ... 291
*Index* ... 317
*About the Author* ... 337

# Introduction

*Reverend Billy, the Stop Shopping Church, and the Religion of Everyday Life*

Intelligence is a moral category. The separation of feeling and understanding that makes it possible to absolve and beatify the blockhead, hypostasizes the dismemberment of man [sic.] into functions.
—Theodor Adorno, *Minima Moralia*

Life is an unexplained miracle. This impossible world is what we have to work with, to enjoy—To have and then leave. This impossible life is the source of our insistence on the possible.
—Reverend Billy, *The End of the World*

## The Overlord's Vessel

Although I had been back in the New York City area for seven years, and back in the city itself for a full year, till that day I had still not made my way to the new Hudson Yards luxury development on Manhattan's far West Side, running from 30th to 34th streets between 10th and 12th avenues. The shiny new subway station for New York's self-proclaimed "newest neighborhood" (Related Companies) is especially cavernous. The escalators are so long from top to bottom that, riding them, I experienced a sense of temporary imbalance, feeling as if I were moving horizontally when I was really moving vertically. It's a feeling I associate with amusement park rides, when, at the end, you're not sure what's up and what's down.

Despite a year in the city proper, I also still had not yet regained all my muscle memory for being, especially walking, in New York. There are habits of the body—routines, cadences, and imperceptible, everyday movements—that keep you from bumping into people, literally and figuratively speaking, in a city of over eight million. Anyone who has found themself less able to read other people due to the protective masks worn during the COVID-19 pandemic understands the communicative importance of the micropolitics of the body—are a stranger's eyes narrowed in greeting or menace, for instance? And different contexts script our movements differently. It's taken years to relearn these habits after more than a decade away in relatively sleepy New England towns around Boston.

Through the looking glass, I move with East Asian and European tourists out of the station and into a twenty-first-century retail plaza for luxury brands. There, I meet up with Valentina,[1] a tenant's rights activist and cosmopolitan Chilean artist in her mid-forties who has exhibitions and residencies in places like Vienna, Santiago, and Barcelona. Especially because getting to Hudson Yards meant taking a subway line I have very little experience with, and taking it to a stop that hadn't existed the last time I rode it, it required concentrated effort for me to get to where I was going. Valentina, by comparison, is someone who is not a native New Yorker but has made this challenging city her own, a leitmotif in the ethnographic fieldwork that grounds this book.

Valentina is one of those people who often seems to be in several places at once: at work in the morning, at an action or protest across town at lunchtime, and at a performance many miles away in another borough come evening. I ask her about her manifest powers of translocation. Despite all of her cultural capital, Valentina, like many of the members of the group that is convening at Hudson Yards on this chilly Friday afternoon in December, often finds money hard to come by. Answering my question, she suggests: "It's precarity. Precarity does that to you."

What the anthropologists George Marcus and Douglas Holmes (2006) call the "fast capitalism" of finance also forces people to try to keep step with the vagaries of capital flows in the so-called real economy.[2] Political economy makes its corporeal impressions on us as workers as we rush, already exhausted by household care responsibilities, to second jobs where we must not only remain awake, but make sure to smile. That is to say that mutually reinforcing political institutions and economic systems are legible on the bodies of their living human conduits whose malnutrition, obesity, overwork, relative leisure, consumptive delight, distraction, anxieties, and pressing needs come to express these relationships of power.[3]

Valentina is a member of the Church of Stop Shopping, a radical performance community with which I had been doing fieldwork for three years at the point we met up on that December day in 2019. For those unfamiliar with the phenomenon that is the Church of Stop Shopping, it is a social action group and community that uses performance to promote what they call "Earth Justice" and to oppose the forces of consumerism on the global stage, taking on the corporate practices of Disney, Starbucks, J.P. Morgan Chase Bank, Walmart, and Amazon, among others. The Church has sung with Joan Baez and toured with Pussy Riot and Neil Young. They have performed at festivals around the world, and together, William Talen, aka the Church's Reverend Billy, and the Stop Shopping Church are recipients of the Obie Award, the Alpert Award in the Arts, the Edwin Booth Award in Theater (City University of New York), and the Historic District Lion's Award. The Church is also the subject of the nationally released 2007 documentary, *What Would Jesus Buy?*.[4]

The group has been importantly unencumbered by secularization theses that have worked to obscure the intensifying "soul-craft" of capitalism. I use the term soul-craft in this book to refer to capitalism's capacities to forge affective bonds and shape social imaginaries. Living under capitalism coerces people into feeling connected to brands, and to other people by way of brands. Capitalism's soul-craft is what makes me feel like I'm part of something bigger than myself when I buy a new pair of celebrity-endorsed sneakers or drive a particular kind of truck (hypothetically, of course). The Stop Shopping Church has always understood that capitalism is not simply a system whereby we produce and distribute goods in the most efficient manner but is, instead, a whole worldview that comes to shape who we are from the inside out. Capitalism *is us*, as Savitri D (the professional name of Reverend Billy's creative co-conspirator and partner in life, Savitri Durkee), the co-founder of the community, often laments, and always hopes to change. Capitalism is, most generally, the assemblage of human hopes, dreams, and desires that have become attached to the exploitative rule of capital and which the Stop Shoppers believe inhibit human life and keep us, in turn, from connecting with the natural world in the ways they feel we absolutely must.

Through its performances, street actions, and social activism,[5] the Stop Shopping Church has been critiquing the religious encroachments of neoliberal capitalism—specifically of capitalist soul-craft—since the 1990s. In essence, Reverend Billy and the Church of Stop Shopping argue that corporations and their celebrity spokespeople operate in much the same way churches do and work to ritualize consumers into accepting the neoliberal status quo. In their critique of the religious power of capitalism to organize our vision of and for the world, what the religion scholar Kathryn Lofton (2017) figures in terms of "consuming religion," the Stop Shopping Church is drawn to the sacred enunciations of urban branding like colorful moths to a white-hot flame. This is why we have come to Hudson Yards this holiday shopping season.

Looking at the retail spaces and storefronts, the yellows and oranges of Thanksgiving have given way to the iridescent white of fake snow. Fifty yards away, international and domestic tourists appeared to have adapted easily to their stage directions as they took pictures and selfies in front of the Vessel, marketed as New York's newest landmark. Billed as a vertical piece of interactive art reminiscent of a honeycomb and "comprised of 154 intricately interconnecting flights of stairs," the Vessel offers panoramas and views of the Hudson River and the surrounding Midtown neighborhood.[6] Each click of an iPhone camera further cemented its financially preordained and instantaneous iconicity. The Vessel, which had opened the previous March is, along with the whole of Hudson Yards, a brainchild of Mayor Mike Bloomberg's administration, which had ruled and transformed New York in the post–9/11 era. It is also perhaps its signature symbol, after the Freedom Tower.

In fact, the Freedom Tower and the Vessel alike might be best thought of as the neoliberal Bloomberg administration's very signature, written on the cityscape as a branded product.[7] The general turn to branding under neoliberalism presents a set of problems and opportunities for activists, scholars of North American religion, and Americanists, that serve as the mediatized, cityscaped backdrop for the interventions of this book. In contemporary North American society, branding is the primary mechanism according to which we become citizen consumers and endow the world we share with meaning.[8] As we will see, branding implies the ritualization and sacralization of economy.

This book argues that, in their activist tracing of the cartographies of contemporary consumer religiosity—that is, *consumption's role in ritualizing relationships and experiences*—the political praxes of the Stop Shopping Church dovetail precisely and generatively with recent work in religious studies, which possesses frames of analysis that are well poised to elucidate the ritual power of consumerism not only for itself but also for a broader readership in the humanities and social sciences. In her pathbreaking and field-defining analyses of neoliberal religion, studies that have yielded lessons the discipline is still absorbing, Kathryn Lofton (2011, 2017, 2019) explores our intensive and intimate reformatting by the disciplines of purchase-as-practice, thus rejoining religion, and those who study it, to a grounding in political economy. Lofton's *Consuming Religion* (2017) is a pivotal scholarly joist that helped me bring together the two central, conjoining, axes of work in this book—my fieldwork with the Church of Stop Shopping and a critique of religious studies as a discipline. By which I mean, the ways in which I take the lessons I learned in the field and explore how they can help me—and other scholars across religion and related disciplines—do our own work differently and better.

Across our subfields, area complexes, and time periods, religion scholars appreciate the power of religious places set apart to govern—ceremonial centers that compel ritual adoration and, through material and existential tribute, further enhance their religious, cultural, and political reach.[9] The power of architectural icons and monuments can sometimes be successfully harnessed and hotwired by resisters, malcontents, and activists in the service of denunciation and critique. This is why Patricia Okoumou, a Congolese immigrant dubbed the Statue of Liberty Climber, chose the July 4 holiday in 2018 to climb the pedestal of the Statue of Liberty to protest the Trump administration separating families at the border and putting kids in cages.[10] It is also why the Stop Shopping Church has come to Hudson Yards on this day. The Church understands that the power of iconicity can be subverted and redirected in the criticism of contemporary capitalism and its iconic brands.[11]

For religion scholars, discussions of how branding entails the production of knowledge and identities through consumer activity, bringing up the role of architecture and place is likely to bring to mind artifacts and archives that can include gargoyles, incense, Birthright Israel trips, and the Hajj.[12] As well they should, of course, if we recall that earlier examples of capitalism's spatial technologies such as the Woolworth Building in downtown Tribeca were meant to evoke the form and function of an iconic religious temple: the medieval European cathedral.[13]

It is certainly right and exceedingly instructive to couch the advent of the billionaire's city within practices of urban branding. However, only through a familiar secular alchemy—to which I will attend ethnographically, theoretically, and historically in this book—does it become possible to disavow the religious aspects of Hudson Yards as a coordinating power. In its own consumerist idiom, Hudson Yards provides pilgrims with the requisite kinds and quantities of capital—both financial and cultural—access to highly valued forms of immaterial goods. With its latticed constitution, the Vessel is a celebration of contemporary capitalism's synecdochical, financialized, and networked global spirit.[14]

If, as Lofton suggests (2017, 13), "*religion* is a word to intensify what we do when we name authority, practice interactions, and interpret life itself," the Vessel is a religious icon of the furtive and dynamic spirit of postindustrial capitalism.[15] This incarnation of capitalism celebrates its rhizomatic structure, is awash in Pixar colorizations, and—existentially structured by the many refractions of commoditized memory—is doused in the sticky sweetness of nostalgia. Consumer capitalism's power is mediated through the feelings it produces.[16] In the twentieth century, especially in the postwar period, the feelings produced by American popular culture were already an important dimension of foreign policy (May and Wagnleitner 2000). As the activists will suggest, in the early twenty-first century, the brand icons of American popular culture are a form of religious media with global reach, purporting to organize the networked world (externalized in miniature by the Vessel) at the expense of vulnerable communities around the globe and the very planet that must support all this living, in the end.

At the dawning of President Ronald Reagan's "morning in America" in the 1980s, the Marxist urbanist and modernist, Marshall Berman, suggested that the denizens of modern cities like New York are marked by our attempts to make ourselves at home in a world in which capitalism threatens to objectify and stifle human creativity at every turn.

While capitalism accelerates the melting of "all fixed, fast-frozen relations" into air, this ominous and dangerous process also "brings our energies and imaginations to life" as we "fight to make ourselves at home in this world" (1982, 348). Valentina is a leading member of a community of singing activists, who has been interpolated by her historical situation to struggle to make herself at home in the world in particularly creative ways.[17]

The Stop Shopping Church has long understood the religious power—that is, the organizing power—of secular capitalism with critical precision and has responded to its sacralizing pretentions in "post-religious" religious kind.[18] They know that it is not only capitalism's Orientalist and romantic appetites for Sadhana practices, Gregorian chants, Catrina masks, and Tibetan prayer flags that we must track, but the religiously disavowed religious power of urban nymphs like the Starbucks mermaid and the magical speculations of corporate overlords like Chase bank, as well. Most particularly to the point for this book, their critical approach entails marshaling the resources of religion to affect the critique of financialized consumerist religion.

\* \* \*

We are ten or so strong on this day when we are instructed by the director of the Choir and Savitri D to make our way to the top floor of the building that houses the shops at Hudson Yards. To avoid bringing attention to ourselves, we break into groups of two and three. We often speak of making our way through physical impediments, like brush or a crowd, but an analogy can be drawn to our spatial relationships with sound as well, especially if what we hear grates on us, wears on us, or otherwise compels us. Anyone who has been at a loud concert or dance club with crowds of people knows that admixture of bodies, perspiration, bad product, and sound amplification that materializes musical notes in more than one sense.

In this case, the requisite bubblegum Christmas music is broadcast in full sonic force. I trudge through it, and through the mall perfume. If, as Guy Debord ([1967] 1994) suggests, the society of the spectacle "has invented a visual form for itself" (14),[19] it is also true that aural and olfactory signifiers should give expression to the society of the spectacle. I fancy myself immune to these particular musical charms (though, embarrassingly, I have been known to ask Alexa to play Christmas music as I bake cookies in December—if somewhat cheekily, I tell myself). The truth is, a lot of professional know-how and money ride on the wager that sound and music compel and give shape to our shopping behavior. Music has also long been understood to be one of religion's most powerful and compelling agents for ritual action (e.g., see Engelhardt 2012).[20] As we will see, it makes good sense for a group dedicated to pushing back capitalism's religious power to take the songful approach.

As we ride up on the escalators (much less daunting than the ones at the subway station and designed to give riders the opportunity to look around this winter wonderland) and walk through the floors, I am struck by the glossiest UNICEF advertisement poster I've ever seen placed amidst the high-end retail stores for international luxury brands such as Piaget and Cartier. I think to myself that this juxtaposition makes a lot of sense, in practice. Especially at this end of the economic spectrum, wealth comes with a sense of responsibility, especially during the holiday season. So long as the felt beneficence is not recast in the register of redistribution and social obligation, contemporary noblesse oblige can't stomach too much feasting without some giving back.[21]

For the elite classes who claim it all, from money to spiritual nobility, it is in the script.[22] Scrooge's redemption is an important part of the story arc. Even for the middle classes, in a different way, the right to enjoy is paid for in the compulsion to give, as any of us who have put coins and dollar bills into the metal cans of Santa Clauses collecting for charity in November and December understands. This kind of mundane, proto-ethical logic of reciprocity might be easy to miss amidst all the critique of consumption. However, as Reverend Billy (Talen 2003, 56) himself concedes, when he is not engaged in polemic and prophetic denunciation, Americans "shop to be together; they shop to belong." He has long understood that easy feelings of solidarity, connection, and care fuel neoliberal consumption.

Once we reach the fifth floor, an impromptu comparing of notes ensues. Leo, a talented singer and actor who came very close to being cast in the original run of the hit Broadway musical *Rent*, notes with clear disgust in his voice that the window displays of the high-end retail shops we marched past were going for something highly theatrical. Is it precisely because the inverted spectacle of it all is so clear to Leo (given his talents and line of work) that the offense is even stronger? For her part, Joana, a young performance artist from Puerto Rico who joined the group after fleeing the disastrous effects of Hurricane María on her home, suggests that the Neiman Marcus display is a combination of the Kardashians and the Last Supper.[23] I remember that my parents had a record of Christmas carols arranged, performed, and produced as disco songs featuring pop icons of the 1970s like Diana Ross. That, today, the Kardashians can find their way to the Holy Manger is actually not surprising.

His voice booming across the abyss like Peter Jackson's Gandalf casting away the Balrog deep inside Moria,[24] Reverend Billy, the titular character in this passion play, begins to sermonize to the shoppers and retailers around us within the belly of the beast. He proclaims: "We're sedated by shopping and colors!" This is a man who has publicly pondered his drenching in the mundane affects of capital for more than two decades. He understands very well that capitalism's everyday practices are more like religious ritual than cold transactional exchange premised on utility and efficiency. As the religion academe had settled into a consideration of the power of religion in the public square,[25] he was preaching on the religious power of the retail plaza.[26]

When Billy wraps up his short sermon, we triumphantly make our way back down the escalators, quite intentionally, as I have learned, *al* Jesus and his disciples on Palm Sunday, the music playing out in tandem with our pied piper performance. As the marketers with whom the Reverend engages in spiritual warfare certainly know, bodies engaged in movement and song can reveal, conjure, and manifest narrative structures, many of which remain hidden at first glance and upon initial hearing.[27] Chanting "Shopping caused climate change/climate caused human change/STOP SHOPPING!," we process back down to the lobby, as some workers, mostly women and people of color, from the food shops and clothing stores that line the way down, come out to take videos with their camera phones, smiling, some of them pumping their fists. A ragtag bunch, we had entered the eye of the consumerist storm. The vibes we were receiving from the crowd were generally good, even heartwarming. Although they remained latent, the cultural resonances with Jesus's prophetic return to Jerusalem in fanfare helped narratively ground the procession, much as they have many a Reverend Billy action. They were a portal and bridge into different matrices of inchoate meaning.[28]

As we were showered in hosannas, I thought to myself: delineating the borders between resistance and more consumption can be very tricky. For these service workers—left behind by the financial gains of Bloomberg's luxury city, but, nevertheless, still its laboring, affective backbone—was our action just better entertainment than the bad Christmas pop, captivating in the moment but bound to end up forgotten in the digital graves of smartphones? Or would it provide a jolt and be remembered? Did a space of negativity break the spell of consumerism, even if just temporarily?[29]

Building security workers join us from behind and escort us to the lobby without force or obvious intimidation. Reverend Billy and Savitri D like to say that there is a vast difference between the behavior and tactics of security in high-end retail spaces and the NYPD, for example. In this, they do not mean to suggest that the former are more enlightened for being mannerly but that they understand, like Bourdieu ([1979] 1984) did, that capital is differentially lived out through our tastes, habits, and dispositions right down to the granular level of the ways in which we respond to situations and carry and move about our bodies.[30] Social life is mediated by symbolically constructed and maintained structures of action consonant with our relative placement within society (Bourdieu [1972] 1977). As a living matter, capital is always and already cultural.

According to the terms in which Reverend Billy often puts it, our everyday gestures are, to some never totalizing degree, *choreographed*.[31] Socialization implies opportunities for resocialization and ritual transformation, as anyone who has studied religion knows. And in his way, Reverend Billy is an excellent student of the somatic materiality of religion and ritual. He has even been known to do warm ups with his merry disciples before a retail action (Talen 2006, 28): "Breaking through the strict choreography of products and retail environments takes body-and-soul readiness . . . breathing and stretching beforehand helps."

At the level of embodiment, capitalization is a scripted, semiotically mediated process, which is a source of both great power and perduring vulnerability.[32] As we will see later on, neoliberal capitalism's consumer performances today imply what religion scholars call *ritualization* and *performativity*. To begin that conversation, I want to recognize that American advertising at either side of the new millennium has understood consumers as being produced by signifying practices that exist prior to the individual and that bring the acting individual to life. In short, brands want us to have no real choice but to consume their pre-directed meanings and look to sell us our straitjackets in the name of practices of freedom. The Stop Shopping Church implores us to not buy the hype. We can back away from consumerism, they suggest, even if doing so will imply its own kind of religious transformation.

I hear two of the male plainclothes security guards, who look like they could be office workers out to lunch only a bit burlier than the norm, discuss an expensive pair of sneakers one of them had recently purchased. Reverend Billy and his merry band of anti-consumer activists have been here before, so the stakes are lower. No one seems worried that the good Reverend is actually the kind of anarchist who carries Molotov cocktails. The preacher asks the guards for just one thing, performatively channeling the strategies of religious social activists from the past: space and time to pray. This further diffuses the tension. In fact, it is not only a defensive action; it's also a rhetorical strategy for roping in the opposition.[33] Reverend Billy educates his flock, forgiving his enemies: "Earth, our great creator . . . these workers . . . we know they have family too."

We step outside, back into the courtyard in front of this twenty-first-century luxury mall. Reverend Billy, then a very youthful sixty-nine-year-old white man in a preacher's costume, paints an absurdist picture of the ills of consumerism *en plein air*. As she often does, Savitri D keeps the singers in time and on the beat from the periphery, snapping her fingers and exhorting us with her facial expressions. An oldie but goodie from Billy's early days as a parodic, right-wing fundamentalist preacher still does the trick. Plaintively, confusedly, he likes to ask: *Are logos and brands our lovers?*

As if the universe has conspired to write an unexpected extra into this well-produced scene of street theater and to sharpen the good Reverend's rhetorical contrast between the cheap grace of consumption and the poignant warmth of human solidarity, a young white man in his twenties approaches. He makes his way through the singers and the melodies with which they accompany Reverend Billy's sermon, and gives the preacher a hug. He explains: He's been at Hudson Yards all week hanging up Christmas lights and has come to loathe the place. All he wants for Christmas is to be done with it. The musical performance had beckoned him away from the hall of products. Given what they call the "human scale" of their world-making program, Stop Shopping Church performances are predicated upon the hope for little moments like these, where personal transformation prefigures the possibilities of collective revolution.[34]

## The Stop Shopping Church

The character of Reverend Billy was originally developed in the 1990s as a piece of performance art and street theater by William Talen, an actor, writer, and musician from the Midwest who was in his late forties when he came to New York City for the theater only to, instead, discover a preponderance of what he calls "retail theater." He began his storied political street theater campaign as the character of Reverend Billy, a mélange of fundamentalist televangelist and Elvis Presley. In its original conception, the character sought, in its performance of parody, to grind together the signifiers of consumer capitalism and right-wing American Protestantism in order to bring attention to their political and functional co-implications. Assuming the mantel of the "new American preacher," Reverend Billy spoke of making the early discovery that "corporations and their celebrity spokespersons operate very much the way churches do" (Talen 2003, 46). He also spoke of consumers being "ritualized" into accepting, again, the *choreographies* of consumer capitalism. As we will see, at millennium's razor's edge, Reverend Billy took on the turbo-technicolored Imagineering of the Disney Company and the commercial romanticism of Starbucks.

Having developed in the subsequent twenty-plus-years into a radical performance community of singing activists based out of New York City with affiliations and connections across the globe, the Stop Shopping Church has conducted actions directed at the corporate practices of, among others, Monsanto (now Beyer), J.P. Morgan Chase Bank, PNC Bank, British Petroleum, Walmart, UBS, Bank of America, Deutsche Bank, and, most recently, Amazon. They have also protested the research priorities of Harvard University,[35] shone a critical light on the

Koch Foundation's patronage of Lincoln Center, been involved in anti-gentrification efforts in New York City, and accepted invitations from around the country and the world to support activists regarding issues of local and global interest.

In 2009, Reverend Billy even entered the New York City mayoral race as the Green Party candidate "in character," opposing Michael Bloomberg's third term.[36] The multiracial, queer, and multigenerational "Church" has been involved on the ground supporting emerging social movements such as Occupy Wall Street and Black Lives Matter, as well as the protests in Ferguson and at Standing Rock.[37] Maintaining an anti-consumerism core, the community prioritizes the work for racial justice, queer liberation, justice and sanctuary for immigrants, First Amendment issues, and the reclaiming of public space.

At the same time, whether this involves joining protests opposing proposed pipelines in the Tristate area, protecting community gardens, protesting the practice of mountain top removal in Appalachia, mapping the use of carcinogenic and bee-killing Glysophate in New York City parks,[38] bringing attention to species extinction, casting a light on J.P. Morgan Chase's financing of climate change, or connecting Amazon delivery trucks to carbon emissions, the struggle for what the group calls "Earth Justice" has taken center stage in the group's activist work and musical performances. The group uses the term "Shopocalypse" to denote the role our consumption plays in the Earth's unfolding Extinction event.[39] Today, as this book chronicles and analyzes, the group calls for a religious reevaluation of human embodiment and an attendant recognition of humanity's constitutive and intimate interrelationships with the natural world.

Together, William Talen and Savitri D have authored five books and have recorded three podcast series chronicling their work with social movements. The Stop Shopping Church has recorded CDs and digital albums of its sermons and songs and, among others, has been in residence at St. Mark's in the Bowery, Theater 80, and Joe's Pub, all in their beloved New York City.[40] They have performed at festivals around the world and have collaborated with activist partner "saints"[41] including MacArthur Fellow and fellow performance artist, Guillermo Gómez-Peña, Code Pink, the Queer Liberation March, and the late anarchist anthropologist, David Graeber.

Figure I.1. The Stop Shopping Gospel Choir at the Millennium. Photo by the Stop Shopping Church.

In 2020, William Talen was offered a contract by WABC Radio, New York, to do a national show based on Reverend Billy sermons on Sunday mornings at 2 am. Also in 2020, Reverend Billy and Savitri D began a new podcast series entitled "Extinction Talk Radio" (aka "Reverend Billy Radio"). Although he is suspicious of digitally mediated life, like other American preachers before him, from Charles Finney to Oprah Winfrey, Reverend Billy has found emerging media technologies can be important tools for spreading, as in this case, the often not so good news.

## Whither and How the Scholars

There is, however, another cast of characters that must also be introduced. This book is *not* a traditional ethnography *of* a group of interlocutors from whom the scholar primarily learns things about the empirical world (e.g., about an outside cultural situation or case) by applying the knowledge and skills they already have entering into fieldwork relationships. The book aims, instead, to interrupt scholarly framings that presume such a clear separation between the ethnographer and the subjects of fieldwork. Indeed, under the present rule of capital, the embodied movements of both scholars and those whom they study are constrained and structured by the same capital process, even if, very importantly, the material benefits of the system that organizes these relationships of value are always unevenly distributed.

Keeping these structured relationships in mind, this book is interested in and committed to an investigation of the interrelationships between the thought and practices of scholars of religion (and the fields and discourses from which we borrow), on the one hand, and those of grassroots activists, on the other. As the members of the Stop Shopping Church have long understood, our climate catastrophe is a direct consequence of consumer capitalism's religious power. Scholars of religion and of the humanities and social sciences, more generally, do well to take inspiration from the Stop Shoppers' praxeological excavations of the spaces between religion and economy and to consider what they do and why they do it in terms of a sophisticated grassroots theorizing in its own right. The group's labors, I will argue, help us reinterpret classics of scholarship and reorient our relationships to them. They also suggest materially minded directions scholarship might take in light of consumer capitalism's religious enclosure of the privatized self.

Drawing on insights from the fieldwork, in what follows, I make the case that both scholars and activists have been ritualized by branding, the cultural process according to which consumer selves are made in neoliberal times. This shared reality has implications that are at once intellectual and political. In short, this book turns to practices of close reading and forms of ethnographic and historiographic empiricism in order to explore the relationship of scholarly thinking to the very broken, often murderous, neoliberal world scholars look to study, mean to analyze, and, increasingly, critique. In the pages ahead, directed convergences of fieldwork description, sociological and historical analysis, and explicit reconsiderations of religious studies theory operate in tandem to identify and suggest caveats and lessons for scholars about the work we do in Shopocalyptic times.

\* \* \*

When I first arrived in Cambridge, Massachusetts, as a graduate student at Harvard Divinity School in 2004, I was anxiously transfixed by the new, glitzy, iPod campaign plastered all over the walls of Boston's bus and train depot, South Station. Silhouettes figured in ecstatic poses beckoned commuters and travelers to plug in and tune out. I was immediately struck by the ecstatic religiosity of the displays but was unable to speak its name, not because they were too *Heilige* (the terrifying and numinous holy) as in Rudolph Otto's ([1917] 1958) work, or even because they are too profane (pertaining to everyday times and places), as in Mircea Eliade's ([1957] 1959). They were, in fact, too *economic*. The turn to secularism studies and, from that, to religion and economy, was still nascent. We had not yet returned, as a field, to considerations of social organization as the study of religious power.

Graduate seminars in theories and methods introduced me to the work of Talal Asad (1993), Daniel Dubuisson (2003), Tomoko Masuzawa (2005), Catherine Bell (1992) and others who, taken together, wove a genealogy of religion's thoroughgoing discursivity. These texts had much to say about the Western construction of religion as a category and about the political self-interest embedded in institutionalized ideas about religion. Especially in light of the ways we discussed them, however, these texts also had oddly little to directly say about capitalism.[42] The curriculum I was introduced to as a member of my generational and disciplinary cohort at Harvard Divinity School presumed a distance between religion and economy. In largely ignoring capitalist economy (implicitly associating it, instead, with loveless, instrumental reason alone in contradistinction to the somatic affects and poetry of religion), whole swaths of religious studies in recent generations remained unwittingly pious in their unstated and unremarked upon commitment to maintaining the chasm between religion and capitalism that none other than the most famous sociologist of religion and economy, Max Weber, had so diligently dug in the case of the so-called Modern West.[43]

There was an implicit consensus since the forging of religious studies as a discipline in the 1960s that capitalism is very precisely not religion. The animating assumptions of Max Weber's ([1904–1905] 2002) spirit of capitalism, it must be admitted, sealed the discipline's original charter.[44] Weber famously argued that although a particular religious history, that of sixteenth-century Dutch Calvinism, had played a necessary (but insufficient) role in the development of the ethos of capitalism in the modern West, a distinguishing feature of secular modernity would be the progressive differentiation of capitalist rationality from religious value, the apogee of which he anticipated to be the case of the United States.⁴⁵ Weber had also assumed that capitalism's "routinized economic cosmos" was characterized by an endemic lack of affect and its strong differentiation from the worlds and interests of psychology and art. As a result of religious studies' indebtedness to the assumptions of postwar social science, matters of psyche and aesthetics became field-adjacent concerns while capitalism was often allowed to disappear from our disciplinary radar.⁴⁶

Whether explicitly or implicitly following Weber, much of religious studies had detached its perseverations upon libidinality from matters of political economy in the decades immediately prior to my arrival in Cambridge. As a consequence, since we had too often framed capitalism in terms of what the historian of American religion and transnational capitalism, Bethany Moreton (2007), calls "cold economic logic" rather than its lived and sinuous effulgence, we collectively tended to miss neoliberal capitalism's stealthy metabolizations of broad affective swaths of human experience, including issues of religious meaning. Panning back to my then unspeakable vision of religion in the bus depot, the afterlife of Max Weber's anathematization of religion and capitalism had, in fact, rendered me mute.

As a scholar, I greatly benefited from Kathryn Lofton's redeployment of Émile Durkheim's sociology in order to reengage with the religious power of nominally nonreligious social systems like consumer capitalism that collectively organize us. Lofton's intervention has given us refurbished tools with which, in a productively full-throated way, to apprehend and begin to speak to the religious power the Weberian taboo had worked to obscure for me at the bus depot and which the Stop Shoppers had apprehended from the start.⁴⁷

The iPod silhouettes, I am able to say now, resonated with the ecstatic, techno-mystical elements of plugging in and tuning out in nominally secular spaces and time.⁴⁸ Apple knows that there is no strict division between body and soul and quite literally banks on the mutual cooperation of magic, science, and religion to sell its machines. Apple has always known that the hierarchies and oppositions between magic, science, and religion are no longer economically productive.⁴⁹ Contemporary capitalism is in no way interested in limiting itself to the interests generated by instrumental reason alone.

Secular enchantment depends on dynamic forces of encounter that connect the human and the nonhuman through forms of technological mediation (Thrift 2010). Already by the mid-twentieth century, marketing magic threatened to expose the con of the heroic, masculine self, pulling himself up by bootstraps attached to boots already suggested to him in advance through the suprarational means of advertisement. As we will consider, especially through an infusion of Freudian psychoanalytic theory beginning in the mid-twentieth century, marketing has long understood that ritualized purchase-as-practice is not wholly dependent on experiences of conscious intersubjectivity.

To be sure, consumer practice has been expertly tutored by accounts of ritual since the nineteenth century (see, e.g., Jackson Lears 1995; Leach 1994; Lofton 2017). New technologies have only strengthened the ritualized and capitalized attachments of the heart. Steve Jobs's Zen master, Kobun Chino, promised him that spiritual health and business were compatible (Robinson 2013). For Jobs, machines could be liberating and uplifting: iPods were precisely designed to be devotional devices. What was an iPod but a means according to which we might calibrate and transform our experiences of ourselves, providing the material means for immaterially restructuring our momentary relationship with the world?

\* \* \*

Critically, at the very moment of my unspeakable religious vision in the bus depot, the Stop Shopping Church had already correctly identified the iPod campaign in terms of the material culture of its main religious adversary. They had not been handicapped by the same ideological blinders I had been. They have been articulately conversant with capitalism's sacred valences for almost a quarter century. A connective thread of this book is this suggestion that the Stop Shopping Church largely sensed "the religious occupation of economy" (Lofton 2017, 9) before religious studies did as a field.

In 2006, Reverend Billy (Talen 2006, 113) wrote this of the community that had formed around him: "Our Church of Stop Shopping always pastes our Reverend Billy posters over the famous shadow dancers of the iPod ads when we see them on the street. Because if we, as communities, don't break out of that sinister corporatization of the body—that's the Death of Place, PERIOD." He wrote these lines more or less at the same time that my younger self, as a new doctoral student in religion, was struck mute by the iPod silhouettes.⁵⁰ I read these lines thirteen years after that moment in South Station, Boston. I was well into the fieldwork but was still working on framing this book. The experience of having Reverend Billy's words transport me back in time was sheer magic. Really.

If we stop and consider how we actually come to think and write, the idea that our scholarly action is influenced only by dispassionate, analytical commitments to knowledge production can seem downright fantastical. For example, the writing of the present book was, in fact, enabled by a correspondence and biographical convergence that provided an affective layer that exceeded that which was provided by what the anthropologist Kath Weston (2018) refers to as the ethnographer's "notional field." While my fieldwork and reading had begun to press me in this direction, my realization that Reverend Billy had so clearly noted the religiosity of the iPod silhouettes just when I lacked the vocabulary and disciplinary authority to do so, convinced me to pursue this book less in terms of traditional ethnography and more as an opportunity to translate the insights of the Stop Shopping Church for readers interested in North American religion and economy.

What we scholars might learn *from* the activists about our scholarly methods became the core interest of this book.⁵¹ Yet I did not finally arrive at this argumentative goal simply as the result of cool calculation. The choice was flooded in memory and the sentiment of biographical convergence, an aspect and consequence of what we might think of as ethnography's sympathetic magic.⁵² It was retrospectively tutored by a moment of media consumption, the occasion for which was a peripatetic commute home, not a serious and sedentary academic seminar or roundtable.

Importantly, in the two decades since I began my graduate studies, led in important ways by historians of American religion, the field's collective blinders have progressively dissipated. With important caveats and suggestions made for more critical engagement with the productive powers of capital,⁵³ the religion scholars Rebecca Bartel and Lucia Hulsether (2019) have suggested that religious studies has made important progress returning to reconsiderations of capitalism and away from (the an-economicism of) the sympathetic study of "world religions," an approach for which Harvard Divinity School is especially well known. In their intervention, these scholars of religion and economy importantly remind us that the doing of religious studies participates in and builds "worlds of capital." That is to say, religious studies discourse has contributed to shoring up and implicitly supporting the social grammar of racial capitalism. Put in Lofton's terms, scholars do not only study organization, we actively organize. We are ritual participants and world-makers.

In her pathbreaking study of the everyday forms of shop-store Evangelical religion in the Ozarks that fueled the (global) Walmart revolution, Bethany Moreton (2009, 270) has brought our attention to the ways in which the economic ideas of Milton Friedman and the Chicago school would never have become living ideas had "the popular faith in Christian free enterprise (not) attracted passionate support among many ordinary people." For clearing the path and for their focus on the role of gender and family values in the neoliberalization of American society, Moreton's studies (2007, 2009) of the "soul of neoliberalism" represented a watershed moment for the study of American religious history and, I want to strongly suggest, for religious studies and scholars with interests in the study of North American power more broadly.[54]

Subsequent scholarship in American religious history has continued to explore Evangelical Protestantism's relationships with the development of modern capitalism. It has generally called into question sundry secularism theses that proposed, midcentury, that the cultural and political power of religious conservatives had so waned throughout the twentieth century that no less a scholar than Harvey Cox ([1965] 2014) would proclaim the advent of the secular city less than twenty years before the Reagan Revolution. For example, taking the Christian book industry as his case study, Daniel Vaca (2019) argues that by the late nineteenth century, American Evangelicalism was already a "commercial religion" since its ideas and strategies were taking shape primarily through commercial logics and practices. If anything has remained constant about the character of Reverend Billy from its inception until now, it's the insistence that conservative Christianity and consumerism have always been fundamentally in cahoots.

Sara Hammond's (2017) biographical exploration of the broader historical significance of two influential Midwestern businessmen in the early twentieth century suggests that entrepreneurial Evangelicals during the Depression and World War II very much asserted their political will and influence through their commercial activities. For his part, Kevin Kruse (2015) makes the Eisenhower consensus central to the story of commercial Christianity. Given that their crusade against fossil fuels is absolutely central to the work they do now, of particular interest for any consideration of American religion and economy through the Stop Shopping Church would be Darren Dochuck's (2019) study of the historical complications of crude and Christianity after its discovery during the Civil War. As the Reverend Billy character always surmised, American exceptionalism, both at the turn of twentieth century and today, has been, as Dochuck argues, simultaneously anointed in oil and sanctified by God.

While these scholars were researching and writing their important work on American religion and economy, Reverend Billy, Savitri D, and the Stop Shopping Church were on the streets performing the spirit of these histories and correspondences, their grassroots performances having divined some of the trajectories of contemporary scholarship on American religion and capitalism. From the beginning, they have been critically drawn to the passionate attachments of Christian free enterprise that Moreton explicates. The Stop Shopping Church intuited, all along, that consumer capitalism's appetites run through libidinized American religious history.

Heath Carter (2015), Richard Callahan (2009) and others have importantly described the ways in which American Protestantism has never been monolithic in either its political conservativism or in its seamless alliances with industrial capitalism. Carter documents the social Christianity that became the idiom according to which late nineteenth and early twentieth century working class Chicagoans negotiated the pains of industrialization. For his part, Callahan explores the Holiness Pentecostalism that influenced union organizing among Appalachian miners in Eastern Kentucky in the early twentieth century. It has even been recently suggested that no history of labor in America is not always and already a religious history (Cantwell et al. 2016, 12). Most recently, however, Lucia Hulsether (2023), urging the field to avoid the temptation to demarcate left Christianity as a "relative moral safe zone," has explored the ways in which interpretations of liberation theology and the social gospel have actually underwritten the "neoliberal institution building" of humanitarian capitalism.[55]

In all of this there are additional correspondences with the performances of the Stop Shopping Church. As strongly as he has personally rejected Christianity as a framework for understanding and living in the world and has desired to bring critical attention to its determinative role in sacralizing the very American order he is intent on challenging, William Talen, like Savitri D, has an appreciation for the role of progressive Christianity in important social movements for justice, especially the legacy of the Black Church during Civil Rights.[56] The character always marked the problem but, wearing a religious costume that in some ways eventually became second skin, Reverend Billy, the preacher decked out in American religious drag, has also delivered the good news. By the same token, the Stop Shopping Church has never wavered from their utter rejection of the logic, often wrapped up in the niceties of progressive theology, that, as Hulsether (2023, 13) puts it, "market exchange (can) under certain conditions ameliorate the worst of capitalist ravages."

As a grassroots icon, Reverend Billy has been capacious enough to speak to the varieties of historical co-implications between religion and economy, hegemonic and resistant, that have existed within the scope and under the umbrella of American Protestant secularism. In all cases, however, whether they are looking to bring attention to consumerism as "fundamentalist religion" or are marshaling religious potentialities to do battle with its religious power, the Stop Shopping Church has always insisted that one important plane of anti-capitalist work and "Earth Justice" activism involves embodied subjectivity and a psychic battle for the "soul" of consumers.

For our part as scholars, for all that has been accomplished in the last twenty years within religious studies to attend to our unwitting separation of religion and economy, we have still not considered carefully enough the ways in which branding is an intensely religious self-making technology, how it represents a significant innovation in the history of modern subjectivity, how religious studies has surreptitiously participated in these transformations of the self, and with what political consequence for the apocalyptic futures of neoliberal capitalism that now inhabit our ecological present. The book turns to the example of the Stop Shopping activists to incite disciplinary engagements with precisely these considerations.

## Book Outline

In what follows, I consider religion at the Stop Shopping Church pragmatically in terms of an interminable dialectic of freedom and control. In a Shopocalyptic age, for the activists, religion is both what must be overcome and the raw imaginative, affective, and organizational material we will need to accomplish that overcoming. Religion is both the poison and the medicine. The religion of everyday life is struggle; it is at once enervating and destructive compulsion *and* the hopeful compulsion to affect life-affirming personal and social change.[57] It is, in short, an expression of the creative experience of history under the present rule of capital.

* * *

This book is an application of existential Marxism.[58] As such, a core methodological aim is to contextualize concrete human action in the ideological world that conditions but cannot determine it. As a consequence of the overarching interests of this approach, its analysis and critique are sharply focused on the mediations between social structures, their attendant ideologies, and the human practices and experiences that operate within and transcend historical constraints. As a genre, in deference to the empiricism of the kind of understanding they achieve, ethnographies often frontload storytelling. Given the particular mediations that are my focus, however, this book is deliberately organized another way.

Since the discourse of religious studies is itself mined for evidence of its own conditioning by the branded logic of neoliberal capitalism, and the critical agency of both scholars and activists in light of this conditioning is implicated by the argument, the book begins with two chapters that foreground and strongly consider the history of American marketing and social theory in religious studies. I provide evidence for the view that at the same time that important religious studies theory had misrecognized its relationship to consumer ritual, the Stop Shopping Church had correctly diagnosed these coordinates and had enacted its activist program accordingly. The intervention of the first half of the book sets up the later chapters, which dialectically shine a narrative light on the world-remaking activities of the activists as exemplary expressions of historically delimited critical agency in the world. In light of their example, the book also asks the reader to consider what the activists' deployment of religion in their performances might suggest to scholars about the work we do, especially as we consider ways to exercise our own critical agency under darkening skies.

As a variant of what we might broadly call philosophical anthropology,[59] this book, based on four years of in-person fieldwork and seven years of content analysis and targeted virtual fieldwork, is written as deliberate pastiche, drawing inspiration from a range of media, archives, experiences, and stylizations and in the types of genres of writing it references and reproduces. The fieldwork is presented through theoretical, literary, and historiographic styles, accents, and forms of writing.[60] I have chosen to write the book this way for a few, interconnected reasons: To reflect some of the performative panache and dynamism of the fieldwork subjects themselves; to establish the significance of the group's work according to the terms of the debate within religious studies; and, finally, to suggest that academic thinking is often caught up in the very consuming power that scholarship in religion generally ignores.

Although my own thought is most closely aligned with existential Marxism and the critical theory of the Frankfurt School thinkers, I needed to directly engage with performativity theory and psychoanalysis in this book because the fieldwork demanded that I do so. Given the Stop Shopping Church's long-standing critiques of the predetermined repetitions of consumer discourse, their interests in the subjection of consumer selves in childhood, and their performative mourning of our "rising dead" within, my intersubjective approach to social critique demanded reconsiderations of critical terms in the study of religion that most closely tacked onto these concerns.

David Graeber (2004, 12), whom the leadership of the Stop Shopping Church worked with and came to trust, describes the relationship of scholars to radical activists this way:

> One obvious role for a radical intellectual is to . . . look at those who are creating viable alternatives, try to figure out what might be the larger implications of what they are (already) doing, and then offer those ideas back, not as prescriptions but as contributions, possibilities—as gifts.

I have also ultimately framed the writing of this book in the spirit of Graeber's suggestion, who, as a respected and celebrated academic and public intellectual, spent more time engaged in direct action work with grassroots organizations than the vast majority of scholars. The task I set for myself was twofold: to unpack the importance of the example of the Stop Shopping Church for a scholarly audience, on the one hand, and to offer up the cultural and political implications of their work, as I see them, to the activists, on the other hand.

Notably, I did not always find myself fully comfortable in the activists' number, mostly as a consequence of my academic introversion. I didn't always agree with this or that community decision and I wasn't always entirely convinced by a particular tactic or practical strategy. Most obviously, I often wished that the group was more interested in directly reflecting on the early days of their activism.[61] None of this, however, takes away from the fact that I learned much from the Stop Shopping Church about the religious character of contemporary consumer subjectivity, and the profound consequences of religious capitalism, or diminished, in the end, my strong belief that religious studies, as a field, as well as American studies, among others, have much to gain from a close engagement with the rich legacy of the group's activist performances around issues of North American religion and economy.

\* \* \*

There are two acts in the drama of this book. Tracing a map of our branded world will occupy us in Act I. This first act brings the discourse of religious studies directly into conversation with the activist labors of the Stop Shopping Church. It flows, as needed, between ethnographic signposts, historiography, and the close reading of illustrative and influential social theory to ask critical questions about religious studies' relationship to social theory in a consumer age.

There is, in Act I's analysis, a mix of good and bad news for religious studies. The bad news is that some important critical terms and theoretical approaches to embodied rationality in religious studies from the neoliberal period, namely *ritualization, performativity,* and *psychoanalysis,* express the logic of branding discourse and are implicated in the historical development of American consumption in ways that have been generally misrecognized and disavowed by the field. The argument is not that the above scholarly triumvirate simply stand in for the whole of religious studies but, rather, that since they have all proven significantly influential within the study of religion of the past thirty odd years, they do serve as concrete examples of the conceptual entanglements I argue scholars need to become more attentive to. There is also good news, however, in these entailments. Our disciplinary understanding of the performativity of ritualization and our disciplinary familiarity with psychoanalytic concepts, I suggest, means that religion scholars and other scholars fluent in these approaches to subjectivity are already in possession of useful schematics of how what I call "post-secular"[62] capitalism's sacralizations and privatizations are accomplished through the activities of ritually branded bodies.

Taking its empirical cues from the Stop Shopping Church's Starbucks campaign from the early years of the new millennium in order to establish the stakes of this work according to the activists, chapter 1 argues that Catherine Bell's account of ritualization mirrors the basic coordinates of branding as an expression of consumer performativity. These confluences suggest an epistemic convergence that the field should continue to explore and that speaks to our own (religious) ritualization by "consuming religion" as scholars.[63]

Chapter 2 asks the question: *How did we become the solipsistic, unjust, and environmentally oblivious consumers that the Stop Shopping Church suggests we are?* Chapter 2 also argues that advertising consultant Ernest Dichter's postwar work to incorporate psychoanalytic ideas and concepts into marketing helped privatize the souls of American consumers. Dichter's widespread influence contributed to a burgeoning proto-performativity that has organized ritualized consumption, influencing the emergence of branding discourse in the present moment.

In the chapter, I also argue that the social philosopher Judith Butler's iconic and influential account of the psychic life of power misrecognizes its own participation in the psychoanalytic history of American marketing. Left social theory, like any other, can unwittingly reproduce the destructive logic of neoliberalism, but I argue that, once materialized, it can, as in the case of Butler's psychoanalytic intervention, sometimes be redirected and redeployed as a vehicle of subversion. Connecting the analysis of the chapter to the performances of the Stop Shopping Church and their insistence of a living otherness "within us," chapter 2 nominates the psychoanalytic concept of social melancholy as one that is especially amenable to anti-capitalist subversion.

Chapter 3 is an intermezzo between acts. It provides the back story of William Talen's development of the character of Reverend Billy in the 1990s and chronicles the emergence of the anti-consumerist activism of the Stop Shopping Church at the millennium with special attention to their early processional actions at the flagship Disney Store in Manhattan. The chapter also presents particularly relevant aspects of Savitri D's biography, setting up her decisive role in firmly moving the community in the direction of political ecology.

The chapter begins to tell the story of Reverend Billy's transfiguration from parodic performance character to serious prophet of "Earth Justice" and the development of the Stop Shopping Choir into a "post-religious religious community." It also describes the critical shift in the group's focus away from the issue of how consumerism distorts human consciousness, toward today's more capacious and radical consideration of our ecological interdependencies, animacies, and intimacies in a Shopocalyptic age.

Act II brings the present day of the Stop Shopping Church very much front stage and looks to their performances as a miming, mapping, and critique of our collective planetary predicament. By pushing back against the sacred power of corporate brands and their harmful environmental effects, the songful community life and activist performances of the Stop Shoppers serve as a kind of somatic imprint of our highly aestheticized and ritualized form of capitalism as well as the intersectional concerns of the contemporary activist moment. Since the focus in Act II is strongly ethnographic rather than textual-analytical, ethnographic storytelling, as a writing genre, is also front stage, along with the activists, in chapters 4 and 5.

Chapter 4 describes the community life of the Stop Shopping Church through special reference to their Sunday afternoon Choir rehearsals and the singular organizational and intellectual influence of Savitri D, the group's co-founder and director. I describe the ways in which the group looks to hone a pragmatic, musical agency that marshals the full sensorium of embodiment to cultivate a praxeological orientation toward "Earth Justice" and the related ability to begin to creatively resist the closed systems of consumerist discourse.

Critical agency for the activists, described in chapter 4, is creative, provisional, interpretative, and intersubjective. Referencing elements of the Stop Shoppers' life stories, this chapter also suggests that while we are certainly collectivized by history (as consumers, scholars, and activists), biographical particularities, existential inflections, and human experiences of chance resist the reduction of anthropology to (consumerist) discourse.

Chapter 5 turns directly to the Stop Shopping Church's theatrical and street-activist performances to argue that they critique the discourse of religious capitalism in an analytically and historically precise way.[64] Having reviewed the social dichotomies and separate spheres of life proposed by Weberian secularism,[65] the chapter proposes that the Stop Shopping Church understands consumer capitalism in decidedly "post-secular" terms and consider ecological intersubjectivity to be a privileged site of political struggle. The members of the Stop Shopping Church strongly appreciate the ways in which the embodied rationality of branding implies the postindustrial annexations of experiential terrain previously reserved, *at least as a formal economic matter*, to religion, art, and psychology. The Stop Shoppers' performances also trace and outline, I argue, key prismatic valences of American religious history and economy. Meanwhile, their trajectory away from parodic critics of American religion to a "post-religious religious" community orientated around the remembrance of "Earth" in all things confounds even deeper histories of religion's supposed transcendence of the natural world.

Chapter 5 describes the ways in which, meeting consumerist spectacle with activist spectacle, the performances of the Stop Shopping Church look to break the closed epistemological universe of financial capitalism by imaginatively reintroducing the extinct fauna, deadly toxins, and rising sea levels (our "rising dead" in Reverend Billy's terms) back into the moral horizons of consumers for whom these have been ritually disavowed and disappeared. I read and interpret the group's activist dramaturgy as a recognition of the necessary mutuality of an indicative analysis of *what is* and a subjective wish for *what could (must) be* in critical social action.

The conclusion brings scholars and activists together in a consideration of our shared epistemic context, this time by way of a new genealogical register. I both recap what scholars can fruitfully learn from activists about North American religion and economy in our present time of climate catastrophe and species extinction and offer up areas where scholars' considerations of religious history can also prove potentially useful to the activists in their grassroots labors. Ultimately, I suggest that activists and scholars can work together to find our human way out of automatic, predetermined consumption and toward a biophilic future that our intensifying ecological calamities increasingly risk and imperil.

ACT I

Scholars at the Shopocalypse

# 1

## Ritualization in the Age of Starbucks

### Scholars and Activists in a Brand-New World

The First Job of a church is to save souls. And pulling out of the advertising/debt/waste cycle of Consumerism is our idea of deliverance.
—Reverend Billy

Reverend Billy sits quietly at a table with devotees and then begins to chat up customers. He works the crowd with an affirming theme but gradually turns on Starbucks. Towards the end, he's shouting. Then the Reverend's devotees hand around anti-Starbucks leaflets. After that, he heads out the door. According to a store manager, he may stand on your tables.
—Internal Starbucks Memorandum (2000)

### Guilty as Charged at the Astor Place Starbucks

In January 2020, my husband and three of our friends met in lower Manhattan at Astor Place to attend a performance of Reverend Billy and the Stop Shopping Church at Joe's Pub on Lafayette Street. We were early and my friend Kathy was eager to get a cup of coffee somewhere. With little time to spare, we did not want to venture too far off so she pointed us toward the (since closed) Starbucks on Lafayette and 8th street. My heart jumped. Here we were about to go to Stop Shopping "Church" but, on our way there, we would first be heading to a sacred pilgrimage site of one of Reverend Billy's most famous brand adversaries for a cup of overpriced joe.[1]

Twenty years earlier, having made his start locked in spiritual battle with Disney, Reverend Billy had turned his attention to what he called "the Caffeinated Satan." He and the disciples who began to gather around him took on Starbucks as part of their stop shopping campaign to address the problems of gentrification and what Reverend Billy and Savitri D call "the rising monoculture." It was also still at the beginning cusp of the group's Jane Jacobs–style turn to the preservation of neighborhoods and local economies. As they do at places like the new Hudson Yards or at Trump Tower today, the Stop Shopping Church of times yore condemned Starbucks coffeehouses' privatized public space as a commodified simulacrum of the commons and performed its existential reclaiming.

Savitri D once suggested to me that the monoculture is, at base, "a sort of industrial manufactured landscape that surrounds us." It is, she would intriguingly add, "increasingly *repetitive* and *predetermined*."[2] In the same vein, Savitri D explained on her walk over to our interview a year earlier, that she was remembering all the funky and gritty New York "subcultures" and shops that had since been crowded out by all the franchises and chain stores.

Chain stores, Reverend Billy (Talen 2006, 24) writes, promise "infinite products" and often try to mimic the independent stores they kill. Starbucks, for its part, he concludes (56), "has systematically taken every movement from labor to ACT-UP and created a coffee flavor." It sends its advertising scouts (or brand anthropologists) out into the culture in search of local creativity that the brand can absorb and re-present to consumers for purchase (Talen 2003, 4). One can read this discursive deflection in terms of capital accumulation and what the sociologist John Holloway ([2002] 2019, 47) describes as the process whereby capital turns "the done (as means of doing) against the doers in order to subject their present doing to the sole end of further accumulation." Capitalism demands a closed system wherein consumer performance leads to theoretically inexhaustible *repetition* and extraction, never a radical breaking away from the law of exchange value.

The passion and verve behind the Stop Shopping Church's crusade against Starbucks cannot be overstated. According to Savitri D, the monoculture, shorthand for the commodification of culture and its attendant exploitation of the Earth and marginalization of "Earth cultures," has "fundamentally changed the ground we stand on."[3] Around the millennium, Starbucks was ground zero for the group's anti-consumerist interventions for good reason. Starbucks became the chosen target because it so clearly manifested the ritualized brand form consumerism had taken.

The depths of commodification are such, Savitri D suggests, that "the conditions that we are under right now" have not "happened (before) in history."[4] For Savitri D, capitalism's reach into the conditions that give rise to both life and death have been extended, in recent times, in exceedingly dangerous and unprecedented ways. Corporate branding is the cultural mechanism through which capitalism has iteratively extended its sacred power in the neoliberal period, especially in the past thirty years. Brands invite consumers to participate in self- and world-making rituals that press particular values, priorities, and ways of seeing upon us. The brand form as it has been identified by the Stop Shopping Church, I will argue, mirrors an important account of ritualization in religious studies, a confluence that speaks to the field's traditional economic myopia but is also a testament to the unique contributions the discipline is poised to make to an analysis and critique of religious capitalism.

## The Stop Shopping Church at the Dawn of the Starbucks Age

As it turned out, I was right to have a lump in my throat as I sipped my green tea inside the Astor Place Starbucks. We were sitting by a window and twenty minutes before showtime, Savitri D and a couple of Choir members walked past and saw me. My head down, there was a knock at the window. In a jolt, I looked up to see Savitri D making a face that said it all: *"Come on? Really?"* This was the one time I felt real judgment from Savitri D, who is known around Stop Shopping Church circles for helping Reverend Billy dial down the delivery of his bombast and righteous anger. The Astor Place Starbucks, with its "pale imitation of an avant-garde café blended with a touch of sanitized mall" (Talen 2003, 3), was once their greatest stage. It is haunted by the memories of many a Reverend Billy action. At that moment, I felt woefully unprincipled and drawn in by the "convenience" that Reverend Billy says drives much consumption.[5]

While I like to avoid Starbucks, here I was sipping out of a white and green cup replete with the brand's iconic mermaid adorning it. As

Reverend Billy explains, even an "ex-consumer" who has learned to "say NO" to the commodity "can easily lose his or her footing, buffeted by all those ghost gestures" (Talen 2003, xiii). Reverend Billy's thinking about "ghost gestures" can help us to understand what religious studies has understood as ritual training. He helps us see how consumption leaves the imprint of muscle memory and inures transformation on and through the body, just as the marketers hope it will. I was, as it were, either guilty as charged or just as I was supposed to be, depending.

* * *

The Starbucks campaign began at the millennium and was phased out as Reverend Billy set his sights on mixing up the 2009 New York City mayoral race with a run "in character" to bring attention to the political dangers of the perceived inevitability of Michael Bloomberg's third term. In their actions at Starbucks coffeehouses, Reverend Billy and his companions sought to "awaken community in the heart of commodification" (Talen 2003, 18) and to loosen the hold of the brand's vacating of historical memory and its choreographing of consumer bodies. The primary point of Reverend Billy's covert actions in retail spaces like a Starbucks store is always to help consumers break out of their "ghost" or (51) "memorized" gestures of ritualized consumption.

At the Astor Place Starbucks, Reverend Billy (Talen 2003, 17) once conjured the memory of the mom-and-pop business the mermaid had displaced: "The Astor Riviera Diner is still here! We remember it, and here it comes! It is returning!" In his exhortations, he even paid homage to the Riviera Diner's "abusive waiters." This gritty and unique past could not be incorporated by the brand, Reverend Billy wagered. The memory of Astor Riviera was not amenable to Starbucks' hegemonic discourse. It was potentially disruptive to the power of the brand.

In their Starbucks actions, the Stop Shopping Church set to disrupt the aura of the Starbucks brand and to interrupt its ritualized strategies for making itself "unending" and "repetitive" (Talen 2003, 8). As Reverend Billy has sermonized within the Astor Place Starbucks, Starbucks is, in fact (14), a "NO PLACE! . . . we are tourists in our own lives . . . our words have a barely discernable echo . . . we have the same relationship to living real lives that these art-school Starbucks graphics have to the real artists who lived on this street. WE'RE IN A FAKE CAFÉ AND WE

CAN'T KNOW THE REAL COST OF THAT LATTE!" While the group would be sure to leave leaflets that contained instrumental information about Starbucks' habit of purchasing coffee from environmentally unsustainable plantations that "employ families at slave wages" and its use of prison labor in the packaging of Starbucks products, the Starbucks actions were always high theater.

One elaborate action that they would perform at the "charged stage" (Talen 2003, 23) of a Starbucks coffeehouse, including the one at Astor Place, was a "trash worship" ceremony. Members of the Choir, dressed up and performing the "upwardly mobile careerists" that comprise the Starbucks devoted—replete with necessary accessories like briefcases and gym bags—would jubilantly wave their green and white Starbucks coffee cups in the air as, absurdly, dancers in skirts, step dancers wearing clogs, or an "elegant Degas-like ballerina" (44) entered through the front door.

Reverend Billy (Talen 2003, 44) would have instructed his merry band of anti-consumer thespians to become the anthropological "other" in order to highlight consumerism's own alienations: "You come from a mysterious culture in which applause takes the form of this ritual Starbucks cup gesture." As the Stop Shoppers looked to make abundantly clear, the Starbucks cup was no hierophany (an appearance of the sacred in historical time), but, rather, a historical product masking its economic exploitation and ecological, political violence with a patina of enlightened capitalism.

One of the longest-standing members of the Choir recounted in an interview that sometimes a group of covert actors would enter the Astor Place Starbucks and get on their phones, pretending to be lost while a friend or date waited on them. "*Which* Starbucks?" "I *am* at Starbucks!"[6] The intent of the drama was to bring attention to the absurd density of Starbucks retail spaces in and around Astor Place, including a second shop just 250 feet away (since closed). This was a ritual means for "punking" the repetitive logic of the brand, inflating its sameness while simultaneously diminishing its difference. The Stop Shopping Church understood that brand power flows through two interacting and mutually enforcing tracks: the consumer's individualized consumption of the meaning of the brand, on the one hand, and the organized cultural repetition, or iterativity, of the brand's discursive meaning in society, on the other hand. In this scenario, brand power implies a closed loop wherein consumers' gestures and ritualized acts of consumption become citations (discursively recognizable and repeated re-performances) of brand meaning. The "cell phone opera" action took direct aim at the space of possible contradiction between the desire for personalized meaning and the brand's actually citational manufacture.

Ultimately, Starbucks' patina of aesthetic sophistication (in Reverend Billy's terms, the brand's productizing of the stylizations of art and activism) was at least as repugnant to the group as the brand's exploitation of workers, its greenwashing degradation of the Earth, and its corporate takeover of neighborhoods. Another favorite retail theater action from the Starbucks days placed the characters of a loudmouthed stockbroker and an everyday Starbucks customer engaged in conversation about how the Starbucks mermaid lost her nipples (Talen 2003, 46): In 1996, as it turns out, as the brand expanded into conservative demographics in places like Ohio, it had no choice but to anesthetize its totem. Or, in the midst of a sermonic fit, Reverend Billy would implore consumers, human extras in Starbucks' brand theater, to take a step back from the brand's rituals and consider it a Trojan horse of postindustrial, urban gentrification: "Look at these walls, these impossibly hip earth tones. Is it Jean-Michel Basquiat? Well, not . . . NOT QUITE. But he used to live in this neighborhood!" (14).

*　*　*

As the communications scholar Tony Perucci (2008) brilliantly details, in 2004, Reverend Billy jumped a counter at a Starbucks on Receda Boulevard in Los Angeles, placed one hand on the cash register, and invited all the consumers and workers present to join him and his group in a "cash register exorcism." A few months later, Reverend Billy received a restraining order preventing him from coming within 250 feet of a Starbucks in the State of California and was summoned to appear in court on charges of "malicious vandalism" and trespassing. The City Attorney argued in her summation that the cash register and the "flow of business" are "things that are sacred" and that Reverend Billy's "cash register exorcism" performance was a kind of "sacrilege."

In short, the performance was deemed a danger because it intended to disrupt the sanctified workings of capital. Reverend Billy was sentenced to three days in a Los Angeles jail and he served two. As Perucci puts it, Reverend Billy was "guilty of sin—the sin of heresy against the God of capital." Reverend Billy's attempt to interrupt the consumer moment was read by his adversaries as a challenge to providential fate, directly revealing, for a moment, the sanctified compulsions that actually underwrite nominally secular and putatively free neoliberal consumption.

In the Stop Shopping Church's Starbucks actions, the goal was always to pry "sippers from a set of gestures, from the completion of a contract" (Talen 2003, 2). In other words, the group wanted to remind consumers that they were not merely iterative citations (or cultural exemplars) of Starbucks' brand discourse as a form of preexisting power. Allegorically speaking, the corporate idea that we have no choice but to accept society's consumer choreographies represents human beings' "original sin" in the Stop Shopping worldview.

I was guilty as charged sitting by the window at the Astor Place Starbucks on my way to a Stop Shopping performance, because I allowed my consumerist gestures to achieve a feeling of predetermined inevitability. In Reverend Billy's terms, I became an extra and tourist in my own life. For the sake of convenience, I simply accepted the stage directions I was given. I failed to back away from the product. My gestures, sitting in the wannabe Italian coffeehouse sipping out of the mermaid cup, contributed to the brand's citational power and added ambiance to its background life, the way an extra adds plausibility to a movie set.

\* \* \*

Reverend Billy (Talen 2006, 199) writes that through consumerism, "we are *ritualized* into acceptance" of a particular "way of seeing the world." Savitri D, for her part, focuses on the ways in which consumerism is repetitive, predetermined, and invested in the logic of what the Stop Shoppers call "identical details." They were accurate and prescient in their diagnoses. The brand form is theorized and applied by marketing discourse as a form of ritualization, which is, as I'll seek to show, conceptually analogous to Catherine Bell's influential academic account of the same. Branding as ritualization serves as the basis of our embodied rationality in consumer society and, hence, has implications well beyond the so-called economic.

Figure 1.1. Exorcising the caffeinated devil. Ithaca, NY. 2006. Photo by the Stop Shopping Church.

As an immediate matter, there is, in these convergences between ideas of ritual and branding, some very good news for religion scholars. The conceptual overlaps between the ways in which marketers and many religion scholars have come to conceive of social action suggest that we already carry around a powerful map of how consumer capitalism works, how it proliferates, and how it depends on mobile, schematizing sacralization to achieve and consolidate its power. Reverend Billy has called the ways in which the "everyday" is ritually endowed with charismatic power, "the mysticism of value."[7] A comparative reading of Reverend Billy's thinking about the mysticism of value with Catherine Bell's work on ritualization and branding theory will help us to further clarify how and why the Stop Shopping Church approaches its anti-consumerist activism in the ways that it does.

In its early anti-consumerist activism, the Stop Shopping Church was aware of and responding in real time to branding's ritualization of consumption and the specifically performative ways in which the repetition of brand narratives works to structure (that is, schematize and sacralize) the social environment, tautologically endowing it with the charismatic authority of the brand. Catherine Bell's account of ritualization, I argue, reflected and expressed the general parameters of late twentieth-century branding discourse while simultaneously misrecognizing its own imbrications in the culture of consumer capitalism. This chapter outlines the ways in which this prominent account of ritualization in religious studies maps onto the brand form, setting up the interventions in Act II, where the performances of the Stop Shopping Church, which look to break the spell of consumerism's ritualized and multisensorial cycles of never-ending repetition, take center stage.

## The Turn to Branding

Scholarship that adopts a post-Fordist orientation often makes much of the disaggregation of markets into partially engineered "lifestyles," wherein marketing seeks not to simply target existing lifestyles but, more radically, looks to actively produce and organize consumers according to mediatized patterns of meaning and identity (see Slater 2005, 191). By the middle of the twentieth century, it was commonly accepted by marketers that markets do not meet already existing demand but, rather, work to "create desires—to bring into being wants that did not previously exist" (Galbraith [1958] 2000, 22).

If the liberal model of the consumer is of a "coherent and calculating self (the Ego) acting in relation to non-rational desires which it can know and rationally pursue," the branded self is in significant ways understood by neoliberal capitalism to be more like the poststructuralist self of recent academic generations. As one sociologist puts it, "a decentered subject, one that deconstructs into the incoherence of multiple discourses, unconscious drives, the amorphousness of desire, the primacy of the body, the endless flow of signs and difference" (Slater 2005, 208).[8]

Historians of nineteenth-century American capitalism such as William Leach and T. J. Jackson Lears remind us that, as Leach puts it, as early as the 1880s, "American commercial capitalism, in the interest of marketing goods and making money, started down the road of creating [. . .] a set of and system of symbols, signs, and enticements" (Leach 1994, 9). Although the brand form is a historical innovation, capitalism had long realized that culture and economy were entwined.[9] Brands, in and of themselves, are not new. The term itself originates with the practice of designating property such as cattle (Pavitt 2000, 21). In a formal sense, branding attaches a name and reputation to commercial entities, often through the use of logos, trademarks, and symbols. What matters most for the purposes of our present discussion is that contemporary branding looks to format subjectivity, not just appeal to it as a preexisting, taken-for-granted dimension of social life.

The cultural critic Naomi Klein (2009, 13)[10] argues that in the 1980s, an economic consensus emerged that companies were weighed down and bloated by their things—their manufacturing plants and the related labor costs. Second, she argues, aging "baby boomers" became increasingly psychologically resistant to "the alluring images of advertising," opting instead to break lifelong brand loyalties and purchase generic goods based primarily on consideration of cost, claiming no longer to distinguish between competing brands. Klein's work shows us that the brand is now the "core meaning" of corporations and advertising technologies provide one way in which that meaning is disseminated in the culture at large. Klein posits: "If brands are not products but ideas, attitudes, values and experiences, why can't they be culture too?" (30).[11] Or, in Savitri D's terms, the *monoculture*.

Klein's popular history is, no doubt, somewhat coarse. She sometimes veers dangerously close to drawing too sharp a contrast between the modern commodification of goods on the one hand, and the postmodern commodification of meaning on the other. Capitalism did not just discover the ruminative potential of meaning in the neoliberal period as some kind of late revelation. However, it is not the selling of meaning per se that is at issue for our purposes but, rather, the specifically iterative ways in which contemporary branding semiotically organizes consumers and products in and through space and time. This is the fulcrum around which scholars, activists, and capitalist culture have epistemically converged.

* * *

The sociologist Celia Lury (2004, 32) argues that by the 1980s and 1990s, there was a sharp increase in "corporate branding," or the branding of a company rather than particular goods and services. No longer did brands simply communicate information to potential consumers about particular goods and services. *Increasingly, they communicated values that extended across a spectrum of products and services.* As discussed earlier, even a global city like New York can be refashioned as a luxury brand. Because they trade in the non-product-specific associations consumers make with corporations (as well as celebrities and iconic places), Lury tells us that "brands are *not* made in the factory but in people's minds" (32). As we will later see, postwar, psychoanalytic motivation research helped to pry open the self and readied it for the making of the contemporary brand in the deep recesses of the consumer soul.

Presently, the brand is the medium through which exchanges between consumers and producers are framed "across disunifed or disparate times and spaces" (Lury 2004, 42), connecting and separating the inner and outer environments of markets, in one sense, and consumptive practice, in the other (7). Brand frames are dynamic but importantly *asymmetrical*. They simultaneously promote and inhibit exchange between production and consumption. Branding reveals some aspects of these relationships, while keeping others hidden (7). Quite directly responding to these ritualized asymmetries during the Starbucks era of their activism, the Stop Shopping Choir would sing that they "don't take slavery in [their] coffee!," and Reverend Billy would demand to know the "real price of that latte!" while inside the coffeehouse.

Brands establish multidimensional relationships between consumers and products and services that exist as cognitive blends that integrate commodity and personal experience.[12] Importantly, the brand is at once a specific cultural form and market modality (Lury 2004, 2). As Lury explains, "the brand mediates the supply and demand of products through the organisation, co-ordination and integration of the use of information" (4). To concretize this suggestion: Online tracking cookies and the ethnography of brand anthropologists help advertisers incorporate the everyday activities of consumers into the design of brandscapes which themselves look to funnel extant cultural tendencies and possibilities into products. Set in motion and sustained by subjects engaged in the ritual action of consumption, the brand form can reshape ancient religious practices and ideas like Islamic categories of *halal* and *haram* (e.g., see Shirazi 2016) and it can transform political institutions like the American presidency (see González 2017). It can ritualize weekly or daily visits to Starbucks that defy a purely economic calculus.[13]

Take, for example, the Rolex company's strategic brand partnership with the tennis icon, Roger Federer. The consumption of Rolex is also a communion with Roger and the classed, gendered, and raced virtues his iconic celebrity represents. The anthropologist Marcel Danesi (2006, 33) suggests that branding is ultimately "a social act" in that it names, encapsulates, and circulates goods, services, and companies into the "web of meanings that constitute a culture," allowing these to become important reference points for consumers. Danesi adds: "Brands have, in effect, been anthropomorphically transformed into personalities with identities that have merged with those of consumers" (33).[14]

In light of branding's interests in the transformation of persons from the inside out, it might not surprise us that the term "brand evangelism" is quite commonplace in contemporary marketing and denotes the view that "corporate brands often engender a loyalty that is not so dissimilar from that found in various faith groups." A corporate brand, analogized as the "faith" by the marketing scholar John Balmer and the corporate brand community, analogized as "the faithful," are "mutually dependent" (Balmer 2006, 39).

The notions of brand "covenants" and brand "mantras" within marketing theory further support this kind of perspective on the sacred valences of brands (Balmer 2006, 38). For his part, Reverend Billy (Talen 2006, 113) writes that consumers have so merged with the dominant consumer culture that we have become like "EXTRAS FROM THE DAWN OF THE DEAD." In their early anti-consumerist activism, the Stop Shopping Church worked to resist the ways in which corporate storytelling transforms people with unique life histories into relatively flat, branded selves (Talen 2003, 22–23). Subverting the figuration of consumerism in terms of religion by advertising, the Stop Shopping Church at the millennium was invested in a reverse process of delivering souls from brand religion, disrupting brand mantras, and releasing consumers from brand covenants.

The specific example of Starbucks, which was a singular focus and reference point for the activists in the first years of the 2000s, further reveals the ways in which the brand form seeks to radically tighten the gap between consumers and consumer discourse, transforming the former into instances of the latter. For the Stop Shopping Church, this kind of possession of persons by brands (what we might think of in terms of the personification of objects and the concomitant objectification of persons) is what they refer to as the unholy state of being "consumerized." As we will also see, the consumerized, branded self closely resembles the ritualized subjects that the religion scholar, Catherine Bell, proposes and analyzes.

## The Starbucks Experience

A 2007 Stop Shopping Church action at a Starbucks in Austin, Texas caught on video by a political commentator serves as a good example of the kinds of dramatic, choreographed actions the group would undertake at Starbucks outlets across the world.[15] The Choir, dressed in red gospel robes, processes down the city streets on their way to their latest retail amphitheater shouting, "Stop . . . Stop Shopping!" Reverend Billy, clad in his bright white preacher's suit, uses his bullhorn to self-identify for the Texans for whom the spectacle is new: "We're a movie, we're a faith, we're common sense, we're common sense—we're trying to get Americans to stop their shopping!" Many of the Choir members carry cardboard shields with the Starbucks logo crossed out. These props will assist them in their miming of the spiritual battle they are about to undertake.

As Reverend Billy approaches the coffee shop doors, he identifies the store as the devil's lair: "I feel the devil right here!" Cautiously, he invites his "children" to enter, behind him. As the Choir enters the store, they chant: "Push back . . . Push back Starbucks!" Using his arms to hold back the invisible evil powers, Reverend Billy eventually testifies in front of the congregation. He summons the "Fabulous Unknown" and asks this power to enter into his hands and through his heart. "What would Jesus buy? Would he buy a $4 latte if the people who made that coffee got less than 40 cents out of that $4?" Reverend Billy exorcises the cash register of its mermaid demon. Overtaken by the spirit of the "Fabulous Unknown," which for the Stop Shoppers signifies, as a kind of negative gap, the final mysteries of life that neither traditional religion nor the religion of consumerism can ever answer away, Reverend Billy collapses to the ground. The Choir helps the good preacher back to his feet.

For scholars with interests in North American religion, the scene is instructive. The religious metaphor—the stylizations of costume, speech, and affect—bring attention to the Stop Shopping Choir's insistence that American consumerism and conservative, Evangelical Protestantism are entwined fundamentalisms (Talen 2006, 56). The heightened affect of the performance also brings attention to the fact that, far from being some dull and instrumental practice of cost-benefit analysis, consumption is very much grounded in an awareness of the fact that "major emotions are markets" (9). According to Reverend Billy, in those early days the "soul-saving mission worked (consisted) of dramatic rituals and plays inside retail environments" (23).

But what is the unseen demonic power being *pushed back* by the group? One way of reading the group's retail rituals in the early years of the new millennium, like the one described above, is that they mimed spiritual struggle against the *immaterial* power of brands, highlighting the ways in which consumerism achieves its sacred power through semiotic and self-promulgating means. By all accounts, their approach closely tracks onto how a brand like Starbucks looks to achieve and augment its potentially inexhaustible cultural iconicity. The social imaginaries of iconic brands, which traffic in sign and soma rather than what Bethany Moreton (2007) calls the "cold language" of the "rational individual," are an expression of the "soul of neoliberalism" because they represent the deepest longings of contemporary economics. It makes sense, then, that the embodied rationality of our consumer age became the privileged terrain of the anti-consumerist gospel of the Stop Shopping Church at the millennium.

\* \* \*

Former Starbucks' CEO Howard Schultz explains that "the people who line up for Starbucks [. . .] aren't there just for the coffee; it's the romance of the coffee experience, the feeling of warmth and community people get" (Klein [1999] 2009, 20). As Naomi Klein puts it: Starbucks is supposed to be an "intimate nook where sophisticated people can share coffee . . . community . . . camaraderie . . . connection" (20). Starbucks coffeehouses make strategic aesthetic associations with books, the blues, and jazz. Aesthetically, she tells us, each Starbucks coffeehouse is conceived around an elemental design: "Earth to grow. Fire to roast. Water to brew. Air for aroma" (139).

Klein further explains,

> everything about New Age chains like Starbucks is designed to assure us that they are a different breed from the strip-mall franchises of yesterday. This isn't dreck for the masses, it's intelligent furniture, it's cosmetics as political activism, it's the bookstore as an "old-world library," it's the coffee shop that wants to stare deep in your eyes and "connect." (136)

For its part, the magazine *Advertising Age* associates Starbucks' phenomenal success with "its tie-dyed, Third World aura . . . for devotees, Starbucks' 'experience' is about more than a daily espresso infusion, it is about immersion in a politically correct, cultured refuge" (112). Starbucks is a particular kind of belonging and joining. In short, people go to Starbucks, not for a product, or even a useful service, but, instead, for the "Starbucks Experience."

Since Starbucks is a "lifestyle brand" that traffics in meaning rather than products, it has sought to break into new consumer domains: Starbucks airline coffee, Starbucks ice cream, and Starbucks coffee beer (Klein [1999] 2009, 20). Once upon a time, Starbucks even sold "Starbucks furniture" on the Internet. Starbucks refers to its "brand extension" as an example of "brand canopy" (148).[16] Klein quips, "this is the true meaning of a lifestyle brand: you can live your whole life inside it" (20). Howard Schultz has stated that consumers have "given us permission to extend the experience" (Simon 2011, 160).

But how, more precisely, does a brand like Starbucks increase its cultural "mindshare," as the phenomenon is sometimes described in marketing discourse? I argue that branding processes that strongly resemble Catherine Bell's account of ritualization can help us account for the brand's success at breaking into new (non-branded) areas like film, music, and book marketing. In ways that are analogous to ritualization, the Starbucks brand equips mobile bodies to re-schematize (that is, sacralize) new social spaces through their very movements as ritualized (that is, branded) consumers. The immaterial and furtive demon that the Stop Shoppers resist, look to "turn back," and exorcise is semiotic and embodied—it is the viral power generated through the ritualized activities of bodies in space and time.

## Branding as Ritualization

According to Catherine Bell (1992, 220), acting through and on the body, "ritualization is fundamentally a way of doing things to trigger the perception that these practices are distinct and the associations they engender are special." Taken together, the definitions of branding given by two professional marketers are strikingly evocative of Bell. One marketer states that "a brand is a collection of perceptions in the mind of the consumer" (Bates 2014). According to another, the branded relationship is driven not by the static image the brand contains in culture, but instead "by the deep and significant psychological and socio-cultural meanings the consumer bestows on the brand in the process of meaning creation" (Klein [1999] 2009, 176).

Through the careful and strategic planning of its consumer rite and its consumer spaces around certain cultural associations, Starbucks is, according to Klein, actively "soaking up cultural ideas and iconography that their brands . . . reflect back on the culture as 'extensions' of its brand" (Klein 2009, 29). Of ritualization, Bell writes that "relationships of power are drawn from the social body and then reappropriated by the social body as experience" (Bell 1992, 207). In the case of Starbucks, the tropes of "jazzy sophistication" are drawn from the consumer body and re-appropriated by the consumer in circular fashion, distinguishing the "Starbucks Experience" from the relatively mundane experience of the local diner where one goes for a square meal and little else. The music selected to be played in Starbucks shops is an essential aspect of how the company ritualizes its customers.

For Catherine Bell, bodies are equipped with particular tastes, habits of thought, and experiences through their engagements with social environments that schematize hierarchies of meaning. Specifically, Bell understands the production of ritual agents as a consequence of the intersection of bodies and structuring environments (Bell 1992, 100). In this process, the ritual agent both generates the ritual environment and is molded by it in return (99).

For example, the mysteries of the Catholic Mass (and, to varying degrees, the authority of the magisterium) are reproduced through the repeated participation of the devout in the liturgy and other kinds of everyday devotional encounters (such as scriptural reading and prayer) that bridge Catholic identity and everyday life. Similarly, the recursive and largely pre-reflexive branded experience at a Starbucks coffeehouse goes something like this: The customer who likes jazz and associates it with cultural sophistication, hears jazz at the Starbucks shop and comes to consider Starbucks to be a brand that is for people who like jazz. The customer is able to express something about themself—their "jazzy sophistication"—through their choice of coffee shop, and their continued experience of brand truth (Starbucks is a place for people who like jazz) reinforces the habit.

For its part, then, the loyal and branded consumer reproduces the cultural dominance of jazzy, "politically correct" sophistication, by participating in and privileging the "Starbucks Experience" as such. At the same time, the branded consumer is creating the consumer environment by enacting ritual activities commonly associated with the Starbucks Experience: The leisurely reading of a book or magazine and the use of laptop computers are two good examples. Those are activities one generally does at Starbucks and not at the local diner or McDonald's (as the taking of the sacrament is an action Catholics generally do during the course of the Mass). In the end, the process is quite circular. The atmosphere and ritual consumer activity help reinforce certain perceptions and associations: sophistication, community, jazziness, connection. A branded Starbucks consumer identifies as a Starbucks consumer according to their perceptions of the brand, and their experience of the brand validates their perceptions of what a Starbucks consumer is.

The typical branded Starbucks customer will "see," in Bell's terms, the "evocation of a consensus on values, symbols, and behavior that is the end of ritualization" (Bell 1992, 110). In other words, they will know what kind of distinctive environment to expect at a Starbucks coffeehouse because encoded on their body are the very perceptions produced by ritual process (e.g., Starbucks is a "politically correct" refuge for jazzy sophisticates). What a branded consumer does not "see" is the way in which their own periodic participation in the Starbucks Experience produces their own consumer subjectivity and continually re-nuances them with "freshly armed schemes of strategic reclassification" (110).

The ritualized consumer does not "see" the ways in which the meticulously ritualized environment of the Starbucks coffeehouse reinforces and re-encodes certain cultural hierarchies (e.g., the cultural dominance of "politically correct" sophistication among elite consumers of the Starbucks brand) that are encoded as perceptions in the ritual body of the Starbucks consumer. This is the reason Bell states that ritual practices distinguish themselves from other social practices that define the self by the fact that "the definition is simultaneously embedded in the social body and its environment" and negotiated,[17] and "rendered prestigious," by the very same privileged status that ritualized activities claim for themselves (Bell 1992, 218). In terms of the Starbucks customer, this recursive logic means that the privileged brand difference of the Starbucks Experience can only be felt by a branded (that is, *ritualized*) customer who is simultaneously generating and molded by the consumer environment.

Bell's account of ritualization, like contemporary branding discourse, assumes a tautological and largely closed account of power. Her account of what she calls "misrecognition" is important to an analysis of the Starbucks Experience.[18] The branded Starbucks customer is, in Bell's language, "unaware of the ways in which the objectified scheme (she) embodies" generates the "sense of integrated reality " (1992, 207). What in fact is schematically arbitrary (e.g., architectural design and ambiance) is misrecognized as being essential and natural. In a similar way, a participant at Mass will generally not directly reflect on the ways in which the incense and music work to produce sacred experience; a Starbucks consumer will not reflect on how the jazz music playing evokes their sense of sophistication. In the case of Mass, religious experience is associated with the inherent power and truth of Catholicism itself. The Starbucks Experience is naturalized and attributed to the power of the brand through commodity fetish. That is, the difference and prestige of the brand are generated through the naturalized and interactive consumer experience and are associated with the brand's power.

The key misrecognition in the case of the ritualized consumer is that the consumer experience is not attributed to corporate marketing strategies but, instead, to the essential meaning of the brand.[19] Ritual loses its efficaciousness if this sense of naturalized totality and "fit" is lost. This is why ritual practice is designed to avoid being brought across the threshold into systematic thought, according to Bell (1992, 93). When one goes to Mass, one's attention is not drawn to the incense, which sets the mood in the background; when one enters a Starbucks, the music is already playing and the smell of coffee is already diffuse. Analogously, Klein writes that the biggest fear of corporations is that their branded lifestyles might "suddenly appear as the ubiquitous goods they really are" ([1999] 2009, 118)—that the consumer might cut themselves off from their Starbucks habit and start going to the coffee cart across the plaza. In its actions within

Starbucks coffeehouses, the Stop Shopping Church very precisely looked to disrupt the naturalized fit of the branded environment.

\* \* \*

Brand logic, like ritualization, is anfractuous and circular. In the second half of the twentieth century, Celia Lury (2004, 8) writes, marketing practices began to incorporate the activities of consumers in their processes of production and distribution. The dynamism of brands "concerns the compulsory inclusiveness of subjects that the performativity of the brand involves" and includes the accumulation and "incorporation of information about everyday activities of subjects—which may be collected with or without their knowledge or permission" (8). What kind of subjectivity is formed—or agency is possible—in relationship to these kinds of power?

The questions of the role of agency in the symbolic constitution of individuals and their social realities are, it always bears repeating, not simply theoretical questions to be vetted in seminar rooms, but also always of very practical concern in our daily lives. For example, today our collective concerns about how the personal data of consumers of social media platforms can be misused by political advertising consultants echo twentieth-century controversies around marketing power like subliminal advertising. They are also a barium drink for mapping the newest incursions of capital into everyday life.

When comparing ritualization and branding, we must ask what branding does for the consumer as a ritualized agent and what implications the ritualization of consumer capitalism has for a critical politics. Bell writes that "ritualization will not work as social control if it is perceived as not amenable to some degree of individual appropriation. If practices negate all forms of individual choice, all forms of resistance, they would take a form other than ritualization" (1992, 22). Put another way, practices of freedom can surreptitiously strengthen the mechanisms of ritual control.

With both ritualization and branding, the tension between sameness and difference remains absolutely central. Bell writes that her term "redemptive hegemony" implies, in effect, that ritualized reality must be patterned in ways that provide social actors with some "advantageous" way to act in the world (1997, 81). Ritualization "structures experience of the world and molds dispositions that are effective in the world so experienced" (1992, 115). In other words, in order to remain effective, the coherence produced by ritualization must be experienced to be in the interests of groups and persons (115).

Similarly, in order to survive, brands must remain both distinctive and flexible enough that individual authenticity and authentic experience can be expressed through the brand. We can learn a lot about how Starbucks produces and sustains its image of authenticity from social historian Bryant Simon's 2011 book, *Everything but the Coffee: Learning about America from Starbucks*. As a Starbucks customers explained to Simon: "I know wherever I go the . . . lemonade will taste the same . . . that's what I want" (2011, 39). Another customer, an American living abroad in Spain, confessed: "I go to Starbucks [. . .] it is nice to get little tastes of familiarity while over here (a little break from the lomo and café con leche!)" (65). There are liturgical elements of the Catholic Mass that are universal. Starbucks uses the same lemonade mix across its global network of coffeehouses.

Brands, like ritualization, are effective when they evoke what Bell refers to as a consensus around values and symbols. Like the Durkheimian "consuming religion" that Kathryn Lofton (2017) analyzes, brands socialize solidarity (in this case: participation in the brand as a taste group) based on the distinctions we make and the hierarchies we hold near and dear. Something we hear in the explanation of a college student whom Simon interviewed who said that she went to Starbucks because "It made me feel older and more studious [. . .] I felt like I was cultured." Starbucks would like the consumers of its lifestyle brand not simply to seek out the instrumental qualities of its coffee but to be drawn into its brand narrative by *and through* the associations the brand elicits.[20]

That college student's experience of sophistication, cosmopolitanism, enlightened benevolence, discovery, and knowledge, is precisely what Bell calls redemptive hegemony, experiences of individual appropriation that prevent the brand from becoming stifling in its ritual control. As Douglas Holt, a marketing professor, puts it, "brands are imbued with stories that consumers find valuable in constructing their identities" (2004, 3). In Bell's terms, brands offer individuals advantageous ways of acting in the world. To return to our example: The college student using Starbucks to feel and project an image of sophistication is simultaneously doing work to shore up Starbucks' ability to be a place that offers consumers a sense of sophistication. Or, in Bell's terms, ritualized experiences of redemptive hegemony work to render the ritual world prestigious.

However, if opportunities for personalization (read: difference) are necessary elements of brand power, Simon points out that sameness and brand coherence are equally important. Brands require "endless repetition" in order to survive, since, as Simon notes, "repetition (remember, Starbucks has thousands of outlets) works in our culture as a teacher" (2011, 108). One kind of repetition might be the music playing, as we've already discussed. Another might be the scripts that Starbucks baristas are given to use with customers in order to "personalize" their experience (11). According to branding professionals, if there is too much difference in the form of eclectic individual meanings, the brand culture dissipates since there is no shared narrative to hold it together or to be experienced as prestigious (Holt 2004, 16).

Without a shared consensus on values and meanings, the brand is no longer socially legible and distinctive. Some amount of predictability is necessary. Simon writes, "There is a tipping point here, however. Too much sameness alarms, rather than reassures, many bobos and creative class types;[21] it cuts into their sense of individuality" (2011, 76). There are unavoidable tensions between "sameness and placelessness, authenticity and consumer desire" (81). McDonaldization or a "functionally geared" model would be deadly for Starbucks (16).[22]

For Starbucks, as with all brands that sell consumer authenticity, the sweet spot is "predictability the individual way," as Simon explains. That is, according to brand logic, activities of consumption ideally reconstitute the brand and simultaneously allow consumers to experience their own individual authenticity, recursively, such that consumer difference is always pegged to corporate sameness.

As Reverend Billy (Talen 2006, 26) puts it: "A Starbucks is dedicated to uniformity but with items that suggest originality, such as mismatching beatnik-like furniture." As we saw, the Stop Shoppers' "cell phone opera" hoped to precisely short-circuit this logic by bringing attention to the coffeehouses' neighborhood-destroying franchise form. However, exploiting the tensions between sameness and difference is only one prong of the activists' full-on assault on the sacralizing power of the Starbucks brand. To break Starbucks' consumerist spell, they would, as we will also see, draw explicit connections between what Reverend Billy has called the "violence" of the franchise's monoculturalization of neighborhoods, on the one hand, and the exploitation of persons whose ritualized disappearances into postindustrial meaning the brand affects, on the other.

## "Starbucks Is the Devil": Breaking the Consumerist Spell

In the end, the authority of a ritualizing brand like Starbucks is dependent on the difference that inheres in sameness and vice versa, or what Catherine Bell refers to as opportunities for experiences of redemptive hegemony. The accretive power of a ritualizing brand is dependent on the (capitalizing) movements of bodies doing things in space and time. Branded (that is, ritualized) agents re-schematize (that is, sacralize) nonbranded space according to their movements in and through the social field (in the activists' terms: through consumerist gestures and choreographies). This, in turn, accounts for the ability of some brands to break into new cultural spaces (and markets) with relative ease. *And*, like all ritual, brands strategically bring attention to certain experiences and relationships while occluding still other experiences and relationships.

The privatization of everything, including cultural critique and subjective authenticity through modes of ritualization, is the fertile ground into which the neoliberal seeds of Starbucks' success were sown.[23] The communications scholar Greg Dickinson argues that Starbucks engages in material and bodily rhetorics of space and place that embed consumers in a "metaphysics of coffee," which is enforced by everyday ritual.[24] These everyday rituals occlude and hide the bodies of global coffee producers from the eyes of consumers, replacing them, instead, with the bodies of affable and inviting baristas who are ready to serve.

As Dickinson writes, "coffee buying and drinking is a ritual that provides indulgences that can cover the sins of living a postmodern life," allowing the consumer to "incorporate" the "naturalness" the brand represents, while also avoiding the exploitations that "underlie the coffee industry."[25] In the early years of the millennium, the Shopping Church intently preoccupied itself with the task of ritually reintroducing these relationships of exploitation back into the horizons of ritualized, choreographed ("Starbucks'd") sippers.

\* \* \*

In addition to proclaiming the sanitized and neutered green mermaid an unholy evil ("Starbucks is the Devil!"), once inside the caffeinated temples that became the group's stage more than twenty years ago, the Stop Shopping Choir looked to break the spell of the Starbucks Experience by interrupting the choreographed sipping of ritualized Starbucks agents with more specific kinds of proclamations that the company would rather silence: "Starbucks is not a fair-trade company! Starbucks is a union busting company!,"[26] the preacher would shout. "Fair trade!," the Choir would chant, in turn.

There was one particular aspect of the Stop Shopping Church's Starbucks era activism that more than one long-standing member of the Choir mentioned as being especially critical. Many of the actions brought attention to the company's attempts in court to block the move by the Ethiopian government to trademark its Sidamo coffee beans.[27] At one such action, Reverend Billy explained to his unwitting retail congregants that the company was selling its Sidamo coffee for $28 a pound, of which Ethiopian farmers received only 78 cents.[28] In the meantime, the farmers' children, he added, were malnourished and the country was dealing with a terrible "child mortality" problem. "They are not fair trade because their advertising is green tinted!," the preacher exclaimed.

Relatedly, and thinking back to our earlier jazz music example, the Stop Shopping Church also made this point clear: Iconic, politically searching music does not ensure progressive politics or manifest social justice. Since "geography is flavor," as a popular Starbucks tagline proclaims, the brand's global music playlist works to strengthen its cosmopolitan appeal. Through its soundtrack for the in-store experience, Starbucks leverages its cultural cachet—that is, its associations (or, in Catherine Bell's terms, "schemes of strategic reclassification") with enlightened capitalism, in order to capitalize on consumers' desire for knowledge.[29] In other words, the coffeehouse music is strategically (and liturgically) designed to compel brand participation in the way sacred music supports religious ritual.

Appreciating, in the Stop Shoppers' own grassroots argot, the role music plays in reproducing the "structuring environments" that shape ritual agents through their interaction with the same in space and time, Reverend Billy once exclaimed at a Starbucks action in London that the coffeehouse "is not socially responsible because they buy Bob Marley, Bob Dylan and Joni Mitchell songs for their Muzak" (Ecotubereview 2009). For the Stop Shopping Church, the moral of the story is that we are never just the *meanings* we consume; the structural violence that enables consumer ritual comes to reside at the very heart of who we are.

If, as we saw, branding strategically organizes an asymmetrical communication between consumers and producers, the Stop Shopping Church, for its part, looked to undo the "division between consumers and workers" so that "we can talk directly to each other" (Talen 2006, 34). In the Starbucks era of their activism, the group brought attention to the fact that in the very same instance that Starbucks stores crowd out and erase local details in their celebration of global diversity, the actual facts surrounding the lives of the global producers of the coffee beans that Starbucks brews into an enticing elixir for the creative classes are unceremoniously obscured and buried by the brand's officious multiculturalism. The Stop Shopping Choir's chosen purpose was one of (religious) rebinding: to rebuild community, as they will say, at the very center of commodified space and pop life.

## Ritualization and Performativity as Cultural Dominant

The "redemptive hegemony" of the Starbucks experience depends on the naturalized fit implied by the ritualization of branded consumers (in the terms of the Stop Shopping Church: consumers' choreographies and ghost gestures) so that consumer experience is a *Starbucks Experience*. In the marketing discourse, branding is understood to be precisely the mechanism whereby the experiences of consumers are integrated, their commitments are shaped, and their worldviews are transformed. It is the chosen mechanism of consumerist soul-craft. The mediatized brand form is part of what we might call neoliberalism's *software*, to borrow Bethany Moreton's (2007) historically apt metaphor.

In the closing pages of this chapter, I want to explore how the Stop Shopping Church's thinking about their own activist performances, and consumer performance's "ghost" and "memorized" gestures, can help us to better understand—and perhaps start to reconsider—how religious studies has theorized embodied rationality in the neoliberal period. The legacy of the Stop Shopping Church helps us to apprehend another way of thinking about a phenomenon with which our discipline has deeply wrestled and to sense more clearly how and why we have sometimes misrecognized important aspects of the situation.

As I have already suggested, Catherine Bell's account of ritualization converges with our everyday consumption at the fulcrum of the brand form and constitutes an important account of embodied rationality in religious studies from the past thirty years.[30] Of this brand form, the sociologist Celia Lury (2004, 7) explains: "the range of performances is not entirely predetermined by the objectivity of the brand, however, but emerges in interactivity. In other words, just as the subject may be seen as an effect of *performativity* (Butler 1990) so too may the ongoing object-ivity of the brand." Put another way, the brand has its own (recursive) logic or "performativity" through which is organized a two-way, selective, and asymmetrical communication between producer and consumers (Lury 2004, 7) that stresses symbolic, communicative interactivity as the ontological meaning of the brand (6–8).[31] Consumer bodies and activities signify.

The concept of performativity that Celia Lury applies to her analysis of branding has had some important analytical purchase in critical religious studies as well, especially through the influence of Judith Butler, best known for their ideas about the performativity of gender. As the religion scholars Ellen T. Armour and Susan St. Ville (2006, 4) explain in their introduction to a popular edited volume on Butler's significance for religious studies, performativity depends on repetition and the fact that language does not merely describe reality but, rather, under felicitous conditions, *does and makes what it says*, in an illocutionary sense. To use the classic example borrowed from J. L. Austin (1962), the wedding ceremony pronouncement "I pronounce you husband and wife" produces a change in the state of the couple, they are now married.

For scholars strongly indebted to performativity theory, description does not merely portray social reality but is strongly involved in its very constitution. Performativity has been applied by scholars to productively think through the ways in which norms, practices, and institutions are both reproduced and resignified. In the Armour and St. Ville volume, scholars of religion apply Butler's work on performativity to make sense of such disparate religious contexts as orthodox Catholic opposition to women's ordination and the Egyptian women's mosque movement of the 1990s (2006).[32]

Additionally, in the same volume, the scholar of Medieval Christianity Amy Hollywood (2006), drawing heavily from Jacques Derrida's deconstructive account of ritual and Catherine Bell's account of ritualization, makes an influential theoretical intervention, noting the ways in which *ritual*, like language, is illocutive—that is, through the *doing* of ritualized bodies, social fields are maintained.[33] Explicitly reading Butler and Bell together, Hollywood's account of ritualization insists that ritual is citational (again, in the sense that it is dependent on recognizable and repeatable re-performances of bodily practice). That is, ritual is repetitive and partakes of a structure in which conventionality (sameness) is always shadowed by the specter of newness (difference), and since repetition is not the same as the reproduction of *identical* citations of ritual meaning, the very structure of ritual signification implies possibilities for improvisation, misfire, and subversion.

Thinking ritualization through performativity, Hollywood argues that the former plays a significant role in social reproduction and social change. Here, we must also recall, Savitri D's description of consumerism as increasingly "repetitive," which is related to a further observation I've heard the Stop Shoppers make of consumerism's obsession with "identical details" (Reverend Billy and the Stop Shopping Choir 2022b). One way in which consumerism works, Savitri D and the Stop Shoppers argue, is exactly by peddling controlled, homogenizing difference. The group's "cell phone opera" ("*Which* Starbucks?" "I *am* at Starbucks!"), discussed earlier, took precise and direct aim at the franchise form as more sameness masking as difference.

For her part, in the same collected volume, the performance studies scholar Rebecca Schneider (2006, 240) is careful to point out that Judith Butler is very much not, in their micropolitics of the body, looking to rehabilitate a voluntarist account of the will.³⁴ Schneider explains: "For Butler, conscious performance conceals discursive performativity." While it is important to recognize at all times that speech, thought, and action are never *sui generis*, Schneider's framing of Butler's poststructuralist insistence that power precedes experience carries echoes of Celia Lury's description of the symbolic and communicative interactivity within which acts of consumption are meant to arise as second-order experience. The problem is that the reiterative and recursive loops of meaning that accounts of performativity traffic in ultimately freeze us into too conservative an account of what's possible. Especially in Butler's largely semiotic approach, performativity theory too strongly emphasizes the semantic construction of agency at the expense of an accounting of subjects' creative, interpretive, and pragmatic abilities to improvise within the constraints of culture. When transported into the activists' context, all of this becomes cause for real concern.

Reverend Billy (Talen 2006, 199) has written this of consumerism's methods and aim: "That's their Orwellian model, the logos talking to each other in the air, with people below pre-persuaded, just consuming, and not in the loop of power. Logo to Logo, transacting: the perfect economy."³⁵ The activists understand brands' semiotic interactivity as the mediatized form of consumption that looks to render consumer desire inevitable and concrete practices of consumption automatic.³⁶ The activists would agree with Kathryn Lofton (2017, 64) that "consumption *is* our ritualization" and might, I would venture, suggest to scholars that one of our leading accounts of ritualization, Bell's (including Amy Hollywood's Derridian rereading of it), offers a useful, granular map into how consumption is actually designed to work through bodies acting in place and time.

Taking all of this into consideration allows us an opportunity to reflect on what we've learned from the Stop Shopping Church so far in order to consider what I see as the problem for readers of Judith Butler in religious studies. Butler themself frames the performativity of embodiment in terms of *ontology* rather than *history*, in terms of a first philosophy of the subject (capable of explaining the ontological conditions of the self) and constitutive social process (what Nancy Fraser [2013, 185] calls an "abstract, transhistorical property of language"). Butler's readers in religious studies have too often failed to account for the historicity of the concept of performativity itself. That is, they risk confusing historical relationships for constitutive ones.[37]

According to the anthropologist Kath Weston, "performativity theory can scarcely attend to the historical circumstances of its production" (2017, 85) precisely because it tends to disappear matters of political economy. Here, I want to suggest the continued importance of Fredric Jameson's (1982, 62) injunction to "*always historicize!*" Cultural productions, including social theory, emerge in place and time and can be understood as negotiations with history.[38] And in neoliberal times, with capital's deep and tight structuring of social value and social imaginaries more broadly, we cannot ever assume that fashions around social theory can ever simply escape or easily bypass the logic of the marketplace.

The feminist scholar Melinda Cooper (2017) places the popularity of performativity within neoliberalism's incorporation of antinormativity, the rise of the nonstandard risk, and the mechanics of credit and debt.[39] The anthropologist David Graeber (2012), one of the Stop Shopping Church's most important academic friends and partners, argues that performativity, which he analogizes as the magical proposition that power creates its own truth, achieved its broad popularity among social theorists during the neoliberal period, when market value became reducible to whatever the market said it was.[40] This tautological structure, he argues, left the economy vulnerable to socially painful bubbles and busts. Importantly, a convergence to which we will return, Graeber also finds that the logic of performativity mirrors "the pervasive Foucauldianism of the American academe of recent decades."[41]

For her part, the anthropologist Kath Weston (2002, 89) specifies that Judith Butler's account of performativity, and of the citational practice of gender, is dangerously abstract since its repetitions are actually accomplished within the economic order, "through the use of mass-produced commodities." Butler's influential account of gender performativity, much as neoliberal ideology would have it, Weston adds, problematically locates gender exclusively within processes of consumption.[42] This accent comes at the expense of labor, despite the patriarchal and anti-queer violence of social reproduction, the increasing feminization of service work, and the harsh realities faced by global, pink-collar labor. It locates gender exclusively within the realm of the visible signifiers and markers of gender.[43]

Weston places the repetitions and citationality of performativity within the cadences of mass production and commodity fetishism.[44] When the norm repeats and accretes, so do the (2002, 84) "chinos and the makeup" and the "timbre of voices and gestures" on offer.[45] As Weston puts it (84), "invariably tick follows tock, the *expectation* that tick will follow tock is something else again, produced through repetition but hardly identical with it."[46] Or, to return to Starbucks, your cup of coffee both is and is not mine, but if we are happily drinking the same brand, our acts of consumption accrete onto the normativity of the brand not unlike the ways in which acts of gender accrete also onto the ruling gender regime.

Over time, the little changes to social norms (the difference that inheres in sameness) statistically add up and the concentrated strength of novel sociocultural citation is able to insist upon its own ability and authority to mark the incrementally shifting boundaries of the real. That is, in an advertising age, repetitive acts of saying so, actually make so. The Starbucks cup, seen in the "right" hands, tautologically reestablishes the brand's cultural appeal.[47] This process is actually not unrelated to the reasons we have celebrities who are famous for being celebrities, or to the money that can be made on the market if you can only convince investors that an idea is better than it actually is. Performativity also underwrites the work of social media influencers, whose repetitions (retweets) can make and remake a product or service through the accretion of authoritative endorsement. Consumer performativity is embodied, ritual process according to which negativity and difference are gathered to the cause of capitalist presence.

Amy Hollywood (2006) was right to insist on the conceptual relationship between performativity and ritualization. And consumption is indeed our ritualization (Lofton 2017). For her part, Savitri D was importantly alighting in her suggestion that consumerism is grounded in the logic of repetition and predetermined meanings. The same is true of the Stop Shopping Church in its diagnosis of consumerism's obsessions with "identical details" (read: the difference that is constitutive of sameness) in our information age. The labors of the Stop Shopping Church suggest to us that scholars do well to embed our own ideas about ritual within the iterative logics that have *consumerized* us, in turn.

* * *

Marketers prioritize the power of abstract discourse; scholars must respect discourse but prioritize practice, *including our own*. We must practice reflecting on the historical determinacies of our chosen theories, rather than afford them opportunities to mask their own contingencies and reflections of historical power. Reverend Billy has proposed that we need to "get rid of labels . . . even avant-garde . . . we need to rediscover experience."[48] Scholars have good reason to consider following this suggestion. Social theories, like marketing, can problematically abstract and remove scholars from the facts on the ground—the intersubjective realms of what we might call social experience.

A return to some kind of a naïve, historically and politically unmediated phenomenology is happily impossible.[49] This is a point that I will take up again in the next chapter, but what I do want to suggest is that it is incumbent upon scholars to test our own theories (in the activists' terms: labels) against the world that grounds them and to which they are necessarily tethered. Our conceptual tools should be part and parcel of the phenomena we study. The encounter between scholars and activists within the branded mediascapes from which we all necessarily drink our proverbial coffee (and tea) suggests that reality-testing our own theories against the social world can begin to help us pry open a window into our own at least partially preprogrammed, religious souls as scholars.

2

## Privatizing the Consumer Soul

Human desire is the raw material we are working with. The strategy of human desire is the tool of shaping the human factor, the most important aspect of our worldly arsenal.
—Ernest Dichter, *The Strategy of Desire*

It is not hard to show that the force of desire alleged to undermine the rigidities of late capitalism is, in fact, very precisely what keeps the consumer system going in the first place.
—Fredric Jameson, *Postmodernism, Or the Cultural Logic of Late Capitalism*

### Remembering the Social Body

In 2018, at the height of activist resistance to the Trump administration's immigration policies, I attended an event co-sponsored by the New Sanctuary Coalition, an immigrant-led and -run advocacy group that works to resist and stop the detention and forced deportation of immigrants, known within the group as "friends." Grounded in New York City's faith-based, progressive networks and social justice communities, it is an organization with which the Stop Shopping Church closely partnered in those days. In fact, its executive director had sung with the Choir, and when he was detained by ICE, Reverend Billy would crack jokes in public sermons, wondering when he was coming back to rehearsal.[1]

On this day, we made our way to 45 Federal Plaza. One of the buildings on the plaza houses the New York field office of US Immigration and Customs Enforcement (ICE), and approximately two hundred people had gathered around it. There were political speeches and an art show on one side of the ICE building and, on the other side, musical and theatrical performances. I took it all in together with the ten members of the group that had come, including Savitri D and Reverend Billy. The music being performed by the all-women Brazilian Samba and Reggae band, Fogo Azul, and the radical marching and dance troupe, the Rude Mechanical Orchestra, provided a caffeinated sonic pulse to the events and reminded me of the sounds and rhythms of movie and television soundtracks.

The main event of the gathering was an interactive art installation in which attendees had an opportunity to think about a person they love and try to pack a twenty-five-pound suitcase for them, the way ICE forces deportees to fit their lives into one bag before sending them back "home" to countries they barely know, where they are endangered by gang violence, or their gender expression and sexuality are criminalized. The exercise was consonant with what Savitri D proposed in her public remarks: that "art is fundamental to social justice," which makes good prescriptive sense since, as we saw in chapter 1, capitalist culture is highly aestheticized and sometimes you must fight fire with fire. Reverend Billy, for his part, reflected on the ways in which the suitcase event reminds us of the irreducibility of a human life and, through a creative and ritualizing form of active remembrance, engenders a loving of persons whom a whole system is designed to "humiliate." In the words of the organizers of the event, the material, everyday lives of immigrants and their loved ones represent an "invisible" layer in the unscrupulous injustices of the "deportation machine."

An event like the suitcase installation accomplishes important critical work even if it must necessarily do so through sorrowful means. Even mass-produced commodities like clothing, shoes, or a valise bear the impressions of persons for whom they become meaningful and intimate. In this case, like the personal artefacts housed at the United States Holocaust Memorial Museum or the photographs of the everyday items left behind by migrants at the US-Mexico border, some of whom were not able to complete their journey and either perished or were incarcerated by border police,[2] the suitcase installation sought to bring attention to what Laura Levitt (2020, 3) calls the "living presence" of the objects that remain and still "hold traces of the blood, the sweat, the tears" of now absent bodies.

To state something of an anthropological truism: Human being is always and already mediated by the material world. Critiques of consumption that underestimate and underappreciate our intersubjective relationships with the things we live by can easily denigrate into ineffective, anthropologically deficient, moralizing finger wagging. Our embeddedness in and entanglements with the material world are never themselves the political problem with consumption. Neither is the human fact of affective attachment. Materiality and desire are not themselves the issue; what is at issue for the Stop Shopping Church—and for us in this chapter—is the fact that consumption libidinally ritualizes intersubjectivity in particularly formatted ways that sever and do violence to constitutive social and ecological relationships. For the Stop Shopping Church, the problem is that consumerism structurally organizes a disappearance of the Earth and conceals society's injuries, spinning injuries out into evermore consumption. In response to the collectivized sacrifice of what we might also call the relations of production and the natural world, the group looks to actively re-*member* the "Earthy" social body that extractive, racial capitalism tears apart.[3]

* * *

I learned early into my fieldwork that memorialization, remembrance, and the redirection of desire are vital to the activist work of the Stop Shopping Church. At the first public performance of the group that I attended, at the Cathedral of St. John the Divine, the Choir processed from the back of the church toward the front, one Choir member at a time taking it upon themselves to shout out the name of a Black person who had been martyred by the racist police state: Sandra Bland, Sean Bell, Amadou Diallo, Trayvon Martin, Tamir Rice, and Eleanor Bumpers, a sixty-six-year-old-woman who was murdered in 1984 by the NYPD during a forced eviction from her public housing apartment in the Bronx. I was eleven when the shooting occurred and I remember that it was often on my mind in those days, both because the incident and the subsequent criminal trial of the police officer who shot Mrs. Bumpers made headline news in the City and because, as a child, I found it especially unsettling that someone who resembled a grandmother could have met such a violent end. The Choir's naming of Eleanor Bumpers gave me a special jolt of remembrance.[4]

After a long, ritual pause, Emmett Till's name punctuated the roll call. Then, after a sung, musical arrangement of Yeats's poem, "The Second

Coming" led by the musical director, Jeremiah, Reverend Billy began his homily by reciting the group's "Beatitudes of Buylessness," a statement of their moral priorities in the genre of Jesus's Beatitudes. Among those blessed by Reverend Billy's homily in the church were workers in the super malls, "ordinary citizens" who "hold onto a patch of the commons," "young women in sweatshops," immigrants, and the "mothers of the children murdered by men in uniforms." That is, he blessed some of the most unheralded, marginalized, vulnerable, and invisible people in global society.

The performative spirit of Reverend Billy's sermon both recalled and resignified the Lucan Jesus, the Palestinian Jewish prophet and social activist many of the Stop Shoppers will tell you they actually respect—the man who fought empire and cared for the poor. But this would not be a moment of Christian conversion: *"I never was in a building that wanted God to come back so bad!"* Reverend Billy exclaimed. They are not interested in what they call "godmen." The Stop Shoppers had a different kind of "second coming" in mind. Within what Reverend Billy called "this hollowed out mountain," the performance, as a whole, urged listeners to pursue justice from the margins. As in Yeats's poem, "revelation is in plain sight." *"Our falconer is the immigrant living in terror in an apartment,"* the preacher proclaimed, adding that whenever activists move to protect immigrants and their families from the police, they are, in fact, meeting the "Earth" there.

For the Stop Shopping Church, consumerism ritualizes a senselessness to the pain, fears, and predicament of others and inculcates a general forgetting of our earthly nature. Important questions follow from the Stop Shopping Church's concerns that scholars of North American religion are, especially in tandem with the activists' example, well positioned to explore: *How did we develop our myopic, truncated, autonomous, and individualistic view of "ourselves," to begin with, and how might we theorize critical subversion from within our ensoulment (the embodied result of soul-craft) by history as persons with particular kinds of desires, attachments, and understandings of the world?*

\* \* \*

In order to think with the Stop Shopping Church about how we have become (and might unbecome) citizen consumers—and to reinforce the necessity of historicizing our religious studies methods and objects of study—we need to go back to the mid-twentieth century to find out how psychoanalytic theory flows through the bedrock of both neoliberal society and religious studies theory and methods, as well as influential social theory from the past thirty years, more broadly. So, while we might be spending some time away from the Stop Shopping Church in the pages to come, our path will lead back to the origins, motivations, and the prescient salience of their critiques.

As we will see, some of the ideas of a classic theorist in the study of religion (one any student in the field is required to read), Sigmund Freud, strongly influenced the development of American marketing and its governance of the consumer soul.[5] North American consumers have long been Freudianized. Both consumer and academic accounts of performativity are also indebted to the influence of psychoanalytic ideas; these connections in turn suggest some critical possibilities. Given its own engagements with psychoanalysis—as informed by the example of the grassroots activists and once it historicizes theory in the ways advised in chapter 1—the field of religious studies is positioned to make theoretical interventions and contributions around the processes whereby we become (and perhaps work to unbecome) citizen consumers.[6]

## Ernest Dichter, Freud, and American Motivation Research

Rather than an economic philosophy, the neoliberal turn of the past fifty years must instead be understood as a cosmological formation that supports a total way of life. The neoliberal worldview gives new primacy to consumption and proposes that human well-being is best advanced by facilitating an entrepreneurial spirit, through the institutional protection of property rights, the liberalization of trade, opposition to union power, and the bolstering of free markets. In short, neoliberalism radicalizes what David Harvey calls "market exchange as 'an ethic in itself'" and implicates in wholescale transformations of "ways of life and thought" (Harvey 2005, 2).

While the performances of the Stop Shopping Church and the work of recent scholars suggest the importance of attending to neoliberalism's co-implications with traditional religion, especially Protestant Christianity, in the development of the American soul of neoliberalism, we also do well to take heed of Kathryn Lofton's (2017) and Reverend Billy's figurations of corporate capitalism itself, on its own putatively secular terms, as religion. Since consumerism is our ritualization (that is, our religious socialization), it is one of the earliest and most direct conduits through which we develop what David Harvey calls neoliberalism's "habits of the heart."

The American reception and institutionalization of Freud's ideas is an important part of this story of how these "habits of the heart" have taken hold. Applying Michel Foucault's concept of self-government to contemporary society, the sociologist Nikolas Rose argues that in our "passional economy,"[7] we are obliged to consume as a practice of freedom. Technologies of consumption fabricate affiliations between consumer desire and the qualities and pleasures represented by products. Psychological techniques have been fundamental, he continues, to the development of these habits. These contemporary "psy-driven" technologies do not crush subjectivity, Rose argues, but, rather, fabricate subjects who can bear the "burdens of liberty" ([1989] 1999, viii). These are the trappings—and traps—of the society Freudian thought helped to build.

According to the social historian Lawrence Samuel, more than a century has passed since Freud's only visit to the United States in 1909, and Freudianism has since insinuated itself into the very DNA of the American story (Samuel 2013). Today, Samuel concludes, the basic assumptions of Freudian psychoanalysis, including ideas about repression and the unconscious, are "deeply embedded in the discourse of American popular and consumer culture" (ix). According to Eli Zaretsky (2005), whereas psychoanalysis in Europe emerged as an alternative positioned against the "traditional, patriarchal order," American optimism and pragmatism transformed psychoanalysis, reorienting its insights toward "personal improvement and productivity" (Samuel 2013, xii). Especially for Americans, Freudianism became "a great theory and practice of 'personal life'" (xiii). Psychoanalysis reshaped American culture and national identity from the inside out. Psychoanalytic ideas and tropes have so greatly influenced popular culture, especially literature, art, and film, that its alliance with the "creative class" became a form of social currency (xvii).

\* \* \*

Although he was not related to Freud, Ernest Dichter, the father of motivation research in marketing—along with Edward Bernays, the progenitor of the field of public relations, and Freud's nephew[8]—became one of the most historically influential interpreters and synthesizers of Freud's ideas. As was also the case with Bernays's public relations, Dichter's approach to advertising skirted the tensions and divisions between individual agency and social control, libidinal freedoms and discipline, individual creativity and mass appeal. For his part, Dichter's greatest detractor, the social critic Vance Packard, famously took strong issue with what he perceived to be a naked attempt at thought control. Packard (1957, 238) concludes in the best-selling exposé, *The Hidden Persuaders*, that corporate interests in loosening (and redirecting) the trajectories of libidinal desire necessarily come at the cost of voluntary freedom.

In the American context, the turn inward toward psychic excavation and somatic excess was an effect of and response to the burgeoning contradictions of secular modernity and its very Protestant antecedent, cultural history.[9] It is within these deeper currents that we must place the early reception of Freud by a rapidly commercializing nation. Given Dichter's efforts, the psychic life of Freudian power would, stateside, prove to be strongly mediated by the economic order from the start. Samuel's (2010, 19) social history of the marketing reception of Freud traces the origins of Dichter's psychoanalytic motivation research methodology in Vienna in the early 1930s through its professional zenith in American advertising in the 1950s to its decline in the 1960s and revival in the 1980s, culminating in its transformation into the "consumer insight" and "account planning research methodologies" of today.

Through their influence on motivation research, Freud's ideas have become essential to the spirit of the market. If the Canadian American economist John K. Galbraith argued that markets do not simply meet existing needs but are expressly in the business of cultivating new needs and desires,[10] Dichter, along with his clients and his followers in industry, enthusiastically agreed. Psychic abundance represented future profit; the shifting, misty cathexes of the subconscious were rich terrain for capital to attach to. Samuel writes, "it was no coincidence that motivation research took off just as the nation's postwar economy kicked into high gear." Dealing just with the "conscious self" may be fine in a subsistence economy, its proponents argued, but not in that of the United States at mid-twentieth-century with so many discretionary dollars floating around with which the self could work to tame its inner disquiet.

Fine-tuning the staging of what he called the "motivational theater" of consumption, Ernest Dichter saw himself as being in the business of "building a better mousetrap" (Samuel 2010, 58). From his perspective, the older models had been decidedly naïve about the realities of human nature. Especially before the 1930s, early advertising was largely based on crude and rudimentary methodologies such as door-to-door interviewing (5), questionable sampling procedures (4–10), and an overreliance on surveys and questionnaires for obtaining consumer data. Although there were important precursors to Dichter's Freudian revolution, it was the psychoanalytic orientation of motivation research that would finally overcome the rationalist biases of early industrialists (9). Going forward, appeals to autonomous consumer choice were disingenuous flattery alone.

Through Dichter's influence, marketers would come to agree with Marx about the "theological niceties" of our proverbial dancing tables. That is, they had jettisoned the conceit that consumption's motivations are merely rational (or, "economic"). As Dichter eventually came to understand it, "each product has a soul—a deeper meaning—and it is only when this deeper meaning is grasped that a real communication takes place between the advertiser and the consumer" (Samuel 2010, 171). These deeper meanings were, applying Freud's psychoanalytic theories to the rituals of consumption, littered with psychological complexes, taboos, and repressed desire (Schwarzkopf 2014). For example, Dichter sold to executives the idea that bathing was simultaneously a purification ritual and an erotic experience for culturally puritanical Americans. As Dichter marketed it: "bathing, in its old, ritualistic, anthropological sense, is getting rid of all your bad feelings, your sins, your immorality, and cleaning yourself, baptism, etc." (Samuel 2010, 34).

In 1947, Dichter wrote in the *Harvard Business Review* that since consumption lagged behind increasingly efficient production, prewar marketing methods had become obsolete. Marketers, he believed, needed to fully commit to addressing consumers' emotions, unconscious drives, and irrational behavior (Samuel 2010, 35). As he refined it at his institute, motivation research methodology incorporated psychoanalytic insights, consumer ethnography, Gestalt psychology, focus groups, free association, storytelling, role playing, and psychodrama (35).

With an aim of understanding subconscious motivations such as greed, desire for security, insecurity, and fear that underlay consumer behavior, Dichter developed the "depth interview" in which a market researcher would have a lengthy (sometimes three-hour) open-ended conversation with a consumer in which the consumer's attitudes, beliefs, and lifestyle would be discussed, allowing their underlying, subconscious motivations to emerge. Dichter also deployed "psycho-panels" in which local Westchester, New York, families who were "sorted by character type, such as secure versus insecure, escapist versus realist" (Samuel 2010, 55) formed the bases for interview sets.[11]

In the 1940s, most American market research focused on learning as much as possible about who made purchases, where, and how information about a product or service reached the consumer. Many marketers assumed that the realities of social stratification and class aspirations provided sufficient data regarding incentives to consume. Ernest Dichter took issue with this simple demographic approach, arguing that only a psychoanalytic approach would help industry understand the underlying, subconscious reasons people part with their money. "Economic man," Dichter believed, "with his (sic) focus on instrumental reasoning and cost-benefit analysis, needed to give way to the complex psychic sinews of 'psychological man.'" The pleasure principle, rather than the reality principle, Dichter insisted, ruled the largely hidden terrain of consumer motivations (Samuel 2010, 27).[12]

"Casual" consumers, Dichter added, are driven primarily by the id, "guilty" consumers are driven by their superegos, and "rational" consumers operate more at the calculating level of ego than other types (Malherek 2014). As Stefan Schwarzkopf (2014) writes, Dichter remained, "a committed Freudian by stressing how sexual motives, ever-present human insecurity, and fear—especially of death, aging, and the unknown 'other'—underpinned our choices as consumers." Often presenting its findings in "literary ways" but nevertheless able to traffic in the clout and prestige of social scientific objectivity, motivation research was all the rage in the 1950s (Samuel 2010, 48). In the late 1950s and early 1960s, Dichter commanded a per diem consulting fee of $500 and could charge a company or organization upwards of $60,000 for a full-scale study.[13] At its peak, Dichter's Institute for Motivation Research employed a staff of seventy researchers and support staff, and around two-thousand part-time interviewers (Schwarzkopf 2014).

Between 1946 and 1956, Dichter performed seven hundred studies for corporate and institutional clients (Samuel 2010, 64). For their part, by then economists solidly endorsed the idea that increased consumer spending was required for sustained economic growth (84). Through the influence of Dichter, who was featured in magazines like *Time*, the *New Yorker*, and *Newsweek*, postwar America's "obsession with all things psychological" coincided with the coordinates of the market, which looked to expand beyond the mass market and move into a "new era of the specialized market" (136). In the 1950s, Dichter worked with major American companies like General Mills, Philip Morris, Mattel (on the launch of the Barbie doll), and the Ford Motor Company to extend their market share by deepening their psychic share in society.

In 1954, the *Wall Street Journal* proclaimed that the subconscious, that "strange wilderness," was at the cutting edge of the "businessman's hunt for sales" (45). Between the 1940s and 1970s, Dichter continued to advise multinational corporations, among them energy companies like Amoco, Shell, Exxon, Mobil Oil; food companies like Cadbury's, Nestlé, and General Mills; tobacco companies like Lucky Strike and Pall Mall; and airline companies like Air France, Japan Airlines, and American Airlines (Schwarzkopf 2014). Meanwhile, although Dichter's motivation research survived the subliminal advertising controversy of the 1950s, secular and religious critics alike expressed worries about motivation research advertising's abilities to engineer consent and to exploit human needs for security, love, and self-worth.

Vance Packard's *Hidden Persuaders*, published in 1957, took direct aim at Ernest Dichter and amplified the brewing blowback against marketing's perceived social engineering. Taking up an ostensibly secular bullhorn, Packard's criticisms nevertheless could stray only so far from the question of religion. An exasperated Packard notes for his reader that, "on (one) occasion, Dr. Dichter (even) pointed out that the public's shift away from its 'puritan complex' was, 'enhancing the power of three major sales appeals: desire for comfort, for luxury, and for prestige'" (Packard 1957, 238). It is no surprise, then, Packard writes, that "religious spokesmen" have been "among the first to speak out in criticism" against motivation research and the growing pressures to consume (238).

Heralding Francis Fukuyama's (1992) fantastically utopian neoliberal dream of a global marketplace peacefully mediating our differences, Dichter proclaimed the dawn of a global age: "a psychological United Nations," grounded in "American psychological values which emphasize the 'good life'" (McKelway 1958). As a postwar political consultant, Dichter also introduced marketing frameworks into political circles. While its professional fortunes would wane in the 1960s (only to wax again in the 1980s) and although new competitors like operations research in the late 1950s (Samuel 2010, 151) and computational approaches in the 1970s (159) emerged, Lawrence Samuel concludes that Ernest Dichter and motivation research left an ineradicable mark on American business. In the end, Dichter's incorporation of psychoanalytic theory into motivation research methodology so changed the very grammar of American marketing (and American society) that, even today, with the rise in interest in the application of neuroscience and ethnographic fieldwork to marketing, Dichter is always, "there by proxy" (3).

* * *

Coming back to the Starbucks-era activism of the Stop Shopping Church at the millennium, we recall that the activists understood that the Starbucks brand works through the power of preconscious suggestion, convincing us in the background that we have no choice but to locate our desires for arty sophistication within its carefully managed brand narrative and retail theater. Before this, Ernest Dichter's mid-twentieth-century incorporation of psychoanalysis helped to squarely move the terrain of consumerism's appeal away from instrumental considerations of cost, efficiency, and price and, instead, toward the vast psychological sinews that support our largely hidden motivations to spend.

As we saw in chapter 1, the Stop Shopping Church correctly diagnosed the specific performative cadences according to which consumer activity is organized. However, when Reverend Billy would denounce Starbucks not only for exploiting workers and farmers but also for daring to attach itself to avant-garde cultural cachet and cosmopolitan signifiers that they felt it had not earned but still used to fool and ensnare consumer seekers, echoes of previous generations' anxieties about the alliance of capitalism and depth psychology could be heard. As it turns out, the group correctly sensed the strongly psychic foundations of contemporary consumption. We will see that, as valuable context for the activist work of the Stop Shopping Church, the iterative and recursive form of consumer performativity we explored in the previous chapter and the marketing turn to psychoanalysis we will explore in the present chapter are, in fact, historically intertwined. And both are anchored to consumer subjectivity's historical grounding in primary experiences of loss.

## Marketing, Ritual, and Iterative Control

Ritual and consumption have been spoken together in the same breath since the nineteenth century. In the mid-twentieth century, Ernest Dichter represents a late capitalist apotheosis of sorts—a proud social scientist and purveyor of Freud's ideas, he comes to view marketers as society's ritual experts par excellence. In fact, he claims, the religious authorities have much to learn from marketers about the psychological foundations of ritual (Dichter [1960] 2012, 112). Marketing rituals, he believes, are related to broader forms of ritual process that marketers, like anthropologists, work to understand.

Dichter ([1960] 2012, 197) writes, "Even from the beginning of kindergarten days we are taught in our lives to ritualize, to squeeze the unorganized day into strict rules." "Practicing cultural anthropology more than anything else," Dichter (112) adds, motivation research marketing is in a position to deeply understand the ways in which consumer media provide resources for living. Explicitly connecting Western consumption to the social rituals of Samoans, Trobriand Islanders, and Balkan peasants,[14] among others, Dichter (41, 190, 197) explains that mid-twentieth-century marketers are, in effect, "merchants of security." Marketers sell the scripts for processes of what he directly calls "*ritualization*" (197) that, in turn, provide technologies for everyday living.[15] Unsurprisingly, he also professed an affinity for the work of the foundational historian of religion, Mircea Eliade, and carried on an ongoing correspondence with the cultural anthropologist Margaret Mead (Schwarzkopf and Gries 2010).[16]

According to Dichter, consumption fulfills the necessary role of ritualization in modern, American society. In Dichter's corpus, consumer ritual is versatile: It offers rewards, it structures the luxury of "me" time, it heightens anticipation, it intensifies our fetishistic associations with consumer goods (Dichter 1947b), it purifies and grounds the self, it binds families and communities, it forms and signals identity, and it transforms and expands the self (Market Research and American Business, 1935–1965).

For Ernest Dichter, consumer rituals could take the mundane shape of oral hygiene practices or, echoing Victor Turner's work on puberty rites, the purchasing of something as grey and dreary as a life insurance policy. Life insurance, Dichter insists, actually signals the transformation of the young person into adulthood (Dichter [1960] 2012, 216) with its attendant responsibilities. Dichter also affirms that the "quest for identity" (282) increasingly compels consumers, and marketers must, in turn, sell solutions to life quandaries and "exert influence to encourage acceptance of change" (215). Motivation researchers can accomplish their manipulations, pushing for transformations of subjectivity and society, because they are trained in a psychoanalytic approach fluent in the pre-cognitive language of the body: *dress codes, facial expressions, symbolic objects, and bodily gestures* (124–125). In short, they understand the importance of placing consumer rites within the "total framework of culture" (148), much as we might say that a good cultural sociologist would.

So where does that leave religious studies' own take on ritual and culture? The historian of religion J. Z. Smith (1982) argues that a basic fact of ritual is that it serves as a "focusing lens." It heightens the significance of some things while hiding and obscuring the significance of other things. With that definition, we could say that, through Dichter's ministrations, it became the work of advertising to suggest and facilitate connections for the ritual expression of self—that is, to manage the terms by which we come to be. Fully absent from Dichter's considerations of this dynamism, however, are the face of labor, the environmental and political costs of doing business, and the social inequalities reproduced by consumption (all the things the Stop Shopping Church would arise to insist we attend to more fully).

Consumers' deep dives into the self are privatized through consumer ritual. Privatization implies the sacrifice of the social and the natural world. As Rebecca Bartel (2021, 4) explains, neoliberal economy gives shape to "affective and internalized repertoires of moral practice."[17] This is as true for consumption as it is labor and the modes of financial self-government Bartel studies. In all cases, through processes of soul-craft, psychic qualities come to mirror economic processes.

Importantly, Ernest Dichter concludes that marketers "*offer a ritualistic framework within which certain deviations are possible*" ([1960] 2012, 200).[18] This idea directly anticipates the concept of citational performativity (of bodily citations) popularized within the study of religion by readers and students of Judith Butler, as we discussed in the last chapter. Dichter's understanding of consumer ritualization establishes, as do Butlerian readings of citational bodies, that embodied ritual is regulated by norms of practice, but must also accommodate, in some controlled way, departures and digressions from the norm. We recall, here, the conceptual entailments between branding and performativity, both of which strongly echo the coordinates of Catherine Bell's influential discussion of ritualization, especially around the iterability of discourse (or, in the terms of the Stop Shopping Church: consumerism's penchant for "identical details"). According to the anthropologist, Kath Weston, Freud's relationship to the rhythms of consumer capitalism should not surprise us. Weston (2002, 84) explains that Freud's thought, contemporaneous as it was to Henry Ford's, was from the start imbued with the assumptions of capitalist time.

Weston specifies: Freud's ideas of "repetition compulsion" are historically entangled with the repetitions and citationality of mass production and commodity fetishism. As an archeological matter,[19] I propose a history of performativity informed by mid-twentieth-century American marketing's account of the subject and the "power" that brings it into existence. This historical revelation in itself, however, would not satisfy the aims and goals of the activists at the Stop Shopping Church, who are directly interested in the ways in which consumers might actively break reiterative, self-perpetuating cycles of consumption. Thus, I will suggest that, as a historical matter, we must consider the constitutive experience of loss that corresponds to our subjection as citizen consumers as important to understanding both what fuels consumerism in the first place and how the activists seem to think we might begin to resist its ritualized disappearances of the many others who make us who we are. To make this argument clearer, and to continue our path back into the performances of the Stop Shopping Church, we continue our discussion of the work of a key scholarly theorist from the last chapter, Judith Butler.

## Judith Butler and the Psychic Life of Power

Judith Butler (1997a, 4) has made the important observation that social theory is at an impasse whenever it assumes an already existing subject who "internalizes" power. How is it possible, they ask, to account for the self that is the subject of social discipline without attending first to the processes according to which that very same self emerges? Although their account of power is theoretical (in the sense of belonging to the "theory" half of scholarly theories and methods) and does not engage with the history of capitalism or with consumer discourse as such, we might think here of the applicability for Reverend Billy and Savitri D, who are very interested in the ways in which children are ritualized by marketing because they understand that consumerism does not just sell to people but, rather, *makes them.*

In their book the *Psychic Life of Power* (1997a, 11), Butler's most extended treatment of psychoanalysis to date, they turn to Freud to explore processes of subjection, or what they call the subject as the "linguistic occasion" for the emergence of living, breathing individuals. Butler is keen to distinguish between the valence of power whereby the semiotic resources of society (our shared symbols) are "taken up and reiterated" by the acting individual (14) and the discursive conditions that make it possible to conceive of oneself as an individual in the first place—as a subject—what Butler calls *subjectivization.* In the terms of consumption, the analogy would be the difference between acts of consumption (e.g., my decision as an adult to buy this or that item on Amazon) and our early ritualization as consumers who are programmed to experience the world in particular ways (e.g., the ways in which advertising discourse is enmeshed with childhood development).

Following Freud, Butler argues that the child's "passionate attachment to those on whom he or she is fundamentally dependent" (1997a, 7) forms the basis for political subordination and agency. They write, "although the dependency of the child is not *political* subordination in any usual sense, the formation of primary passion in dependency renders the child vulnerable to subordination and exploitation, a topic that has become a preoccupation of recent political discourse" (7). Butler's underscoring of the subject's *primary dependency* is central for the cross-readings I will propose between their work and that of the Stop Shopping Church, connecting their points of shared interest.

Subjects, according to Butler, invest libidinal energies (desires and urges) onto regulatory ideals (societal norms and rules), a process that simultaneously implies a self-recoiling thwarting of potential desire while simultaneously being expressive of a desire to persist, that is, *to be* (1997a, 9). Existence comes at the price of primary psychic ambivalence and foreclosed possibility. Subjectivization implies a socialization anterior to autobiography; to become an individual is to have certain life options foreclosed at psychic levels prior to the experiences of conscious individuality. In other words, discursive conditions program existence in advance of individual consciousness. Or, to continue with our analogy to consumerism, our psychic space is preprogrammed by advertising to consume before we even become conscious consumers. In the process, we find it hard to conceive of a world outside of consumption because such alternatives are psychically foreclosed by our collective socialization—by our religious formation as consumers.

In order to theorize subjectivization, Butler proposes to read the "Foucauldian notion of a regulatory ideal" (1997a, 25) and psychoanalysis in light of one another. They believe that Foucault was quite right to insist that the norm (or the power of the law) conditions experience but cannot explain how individuals are, from the start, shaped by the authority of the norm from the inside out. Proceeding to ontologize psychoanalysis as a first philosophy of the subject, a move to which we must return, they write: "the subject who is at once formed and subordinated is already implicated in the scene of psychoanalysis" (6).

Reading the Foucauldian concept of the norm in psychoanalytic terms, Butler argues that the repression of the libido which the norm (or the law) requires is always to be understood as itself a "libidinally invested repression" (1997a, 79).[20] Libidinality therefore becomes an agent of its own repression. The process of psychic foreclosure both reproduces the norm within a life that bears it anew and renders the norm, as it is lived, ambivalent and incomplete by nature. For example, subjectivization within a culturally heterosexist matrix is underwritten by an ungrieved foreclosure of homosexual possibility that continues to haunt the subject, if often below the surface of consciousness (139).[21] Despite appearances, the heterosexual man's desire (and his disavowal of same-sex attachments) actually remains psychically unresolved. In Butlerian terms, homophobia is, therefore, an aggressive effect of the psychic remainders of socially regulated sexual desire.[22] Desire is, as it were, trapped and incited by its own embodiment. However, sexuality and sexual identity, as we will discuss, are by no means the only possible welter and crux of our psychic ambivalences in a consumerist age.

Turning to Freud's discussion of mourning and melancholia,[23] Butler reads the socialization of normative identities in terms of *melancholic incorporation* (1997a, 142), which implies that affective attachments (cathexions) that must be given up still remain somatically present, within the ego. Our identifications with the norm can only be *ambivalently* accomplished because the objects we refuse are psychically preserved.[24] Summoning Freudian psychoanalysis to advance their understanding of social discipline's constitutive slippages, they add that "being psychic, the norm does not merely reinstate social power, it becomes formative and vulnerable in highly specific ways" (23). As David Kyuman Kim (2007, 118) explains, "the psychic strain of difference that results in melancholy reflects the ambiguity, ambivalence, and uncertainty about self-possession." In Butler's account, melancholia is the psychic form that *difference* takes, which is why in their thinking the slippages of language and the psyche remain so strongly connected.

A necessary aspect of the above social processes, the law's prohibitions—with which the ego has now come to identify—come to police interior compliance. In Butler's psychoanalytic reading of Foucault, power implies the ego's concomitant self-beratement such that the subject's own voice becomes the "regulatory instrument of the psyche" (1997a, 19). For example, it is we who might come to finally decide that we are not fit or healthy enough (that is, that we deviate from an unmet internalized norm) and must, therefore, pursue a strict regime of wellness.[25] Such a bargain with the regulatory power of contemporary wellness would necessarily come at the loss of other competing attachments and uses of our time, energies, and money (and the expressions of who we are that these other activities would perform). But in Butler's account of the melancholic structure of subjectivity, what we let go of to comply still remains (stilly remains).

In a Butlerian reading of subjectivity, incompleteness and loss always haunt normativity. As such, we might suggest in this vein that the power of the norm over even the most consciously committed consumer of contemporary wellness might remain irresolute and fluctuating. In American society, the lingering desire for hamburgers and beer (and the jovial communion and sociality we might associate with these) is, as such, an experience of serious anthropological interest.[26] Or, most to the point for what ultimately interests the Stop Shoppers: Perhaps the loss of the biophilic ways of life we have given up in order to keep consuming continue to tug at our preconscious sense of social possibility in ways that activism can exploit?

* * *

In a basic way, Judith Butler's Freudian account of power depends on the concept of *performativity*, with its repetitions, preconscious movement of difference, and the constitutive vulnerabilities of signification.[27] But, since they treat psychoanalysis as a kind of first philosophy—the epistemological framework with the most and best explanatory power—and divorce their considerations from the history of capitalism, they fail to appreciate the ways in which the repetition and iterability of performativity mirror Dichterian consumption's "ritualistic framework within which certain deviations are possible," the branding discourse that develops from within its historical coordinates at the end of the twentieth century, and the activists' diagnosis of consumer capitalism's "predetermined repetitions" and obsession with "identical details."

Once we bring theory to the level of street action, it must also be asked: Can theories like Butler's cede so much of the terrain of critical agency to preconscious processes and still be effective in the ways activists like the Stop Shopping Church need them to be? This is an especially critical question since psychic plasticity and ambivalence are actually necessary to the life of consumer capitalism, which ultimately capitalizes upon our ritualized losses and experiences of lack to sell its wares and vision of and for the world.

## Cross-Reading Judith Butler and Ernest Dichter on the Psychology of Consumer Subjectivization

What more exemplary expression of self-governance in the name of formal freedom but under the actual tutelage of a ritualized psychic lack is there than contemporary consumption? We never have enough; we never experience intensely enough; we never *are* enough. Kath Weston (2017, 85) concludes: "(the) turn to psychoanalysis at the expense of political economy makes it difficult for performance theory to gauge the limits of its own applicability. Lacking any historical perspective of its own, performativity can scarcely attend to the historical circumstances of its production." If it is not historicized within its reception by American capitalism, it is easy to miss the ways in which the flexible iterability of consumption (whether, say, that of those committed to the "good life" advertised by celebrity culture or devoted to socially prescribed ideals of beauty and wellness) depends on psychic abundance (the misty cathexes of the *preconscious* self rather than the calculating rational ego) and experiences of psychic lack.[28]

Judith Butler was very right to appreciate the importance of psychoanalytic ideas to the reproduction of contemporary North American power, but fails to register their relationship to the history of capitalism. This is not really a problem in and of itself, as Butler did not set out to study the history of capitalism and fail. They set out to think critically about how power works. The problem is that there's more to how power works than their methods and theories can account for and, in their immense usefulness, they've shepherded in a dominant method of critique that has led to the treatment of psychoanalytic theory as a method, but not an object, of study. What thinking with the Stop Shopping Church, and about figures like Ernest Dichter, allow is for us to disengage from Butler's paradigm and account for psychoanalysis not as an epistemological method, but as an instrument of capital. A cross-reading of Judith Butler and Ernest Dichter can begin to make these entanglements and co-implications more legible.

\* \* \*

For American marketers, the consumptive construction of value and identity is, in a significant way, a preconscious affair in much the same way in which subjectivization is for Butler. In Dichter's ([1960] 2012, 45) view, many "human motivations are irrational, unconscious, (and) unknown to the people themselves." Marketers well-versed in psychoanalysis are, per Dichter, poised through their tools of persuasion "to bring about behavioral change" (12) by manipulating the prideful, "self-authoring" will (170). That is, marketers are able to readjust the norms that ground subjectivity.

The role of psychoanalysis in the construction of consumer power (and potential resistance to it) becomes an especially urgent question, however, as it becomes clear that infants and toddlers—for whom the pretenses of rational choice do not even apply—are able to recognize brand logos. This suggests early passionate attachments to the signs of capital and pre-rational socialization into the culture of consumer capitalism. Advertising to children and teens has become big business (Linn 2004; Quart 2008; Schor 2008).

While Judith Butler is rightly known for their groundbreaking work on the performativity of gender, in material practice the ritualizing effects of toy consumption, for example, play a significant role in early gender socialization (Weisgram and Dinella 2018). This kind of sociological detail gets lost in Butler's more abstract discussions and is symptomatic of Butler's broader tendency to cleave matters of language and desire (e.g., issues of corporeal materiality and cultural representation) from matters of political economy.[29]

This tendency to bifurcate soma and sign, on the one hand, and direct considerations of capitalism, on the other hand, has a deeper history. As Rosemary Hennessy (2000, 69) explains, bourgeois ideologies since the nineteenth century have worked hard to separate sexuality (and we can add race and gender) from class analysis so as to guarantee that "desire takes on a life of its own." It is therefore all the more critical, she adds, to examine "the social forces out of which the desiring subject and the subject of pleasure are formed" (69). While Butler productively registers the psychoanalytic dimensions of American power, they elide their imbrication in the entwined histories of American religion and capitalism within the neoliberal order.

As we saw, Judith Butler, turning to Freud, argues that *subjectivization*, the process whereby we become historical subjects, implies a primary submission to power mediated by the affective labors of the parent figures who provide the earliest training in social discipline. For his part, already by 1947, Ernest Dichter turned to Freud to point out the importance of involving both the mother and the child when selling children's shoes. Dichter promoted research into "the psychology behind children's attitudes towards their clothing" and advised different kinds of sales pitches by sales staff depending on the age of the child (Dichter 1947a).[30]

For Dichter, it was obvious that parenting and childhood development were wrapped up in fields of consumption. If consumer society is like the water in a fish's bowl (so basic that we can fail to register it), we receive training in its laws and demands at an early age through the mutual cooperation of caregivers and advertisers. *Also, then, true*: If, as we saw, Butler argues that libidinal attachments to primary caregivers render the child vulnerable to later "political subordination" (Butler 1997a, 7), this is no doubt true of economic subordination as well. Today, it is manifestly accepted within advertising that young consumers are, in fact, discursively produced and that the desire of consumers is, in Butler's terms, "the effect of prior power" (2). Applying Butler's terms to the field of consumption, our passionate attachments to the regulatory processes of consuming are established in early childhood.

In the mid-twentieth century, motivation research was at the vanguard of the turn to a paradigm of consumption, which emphasizes not a hermetically sealed rational chooser but, rather, the fact that the social categories that themselves establish the subject in language *are mediated by fields of consumption*.[31] In this sense, advertisers have now long understood that, as Butler puts it more abstractly in their discussion of the psychic life of power, norms are "vulnerable to both psychic and historical change" (1997a, 23). As Butler highlights the ways in which performance (the subject consciously taking up and reiterating the norms of culture) conceals its grounding in performativity (the semiotic regime that preconsciously constitutes experiences of subjectivity) by flattering the former's assumed singularity over and against its conventionality, so too does conscious (Dichterian) consumption disavow its discursive dependencies on marketing discourse in similar fashion. This actually recursive form of social discipline, in turn, engenders the hallucination that we are autonomous individuals and that consumption is primarily a matter of choice.

In short, for Dichterians and Butlerians alike, if you want to change society, you must change its rituals and the anterior terms and conditions of human existence these can bring to life. Moreover, in the psychoanalytic accounts of both Butler and Dichter, the subject's naturalized reticence *and* its actual plasticity are predicated on the fundamental experience of psychic loss or longing.

Judith Butler argues that we attach to and live out social norms in ambivalent ways that implicate the psyche's melancholic structure. The ego aggressively turns back on itself, taking the law as its own and policing the self in its name. The norm's demand for obedience means that we get caught up in cycles of psychic satisfaction and dissatisfaction. In a world in which we cannot be cool enough, beautiful enough, young enough, smart enough, unique enough, and the like, consumption's many concrete uses for psychoanalysis are patent.[32]

\* \* \*

In 1960, Ernest Dichter (1960) argued that "ambivalently regarded whole objects" that obese women fear to lose are incorporated by the body as excess food, leading to a somatic expression of melancholic loss. Dichter's tellingly gendered and misogynistic account of melancholia implies a never-ending consumer binge in which constitutively ambivalent psychic attachments are projected onto a chain of commodities that are consumed, but whose cheap medicine is unable to heal primordial psychic wounds.

In a consumer society, the social norms that figure the psyche through ritualized processes of melancholic incorporation drive purchase as practice. Psychic ambivalence (again, the recriminations of the ego turned against itself as its own cop) encourages the expenditure of discretionary dollars. Not unrelated to capitalism's insatiable drive to mine the earth for extractable resources, the capitalist desire to mine the consumer psyche is, as conceived, inexhaustible. We are compelled by a never-ending search for our "best self." Analogies to the mystic's *via negativa* and impossible desire for God easily present themselves except that consumption's constitutive attachment to the logic of identity renders consumer mysticism decidedly un-apophatic.[33]

Within marketing discourse, capitalism's need to generate demand and to capitalize its gains rather than promote consumer satiety are well-served by Dichterian psychoanalysis. The subtitle to Kathryn Lofton's introduction to *Consuming Religion* is "being consumed." In a society suffused with capital and disciplined by advertising, a nagging sense of loss (*experienced as the inadequacy of the self*) is one of the ways in which what phenomenologists and existentialists call *being* is commodified. Within neoliberal capitalism, the Dichterian norms we inhabit and that give rise to us cannot, for financial reasons, acknowledge a surfeit of loss. Having incorporated even antinormative desire in the neoliberal period, consumer markets seek to manage deep psychic abundance within the rule of exchange value. In the end, once historicized within the history of American capitalism, Judith Butler's insistence that power forms us and is predicated in our experiences of (and deviations from) the norm is exceedingly useful for our thinking about how the rule of consumption works at the psychic level.

## Toward a Melancholia of Capitalism

In his sermons, Reverend Billy emphasizes the fact that "personal transformation is as necessary as political revolution." If the Stop Shopping Church foregrounds the horizontal intersubjectivity of social life (our moral responsibility to persons at the margins), as they certainly did in their performance at the cathedral where we opened this chapter, they also importantly implicate interiority and the space of psychic intersubjectivity in the anti-consumerist struggle for Earth Justice. On the importance of "soul-craft" to power, the Stop Shoppers most certainly agree, as they also agree with the idea that our losses accumulate within the psyche. However, rather than focus inordinately on loss in terms of our deviations from regulatory norms (which remains important to understanding processes of race, gender, sexuality, and other dimensions of cultural embodiment), they also prioritize the concrete persons, flora, and fauna whose suffering, even mechanized deaths, by capitalist production make us who we are as citizen consumers but whom we are also ritualized not to know to grieve by the law of capitalist exchange.

Reverend Billy often speaks to the constitutive pains and losses of our living otherness under capitalism. Of our financialized consumer society, the preacher laments, "we are sitting in a financial bubble that has hurt people who are not here" (Talen 2006, 90), adding that "a Big Box," that is, a mass-produced commodity, always has "lives buried under it." To break the commodity chain, and transform ourselves, the preacher finally declares, we must acknowledge that our internalized "dead are rising" (90).

The most consistent claim Savitri D and Reverend Billy make these days is, as Savitri D explained to me: "everything we do is like the earth . . . we're not separate from the earth."[34] "We are the Earth . . . the Earth is inside us." Savitri D and Reverend Billy explain that consumerism has crowded out the Earth from within us, reformatting our imaginations with its corporate stories. Linking the anti-consumerism of their early work and the radical ecological critique that has developed in the past almost twenty years, they strongly implicate advertising's commercialization of childhood memories in our predicament.

According to the activists, even though we have the inner capacities and psychic capaciousness to remember Earth in all things and build a "post-product personality," the problem is that marketers "attach product placement deals to our earliest impressions" (Talen 2006, 213). At a Starbucks action in the UK, Reverend Billy used his bullhorn to shout that if there is to be life after shopping, we must "pull the advertising out of our children!" Here, important academic theory, the history of American consumption, and activist labor have converged around this pivot point of consumer socialization, childhood development, and the making of the preconscious self.

\* \* \*

A year after the suitcase event, I had the opportunity to sit down for a meal at the Tick Tock Diner, an iconic retro-style eatery near Penn Station in New York City, with Jeremiah, the young man who was, at the time, the virtuoso musical director of the Stop Shopping Church. At least on the face of it, the background music that provides ambiance at such places provided a contrast, in its everyday innocuousness, to the ways in which Jeremiah foregrounded the singular importance of music in his own life.

Jeremiah's first memories of music, he explained, when I asked him how he came to music and activism, are of composing and singing a song to cope with the loss of his cat as a young child.[35] He was five or six years old at the time and even though he came from a musical family, he was considered still too young by his father, a pastor in the United Method Church, to receive formal training. So, when Tiger, the family cat, escaped and was hit by a car, Jeremiah had to improvise his musical lament at the ivory keys.

As Jeremiah recalls the incident today, it was in that moment that he realized the power of music "as an outlet." It is when he is making music, I learned, that Jeremiah feels most able to act on the world. While I will turn to the preeminent role music itself plays in the communal life and activism of the Stop Shopping Church in chapter 4, I introduce this vignette to inaugurate considerations that foreground the roles disavowals and avowals of loss play in the formation of agency, subjectivity, and criticism in a consumerist age.

For Jeremiah, who grew up in Jackson, Mississippi, his love of music and its agential potential, however, is not something that simply emerges in his grieving over the death of his cat, as a way of coping with the grief of that particular loss. Reverend Billy likes to say that the Stop Shopping Church has become a rooming house for preachers' kids (PKs). Jeremiah is a "PK" who claims his wounds from that experience. He explained that he first actively learned music at church as a child, while he navigated the pain of growing up gay in a non-affirming United Methodist Church. There is, I detect, a noticeable trace of sadness in Jeremiah's voice when he speaks of the profound spiritual depths of his relationship to music. During our conversation, this tone of melancholy was perhaps strongest when he was recalling a poignant and resplendent experience he had as an adult, when he was already an established, professional musician.

Jeremiah explained: He had been asked by a friend to come to Portland, Oregon, to help with a concert of David Bowie's music his group was putting together and performing. At that point, Jeremiah was not too familiar with Bowie's music, so he took to practicing on the street, his earphones in, walking along downtown and singing the song Bowie recorded with Queen, "Under Pressure." Partly a reflection of his incredible singing voice, at some point he realized that he was being flanked by total strangers, who were singing along with him.

Jeremiah was immediately struck by the fact that members of the local unhoused community accompanied him in song as he sang these particular lines from the famous song: "Cos love's such an old-fashioned word / And love dares you to care for the people on the edge of the night / And love dares you to change our way of caring about ourselves / This is our last dance." In this magical coincidence, where, if just for an instant, form meets content and art is life (and an ethnographer's ears perk up upon the retelling of such a moment), we might say that alienation has ebbed more than it normally can in our world.

Jeremiah likes to say that singing brings people together—that anybody can stand next to each other in song, as in the poignant example of his very unexpected and unrehearsed rendition of "Under Pressure" on the streets of Portland. Despite no longer considering himself a Christian, he bemoans the fact that as fewer Americans attend weekly church services, there are fewer opportunities for people to sing together. As someone who has experienced forms of racist and homophobic exclusion, Jeremiah considers music the most powerful technology there is for tapping into our abiding sociality.

The poignant regard with which Jeremiah often speaks of music's beauty and its power (during our conversations but also when he addressed the Choir) is, I believe, connected to the losses he recounted: from the homophobia he experienced within the Methodist Church, to his concern that we have fewer and fewer opportunities to come together through song, even the death of his childhood pet cat. For Jeremiah, experiences of loss support the impulse to gather together with others, especially those who find themselves at the margins of society. Reverend Billy, Savitri D, and the Stop Shopping Church strongly urge us to seek out and avow the marginalized and the exploited.[36] Importantly, they remind us that those exploited by capitalism make us who we are and are, as it were, *in us*.

This grassroots activist account of psychic intersubjectivity draws a sharp contrast with Dichterian consumption's ritualized solipsism. Kathryn Lofton (2017, 1) begins her introduction to *Consuming Religion* with the pithy paradox that "consumption is loss." Inevitably, Lofton adds, "something is gone: gone because of use, because of decay, or because it was destroyed" (1). Unlike Judith Butler, who altogether elides the role of capitalism in their account of the psychic life of power and renders loss in psychic terms alone, or Ernest Dichter, who disavows the many costs of doing business, Lofton reminds us that consumption always entails social sacrifice. Gasoline will run low (we got it somewhere, somehow), energy will be used (contributing to environmental degradation), and capitalist alienation threatens our humanity (we are abstracted by the valuations and measurements of profit). Sacrifice is a kind of paradigmatic ritual (105–121). This is no less true within the context of consumer ritualization. The losses that accompany consumption can help us frame the psychic dimensions of the cannibalizations (of persons, institutions, and the natural world) that Nancy Fraser (2022) argues renders capitalism systemically unsustainable and unstable onto itself.

Given that American consumerism has Freudianized us, Freudian ideas are potentially valuable and useful tools in the project of subverting the power that has made us. As Amy Hollywood (2016, 86) powerfully states: "to disavow the subject's melancholic constitution is to disavow the complex constellation of others who make us who and what we are." Melancholy is important to the analysis and critique of consumer capitalism because it registers the processes whereby branding ritualizes the self's internalized sense of lack, spurring iterative acts of consumption. It is also important because it can be used to frame the coordinates of the kind of relationships that are required, the activists will tell us, if we are to survive the Shopocalypse.

What if we consider our consumer disquiet not simply in terms of individual lack, purchase, and the cyclical, self-perpetuating desire to be better but, instead, open our souls to an accounting of the social suffering that underwrites the enterprise as a whole?[37] What would it mean to reject the ideal of your "best self" and turn our attention elsewhere?[38] For the activists, the "constellation of others" who make us who we are

Figure 2.1. Mourning the victims of democracy's demise. US District Court. Manhattan, 2023. Photo by the Stop Shopping Church.

include the sweatshop workers and immigrants whose labor serves as the physical backbone of abstracting and exploitative systems of finance as well as the honeybees and Central American tree frog whose deaths are demanded by our way of life. In Savitri D's terms, self and society are always and already a matter of *ecology*.[39]

### Epistemic Convergences and the Uses of Social Theory

Our encounters between the history and discourse of American consumption, social theory in the study of religion, and a foretaste of the activism of the Stop Shopping Church have suggested the outlines of our shared epistemic context. In religious scholar speak, we can say that contemporary branding is ritualization. We can say that consuming power is citational, iterative, and recursive. An iconic brand like Starbucks establishes the basic contours of the meaning of the brand and acts of brand consumption add to and reinforce brand meaning, much like acts of gender reinforce norms of gender.

As was the focus of the previous chapter, consumption is citational and recursive because it is dependent on preexisting significatory practices and conventional cultural meanings that render acts of consumption concrete. Consumption is iterative because it is always a process of restating conventional meaning in some newly resonant experiential way, rather than the expression of some unbending, fixed meaning. That is, the citational desire to shop is always a desire for new possibilities within existing constraints. Consumption follows the logic of personalized repetition or, in Catherine Bell's terms, redemptive hegemony.

As has been our focus in this chapter, we can also say that, given advertising's Freudian history, the occasion for consumption is loss. Judith Butler's work on the psychic life of power is of critical importance to an analysis and critique of North American consumption because it reads performativity and psychoanalysis together, in terms of one another. However, it must also be admitted that capitalism and its consequences are grossly missing from Butler's framing, as they are from Catherine Bell's analysis of ritualization, both of which are influential academic accounts of subjectivity (or embodied rationality) from the neoliberal period and both of which strongly mirror the mechanics of contemporary consumption, in the end.

In light of the preceding analyses, I submit that the activists have sometimes had a more grounded and complete mapping of what we might call contemporary "power" than scholars have. The activists have long understood that capitalism is not merely "economic." For one fundamental thing, it shapes subjectivity at the core. The activists readily concede that consumerism has at least partially formatted their interiority and the speech, thought, and action that follow. Scholars should, I think, follow suit.

* * *

The danger I have addressed thus far is this: If we turn to theorists like Catherine Bell and Judith Butler, heavily influenced by Foucault in both cases and strongly influenced by Freud in the latter case,[40] simply to attend to philosophical and theoretical quandaries in contexts that are not expressly our own (e.g., intellectual horizons that do not account for our own consumption, labor, and ritualization by contemporary capitalism), we run the risk of not seeing how our use of these thinkers also cites and reproduces power right beneath our feet in our real time. In other words, we must always remember that social theory always reflects historical power; it can never simply escape it.

Religious studies, as a field, has recently been called to account for "our unstated principles and observable practices about money and labor" (Lofton 2019) and to situate academic practices within political economy and the determinate relations that materially support these (Bartel and Hulsether 2019). A lesson that also holds true for humanistic and social scientific practice generally, I submit that a precondition for such efforts is to consider the entanglements of our own "academic" thinking about the social world with the ideas that promulgate the rule of capital. In other words, to the urgent reminders above, I add the importance of historicizing our own thought and the need to resist the consumerist temptation to grant theory the power to simply free-float above the social world, as an autonomous analytic tool.[41]

This can be a painful suggestion because our iconic, special, and ritually set-apart theories have helped us, and will continue to help us, to do good and important work within the context of our scholarship. There are important reasons we cite and recite our favorite social theory again and again, contributing to their iconic authority. Most notably, Judith Butler's work on gender has understandably become a beacon and a life force for many disciplinary travelers. Importantly, though, even it does not escape the ritualizing coordinates of contemporary consumption. However, the fact that social theory is never historically innocent is no reason to despair. Rather than a return to any kind of vulgar ideology theory or conceiving of culture as superstructural efflux, what is called for is a pragmatic understanding of social theory.[42]

I strongly agree with Robert Orsi (2016) on the explanatory direction between fact and theory such that empirical investigation precedes theoretical analysis.[43] As we already know, important empirical opportunities to learn about the world present themselves when we first stop to ask how persons and communities outside of the traditional academe organize their lifeworlds, theorize the demands of historical living, and understand the responsibilities of freedom. Increased *self-awareness* around the same (the social facts of *our* lives—*our own religious collectivization*) can only help us do more thoughtful work, in the end.

* * *

And with this, Act I draws to a close . . .

Now, a little intermezzo before Act II begins . . . Next up: a retrospective of the history of the Stop Shopping Church. They have honed their craft by meeting spectacle with spectacle. They respect their own religious ritualization by the very consumerist discourse they seek to undo. They perform "post-religious religious" breaks with its closed loops of endless soul-making repetition with musical flair.

New York . . . at the millennium . . . (The curtain rises)

INTERMEZZO

# Reverend Billy and the Stop Shopping Church at Millennium's Edge

# 3

## Crucifying Mickey Mouse to Save the Earth

### *From the Critique of Fetish to New Animisms*

Who's the leader of the club? That's made for you and me . . .
M-I-C-K-E-Y M-O-U-S-E.
—Mickey Mouse Club Theme

We thought there might be more magic but we sold off our most ancient power . . . It's the end of the world, only so many beautiful days on Earth.
—The Stop Shopping Choir, "End of the World"

## Enter Reverend Billy, Stage Left

At the edge of the new millennium, the first holiday season of the twentieth-first century by the accounting of secular, capitalist time,[1] a prophet enters a crowded New York City subway car and begins a public exhortation over the clanking shrieks of the train moving uptown from Greenwich Village toward Times Square. Riders familiar with the subway have heard variations of the opening lines of this genre many times before: "Ladies and gentlemen, I am Reverend Billy from the Church . . ." Those paying attention will notice a change of script. "I am Reverend Billy from the Church *of Stop Shopping*," he shouts, rather agreeably, as far as these performances tend to go.[2]

The man, white and middle-aged, in a preacher's outfit hidden by his navy blue wool winter coat but for the visible white priest's collar, is standing next to a young man holding a wooden stick onto which a crucified three-foot-tall Minnie Mouse plush doll is attached. Down the subway car, someone else is carrying a crucified Mickey Mouse. The preacher explains that he and his collaborators are on their way to the

Disney Store at Times Square to "disrupt the shopping process there" (Post and Palacios, 2002). For this preacher, it is of no minor importance that along her agonizing procession to Calvary, Minnie just keeps smiling, her frozen expression a sign of her spiritual and material power. These dolls, he argues elsewhere, just smile at you, "with an air of assumed knowledge about your personal life" (see Lane 2002).

As an actor, writer, and jazz musician, William Talen had arrived in New York City in 1994, to the doorstep of what he believed was the American mecca for theater. Instead, as he would later write:

> By 1998, whichever direction you walked, from Drama Books south, or from Joe Allen's east, or the International Center of Photography west, or the Port Authority north, there wasn't a thing of substance to stop you and force a personal question. You could really work on your tourist drift, your bovine browsing, your "nice time." (Talen 2003, 31)

In the place of great theater, what Talen discovered along the "Great White Way" was "consumer Theater, whose leading actors perform on the shoulders of Diane Sawyer or Bryant Gumbel" (31). The streets of New York City's internationally recognized theater district, he believed, now resembled the over-policed and over-surveilled "hallways of a mall" (31).

\* \* \*

The capital of the American stage, by the 1930s, Broadway was already being crowded out by the cheaper, mass accessible picture shows. Moreover, approaching from the West, Hollywood's shadow loomed increasingly large in the postwar period.[3] By the 1970s and the 1980s, Times Square had also become a haven for massage parlors, sex work, and pornography. However, by the time Reverend Billy arrived on the scene in the 1990s, Times Square had become the very "emblem of the safe, clean, and orderly New York" (Traub 2004, xiii) of the Giuliani administration's aggressive rebranding of the city as the "Capital of the World." Its capital flows were, according to the performance studies scholar Jill Lane (2002), increasingly transnational rather than local. Times Square is a place well-suited to becoming the must-be destination for a crusader who pits himself against the rising tide of the consumer "monoculture."

Today a symbol of the "hollowing out of urban life, (and) the decay of the particular in the merciless glare of globalization" and the "corporate-theme-park version of urban life" (Traub 2004, xiv), Times Square, with its affectively intense and condensed brew of entertainment, tourism, retail consumption, and the Nasdaq ticker to mark financial seriousness, is emblematic of the spirit of global capitalism. There, from the beginning, Reverend Billy sermonized about "Logos as Lovers" (Talen 2006, 12), has read advertisements as gnostic inversions of human impulses (14), and has warned against the six-foot-tall "horny looking supermodels... draped down the sides of building" (Talen 2003, 7), even likening the giant heads of billboard models to "the heads on Easter Island secreted through wires and emerging on flickering glass walls" (Talen 2006, 14). Despite secularism's fanfaronade to the contrary, he is convinced that this place is exceedingly religious. As Kathryn Lofton suggests, "porn, Victoria's Secret advertisements, and Showtime programming constitute subjects of intense consumer practice" (2017, 28) equal to that of extreme religion.

Less than a year after the subway ride with which we began, the preacher, along with his partner, now spouse, and chief collaborator, Savitri D, would watch the devastation of September 11 across the river from a balcony in Fort Greene, Brooklyn. The organizers of the attacks targeted the Twin Towers (like Times Square, on New York's map of hotspots for pilgrim tourists) not because they represented the *absence* of religion but, instead, the presence of "the *wrong* religion," two "extremities facing off with each other" (Lofton 2017, 28). The then hidden environmental fallout from that catastrophe introduces themes we will take up toward the end of this particular account of the prophet's passion play. For now: *foreshadowing*.

\* \* \*

Panning back to the preacher's subterranean performance inside the New York City transportation system, Reverend Billy continues his sermon to some call and response *Amens!* and *Hallelujahs!* from the small band of disciples who have accompanied him and have dispersed the length of the subway car.[4] He explains that the action they plan to undertake at the Disney Store hopes to "talk people into understanding that this is a sweatshop company and that the people that create the

Disney toys work in places like Sri Lanka and rural China and make as little as 16 cents an hour whereas . . . the President and CEO of Disney, Michael Eisner, makes $330,000 in that same period of time." He ends with what in business speak is called an "action item": "please boycott Disney and find out what other companies do this kind of thing!" Some passengers give him a quizzical side-eye glance and others look amused and laugh softly.

Exiting the subway and moving above ground at 42nd Street, Reverend Billy and his merry band walk past an advertisement for the Broadway show based on the Disney film *Lion King*, covering the ground-level scaffolding. The bright lights from the buildings grow even sharper as night falls. The group is carrying the crucified Disney dolls at the front of the procession, Reverend Billy himself carrying Minnie Mouse. The preacher shouts, "boycott Disney, the sweatshop company . . . stop shopping this Christmas," as he enters the lion's den, Mordor, or Jerusalem, as the case may be. The magical place to which he is headed, on 45th Street and Broadway, is enveloped by a miasma of consumerism. From the cologne and perfume of global visitors, to the glossy look of branded boutique store shopping bags, to the smell of the hotdogs and pretzels, and sidewalk incense vendors, the space is emblematic of what Reverend Billy opposes (but also admits he cannot escape). It is a place in which we become what he calls "consumerized"; "ritualized" into accepting (Talen 2006, 199) the stories that the brands tell us about ourselves.[5]

To the preacher's grave dismay, the pinnacle of the American theater has "finally flowered into Goofys and Sleepys and Donald Ducks and the thousand screaming anthropomorphized animals now dancing on the shelves of Disney's 42nd Street address" (Talen 2006, 197). There are distinct echoes in this nightmare of Marx's idea that wooden tables, once they are reborn as commodities, evolve out of their wooden brains "grotesque ideas, far more wonderful than if (they) were to begin dancing of (their) own free will" (Marx [1867] 1983, 445). In front of the magical world of Disney, the preacher addresses his co-conspirators, readying them for the latest and, at the time twenty-ninth ever, Church of Stop Shopping action.

The religion scholar would do well to pause the action and freeze the frame, here. Of what concern is this scene to those who profess scholarly interest in religion?

## The Problem of the Billionaire CEO's Fetish

If, as Kathryn Lofton argues, "religion describes what humans do when they harness—or talk about harnessing—material means to access immaterial power" (2017, 31), the Nike swoosh's provocation to "Just Do It!" is religious jubilee (or fire and brimstone, depending) and the dolls crucified onto the anti-consumerist activists' wooden sticks are rodentian fetishes of the unquiet, sentimental heart—entry points into experiences of childhood nostalgia, culturally sanctioned Pollyanna, or cheeky irony, millennial capitalist sentimentality's gag reflex. Plush oversized Disney dolls are religious objects that are emblematic of some of what and who we are as Americans and, increasingly, global citizens at millennium's razor edge.

Given that a man dressed as a preacher, one with a Calvinist religious childhood as it turns out, is preaching salvation from the sins of consumerism right in front of what he calls "the high church of retail," his relationship to other preachers, Max Weber's this-worldly Calvinist saints, is a compelling question. To preview: We will engage the thresholds of the secular, as we walk with Reverend Billy into shifting tides. But immediately before us in the preacher's absurdist twilight zone stands a pair of peculiar and particular crosses. *What do we make of them as scholars of religion?*

Walter Benjamin ([1921] 2005, 259) leaves open the possibility that capitalism can be best understood as a "religiously conditioned construction" or as an "essentially religious phenomenon" in its own right. However, before either of these historical possibilities, there were, as the anthropologist William Pietz explains, proto-capitalist trading relationships between West Africans and Portuguese merchants in the sixteenth and seventeenth centuries out of which would emerge "the fetish, as an idea and a problem" (Pietz 1985). This is the ideological wellspring and constellation of meanings that would hand consuming religion's most famous adversary, Karl Marx, the recipe for one of his most famous counterspells, the concept of commodity fetishism.

The concept of the fetish is a historical crucible. Pietz explains: "The idea of the fetish originated in a mercantile, intercultural space created by the ongoing trade relations between cultures so radically different as to be mutually incomprehensible" (Pietz 1987). Although one might presume that the concept, as it was wielded by pre-Enlightenment Portuguese and Spanish merchants, was influenced primarily by Christian theology on idolatry, Pietz argues that the West African cultural practices (e.g., among the Beninese) that became the source material for European ideological claims about "Africans," were mediated more directly through the lens of Christian law rather than Christian theology (1987). This is because *feitiços* were understood in ways that had less to do with belief in "false" gods external to the self and more with the personification of objects and, recursively, in turn, the objectification of persons.[6]

Pietz proposes this: "The discourse of the fetish has always been a critical discourse about the false objective values of a culture from which the speaker is personally distanced" (1985). If early modern Europeans marveled at the "trinkets and trifles" (1985) they were able to trade for objects of "real value," mainly gold, it is because they had their own ways of arranging and ordering the world. Once fetishism entered social scientific discourse, it could also be used to mark excessive intersubjective investments *within* European cultures, such as deviant sexual investments, as in Freud's work, or the illusions and fixed consciousness of commodity practice, as in Marx's writings (1985).

As a general rule, the sin of excessive and disordered affective investment has historically been forced upon persons of color, women, sexual minorities, religious minorities, and the working poor. We see contemporary echoes of this history in the racialized and racist American discourse of looting, the classist ogling of Black Friday shoppers, homophobia and transphobia which point fingers at the consumptive elements of gender reproduction when it pertains to gay men and trans-women but not heterosexual cisgender men, the JAPs and shylocks of anti-Semitic discourse, Islamophobic mockery of Muslims' offense at forms of secular blasphemy, and the generalized cultural association of consumption with the feminine.[7]

Coming back, now, to our preacher and his merry band of fools, standing in front of the Disney Store, about to engage in the ritual disruption of consumer ritual, what does the problem of the fetish have to do with them? The anti-consumerist warriors at the Disney Store cannot escape the background history of the critique of the fetish or the critical dangers that attach to its wielding. It is important to rewind back to something the importance of which we might have missed the first time around. Reverend Billy did not aim his subway sermon at our excessive consumptive desires, as a Neoplatonist would. He did not accuse us of being trifling, silly, and depthless and did not, like Theodor Adorno, preach the virtues of high modernist art as an antidote to all the dreck.[8] Instead, he seized upon modes of entertainment, celebrity, and religion to engage in millenarian situationist street theater that sought to reconnect and repair the intersubjective relationships that neoliberal relations of production routinely destroy.[9] The Disney mice were sacrificed to bring awareness to the sacrifice of global labor that endowed them with their unseemly powers.[10] It was done to bring attention to the "rising dead" that haunt the interiority of consumer ritualization.

A turn of the spirit (*détournement*) (Sandlin 2010) was the goal:[11] that we might avow the losses we currently disavow, in terms of the exploitation of labor, that make consuming Disney possible. As was later written down in what became one of the Church of Stop Shopping's grounding texts, "The Beatitudes of Buylessness," "Blessed are the young women in sweatshops. The things you make will fly you like magic evening gowns to the City of Light/Blessed are you who disturb the customers. You might just be loving your neighbor" (Talen 2006, 180). Even if the group is still developing this approach at the millennium, reclaiming some amount of autonomy of will and critical distance from the power of consumer fetish is not an ethical end in itself; this turning of the soul serves the purposes of a broader critique of political economy.

The villain in the preacher's tale of woe is Michael Eisner, the then billionaire CEO of Disney who was making a killing on the backs of an army of pink-collar sweatshop labor. The numbers speak to Eisner's overvaluation and undervaluations. Greed and being comfortably adjusted to capitalism's devastating inequities is the perversity to be damned.[12] The mixing and matching of the visual and aural signifiers of American religion and politics is *in itself* not the point: The point is to expose the historical and material conditions that make it possible for American consumers to experience the magic of Disney. The exploitation that underwrites our trips down memory lane and tourist pilgrimages is the moral of the story.

As Talal Asad argues, we are, in our financialized world, governed by a tyranny of numbers. "Secular reason," he writes, "employs increasing abstraction and calculation for formulating and resolving problems"

(Asad 2018, 150).[13] A common example of this is the dogma that, if we look at the world through the measures of economic growth, global capitalism is, in the aggregate, good for humanity and good for the so-called developing world. But, *as consumers*, it is also true that we are trained to lose ourselves in stories rather than numbers for a reason. For one very important reason, corporate storytelling offshores the face of labor. Reverend Billy and his comrades, like the adbusters and culture jammers of the millennium, understand this very well.

Their wager is that their performances might break the iterative, proliferating, sacralizing sign chain of the Disney brand—that is, its objective performative power. Through their spectacles, the Stop Shopping Church rejects the obscurantist accounting of secular reason and brings attention to the inviolable moral worth of every human being, no matter how distant and undervalued by the market. On this count, above, a telltale characteristic of Protestant secularism remains, embroidered on the performance. For the group, conversely, the fetish is the numbers, and the idol is the faith in progress that capitalism's numeric valuations and measurements demand from us.[14] Here, Reverend Billy seems to resist the accounting of secular time. In recoiling from the productive power of the fetish over the self, however, he is simultaneously an heir to Enlightenment anthropology, modernity's theory of the human. The effect is historical bricolage.

## The Actor, the Character, and His Mask

The group huddles for one last exhortation before entering the store and setting into motion, as the preacher puts it, "the beginning of the revolution against consumerism" (Post and Palacios 2002). The mythic framing is delivered with ironic distance. A young man playing the role of an ecstatic disciple wails as the preacher asks the group to address their intentions to the "sky still not covered in logos" and exhorts them to go inside and "challenge those products! . . . those neurotic Goofys and Plutos and Aladdins!" A woman who has happened upon this scene asks, "Are you a real priest?" Deadpan, falling out of character for a moment to set the record straight, William Talen responds, "No, I'm a fake preacher." You can see in his facial expression and hear in his voice clear frustration that this was not already obvious to the spectator.

Having removed his coat to reveal his costume, Reverend Billy moves inside the store to the middle of the retail stage and begins his sermon. "We are here today, Children . . . Praise be! Do I have a witness? We are here today to discourage the purchase of these neurotic Christmas tchotchkes!" The store manager, a middle-aged white woman who clearly already knows this cast of characters, approaches Reverend Billy and calmly asks the preacher to leave. Retail environments have their own stage directions, what Erving Goffman calls interaction rituals (Goffman [1967] 1982), and the store manager plays her part well. From the perspective of the store, the best thing to do is defuse and take the air out of the situation.

Reverend Billy projects: "I am right here in the center, Ground Zero of evil." With some Snow White and Ariel pen and crayon bags behind him, he continues, "*those neurotic little tchotchkes are staring at me . . . they come all the way from China, where people made them for nothing an hour, where they couldn't even take bathroom breaks, no possibility of a union, we have no idea what right is and wrong is anymore. This is it! This is wrong!*"

The preacher does not seek to move beyond good and evil but, instead, to use the trappings of American religion to pragmatically affect prophetic denunciation. Mickey Mouse is the Antichrist, as the Reverend Billy enjoys shouting, because he is found to be demonic on material economic grounds. In Reverend Billy's hand, "Mickey Mouse morphs from the Disney-sanctioned symbol of everlasting childhood and nostalgia to the leader of the evil, child-labor-sweat-soaked empire of Disney" (Sandlin and Milam 2008). As we have seen, though, deeper, religious histories also inform this political theater.

\* \* \*

Reverend Billy's sermon picks up steam. "*This* is evil," he explains, dropping the parody and delivering the punch line with an arresting dose of what he has come to call "sincerity." "We need to start our own church that . . . isn't about the worship of the retail moment . . . that isn't about the worship of the commodified moment." He continues, "we do not need Disney to mediate between us and our own lives. I don't need Peter Pan to fly through the air to have an imagination. I don't need the Little Mermaid to walk on land to lose my cherry. My life isn't a Disney production!"[15]

While the point of the sermon has been, up to this point, a fiery condemnation of the billionaire CEO's fetish, a kind of materialist (in this case, neo-anarchist[16]) critique of secular capitalism, the good Reverend also becomes possessed by a common modern secular fear: that of the fetish's power to invade and control the self. For him, Disney is a foreign power that threatens to rewrite our imaginations and childhood memories (Talen 2006, 88). He ends the performance by exorcising the soul of a customer who plays along, telling her to go forth and "stop shopping!" Moving out of character, he speaks to the gathered retail theater audience and engages in a bit of postscript: "I hope that some of us shared some information about what Disney is doing around the world . . . hopefully we slowed down the commodification process just a little bit." He thanks the store manager for her patience but recommends that she look for "another job."[17]

Outside the store, back in character, Reverend Billy gives an encore. With a group of curious tourists looking on, the preacher explains that in this place all "storytelling is by the credit card," which creates a "kind of enforced silence." "We are turning into a society of extras from Dawn of the Dead." We need to revivify relations that have been starved of communication, he argues, "because when they abuse people on the other side of the world, they abuse us." Putting all the pieces back together, the preacher connects Disney's law—that all expression must be mediated by commodity practice with its corporate brand (the predetermined details of consumer ritualization, in the terms we interrogated and established in Act I)—to the abuses of labor on the other side of the world. We can disrupt the cycle, he exhorts: "Let's not pick up Mickey!" Meanwhile, Giuliani's police approach.

This time, William Talen and his friends are told to move on. Talen says he did the best he could, given the highly charged situation, but worries that he might not have "sounded like a preacher" in stretches: "I lost my character." Talen's performance of self-possession is a part of the show. William Talen has not yet become his character; the fetish has not possessed him, and he has used entertaining bombast, a performative distance from the preacher, and his critical reason to circulate important instrumental information for his own political purposes. He has disrupted the flow of commoditized time. This is the William Talen who claims Thomas Paine as a teacher.

A revised account of Reason is still the ultimate cure for the productions of the Church of the Poison Mind.[18] Not interested in the conceit of pure reason or in parroting Weberian *Zwekrationalität*, this critical performance of reason engages in self-critique and is well aware of its limitations. The performance resembles critical theory's account of reason's self-critique in the name of reason (Lane 2002).[19] As Talen once explained over fair-trade coffee, iced tea, and soup, his early work was predicated on the production of irony and parody by "developing distance on the character to manipulate the mask."[20]

Still, the permeabilities between the actor and the prophet, the self-intending subject and the subject who is done and made from the outside are already there in this early action. Having already slid down a bit, the zipper of the secular's costuming will become undone. If William Talen assumed himself to be a "fake preacher," "religion" was a role to perform, and the cross a tool to take up and use in his critique, this would become an increasingly difficult story to maintain. As Ann Pellegrini (2007) has suggested about the actors who stage Hell Houses, ostensibly Reverend Billy's performative mirror opposites from a religious and political perspective, the mask is leaky. The border between front stage and back stage is dangerously porous.

## A Prequel: The Origins of a New American Preacher

Because history is reborn and remade in practice, origin stories are especially slippery to write, as any religion scholar will tell you. Still, I will give it a whirl.

William Talen, a man who characterizes his Dutch Calvinist upbringing in the Midwest as abusive,[21] and who did not "want to so much as spoof a Christian" (Talen 2003, 41) has, by now, spent almost three decades with Reverend Billy. The Calvinist minister is still exhorting us to curb our consumption, as Max Weber might have predicted. In Talen's postindustrial restaging, however, the Calvinist minister's exhortations serve the purposes of a *criticism* of capitalism—a chastising of our structurally ignorant expenditures rather than a call to capital accumulation. Reverend Billy has never mentioned Max Weber or the secularization thesis to me and I have not come across them in his writings. Talen speaks of reverse mentors. Perhaps Weber's ideal-type of the proto-capitalist was surreptitiously one of his?

Although he once confessed to me that he always had a general contempt for formal acting "because you were always performing another person's script," acting in the sense of exercising human agency is always mediated by the scripts of haunted history. Importantly, despite the uneasiness he ascribes to acting out scripts written by others, Talen readily concedes that he received a lot of help from an important mentor as he conceived of and scripted the character he first began to play over a quarter of century ago and which, I am arguing here, he has also in some important way *become*. As Talen frames it, his mentor's story is worthy of its own prequel.

When William Talen, who turned seventy in 2020, arrived in New York City in 1994, he was already in his mid-forties. It is incredible, remarked Sebastián, a long-standing member of the Choir, that the Reverend Billy Project, now approaching its quarter century, represents William Talen's second act in life. In the first act, he worked at Life on the Water, an experimental theater in San Francisco, where he wrote and staged his own work and produced monologues, performances, and plays. At the time, he was especially taken by monologists like Holly Hughes and Spalding Grey. It was at Life on the Water that Talen met Sidney Lanier, a former Episcopal priest twenty-six years his elder, who, along with Wynn Handman and Michael Tolan, had founded the American Place Theater in New York City in 1963, working with the likes of Danny Glover, Robert De Niro, Faye Dunaway, Morgan Freeman, and Dustin Hoffman.

Lanier saw talent in Talen but not of the sort Talen had hoped for. "You're basically a Calvinist preacher in disguise," he would conclude. Lanier himself knew much about the confluences and tensions between religion and theater. Having arrived in New York City in 1959, he took up as second rector at St. Thomas Episcopal Church on Fifth Avenue and 53rd Street. In Talen's telling of it, one day, on the surface of it not unlike any other, Lanier, preaching from the pulpit, became such a pure vehicle for the delivery of his script, the Gospel story of Jesus running out the money changers in the Temple, that, "Jesus Christ couldn't have said it better!" (Talen 2003, 36). His monied parish, however, "a redoubt of Episcopalian WASPness on the Upper East Side," was so thoroughly bothered by his suggestion that a Church, were it in Times Square, would have to minister to hustlers, unemployed method actors, and pimps (37), that Lanier was removed and sent to St. Clement's Episcopal Church in Hell's Kitchen, where his prophecy about preaching the Gospel to characters out of a De Niro film finally came true.

In 1962, Rev. Lanier, who was the first to convince Talen that Church is actually theater, began a ministry to the theater arts at St. Clement's. He conceived of it as a "communion" between worlds. As Reverend Billy puts it, Lanier and his friend, Wynn Handman, "collapsed the sacred and the dramaturgical" at a time when that was not yet being done.[22] The sanctuary was eventually converted into an Off-Broadway theater. To this day, an altar remains in place "on the set of whatever show is currently performing" (St. Clement's Episcopal Church, n.d.). Three short years later, Lanier left the priesthood, explaining that he was "ready to escape the prison of the stereotype of the clergyman" (Vitello 2013).

A teaser: Lanier's student, William Talen, is today so identified with Reverend Billy, the (once) parodic embodiment of a right-wing, fundamentalist televangelist, that as Savitri D has explained to me, the only way for him to get away from the character now will be if Reverend Billy somehow gets killed off the show. A parable for all of us: In our society, even the great actors do not get to blithely move in and out of roles. In a consumerist age, freedom's task is much more daunting than a costume change can convey. More than this, however, in Talen's particular case, the task of freedom is further complicated by the celebrification, at grassroots activist levels, he has undergone in his two-decade crusade against corporate celebrity as the co-leader of a "Church."

When Lanier met Talen and began to coach him on his vocation as an artist, he himself was no longer a priest. Along the way, the master introduced his student to the thinly veiled biblical allegories of Tennessee Williams, Lanier's distant cousin, the scholarship of John Dominic Crossan and the historical Jesus school, Elaine Pagels's work on the Gnostic gospels, and the comedy of Lenny Bruce. Lanier eventually sensed Talen's thirst for social justice issues. Therefore, together they digested political theater: the theatrical activism of the Yippie Abbie Hoffman, Bertolt Brecht's Marxist dramaturgy, and Augusto Boal's Theater of the Oppressed. They also analyzed the narrative structure of the Christian passion play as a powerful stratagem for activist organizing. After many peripatetic conversations, Lanier convinced Talen to move to New York City, ostensibly to begin what would become the Reverend Billy Project.

Also in his path, at once immediate and genealogical, Talen had important forerunners and contemporaries. The culture jamming street satirists, the Yes Men, and Billionaires for Bush, came up at around the same time. In the background, Talen and the Stop Shopping Church took direct inspiration from the street theater of ACT UP, the Wobblies, and Emma Goldman. Reverend Billy also appeared in Times Square at a specific cultural and political moment. Upsetting fashionable predictions of the advent of the secular city, white American Evangelicals, who were largely free-market enthusiasts, had returned to the public square with a vengeance and televangelists had become popular celebrities in their own right. Looking to grind together two fundmentalisms that threaten our ability to think for ourselves, the character spoke to the co-constitution and consanguinity of American religion and economy.

The "new American preacher," equal parts Jimmy Swaggart, his "reverse mentor," and Elvis, donning a blinding white suit, "boots for the battle," cleric's collar, and a golden-haired pompadour, was born as a parody of figures like Don Wildmon, founder of the American Family Association, and Jerry Falwell, leader of the Moral Majority. By confounding people's expectations, the aim was to jolt people from their sentimental attachments to the characters of religious and consumer theater.

At the same time, Talen readily admitted to his own attachments at millennium's dawn, admiring "the politicized activism of so many African-American churches," the delivery of Baptist preachers, and sacred music he would experience at Mariner's Temple Baptist Church, where Bill Henry, his first organist, would play (Lane 2002). By actually tipping his hat in a gesture of sincerity to the role of the Black Church in organizing for progressive social change, Reverend Billy differed in important ways from the "ironic amusement" and "ironic televangelic fandom" of the alternative underground of the 1980s and 1990s Denis Bekkering (2016) analyzes. In short, there were, from the start, important limits to the irony of the performance.

## Losing His (Fake) Religion

At the height of their popularity and public visibility in the first half of the 2000s, Reverend Billy and the Church of Stop Shopping were thoroughly invested in parodic practice. The Choir that viewers saw portrayed on the big screen in the 2007 documentary about the Stop Shopping Church, *What Would Jesus Buy?*, certainly appropriated aspects of American Protestant Christianity to positive counter-effect: sermonic delivery, call and response, gospel choreography, and the resignification of hymnody.

The fake church Choir also had a lot of experience with the real deal. Paul Broussard, the Choir director from 2004 to 2009 whose choreography is featured in the film, was a preacher's kid who grew up in the African Methodist Episcopal Church. A gay man who felt the impact of "church hurt" and speaks of his "fractured childhood in the church," Broussard experienced his participation and leadership role in the Choir primarily through the lens of musical theater, an artistic passion that had brought him to New York City in the first place. Broussard explained: "I was the Real McCoy . . . I wasn't an imitation Gospel performer. I was a real Gospel performer."[23]

From the start, the signifiers of African American religiosity were marshaled to lend the Reverend Billy Project an aura of authenticity and credibility.[24] As such, even then, there were structural limits to the parody of religion. Importantly, however, the symbolic pastiche of right-wing white fundamentalist televangelist and the Black Gospel tradition sometimes unintentionally alienated Black audiences in those early days.[25]

At the time *What Would Jesus Buy?* was filmed, the respect for the cultural power of American religion was quite real. Since, as Talen explained to me almost fifteen years later, American society is structured by the narratives of Christian parable (the idea of divine providence is an example), the project of social criticism demanded his intimate involvement with those narrative *ur* structures. Relatedly, he reads the character of Jesus as an activist from 2,000 years ago who did very good work combating empire. Simple mockery was never in the cards and parody of the right-wing preacher never went all the way down.

Although she engagingly and productively explores the dimensions of the Sisters of Perpetual Indulgence that constitute them as a queer religious order in their own right, Melissa Wilcox (2018), like most academics who have written about Reverend Billy, underestimates the instabilities that inhere to the life of the character. Wilcox writes: "The

Church Ladies do not claim with any sort of seriousness to actually be church ladies, nor does Reverend Billy claim to be a real Evangelical Preacher. The Sisters, on the other hand, are quite serious that they are nuns" (69). This is not quite accurate. The Sisters do not claim to be *Catholic* or *Orthodox* nuns. These days, Reverend Billy does not claim to be an *Evangelical* preacher, *Pentecostal* preacher, or any kind of *Christian* preacher, but clearly he has adopted the mantle of *a preacher*. The personal history that has led to the Green preacher that he is today runs through what he sometimes calls the "early days."

* * *

William Talen confesses that when he would walk around in full Reverend Billy regalia in the "early days," he would inevitably have "mothers come up to me to bless their child."[26] Sometimes, the parent would make the approach winking but, often, there was ritual misfire and misrecognition at play. When this happened, he usually decided "to just let the blessing take place." That is, Talen would be taken for a religious minister and asked to serve in that capacity and he would.

More recently, I witnessed something similar when, at an immigration rally with the group in Minneapolis in 2018, I saw a group of congregated clergy wave him over to join their small-group confab. They did not think he was an ironic or parodic preacher but, reading the text written on his body, assumed he was one of them. The politics of visibility in which accounts of performativity traffic speak to real effects in the world even if they also obscure as much as they reveal about cultural production (Weston 2002, 16). One moral of that story is, no doubt, that just as theories of performativity would caution, even a master performer like William Talen is never in full control of the significations he wields.

When Talen tells the history of the Stop Shopping Church, he highlights the importance of two national events a few years this side of the millennium. First, 9/11 and the grief, trauma, and anxieties it manifested, he explains, demanded "compassion" and "sincerity" rather than "irony" and "parody." Talen shared that one day, in that immediate era in the aftermath of 9/11, he was biking over the Brooklyn Bridge and someone yelled, "hey, pastor!" Talen stopped and ended up in conversation with the man for more than an hour, comforting him as the East River flowed beneath them. This is the point, Talen believes, when "I became a pastor and the distance I had on the performance art project was dissolved."[27] Second, the Great Recession (2007–2009), with the human suffering that it occasioned, created a need for a community of care. Eventually, "over-cultured agnostics" at Burning Man even had him "conducting funerals and weddings" and he was even invited to counsel teenagers dealing with addiction issues.[28]

As I have contended, William Talen moved into the Reverend Billy character to track and counter what Kathryn Lofton (2017, 9) has called the religious occupation of the economy, still associating the religious with the curtailment of autonomous freedom. In the end, religion also *came upon him*, refashioning his critical agency. Savitri D explains that whether Talen was ready for it or not, historical circumstance had occasioned "a peeling away of the satirical and of the irony . . . some of the fake went away."[29] In fact, as she sees it, Talen became a preacher as soon as he cared about what he was saying and the "text wasn't fictional" (Durkee and Talen 2013, 233).

I once heard Billy, in one of his sermons, call the handkerchief, one of the preacher's sartorial accessories, a "preacher's flag, pain, and drama." Eventually, this fetish became less theater prop and more an emblem of who William Talen had become. Accepting, however, that the porousness of subjectivity extends beyond the issue of fetishism's objectification of persons is something that Savitri D would eventually help Reverend Billy come to accept and make central to his soul-saving mission today.

As a related matter, Reverend Billy will no longer roll his eyes at someone who identifies him as a "real" preacher.

## Savitri D and the Turn to Eco-Sincerity

On more than one occasion, William Talen has told me that if his own origin story might be important to understanding the emergence of the performance character he is sometimes at pains to distinguish himself from, Savitri D's story is most crucial to understanding who the group is today. Part of the reason for this is that he feels that the iconicity of Reverend Billy has been a double-edged sword: It has added to the recognizability of the group's work and has been useful in drumming up second-order interest from journalists and academics, but has also served to occlude the singular creative and organizational importance of Savitri D. As I was told by Choir members when I came on board, it has most definitely been Savitri D's influence that proved decisive in folding Reverend Billy's anti-consumerism into a broader agenda of ecological justice.

Savitri D's parents were Greenwich Village bohemian artists who, she will tell you, were proto-Hippies who helped model a way of life that was later taken up by the Baby Boom generation. Born in the 1930s, they were caught between the Beats and the Hippies. In 1967, Savitri D's father, then known as Stephen Durkee, and her mother, then known as Barbara Durkee, co-founded the Lama Foundation, a spiritual retreat center and intentional community near Taos, New Mexico. Taos had already come to loom large in the religious and philosophical imaginary of early twentieth-century Greenwich Village artists who projected onto the nearby indigenous community, the Taos Pueblo, their own romantic, antimodern ideals.[30] Zen masters like Joshu Sasaki Roshi and Tibeten meditation masters such as Chögyam Trungpa and Kalu Rinpoche traveled through and became associated with the Lama Foundation.[31]

Savitri D's father, who worked with the famed American psychedelic mystic and guru, Ram Dass (né Richard Alpert),[32] and held a spiritual interest in the religious philosophy of Meher Baba, helped found a multimedia art collective, the Company of US (USCO), that, among other things, used kinetic art and surround sound to produce light shows for Timothy Leary's Psychedelic Theater (Byerly 1996). Decades before Silicon Valley venture capitalists discovered their passion for radical art at Burning Man, Harvard Business School (HBS) took an interest in USCO's work. One of Stephen Durkee's friends was invited onto the HBS faculty, while two core USCO members founded Intermedia Systems Corporation in Cambridge, Massachusetts (Byerly 1996).

Positioning itself between art, psychology, and business, Intermedia sold a multisensorial capitalist rationality to American organizational management. George Litwin, an HBS professor, described the scope of the work of USCO this way (Kranz 1974): "(in using) mixed media—multimedia technology—to create environments that have particular kinds of psychological effects." While he wasn't a formal member of USCO, Stewart Brand, the founder of *Whole Earth Catalog*, which blended counterculture and networked consumerism, spent time with

USCO and its work (Turner 2006, 49). A fascinating historical detail given the ardent anti-consumerist his daughter has become, Stephen Durkee's work with USCO can be placed within the historical currents within which dramaturgical hippie expressivism becomes affective, "post-secular" consumer culture.[33] His second act, however, would take direct critical aim at the same consumer expressivism.

At the height of the American counterculture, the great British Marxist cultural theorist Stuart Hall (1968, 182) suggested that the hippies' "emphasis on expressiveness is a counter-thrust to the bottling up of emotions and the role-doubling which they feel to be so central a part of the dominant personality types of American modern society."[34] However, today, in the age of the Google playroom, the emotionally truncated grey-suited organizational man is no longer the corporate ideal.[35] The power of Dichterian consumption and branding, as we saw, lies in its ability to actually govern through social imbrication, with one hand, but to sell its historical form of social control through appeals to creative, individual freedom (Catherine Bell's "redemptive hegemony"), with the other. The contradiction the sociologist Daniel Bell ([1976] 1996) posed between economic rationality and cultural expressiveness has been dulled by the fusions of a "post-secular" capitalism that is at once instrumental and enchanted.

In the early 1970s, having already become an exemplar for New Age seekers, Savitri D's father, Stephen, converted to Islam and eventually came to be known as Shaykh Abdullah Nooruddeen. In 1979, he helped found Dar al-Islam, an Islamic community in Abiquiu, New Mexico. He penned important translations of Sufi classical texts and an English translation of the Qur'an. Shaykh Nooruddeen became influential in the growth of American Sufism and is thought to be the first American-born Sufi Shaykh. His "middle-way" approach to Islam attempted to stand between the seekers whom, he thought, sought to transform everything into metaphor and the fundamentalists whom he accused of reducing the world to form and law.

When Savitri D's father converted to Islam, he sought to convert the Lama Foundation into an Islamic center, even sponsoring a visit by Muslim scholars in 1977 to sell the community on the wisdom of a new Sufi path. Barbara Durkee and the community members stood their ground, testifying to the value of the Lama Foundation experiment in their lives.³⁶ Stephen Durkee's transformation into Shaykh Nooruddeen changed Savitri D's life forever. In an interview, Savitri D recalled that her father's conversion to what she considers a fundamentalist form of Islam was an important turning point in her life.³⁷ Along with her schooling in New Mexico, where the majority of her classmates were Chican@ and Native American, she credits her travels around the Middle East with her father as a white child with learning, through experience, what it is like to live in the world as a cultural and racial minority.

As Savitri D will also say, her childhood experiences at the commune her parents had founded are still very much in her soul. Sitting adjacent to the Carson National Forest, the Lama Foundation is premised on "a connection to the land," the tenets of permaculture, and overall sustainability. Everyday life involves daily meditation practices of "consensus decision-making," seva (selfless service), daily communal check-ins called "tunings," dances of peace, and shabbat. Communal life is grounded in the charge to treat "everyone and everything with love and respect as a unique being."³⁸ While the concept of community is fundamental to what the Lama Foundation seeks to embody, like the Stop Shopping Church that Savitri D leads, the point of community is never to eradicate individuality but, rather, to honor "the unique role and perspective of each individual."

When we engaged in conversation, Savitri D further explained that the commune where she grew up was on the "spirit path" of the Taos Pueblo and that she would often see Taos Pueblo men on horseback "performing their rituals." Her mother, who adopted the name Asha Greer and did not follow her husband down his newly chosen religious path, remained, Savitri D explained to me, a "highly ecumenical mystic." While she was known for developing her "Vast Silence," a long-term meditative practice, Asha Greer always did hospice and care work. Her mother's path of service, Savitri D believes, is ever in the background of the community work she does with the Choir. As she explained: "What I like to do with the Choir comes directly from that community work."

Given her experiences with racial, cultural, and religious difference and the Lama Foundation's insistence that the uniqueness of individuals and the goals of collective living can coexist and mutually reinforce one another, it makes sense that Savitri D would espouse a kind of grassroots, existential deconstruction.³⁹ The fastest way to defeat the (consumerist) monoculture (what we might call the hegemonic corporatized sameness that domesticates all difference) is to "look into someone's eyes," she once told me. "When I'm connecting to you," she added, "there is no monoculture . . . then we're in this strange wild territory, right. That's wildness, like this is the wildness of an animal looking into the eyes of an animal." Today, Savitri D is known for the "Stop Shopping!" slogan of the group she leads. However, it is worth noting that her relationship to the work to which she is tirelessly committed cannot be reduced to this anti-consumerist copy. In other words, Savitri D's personal experiences with sustainability, religious ecumenism, religious fundamentalism, countercultural consumerism, and cultural difference remain deeply and tightly woven into the group's collective representations.

Savitri D considers her early life living in New Mexico to be determinative in teaching her that human beings are part of the land, not separate from it. These days, when Reverend Billy exhorts us to grow into awareness of ourselves "as Earth," Savitri D's profound influence on the directions the Stop Shopping Church has taken in the last two decades is strongly evident. Reverend Billy credits Savitri D's example for helping him truly understand, in the aftermath of Hurricane Katrina in 2005 and the drowning of New Orleans, that anti-consumerism must, in fact, become Earth activism. This turn to the environmental consequences of consumption implicates the discussion of the fetish with which we began.

The first iteration of Reverend Billy trafficked in the modernist critique of the fetish. The street preacher assumed that the basic problem with consumerism was that false and foreign marketing semiotics threatened to kidnap consumers, taking us away from our own lives, enveloping us in the brand stories of the likes of Disney and Starbucks, and making us complicit in systems of corporate exploitation in the process. The crucifixions of Mickey and Minnie Mouse were designed to bring attention to the ways in which brands ritualize a personification of objects that simultaneously induces an objectification of persons. The aim of the ritual was to eventually return consumers to a space of autonomy wherein the devil had been exorcised. That was then.

Today, in strong measure a testament to Savitri D's preeminence within the history of the community, the Stop Shoppers reject critique's aim of achieving autonomy from religious power and the traditional humanist metaphysics upon which such a goal rests. Their fundamental tenet today is the idea that human beings are not separate from the Earth. Now, success against the power of the brands is understood to depend on a primary awareness of the self's porousness within the relations of political ecology. The contemporary Stop Shopping community rejects the inviolability of the self and religiously transfigures selves into "Earthly" creatures. Concomitantly, parody, a tried-and-true tool of the earlier work, has also transformed into more direct and earnest kinds of intentions.

\* \* \*

Savitri D believes that academics generally lag behind the cultural contexts they aim to study because of the slow and deliberate rhythms of academic work.[40] While Reverend Billy was busy losing his parodic religion, many academic treatments in diverse disciplines like performance studies, organization studies, marketing, pedagogy studies, and communication studies focused attention not on his awakening as a sincere preacher but, instead, on his "parodic overidentification" (Murtola 2012), Bush-era "ironic and artistic activism" (Lechaux 2010), "carnivalesque activism" (McClish 2009), and culture jamming pedagogy (Sandlin and Milam 2008). The Stop Shopping Church was read as an example of modern-day mummery (Berthon et al. 2011) and the burgeoning postwar American phenomenon of "fake religions" (Simpson 2011).

Some academic treatments of Reverend Billy and the Church of Stop Shopping have noted the importance of religion to the activism of the group. The communications scholar Brian Kaylor (2013) suggests that William Talen's rhetorical strategies can be productively read through the lens of biblical prophetic discourse. The performance studies scholar Diana Taylor (2010) reads a performance of the Stop Shopping Church at a conference sponsored by the Hemispheric Institute of Performance and Politics at New York University in Victor Turner's ritual terms: as the temporary creation of a *communitas* of democratic space shorn of corporate rule. Taylor also notes connections between the group's performative style and the politically energizing diasporic African practices and embodied religion that help "build a sense of hope."

Alisa Solomon (2013), who also notes the political power of ritual in the work of the group, places Reverend Billy and the Church of Stop Shopping within traditions of premodern dramaturgy that trouble and disrupt modern categories of religion and theater in the contemporary context of radical performance. Jill Lane (2002) places the work of the group within a negative dialectics that continuously blurs the distinction between "real church and real theater." Her important early treatment of the Stop Shopping Church associates Talen's critical deflections of a positive identity with his "most spiritual act." Lane (2002) proposes, "as long as he doesn't actually become the preacher he continuously pretends to be, his performances will continue to refract, deconstruct, and open rigid understandings of spirituality and materialist critique." Recognizing a shift to which I will turn, Solomon (2013) sounds a similar note a decade later: "only comic irony prevents Reverend Billy from tumbling into self-righteous moralizing; his performance must always remind spectator-participants that he is wearing a disguise, transparent as it may be." Importantly, however, recent treatment within religious studies (LeVasseur 2020) analyzes the Stop Shopping Church not as parody but, rather, within the framework of religious *animism*.

When I first began my fieldwork with the group, Talen and Savitri D suggested a strong relationship between what they call the group's

Figure 3.1. Savitri D and Reverend Billy. East Village, Manhattan. 2023. Photo by the Stop Shopping Church.

gradual turn to "sincerity" in the past twenty years and the decline in academic interest in the project. I propose this: *For religious studies, at least, there should be ripening interest.* While ingenious and of continued interest, Talen's visible, conscious performance of Reverend Billy is not the only matter of religion to which we ought to attend. If we are mesmerized by his playful and performative confounding of discursive boundaries, we will miss the spillages and slippages which he and the Stop Shopping Church have now taken up, in unfunny lament.

## Between Religion and the Secular

As David Feltmate argues, religious satire is religious in two ways: "It is religious in part because its content deals with 'religion' and it is religious because the desecration of an opponent is the sacralization of one's plausibility structure" (Feltmate 2017, 25). In this sense, while the tensions were already present in the early parody of the right-wing televangelist, as the Stop Shopping Church became a community for its members and structured a positive orientation (Long 1986) toward the world, this parody of religion was actually destined to fall into religion. That is, as soon as performance became community, religion, in a Durkheimian sense, grew deeper roots even if the visible signifiers of American religion were consciously dialed down.

If Reverend Billy were simply the headliner of political vaudeville, he would have been able to performatively maintain the negative dialectics the academic community knows him for. Religion happened to William Talen because a community of interest formed around his work. Today, in addition to its social justice activism core, the Stop Shopping Church members, which generally number between thirty and thirty-five at any given time, provide childcare for each other, pitch in to help send members' kids to summer camp, assist members with housing and employment searches, and have been ritually meeting on Sundays since 2003 for weekly rehearsal and what they call "fellowship" despite the Christian resonances. As Jeremiah once explained to me, "as people got together and married and had children, we realized it wasn't a fake church anymore."[41]

* * *

In addition to the structural matter of the community functioning as a religious community, Reverend Billy and the Church of Stop Shopping also actively cultivate a space of what they call "radical instability" and, in my view, exploit religion's (*and the secular's*) lack of essence in order to do so. Kathryn Lofton argues that, like all binaries, the sacred and the profane exist within "a tense purlieu of differentiation" (2017, 28). As Janet Jakobsen and Ann Pellegrini (2008, 7) usefully unpack, secularism, "as a political project that deploys the concept of the secular," posits oppositions between the secular and the religious in order to advance the political purposes of modernity. They write: "a secular society is one not bound by religion. Thus, a network of associations is established between the religious-secular opposition and that between bondage and freedom" (Jakobsen and Pellegrini 2008, 6). Whereas, as Lofton (2017, 28) observes, "the last ten years of scholarship on secularism ... has worked to show that secularism is not the least bit minimal in its engagements, classifications, bureaucracies, or habits," we are nevertheless ritualized in society to associate secularity with autonomy and agency and religion with the curtailing of agency and autonomy. From the beginning, Reverend Billy conjured away the smokescreen, turning to consumerism to expose the secular's strict disciplines and undemocratic phantasmagoria. Complicating matters, the group's actual critical rigor can also be the cause of lived anxiety for some community members who long for a place of freedom to step into that is safe and set apart from religion as social control.

Mixing and matching leftist politics and the signifiers of right-wing American Protestant fundamentalism, one can read Reverend Billy as an example of what Melissa Wilcox (2018, 85) calls *religionfuck*, challenging and undermining "cultural assumptions about the ways religious identities, roles, practices, beliefs, and appearances cohere." Given that secularism is, in fact, *Protestant secularism* (Jakobsen and Pellegrini 2008), that William Talen chose to don the habits of a right-wing televangelist was a precise and strategic move. Not only was the effect of the performance to spark the question, *what do we mean by religion, anyway?*, it also brought attention to the close historical relationship between free-market enthusiasm and forms of American Protestantism.

If Protestantism and capitalism were, from the start, "coimplicated" (Jakobsen and Pellegrini 2008, 3), the American situation within which Reverend Billy arrived had radicalized the historical relationship between American Protestantism and American capitalism by announcing it with affective intensity and publicity. The Reverend Billy character engaged with American religion in its overdeterminations: as a response to consumer capitalism's soul-craft, as a marker of the historical alliances between conservative Christianity and neoliberal markets, as a performative repository of condemnatory critique, and, finally, as the lynchpin of an emergent grassroots community. For William Talen, the character became the privileged medium for exercising political agency and "saving souls" (Talen 2006, 23). The activism that developed around his shared work with Savitri D is a form of *religious activism* precisely because it has traditionally moved with, between, and against these different valences of American religious history.

In a society in which theme parks and museums dedicated to selling free enterprise go hand in hand with the rise of pro-capitalist Christian entrepreneurial education (Moreton 2009), the experience economy has given rise to Bible-based theme parks (Bielo 2017), Black televangelists sell capitalism through techno-mediated inspiration (Walton 2009), and working-class Latin@ neo-Pentecostal worship sometimes blends religion and the secular performing arts in the advancement of "spiritual warfare" (Elisha 2017), the Reverend Billy Project strongly appreciated, from the beginning, neoliberal recombinations of "religious" and "secular" affects and effects.

The Stop Shopping Church was, from its inception, prescient to understand that despite the lingering conceit of separate spheres of life, everyday libidinal dramas intimately link the sacred and secular in neoliberal times. As Nigel Thrift (2010) argues, economies must always generate passionate interest. Talen and his early disciples certainly knew this as well. They also understood that critical praxis and resistance demanded affective interest in turn.[42] However, vital to understanding the transitions and transformations the Stop Shopping Church has undergone in the last almost quarter century and why is appreciating the fact that neoliberal capitalism has not just erased the borders between the religious and the secular but that these movements also imply the confounding of the borders between culture and nature. Most to the point, for the Stop Shoppers, what matters most is that the

Shopocalypse forces a reconsideration of the borders between the self and the natural world that occupies and constitutes the human body.

## After "Religion," at the "End of the World"

Twenty years after he entered the Disney Store to proclaim Mickey Mouse the Antichrist, Reverend Billy leads a new group of radicals, some of whom were there at the beginning, into a branch of J.P. Morgan Chase. They are carrying a big blue tarp and begin working it, miming the waves of the sea. The group chants "we are the river/we are the sea" while Reverend Billy delivers a sermon condemning Chase's financing of climate change for slowing down sea currents and accelerating the species extinction of marine life (Reverend Billy and the Stop Shopping Church 2019). In these latest episodes of Reverend Billy's street theater, Chase CEO Jamie Dimon, and Amazon's Jeff Bezos often play the role of the billionaire villains.

In the beginning, the Stop Shopping Church was known for its flowing gospel robes and rhythms. The robes have since been retired, the musical and performative style reaches beyond gospel into pop, country, Brechtian theater, classical, and even disco. These days, Reverend Billy is more apt to wear a pink, green, or orange suit than a white one, meaning that one is much less likely to misrecognize him as a Christian preacher. The group preserves its anti-consumerism core in its work and in its name and continues to advocate for the preservation of neighborhoods and local economies. Having been a presence at Occupy Wall Street (2011), Ferguson (2014), and Standing Rock (2016), it has been very much involved, at the local level, in the new sanctuary movement, Black Lives Matter protests, queer liberation, and First Amendment issues. It continues to be invited abroad for activist festivals and events, most recently in the UK, Greece, and Australia.

Savitri D, of course, now directs the group.[43] Jeremiah became the group's musical director in 2009 and served in that capacity when I did my fieldwork with the group. Together, Savitri D and Jeremiah retired the gospel Choir for the sake of greater musical experimentation and flexible choreography better able to nimbly respond to the situation at hand.[44] Most days, there is little irony to be found in the work. If the commodity fetish, once the main attraction, and its attendant issues of agency, autonomy, and intersubjective relationships, was the focus of the group's earlier attention and work, the fetish has now been swept up into deeper, planetary currents.

From the beginning, Reverend Billy lodged humorous critiques at scientism, mocking the "happy men of science" who look to solve the mystery of Love through the study of pheromones certain to be of interest to the corporations and marketers (Talen 2006, 8–9), consumer capitalism's ritual specialists if Ernest Dichter, we recall, is to be believed. Then, what the group calls "the Fabulous Unknown" was akin to what the anthropologist Michael Jackson puts in phenomenological and existential terms: the mysteries of life that remain at the limits of human understanding and control (Jackson 2009, 232) and are often best expressed in the language of art. The group now often deploys the term in a more metaphysical capacity, to mark the sacred mysteries of the Earth.

Savitri D suggests this: "we have to know and trust an intelligence there that we don't need to describe in our terms but need to respect" (Reverend Billy and the Church of Stop Shopping 2018). Fundamentalist religions, including consumerism, Savitri D and the other Stop Shoppers will tell you, keep us from asking questions and traffic in the currency of false resolution to life's mysteries. As I discovered, while on the surface the group seems less and less interested in engaging in what Melissa Wilcox (2018, 85) calls *religionfuck*, the role of religion in the life and work of the community has become an even more interesting question. The group's recent work actually returns it in an even more direct way to the deeper religious histories of mercantilistic encounter with which we began.

These days, Reverend Billy sermonizes about the need to "be the Earth" and to "listen to the Earth." Savitri D once explained to me that activism is about "a body confronting power . . . there are huge, huge forces that go through your body when you confront power."[45] If in the early work those forces were read through the lens of capitalism's mediating affects and were alien forces that required *exorcism*, today those forces include the Earth,[46] a power the group looks to *channel*. Accepting the porousness of life, Savitri D and Reverend Billy are fond of saying that the "body is the plan," which is to say that politics must start from an acknowledgment that "we are the Earth."

For the group, "weather events" like the Canadian wildfires (2023), California wildfires (2020), Hurricanes Katrina (2005), Sandy (2012), and María (2017), and the Australian bushfires and Brazilian forest fires (2020), as well as accelerating species extinction, the environmental impact of chemical agribusiness, and destructive practices like mountain-top removal and fracking are the warning signs of a human-induced apocalyptic climate event. They conceive of them as communications from the Earth that should compel us to change. As William Talen once explained it to me, "the climate crisis and species Extinction forced us to integrate the issues. And I think that it's true that I've seen earlier efforts in a new light as a result of what's happened since."[47]

\* \* \*

At a rehearsal I attended, Savitri D explained to the gathered group that, in the end, she does not hope to be remembered for her human form but, rather, for having simply returned "to the Earth." There was no irony or poetic license in her delivery. As she once put it in a podcast, we need to "take humans out of the center of the story" (Reverend Billy and the Church of Stop Shopping 2018). At present, for the Stop Shopping Church, to "be Earth" is sometimes understood, whether in activism or on stage, to perform intuitively, in dynamic, interactive, self-organizing ways.[48] The negative dialectics that prevented religion from having a positive identity in the early work have been relaxed. The flowing robes of gospel choir as set piece have been retired. Now, form meets content: The group's activism and musical performances form what they experience as the sincere ritual of a community of values. In everything they do, Talen and Savitri D will tell you, the community tries to listen to and embody the rhythms of the Earth. These days, Reverend Billy does not shy away from describing the project this way: to make an "Earthy religion" (Talen 2012, 98).

The superstorms are insisting on this basic fact, Talen declares: We are nature, nature is us (Talen 2012, 100–101). Our actions and their consequences, Talen inveighs, suggest that we are a part of the Hollywood movie–sized F5 tornadoes that bring devastation with greater frequency because we caused them. We terrorize ourselves in more than dreams. If we are what we eat,[49] today that means human-produced carcinogens and $CO_2$ greenhouse gas–emitting beef. To be Earth today is to have our own deadly effects boomerang back at us (for example, the microplastics that have taken up residence inside human lungs). Given the environmental devastations capitalism wreaks, our intimate relationships with the Earth are more than sometimes toxic and deadly (Weston 2017, 196).

* * *

Of the fetish, William Pietz (1988) concludes:

> It lies at the core of the idea of fetishism and provides a key, I would suggest, to showing a common conceptual ground among such diverse theorists as Kant and Tylor: the notions of purposiveness and of animism derive from the same problematic that engaged both thinkers in their writings about the problem of fetishism.

In E. B. Tylor's ([1871] 2016) case, the personification of impersonal forces in nature is characteristic of the primitive mind, which is ignorant to the scientific view of causality. According to Tylor, primitive religion, characterized by its animistic ideas about souls dwelling in the world, would eventually develop through spirit cults and polytheism into abstract monotheism. Within Tylor's view, humanity progressively gains increasing independence from a subordinated "nature" revealed to be inanimate, leading to the self-intending posture of the Enlightenment scientist and his cultural Christianity (Tambiah [1990] 2004, 48).

The early Reverend Billy was spooked by the porousness of human beings because that is how corporate capitalism comes to possess us from the inside out. Today, Reverend Billy starts from a place that has reckoned with the "intimate matters of infiltration and interdependence" (Weston 2017, 11), intimacies and animacies, that attend to the environmental destructions of the capitalist Anthropocene, his journey tracking shifts in anthropological discourse. The "Shopocalypse" is a space-time the anthropologist Kath Weston calls "not your great-great-grandmother's animism" (33), wherein the spirits of financial markets compel some consumerized bodies to take up more radioactive isotopes and coliform bacteria into their bodies than others (33), and industrially produced synthetic hormones flow from bovine bodies back into human bodies (4).

In Weston's view, the idea that religion, society, and political economy are separate spheres of life and at metaphysical remove from "nature" is a dangerous con. For her, the turn to "new animism" has less to do with philosophical vitalism and the question, though important, of whether and how Western scholars might account for indigenous communities' nonhuman persons, and more to do with the desire to mark in an affectively effective way how the planet has been occupied by a dangerous mode of production. "Embracing destruction in order to defeat it" (2017, 198), late-stage capitalism, she suggests, has erased the ontological border between person and thing and summoned the twilight. We have the animacies of the material world on the brain, she proposes, because of where, when, and how we are standing.

Weston suggests, "new animisms literally reconceive humans as the products of an "environment" that has itself taken shape through embodied human action, often in pursuit of profit" (2017, 4). For his part, Reverend Billy condemns the "nature-hating gods" (Talen 2012, 98) that taught us that "nature is separate, somewhere in the background of sanctified and patriotic human life." If we "stop demonizing the weather," Reverend Billy similarly wonders, "then perhaps we will also separate ourselves from the wars" (101). Wars such as the ones that set the stage for the crumbling towers on 9/11, an event that has caused cancer rates to be higher in Ground Zero first responders, more than twenty years later?

The pretenses of Western religion's claim to a human transcendence of nature have dissolved; our affective connections with the world are much more intimate than our nostalgic attachments to our favorite Disney film. Our technological capacities and our "continuous sensory engagement with industrially sourced experiences of consumption" (Weston 2017, 198) have brought us to a brink where we might have caused Foucault's ([1966] 1984, 387) premonition of the disappearing human face in the sand to come true in spite of ourselves. As Reverend Billy often preaches, while Disney animations and Hollywood films turn our environmental catastrophes into saccharinated utopias, buddy films, and happy endings, intoxicating us with the dazzling displays of American circus (and no bread), the "end of the world" is nigh.

For the Stop Shopping Church, the "Shopocalypse" is "Western Civilization's recent way of life, or vast drunk party, which is a terminal process in the life systems of the earth, where the importance of fourth quarter corporate meanings control any possible resistance to mass suicide" (Talen 2006, 213). Now it has been broadened to incorporate a primary focus on the ways in which social and political problems like racial capitalism, neoliberal/neocolonial economics, and immigration justice are always and already deeply ecological issues as well. If consumerist fetish was, from the start, a crucible for racial histories and issues of gender and class and these valences have become ritually obscured by consumerism, the Stop Shoppers do not tolerate a truncated view of the stakes. However, they will also tell you that all of us, whoever we are, are about to be flooded out of ecological complacency and lit on fire.

According to the Stop Shopping Church, we, the intellectual descendants of modernity's birthing of religion and progressive time, are blinded by our own Imagineering and addictions to lucid dreaming. We have too long "meddled with the REAL gods. This is an Apocalypse, not bad weather," proclaims the prophet (Talen 2012, 99). Given the ecological effects of our consumptive practices, we have objectified ourselves in ways, some anthropologists will tell us, that are quietly undoing the religious metaphysics of Western personhood heralded by secular modernity, with its account of inanimate "nature." In this context of all-consuming, highly intimate, "post-secular" capitalism, animism, a "survival out of time," is perhaps more to the point than even religion, and certainly the parody of religion. *Better stated: The only religions that can save us now, the group believes, are ones that can teach us to live without religion's bounded assurances.*

ACT II

Activists at the Shopocalypse

# 4

## Becoming the Beloved Community of Musical Earth

Devotion . . . is no more than the chaotic jingling of bells,
the mist of warm incense, a musical thinking that does not
get as far as the Notion.
—G.W.F. Hegel, *The Phenomenology of Spirit*

You're in community when you're singing.
—Savitri D

### Musical Agency and the Sounds of Capitalism

For a child of the late 1970s and the 1980s, there are certain sounds that still manage to jolt the body and quicken the heart in anticipation some thirty-five years later. Like many from my generation, the 20th Century Fox strobe lights followed by the "Star Wars crawl" and John Williams's magisterial score are forever etched in my sonic imagination. The then shiny and new cable television channel, HBO, opened its feature presentations with synthesizer-generated orchestral music designed to remind the viewer of the movie house experience. For someone whose parents could not afford to take us to the movies on any kind of regular basis, it was my synthesized door into the magic of Hollywood.

Under late capitalism, personal and social history are lived with an attendant score, through flowing tapestries of sound and musical soundscapes. As such, the birth of Internet life, for example, is seared into my own memory by the then ubiquitous Windows 95 startup sound.[1] And, in the age of Spotify, political history has thoroughly incorporated the concept of the soundtrack. On the eve of the publication of his memoir, President Obama tweeted a playlist of twenty memorable songs from his administration.[2] Not to be outdone in his consumption of youthful "relevance," Obama's successor, Joe Biden, dropped an inauguration playlist. There has even been speculation about Pope Francis's personal playlist.³

As marketing adopts more anthropologically sophisticated uses of sound and music, it becomes increasingly difficult to dismiss Harvey Cox's (1999) view that the market is "inside us, informing our senses and feelings." Music helps the market hail us as consumers and therefore participates in the making and remaking of social identities from the inside out. A testament to the specific contours of my own particular biography, my childhood is marked not just by the commercial music of bland Americana—(I'm not sure if Dr. Pepper made a pepper out of me or not, but the jingle certainly made an impression on my group of friends as pre-teens in the 1980s⁴)—but also strong sonic reminders of my East Coast Latino childhood.

We should not underestimate the role that seemingly innocuous television and commercial music can have on the construction of personal and ethnic identity.⁵ In addition to the theme songs for the countless telenovelas my mother would watch when I was a child (some more memorable than others) or the clownish boings of the theme song to the ubiquitous "El Chavo Del Ocho" (the most successful Spanish language comedy in television history), television music has played its own important role in the creation of US Latinos as a market segment and generic cultural identity. "Latinos Inc.," as Arlene Dávila ([2001] 2012) explains, has come to metabolize and subsume a plethora of cultural particularity within it. US Chican@s, Puerto Ricans, Dominicans, Costa Ricans, Cubans, Peruvians, and others have come to share musical references like the theme songs to the popular Chespirito TV comedies that work to traverse and bridge otherwise divergent ethnic and immigrant histories.⁶

While marketing has, since its advent, "been involved in the making of public identities" and the "Americanization" of immigrants, the globalization and neoliberalization of the economy has upped the ante with respect to the encroachment of capitalism into everyday life, interpolating consumers through niche identity markets (Dávila [2001] 2012, 10).⁷ If consumers have become central bastions of contemporary politics, commercial music is one of the technologies according to which consumers are *ritualized*. Organizing sounds and programmed music help produce the architectonics of commercial space, whether *physical*, such as at a Starbucks store or a shopping mall like Hudson Yards, *digital*, as the sonic background for our monetized surfing on the Internet, or *psychic*, through our sensuous entanglements with these aesthetically immersive spaces.

Commercial music runs through the cutaneous membranes of our bodies as we receive its vibrations and pulses and metabolize human meaning through our interaction with these sonic inputs. Even if experience is damaged by its entanglements with capital, as Adorno argued,[8] commodification does not thereby obliterate the potency of desire or negate the visceral livingness of human experience. Commercial music makes its rhythmic way into muscle memory. Just ask Rocky Balboa's cinematic fans or any spin instructor. We dismiss its power on aesthetic grounds at our own political peril. Especially under the rule of neoliberal rationalities, capitalism's enchantments are musically present to and "in us" in ways that cannot be simply undone by right thinking and access to healthy reading.[9]

At midcentury, Henri Lefebvre argued that consumer capitalism purports to absorb and deflect human brokenness and hope in an effort to sell us productized solutions we then come to experience as very real medicine. This move, however, concomitantly reproduced a necessary opposition between religion and freedom that still problematically haunts social critique to this day.[10] Much more usefully, however, one very prescient aspect of Lefebvre's argument is the idea that critical social theory must be able to attend to the *affects* and not just the institutions of capital.[11]

With the ubiquity of sonic advertising in our everyday lives and in the face of the reality that, today, much radio music is birthed into the world as advertising music first rather than appropriated as advertising music on the back end (Taylor 2012), it might be tempting to overemphasize music's role in social control and the neoliberal collectivization of human desire. The commercialization of the world, however, is never actually as airtight as advertising would like it to be.

At their most effective, the creative tactics of the weak that Michel de Certeau (1984) stresses can prevent social action from existing as flat and predictable instantiations of hegemonic social processes. For example, as we will see, in the diaphragms, throats, mouths, torsos, arms, and ears of the Stop Shopping Church, who often refer to themselves primarily as "singing activists," music is a hopeful practice of freedom and sonic agency. For the Stop Shoppers, singing expresses the creative prong of their entanglements with the religion of everyday life. Central to understanding the musical critique of the activists is contextualizing their performances within the sonic landscape and musical character of the branded empire they take on.

* * *

The study of American religious life is rife with rich and textured examples of the ways in which the sociocultural production of what Isaac Weiner (2014) calls "sonic experience" generates opportunities for the dynamic negotiation of power, including, in some of these registers, acts of existential and political resistance as well. For example, we might think of Albert Raboteau's ([1978] 2004) classic discussion of slave spirituals as technologies for interpreting experiences of radical dehumanization within a religious system of meanings that preached the deliverance of slaves, happiness in the world to come, and the importance of communal bonds in the present. We can also consider the plethora of scholarship written on the organizing power of freedom songs of the 1960s[12]—a power that depended on the ability of song to instantly historicize civil rights within biblical narrative, the political and religious history of African Americans, and the oral tradition of the spirituals, in particular (see Reed 2006). And, as the filmmakers Abel Sánchez and Andrés Alegría (2021) document, the farmworkers movement of the 1960s and 1970s was supported by the music of popular musicians like Joan Baez, Neil Young, and Taj Mahal.

Examples of recent scholarship in religious studies that directly consider the relationships between music and American Protestantism include Ari Kelman's (2018) study of the role of Evangelical worship music in the production of religious experience and Vaughn Booker's (2020) study of the religious valences of twentieth-century jazz celebrities.[13] In a more Durkheimian direction, music can also be vital to what is sacred to subcultures. As Octavio Carrasco (2022) suggests, popular music can become a "lodestone" for devoted fans, even assuming a religiously orienting force in their daily lives.[14] Today, as in the past, popular music can open spaces for marginal communities to congregate and engage in a critique of the world.

Even as it, like other popular musical forms such as punk rock, has often reproduced patriarchal and homophobic norms, the roots of hip-hop can be found in the artistic responses of African American youth to the contradictions and social neglect of postindustrial urban cities like New York at the start of the Reagan era. As Joseph Winters makes clear, however, such mediatized critique must always be historicized. He writes (2011) that hip-hop, for example, "has always been constrained and limited by the dominant norms, expectations and standards of the broader social order."[15] As important as it has been to counteract the influence of crude and unempirical forms of Marxian economism with an attention to the ideas and practices that give rise to human experiences of the world at particular times and in particular places (a sensibility that is now a hallmark of religious studies as a discipline), it is equally important to remember that critical, even liberationist, cultural and linguistic expression and the affective life these help bear can be strongly disciplined by capital in a postindustrial and financialized society like ours.

Theodor Adorno and Max Horkheimer ([1947] 2002) famously worried that the culture industry manufactured our dispositions, displacing the grounding of tradition and obliterating the possibilities for criticism in the process.[16] There is, however, a dangerous domino effect of cascading implications for social activism that follows from such a pessimistic understanding of how capitalism indoctrinates and reifies experience. For one thing, we might come to underestimate or misrecognize the viscerally *lived* dimensions of consumer capitalism.[17] And while we might more readily grasp the social control implied by consumer ritualization, we might also find ourselves unprepared for the task of actually building a world outside of capitalism. While we overlook the Stop Shopping Church's acumen as diagnosticians of the discipline of consumer capitalism to our detriment as scholars, it is actually toward their theatrical manifestations of present and future possibilities that the group itself most clearly looks to draw our attention.

If consuming power has taken root in the recesses of the branded soul (even constituting psychic space) through modes of consumer ritualization, just as Ernest Dichter hoped it would, the ritual transformations of radical practice (rather than textual analysis alone) would seem necessary to the goal of piercing the closed loops of capitalist subjection. The religion scholar Eddie Glaude (2008, 96) has suggested that Judith Butler's account of performativity and agency, discussed earlier in this book, is unresponsive to the actual vicissitudes of creative, human living. As scholars, he argues, we can attend to the necessary critique of the conceit of the autonomous will without reducing lived struggle to its semantic conditions alone.

Glaude's is a key insight generated as well by an ethnographic encounter between religious studies and a grassroots community like the Stop Shopping Church. To unpack the stakes: Performativity theory's hypernominalism not only mirrors the logic of branding, as we saw, but also flattens out social experience by privileging visuality over and against other aspects and dimensions of sensuous embodiment. For the Stop Shoppers, if agential acts of resistance to consuming power are to stand any chance, we must ground them within the whole range of our senses.

Even in the most oppressive circumstances, human beings are not simply the effects (or iterative citations) of prevailing regimes of power. Neither are we reducible to visual signs and signifiers.[18] If another world is indeed possible, the grassroots activists suggest through their labors, we need to enlist the fullness of who we are to begin to even imagine it. As Reverend Billy likes to put it: Liberation is not an idea, it is physical. And music (*and religion*), he and his co-conspirators know very well, can move whole bodies and souls.

\* \* \*

As Jason Bivins's (2015) study of American jazz explores, music, like religion, is characterized by definitional slipperiness and experiential polymorphousness and exceeds the definitional limits of language at the level of lived practice. This is why Max Weber ([1922–1923] 1946, 281) suggested that religion and music resist final intellectualization and rationalization in similar ways.[19] In the present day of the discipline, Francis Stewart (2017) productively explores and details the descriptive poverty of current scholarly accounts of religion in her brilliant ethnography of punk subcultures as "implicit religion." The affective, suprarational force of music in the lives of punk communities is one of the reasons the categories of religion and non-religion are rendered so unstable in her study.

Organizing binary pairs such as secular / religion and inside / outside fail to signify the ultimately "non-ascribable experiences" (Bivins 2015, 274) that music can elicit. One religion scholar has even suggested that, in their attempt to elicit ineffable and intensely emotional responses, John Williams's "Star Wars" chorales can be understood as a kind of worship music (Thornton 2019). The iconic role George Lucas's nominally "secular" space opera plays in the lives of its fandom would demand no less. We might recall Henri Lefebvre on this point: Consumer narratives, much like the culturally pervasive Catholicism of his twentieth-century France,[20] offer opportunities for the consumers of media to insert ourselves into transcendent stories that bridge experiences of self and other, providing, in turn, meaning-making resources for the prolonged scope of particular human lives.

Music carries consumers through and across intersubjective netherworlds that might more easily recall Wonderland (or, at least, home movies, MTV, and TikTok videos) and so-called sacred experience than an ideologically fetishized "rational" world in which time is linear, the laws of scientific causality apply, capitalist rationality governs exchange, and the scholarship we do has absolutely nothing to do with the late-night television we watch. Music provides misty access to what Michael Jackson (2018) calls our "off-modern condition."[21] It provides existential signposts; it can return us to experiences that have wounded or enlivened us; it can alter our mood in one direction or another; it can take us away or ground us; it can, in the end, transform our experience of self and world.[22] In short, music can serve as a vehicle for many a magic carpet ride.

Music, like lived religion, works on the full sensorium of human experience, generally privileging feelings over ideas and the body over the mind.[23] "Post-secular" capitalism is highly musical because music and sound help move the consumer soul along its interminable and loss-strewn journey toward its best life. And keeping in step with this sensorily dynamic and amorphous embodied strategy, it becomes impossible to neatly delineate between the assertions of the will and the environmental influences that inform and structure but do not fully define human action in the world. Having arrived at something of the very same conclusion, for the Stop Shopping Church, *doing* music, like *doing* religion, does not admit of binary talk of agency *or* control.

\* \* \*

For the religion scholar Robert Orsi (2012), the fates of human and divine purposes are ultimately linked in a particular way. Although epistemic modernity has often assumed their eventual disappearance, "gods" (for Orsi, a synecdoche for the special beings that humans maintain relationships with in their "religious imaginings of reality") permeate the crevices of modernity's vaunted borders, exposing their constitutive instabilities in the process. As it is lived,[24] religion surreptitiously unmasks the conceits of modern secularism's separation of spheres and the scientific worldview's insistence on rational, linear progress.

Orsi's account of religious subjectivity is, for our purposes, importantly *praxeological*. It is essential to note that, in his account, it is intersubjective life rather than the slippages of language that performs the upending of secular metaphysics. Orsi's "third way" to the study of religion—one that is attentive to the spectrum of religious worlds that actually exist despite secularism's attempt to conjure them away—not only demands that we attend to the "real presence" of the gods but that we also closely heed the "real" human agency of those who enter in and out of relationship with them.[25] Orsi's approach resists the dissolution of agency into discursive meaning since what actually matters to human beings is not reducible to scholars' attempts to explain, authorize, and police the social world or the attempts of religious elites to do the same.

One thing religion does is express the interminable and tempestuous dialectic between freedom and control.[26] In the end, music, like religion, is also never in-of-itself either liberating or disenfranchising.[27] As Tracy Fessenden's (2018) study of Billie Holiday suggests, popular music can exist as a dynamic crossroads within which history and biography (and the so-called secular and religious) "trade skin" and riff off one another. At his most humanistic, Marx ([1852] 1983) understood that the fact of historicity does not in turn foreclose our ability to shape history.[28]

For the Stop Shopping Church, the modern antinomy between agency and control is, finally, (*musically*) false. The dialectic between freedom and control is also one reason, I have been suggesting, that

American religion became the performative fulcrum it did for the Stop Shopping Church. For the activists, religion references and performs the dual nexuses wherein consumer choice is both exposed as radical social construction (the "consumerization" and pious gestures of ritualized branding), on the one hand, and the grounds from wherein we struggle to release ourselves from environmentally destructive forms of psychic and bodily capitalization (religion as performance community), on the other hand.

Religion is a privileged category for the Stop Shopping Church precisely because it is historically overdetermined and dramaturgically open. As a lived, social phenomenon, the religion of everyday life is caught up in the historical forces of social control *and* provides the moving and compelling resources for their creative appropriation and subversion. The highly corporealized Stop Shopping community, as the journalism scholar Alisa Solomon (Durkee and Talen 2013, 15) suggests, has become piously devoted to the ideal of creative agency. The Church's convivial practices of musical freedom in a time of branded ritualization, ecological catastrophe, and the reign of "post-secular" capitalism's pantheon of hungry, all-consuming gods lay the foundations for the group's "post-religious" performances of the twilight of ecologically destructive religion.

## "The Plan Is the Body": Working in Concert

During my first ever conversation with Reverend Billy, he suggested that the time lag I was experiencing with my Institutional Review Board application was evidence of the counter-revolutionary nature of the university as one of society's big and morally disappointing institutions.[29] He also wondered if I had ever considered working outside of the university, without its conservative controls and restrictions looming over me. I have, in fact, worked in social services as a case manager, work about which I have profound reservations given its bureaucratic ruthlessness, but which I do sometimes miss. Reverend Billy's suggestion provided a jolt, causing a dustup of my own sometimes ambivalent feelings about the academe, its penchant for echo chambers, and its own propensities for magical thinking.[30] I was more uneasy, coming into the fieldwork, than I had imagined I would be.

From our conversations and exchanges, it was clear to me, coming in, that more than their formal performances on stage, it was the community that has developed around Reverend Billy's emergence onto the scene that he and Savitri D consider to be the hallmark of the work they had been doing together for two decades. The Stop Shopping Church practices community as the form it believes radical living today must take. Savitri D elucidated in an interview[31] that at political actions, often under duress due to the actions of police or counter protestors, the Choir practices "being human in public space together." This is necessary, she suggests, in order to chip away at the "cult of the individual" that serves as the basis of consumerism.[32]

For Savitri D (Durkee 2021), singing together as activists is radical because it provides support for acts of both "collective transformation *and* generous invitation." The "repetition" of the song's "melody-tone tempo," she explains, provides a shared sonic "meeting place" and "stage" where our emotions can temporarily liberate individual identities. What Savitri D (2021) calls the "transformational potential" of singing with other people suggests that it is at once "structure and anti-structure." This view mirrors the citational logic of branding (where sameness is shadowed by its constitutive difference) but, as we will see, for Savitri D and the Stop Shoppers, music and performance offer opportunities for encounters and experiences that can work to ultimately arrest the proliferation of endless consumerist repetition. Through her life's work, Savitri D proposes that activist communities anchored by a choir (what she and outside collaborators have called "choirs of assembly") (Durkee 2021) should respect the fact of our ritualization but also, at the same time, present opportunities for expressive breaks with the repetitive beats of capitalism.

In my estimation, Savitri D's theorizations of the intersubjective capacities of singing share important resonances with academic theorizations of assemblage (Puar 2007), critiques of "possessive individualism," and something like Hardt and Negri's (2004) ideas about assembly as a contestation over neoliberalism's powers of subjection. In their work, perhaps surprisingly for a group devoted to an "Earth"-based ontology, the general praxis of the Stop Shopping Church resembles Edward Said's critical humanism and pragmatic thought. It shares their focus on provisionality, the questioning of totalizing claims, and the broader project of "living lives oriented towards justice and inclusiveness" (Chatelier 2018). The focus for Savitri D is always assembly as a musical act and a verb rather than an analytical noun. In its musical agency, the group's approach very strongly resembles the pragmatic philosopher Cornel West's (1999, 23–24) musical lens for marking moral agency's dual aspects of freedom and control.

For grassroots activists, any analysis of discursive conditions must ultimately give way to the practical considerations and needs of what Edward Said (1983, 221–222) refers to as "engaged political workers" working in "ensembles of relationship."[33] Given her abiding interests in the decision-making around the immediate questions that confront activists, Savitri D's view of collective organization seems, in the end, to have most in common with David Graeber's (2004) articulation of anarchist struggle.[34] How does the Choir become the kind of choir that can be light enough on its proverbial feet but strong enough in its shared creativity and commitments to meet the police head-on, with disciplined nonviolence? How to organize together for freedom through coordinated action is the question Savitri D will ask out loud as a way of keeping the Choir grounded in and considerate of its purpose.

For his part, Reverend Billy is also a jazz musician, and the Choir he and Savitri D lead is trained to experiment, improvise, and play with the cultural and physical structures of capitalism in ways that are reminiscent of how scholars write about religion and jazz (see Bivins 2015). Synergistically, musical performance is rehearsal for the acquisition of certain political sensibilities and the development and refinement of a pragmatic rationality that is able to respond to the changing, ad hoc demands of political street theater. Weekly rehearsal is where, as Savitri D explains, the Choir learns to trust one another and becomes street ready, able to act *in concert*.[35]

As Jeremiah, in his role as music director, once suggested over meatballs and a martini, music hits emotional chords more deeply and quickly than language alone can.[36] If post-Fordist capitalism is fueled by immersive, cultural labor, Sunday rehearsal is where like begins to meet like™ in a spirit of creative, subversive resistance rather than compulsory compliance. It is a communal ritual through which a group of local New York City–based activists and singers begin to cohere as a globally renowned choir and radical performance community. The work of the

Stop Shopping Church is itself a "strategy of desire" and keenly understands that the anthropological (and religious) seriousness of branding as consumer ritualization must be met in kind, if, subversively, with the opposite goals in mind. The antidote, they know, is brewed in the sickness.

\* \* \*

While I had, at that point, already seen and heard the group perform at the Brooklyn Commons Theater and side by side with the likes of Slavoj Žižek and Sister Helen Prejean at the Cathedral of St. John the Divine, and I had also joined them for a political action at Trump Tower, my first time attending one of the group's Sunday rehearsals at the Lower Eastside Girls Club in Alphabet City provided the real introduction to how the activist sausage is made. Reverend Billy had already told me that Savitri D does not tend to suffer fools lightly and, thinking, too, of his suspicions of the university, I was full of worry as I made my way to rehearsal. I had stable academic employment with state benefits and a pension, lived in suburban New Jersey, and was not in the recent habit of putting my body on the line at political actions. Worst of all, I was in a NYC yellow taxicab of all places, on my way to meet people who regularly make material sacrifices on behalf of the commons I had never considered in my most politically defiant dreams, least of all dared to do. I felt embarrassingly bourgeois.

With apprehension, I rang the bell of the Lower Eastside Girls Club.[37] Its full glass façade provided an apt metaphor for how exposed I felt. Paulina and Kevin, whom I had met at my first Trump Tower action, were the first to greet me and seemed genuinely pleased to see me. It occurred to me later on that, on some general level, my anxieties were also quite familiar. They reminded me of the first few times I attended coffee hour at Manhattan's St. Michael's Episcopal Church in the early 2000s, the last time I had attended church services with any conviction and regularity. Then, and now, though, things usually turn out fine. Although she was reserved, Savitri D welcomed me in a way that felt warm if also contingent. As she later explained to me, academics can be dangerous for the group because they can demand forms of self-reflection they do not always have the time to do. I wonder now if she worried at the time that my presence might prove to be such a distraction.

Folks I had yet to meet but had caught glimpses of at the Trump Tower action nodded in my direction from afar.[38] Others came over to say hello. Reverend Billy was busy mingling but briefly came over to pat me on the back and say hello. Panning around the room of about twenty-five people, I found the racial and generational diversity of the Choir quite striking. There were even children present, Savitri D's and Reverend Billy's then preteen daughter and the toddler children of longstanding members of the group. The group's diversity at the time was an observation I would make time and again during my visits with the Choir.

At a later rehearsal, Shirley Williams, an incredibly youthful African American performance artist in her mid-forties, would eloquently celebrate the Choir's diversity during the community meeting that follows the singing practice. Savitri D and Reverend Billy, I learned, are quite intentional about cultivating a heterogenous choir. As they explain, movements for social justice have generally been led by people of color, indigenous communities, women, queer folk, and the poor, communities and persons that have the most at stake when institutions fail society and the "Earth."

Importantly, Savitri D has led the group into thoroughly intersectional terrain as an organizer. Although she considers "Earth activism" her primary work,[39] Savitri D has been, by all accounts, instrumental in moving the activist focus of the Stop Shopping Church into areas like immigration justice and the Movement for Black Lives.[40] In Nancy Fraser's (2022) terms, Savitri D, Reverend Billy, and the Stop Shoppers understand that our ecological crisis cannot be separated from issues of livelihood security, public investment in institutions of social reproduction, the exclusion of migrants, the militarization of everyday life, and forms of ethno-racial and gender oppression since all of these are symptoms and effects of the same systems that drive climate change.

In recognition of and deference to what academics might consider the precarity and dispossession of the communities of color with whom the Stop Shopping Church looks to partner and aid, Savitri D believes that, at least more often than not, white activists should offer to help, rather than lead. This philosophy was on full display at the height of the Black Lives Matter protests during the summer of 2020. Savitri D and other members of the Choir intentionally took their cues from Black organizers, choosing to "show up, shut up, and show up again," as Savitri D puts it.

Importantly, the group's determination to not perpetuate everyday forms of racial hierarchies within activist organizing also looks to avoid collapsing into the kinds of dangerous reifications of race and identity that could themselves ultimately run counter to the general anarchistic tenor of the community and its vision for the world.[41] For example, when the initial video of white Covington Catholic High School students confronting a Native American elder went viral on social media in 2019,[42] some incensed Choir members brought it up during the community meeting. Savitri D and Bea, a formerly unhoused African American soprano, asked the group not to freeze the situation and to remember that social media has a way of distorting context. We were not privy to the full picture, they suggested. Savitri D explained: Media is never a mirror. It is curated to make a point and we must approach its (visual) rhetoric as such.

Along similar lines, I have heard Savitri D decry Internet "call-out culture" as juvenile and contrary to the purposes of justice-seeking, as she understands it, because it can be so "dehumanizing," its frames of reference too often shorn of the inconvenient details of actual human situations. In an interview Savitri D suggested that she is "violently opposed" to call-out culture as "anti-generative" and "anti-creative." It is, for her, part and parcel with all fundamentalist border policing that finds what she calls the "complexity of human behavior" embarrassing. If we are simply content to wag fingers, where are the possibilities for contentious transformation, Savitri D wonders?

\* \* \*

As I settled into my first rehearsal, I thought I might be able to get away with sitting in the back while the singers congregated at the front of the room, by the electric piano, according to their vocal parts. I was dreading the idea that I might have to actually sing. I enjoy singing and have always wished I had pursued music in some way. But, having next to no musical training and no discernable talent for music, I was also worried about appearing foolish in front of my new ethnographic interlocuters.

As I would later learn, though, Savitri D and Reverend Billy are increasingly looking for the Choir to maintain a patina of visual and sonic roughness and, hence, grassroots authenticity. They are not a professional choir, they insist, even if they have, over the years, counted among their number Broadway singers and television actors. Paul Broussard, the music director for much of the first decade of the 2000s, shared his reservations and personal regret with me about the fact that the Stop Shopping Church increasingly pivoted away from the professional choir model during his time there.[43] However, a rejection of the logic of excellence at the complete expense of the needs of community is an important characteristic of who the Choir aims to be today.

For the group, art and politics are not finally grounded in different rationalities, as they were for Max Weber. Instead, the members of the Stop Shopping Church will explain, effective critical social action is necessarily artful. The full sensorium of experience must be engaged, the Stop Shopping Church believes, both to sustain the activists themselves in the face of the rigors of street politics and to best serve the kind of transformations of self they seek to inspire. For the Stop Shopping Church, it is important for *being* to always remain active rather than static. The Choir and the community, like the world, they believe, are always changing—that is, in process. We might think of this view as expressing a commitment to the critical importance of preserving some space of self-alienation (as a font of potential creativity and transformation) and a related refusal of professionalization (a kind of negative dialectics designed to disrupt the commoditization of what they do).[44] In the community's view, too much of life's immediate textures and tones are sacrificed when performance is overproduced and experience becomes a commodity-thing. Smooth jazz is decidedly not the inspiration here.

Especially in his earlier days, Reverend Billy, a "clown" in the estimation of one long-standing choir member,[45] liked to speak of the political importance of the state of "exalted embarrassment," a "holy oddness" (Talen 2007, 212) that can compel its acolyte to say and do all the right things in the wrong places. According to Reverend Billy and Savitri D, this is an electric capacity that can help us break through the scripted movements and pious gestures of consumerist society. Which means I shouldn't have been too surprised when I was asked to come forward and join the fun.[46] The professor, as it turned out, would not be spared the experience of discomfort. The fact that I was so hesitant and uncomfortable made my obvious embarrassment all the more entertaining, I think, in the eyes of my new friends.

I had participated in my high school chorus for two years, but that was the only instruction in singing I had ever received. At that time, my chorus teacher was not ultimately sure if I belonged among the low tenors or the baritones. I would start off singing tenor with the Stop Shopping Choir and eventually moved my way to sing with the basses and baritones. My voice is caught between parts. In the end, baritone would probably be an easier part for my voice, Savitri D would later explain. For my part, I needed to be pragmatic about the situation. I could not become a distraction to the Choir and I needed to blend in, both musically and from the standpoint of the fieldwork itself.

Taken as a whole, my experiences singing and practicing to sing with the Choir proved to be an experiment in performance anxiety.[47] In fact, it often felt like an exercise in tragicomedy. Being taken by the situation well outside of my comfort zone and still wearing sensible shoes and neutral colors to Carnival,[48] I was reminded of the limiting horizons of professionally regulated competencies—that is, how the borders of specialized forms of training and mastery can hide and deprive as much as they also provide support and make certain things clearer.

For scholars, spending time in libraries to the exclusion of more popular archives or to the exclusion of self-reflection on the ethnographic situations of our own lives can distort the lens through which we come to an understanding of the very world that grounds and supports our academic analyses of it. When scholars of religion routinely edit out our own consumption, it becomes easier to disavow the "consuming religion" that ritualizes even the most ardently irreligious among us. According to David Graeber (2004, 71), contemporary left academic thinking has come to so stress the importance of discourse (the sedimented "totalities," *mentalités*, or historical structures that Jean-Paul Sartre would consider the proper object of analytical reason) (González 2015, 202) because doing so flatters our own sedentary competencies while simultaneously incentivizing a forgetting of the institutionalized privileges that support such a reduction of politics to textual-analytical matters.[49] In the end, academic labor ritualizes and, like all ritual, it obscures just as much as it accentuates. It can disappear our participation as scholars of religion in the religion of everyday life.

\* \* \*

As a synecdochal matter, my first day at rehearsal introduced themes that would continuously present themselves during my time practicing with the Choir. First, the deep interest Savitri D, as a trained dancer, has in the kinesthetics of voice was readily apparent. As we sang, she asked us to extend our bellies, which was amusing to me because I found that my belly was already extended enough.[50] Then she asked the singers to bend over and work on loosening the sphincters of two of our bodily orifices: the one we make sound from and the other the one through which we evacuate our bowels. Savitri D was not the first Stop Shopper to bring attention to bodily nether regions. During a sermon he delivered at the public gardens at Trump Tower, Reverend Billy had proposed that in our contemporary global predicament, we need "Dadaists" and their "grunts and farts." The "new language" we need to develop in the age of rising totalitarianism and environmental catastrophe must include humor and whimsy, he proposed.

I blushed at Savitri D's instructions. And I thought: how might singing and farting somehow be connected for the Stop Shopping Church? I was immediately taken aback by my own seemingly screwball thought and have since reflected on my prudish hesitancy. Especially when it comes to our own knowledge production, academic labor in religion very much continues the general division of body and thought. There is much evidence to suggest that we actually know better. Whether that of Medieval Qur'anic communities (Asad 1993), the ritualizing texts and performances of eighteenth-century imperial China Angela Zito (1997) details, the branded Starbucks consumers analyzed in this book, or the songful resocializations of scholarship students from Latin America into a neoliberal reframing of their experiences Bethany Moreton (2009) considers, the social poetics of cosmology are always materialized in and through the sensible body. One central suggestion of this book is that North Atlantic scholars of religion are not simply students of the catalogued varieties of such embodied cosmologies but are also (the mostly loving) embodied subjects of one particular historical formation of such.

Of course, it is clearer to me now from the vantage point of the kind of hindsight that fieldwork notes can enable that any critical attempt to meet capitalist powers of subjection head-on will need to mirror its interests in the materiality of the body rather than attempt to aestheticize and circumvent embodiment's griminess.[51] Of the Choir, Savitri D said this to the gathered group at my first rehearsal in 2017: "We incarnate commitment" and "our bodies are the Earth."[52] For Savitri D, Reverend Billy, and the current incarnation of the Stop Shopping Church, ultimately what is at stake is a humanistic reversal of the humanistic chain of being. We are ultimately human,[53] they readily admit, but our human capacities must be engaged, developed, and deployed to decenter humanity from the center of cosmological storytelling. The Stop Shopping Church looks to move our primary orientation as a species toward the primacy of life in all of its dimensions, known and unknown.

In the experiences and a/theology of the Stop Shopping Church, the body, which cannot be separated from creativity or divorced from imagination, is the filter through which communication with the "Earth" must always pass. As Savitri D and Reverend Billy understand it, rehearsals hone the Choir's communicative capacities with life. So devoted are they to luxuriating in the liminal spaces that suture body and "Earth" that they have even partnered over their years with the feminist sexologist and performance artist, Annie Sprinkle, and her adoption of the ecosexual position.[54] However, while the Stop Shopping Church strives to embody the sexual politics of its anarchist forbearers and the queer liberation of more immediate activist forbearers, singing activism, not sex, is the primary vehicle through which the group strives to meet the vitality of life as an embodied, sensuous practice.

Under the long, deep shadow of contemporary consumer capitalism's musical personality, the members of the Stop Shopping Church are convinced that music, which Savitri D identifies as one of our most ancient "technologies," needn't simply bring us back to our screens and new monetized moments of ritualized consumption (our binge-watching of new Disneyfied Star Wars stories or influencer TikTok videos, say). Singing together, like walking together, Savitri D believes, is a form of collective behavior that can be used to train our insurgent capacities for "being Earth."[55]

* * *

Singing together brings the Stop Shopping Church together as a kaleidoscopic community. This perspective was foreshadowed at my first Stop Shopping Church performance as a member of the audience. Before the concert began, Reverend Billy introduced me to Peter, a white man who had by then been singing with the Choir for three years, though he had only taken up singing in his forties. In conversation, Peter suggested that what he most admired about the group was that the Choir looks to "make every voice shine and contribute." Peter, like many I have met within the group, was exceedingly well-read. Eventually, we proceeded to touch on the thought of the anti-ecclesial, nineteenth-century philosopher of religion, Friedrich Schleiermacher. Schleiermacher ([1799] 1996), influenced by the Romanticism of his day, argued that the Christian community was a "choir of friends," manifesting the fullness of the universe by way of its dynamic, internal diversity. The uniqueness of persons, for Schleiermacher, is enhanced by our engagement with others. While the group is decidedly "post-Christian," Peter found this analogy concretely useful.

For his part, Schleiermacher himself can be read more for what he has to say about the organization of creativity than for what he has to say about explicitly Christian theological considerations. According to the historian of religions, Charles Long (2018, 7), a basic tenet of Schleiermacher's thought is his consistent interest in the dynamic interrelationships between part and whole in human expression, such that the whole is experienced as ultimately greater than the sum of the parts. There are resonances of this kind of concern in the life of the Stop Shopping Church. The Stop Shoppers look to avoid trapping all of experience within inescapable hermeneutic circles in which there is no room left for facets of life that escape the powers of the rational mind. There is, for them, always a "more" that remains on the far side of conscious life.[56]

The elegant reconciliations promised by closed systems of thought are musically resisted by the Stop Shopping Church. "The clashing makes it beautiful," Jeremiah, the music director at the time, once assured us while we were practicing one of the group's staples, "Imagination." We must push our voices to a place that is no longer "pretty and comfortable," Savitri D similarly suggested as we practiced an arrangement of "Blackbird," the Nina Simone standard. In that moment, I felt in control of nothing. I was fully outside of my musical and emotional comfort zone rehearsing that iconic and gorgeous but also brutalizing song. I discovered over time, though, that even if I had failed to improve as a singer, this would not have been enough to wear out my welcome.[57] An openness to a diversity of singing capacities and musical competencies mirrored other kinds differences the Stop Shopping Church looks to embrace and carefully attend to.

\* \* \*

At one rehearsal, Reverend Billy, who had been practicing his stock preacher gestures in the back of the room while we sang, lamented during the community meeting portion of the evening that we are all "possessed" and that we carry around the "walls" of sexism, racism, homophobia, classism, and ableism within us. These are the walls that singing together, on the street, and "breaking into public space together" can help us begin to tear down, he suggested. Of course, there is another angle for analysis that, in a consumerist age, cannot be ignored. As it does for the global brands against which Reverend Billy sharpened his critical teeth twenty-plus years ago, announcing a commitment to equity and diversity in a post-Fordist era can increase and intensify capital flow.[58]

In the circles within which the Stop Shopping Church travels, diversity adds marketability. Unless you look more closely, a critique of marketing can sometimes look like just more marketing. If we are being honest, in the age of social media, academics know from experience the anxieties that can stem from this kind of quandary. Are left academics' social media posts of solidarity with the pains of the world expressions of genuine concern or performative practices of virtue signaling and attempts to fish for cultural capital? Both? And in terms of the Stop Shopping Church itself, what do we make of the fact that while the current members of color I spoke with feel very much at home in the community, some alumni of the group expressed the concern that the bodies and voices of African Americans, especially, were strategically mined and managed for their association with authenticity?[59] The discourses of early twenty-first-century North American identity are not easily disambiguated from the logic of marketing and the processes of consumption.

Like the walls that thwart it, inclusion, though, begins at home. For example, as one choir member once explained while we were walking toward rehearsal, the group looks to nurture its "neuro-chemical" diversity, meaning that it looks to destigmatize issues of mental health and works to avoid reproducing the assumptions of a neurotypical world. During my time with the Choir, especially under the personal influence of Jeremiah,[60] at least a couple of transgender singer-activists of color were also welcomed into the fold. Members have also welcomed undocumented individuals into their homes to keep them safe from Immigration and Customs Enforcement (ICE). The Stop Shopping Church should act as a beacon for those who are undocumented and afraid, a reminder that there are still some safe spaces left in society, Savitri D once explained.

And Ruthie, one of the first ever professional American Sign Language interpreters who honed her craft in New York City in the 1970s, would make the group's performances and actions accessible to her beloved deaf and hard of hearing community whenever she was able to.[61] She once explained to me that her facial expressions and the ways in which she moves her hands help her audiences listen to and enjoy music as a matter of visible movement and the synesthetic miming of sound.[62]

Savitri D has suggested to me more than once that she is exceedingly proud of the fact that, especially given the current state of activism in New York City, which can veer toward separatism, the Stop Shopping Church remains as diverse as it does, both in its membership and in the kinds of issues it takes on. Still, the politics of identity at the Stop Shopping Church are not without their own very real and understandable tensions. A case in point: During my first rehearsal, when Savitri D, Reverend Billy, and the music director make important announcements and the Choir is asked to come forward with their own announcements, questions, or concerns, Lorraine raised her hand with a look of deep concern on her face.

Lorraine is an African American "movement-based" performance artist, urban farmer, and NYC-based adjunct instructor in performance studies who at that point had not used a credit card in more than ten years. Expounding upon the source of her unease, Lorraine explained that rehearsing the group's musical vamp, "First Amendment," which puts constitutional text to music, proved very uncomfortable for her. Detailing in conversation with me later on that she was thinking specifically of Saidiya Hartman's classic study of the racialized subjectivity of

American slaves, *Scenes of Subjection* (1997), Lorraine explained to the group that, given the document's key role in the founding of the racial state, it was difficult to sing an uncomplicated ode to the Bill of Rights and its importance for grassroots politics.

A conversation then ensued in which other Choir members agreed with Lorraine and still others agreed with Savitri D and Reverend Billy, who explained that the song was born of the group's experiences protesting war in the aftermath of 9/11 and suggested that it is important to lift up a right, free speech, that, as they understand it, is the one guaranteed right that is not directly linked to the ownership of property.[63] In whatever way one theoretically adjudicates the issue of the First Amendment's proposed radicality, on the merits, I was struck by the level of erudition of the discussion as a whole. I felt almost transported back to a seminar classroom. With pragmatic flair, some of the Choir members even added that it is toward the unmet freedoms of democracy that we must continue to strive. But freedom is bound to history, even if a collapsing of these horizons is finally unacceptable to the Stop Shopping Church. There was, for me, no doubt about this, however: Where we stand today, the group, like all of us, does not escape racial history, its co-implications with capitalism, and the painful fissures and wounds these continue to inflict on the living despite anyone's good intentions.[64]

* * *

My participation at the group's rehearsals gave me a living sense of the shared values and vision of and for the world that motivates the Stop Shopping Church as a community. For the historian of religions Charles Long, religion implies *orientation*. Elaborating, he writes (1986, 7): "Orientation in the ultimate sense, that is, how one comes to terms with the ultimate significance of one's place in the world . . . the religion of any people is more than a structure of thought; it is experience, expression, motivations, intensions, behaviors, styles, and rhythms." If we pragmatically apply Long's definition to the life and times of the Stop Shopping Church, one thing that I hope is immediately clear is that, as I once heard Savitri D say, the community is not conceptual or abstract. It is not an art project, even if Reverend Billy, the character, had its origins in the spirit of that kind of approach. For the Stop Shoppers, their community, as church, is not an abstract idea or the two-dimensional repository and teacher of a particular "structure of thought," but, rather, an active, ritualizing communion with a particular worldview. It is "Earth"-grounded ritualization that moves in time to the beat of a particular anti-capitalist cadence.[65]

For their part, from the very start, the group has been hip to "postsecular" capitalism's musical cravings and etiolating "effects" and has developed a musical form of resistance, in turn, rooted in the physicality (Durkee and Talen 2013, 232) and the movement of the body and not only the mind: just the kinds of experiences, expressions, motivations, intentions, behaviors, styles, and rhythms that Charles Long associates with religion as orientation.[66] What, in the end, are those orientations? They start with the body. Again, "the body is the plan," Reverend Billy sermonizes.[67] Human bodies are ritualized into the stock gestures of points of purchase, but musical freedom also starts with the body and the kinds of re-imaginings it can begin to materialize.

The Stop Shopping Church understands that dispassionate reason is never sufficient to the task of taking on what Bethany Moreton calls the "emotional content of economics."[68] Music, the Stop Shopping Church knows well, is something human bodies "can feel all over," to hum Stevie Wonder's magisterial ode to music. In the case of the Stop Shopping Church, it prepares activists to confront social forces that dwarf and outdraw them through the means of head-to-toe encouragement.

\* \* \*

As I learned the first day at rehearsal, when Reverend Billy pointed out all the couples that had met at Stop Shopping Church,[69] the community respects the libidinal attachments that make collective struggle and activism possible in contemporary society. What they mean by what Reverend Billy often calls "love" is, in the end, however, more than Freudian sexual desire or Protestant agapeistic "fellow feeling"[70]—it is an affirmation of life itself as a vital force that transforms persons and builds community. In this belief, Savitri D and Reverend Billy like to paraphrase Emma Goldman's idea that love is the strongest molder of human destinies.

Justice work feels good, Savitri D and Reverend Billy will say, and should bring people together in the sensuous practice of "being human

Figure 4.1. Behind the scenes with the Stop Shopping Choir. Joe's Pub, Manhattan. 2015. Photo by the Stop Shopping Choir.

together," a comingling of persons that leads to free discourse, lots of music, and sometimes even moments of romance. This approach to activism as a cultivation of élan vital was put to song by the group's queer resignifications of Donna Summer in their arrangement of her disco classic, "I Feel Love,"[71] which Jeremiah once explained to me as a "sweaty" reclaiming of the song for a queer community that had made Summer iconic but whom the singer had betrayed and condemned for religious reasons.

During my first day at rehearsal and many times thereafter, it occurred to me that among the many abstractions they defy without philosophical fanfare, the Stop Shopping Church does not imagine the Apollonian and Dionysian elements of what they do in binary terms. Academic debates that pit analyses of power against critiques of domination, or ones that disappear either the sensuous body or our libidinized political economy in the name of critique, would be thoroughly unintelligible to the group. Similarly, separating the struggle for sexual and gender justice from struggles for economic and ecological justice would be impossible for the Stop Shopping Church to countenance.[72]

## A Church at Many Crossroads

I am sometimes asked about the political orientations of the Stop Shopping Church—that is, where I would place them in the American political landscape. A story once recounted to me by Pan, a white actor, photographer, and former Guardian Angel in his fifties who has been by Reverend Billy's side since the Starbucks days,[73] begins to speak to the political fault lines the group has skipped and skirted. Apparently, in the aftermath of the distribution of *What Would Jesus Buy?* in 2007, the now infamous anti-gay Westboro Baptist Church attempted to contact Savitri D on several occasions, leaving messages on the group's answering machine that voiced great pleasure at the group's anti-consumerist message. As Pan described it, due to their dogged persistence, Savitri D had a hard time avoiding the overtures of a church that the Southern Poverty Law Center calls "arguably the most obnoxious and rabid hate group in America."[74]

Then and now, there were important limits to how open to political enemies the Stop Shopping Church could and should be, given its collective values and commitments. Around the time Westboro wanted to be in touch, the group's star diva, Derrick McGinty, was a gay, African American man living with HIV / AIDS, precisely the kind of person Fred Phelps, Westboro's infamous leader, routinely condemned to hell. Phelps, a Kansas Democrat, surfed the waves of change in his political party, which eventually embraced a marriage equality platform, nationally, but had also, in that time, continued to distance itself from labor and "flyover" populism in favor of the technocratic worldview of bicoastal professionals and creative class elites (Frank 2016). What if the Democratic Party had not separated itself from organized labor? What if the AIDS crisis of the 1980s and early 1990s had not pointed visible American LGBT organizing squarely in the direction of working truces with neoliberal capitalism?[75] Would Fred Phelps have so easily assumed that an anti-consumerist organization was not also an ardently queer one?

For his part, Micky, a delightfully spritely member of a schismatic New York City–based order of the Sisters of Perpetual Indulgence in his seventies,[76] tells the story of how, at the Obama inauguration in 2008, caught in the emotion of the moment, he began to sing lines from a song featured in

*What Would Jesus Buy?*. Upon hearing him, a group of older women from a theologically conservative Baptist church turned to him and asked him if he was a member of Reverend Billy and the Church of Stop Shopping. Apparently, their community had been economically devastated by the recession and they had, through the film, rediscovered the true meaning of Christmas. The congregation had decided to make, not buy, gifts.

In practice, agency and control are experienced as a blend. Another way of putting this is that critique does not simply free-float above the conditions of the social world. The problem is that the critique and critic are part of the same historical and experiential brew.[77] Since agency implies control, we cannot, despite our adaptive and tactical abilities, fully manage all the ways in which we might be heralded by others with their own understandings of how we fit into their visions of the world.[78] The Stop Shopping Church's unexpected appeal for Fred Phelps, who actually considered one of Reverend Billy's "reverse mentors," Billy Graham, *soft on homosexuality*, indicates that the group's performances are not reducible to the meanings they themselves give them.

On this occasion, circumstance ("history" to be more dramatic) outdid the group in its ability to performatively script an absurdist plot twist. Performance does always imply performativity, in other words, even if my argument has been that we misrecognize the stakes when we fail to historicize the remarkable popularity of performativity theory within the coordinates of neoliberal capitalist society. The fact of conscious intentionality in performance (in this case, William Talen's "character") does not abnegate the fact that the possibilities of signification exceed the horizons of conscious intentionality as a matter of course (Reverend Billy's envelopment by Westboro's theology or William Talen's own transformations by the Reverend Billy mask, for that matter).[79] Because the group confounds the borders of contemporary politics by rejecting both the "gentle spirit" of enlightened (even "Woke") capitalism and the religious character of American conservatives and, in this way, does not fit neatly within the political coordinates of mainstream left and right, it might be especially vulnerable to misidentification and projection.[80]

* * *

One way in which human beings seek to control the meaning of ideas that matter to them is to embed them within institutions. Institutionalization is ultimately about the survival of meanings and ways of valuing. As religion scholars, we learn that Max Weber ([1915b] 1946, 297) proposed that primary religious charisma is dulled by religious rationalization and bureaucratic routinization.[81] The institutionalization of religious energies, Weber suggests, strikes a wager with time, allowing religious ideas to perdure but in a safer, intellectualist form.

In the end, it is not possible to fully predict in what form the Stop Shopping Church will continue into the future and whether the creative bursts of the past two decades of the community and twenty-five years of Reverend Billy will continue to burn bright. During my time with the group, however, it became clear that the question of the community's persistence and continuance was indeed on the collective brain. It was a community at an organizational crossroads.

When I began my fieldwork, I learned quickly that the group was trying to remedy some organizational weaknesses they thought were undermining the sure footing of the work itself. Even before the COVID-19 pandemic forced the group to pause its 2020 performance season, the question of funding the community's activism was a lively issue. Grassroots activism is not remunerative.[82] Formal performances in theaters or at schools and churches do not bring in the funding stream needed to pay two salaries, Reverend Billy's and Savitri D's—and especially three salaries when the group is paying a music director. In fact, in order to keep the community afloat, there have been times when Reverend Billy and Savitri D have not paid themselves a consistent salary. The group is too dependent on the generosity of several well-heeled donors, Reverend Billy has more than once conceded in conversation.[83]

Financial insecurity has been a cause of some interpersonal tensions. Although the group actively seeks to ground itself in the virtues of inclusive community, the most polished singers and performers are generally the ones who are called upon to join the Choir when the expensive plane tickets must be purchased to travel to a paid gig. Singers who are otherwise active in the group and show up to rehearsal on a consistent basis can sometimes feel slighted when someone who does not embody commitment in the same way but might be a Broadway-ready soprano, say, is chosen over them to represent the group at an international festival or marquee tour. While there have been times when Reverend Billy and Savitri D have been able to consistently pay performers for their participation in gigs, the Stop Shopping Church's inability to firmly establish itself as a paid rather than volunteer choir has also led to some hurt feelings and departures over the years.

The Stop Shopping Church is housed within a legal nonprofit, Immediate Life, Inc. It has a board of directors comprised of professional friends, and works with lawyer friends to help get members (often Reverend Billy) who have been arrested at an action, out of jail. One of the first matters I understood to be important within the Church was the need to delegate. As one Choir member explained to me early into my fieldwork, Savitri D and Reverend Billy still took on too many of the daily tasks and made too many of the decisions. Savitri D's and Reverend Billy's philosophical commitments to egalitarian forms of organization needed to be better institutionalized within the Stop Shopping Church itself, I was told. If the project were to survive into the future, authority and power would need to be more fully democratized and shared.

It therefore came as no surprise to me when Savitri D announced in May 2019 that a small group of members of the Choir had been convened to establish a rotating Choir Council, something that sounded a lot like a church vestry. When she announced the initiative at a rehearsal, Vid, a young Latino CUNY college student and then aspiring neuroscientist, raised his hand to ask what would become of the group if Reverend Billy is ever no longer able to participate. The Stop Shopping Church is a "social project," Savitri D explained and, as such, Vid's concern was precisely the kind of inevitability the group must prepare for.

The conversation reminded me of Weber's ([1915a] 1946, 327) ideas about the rationalization of a way of life. Savitri D offered that it is important to "de-psychologize interactions" and build systems into the group's daily routines. An anarchist friend of mine swears that anarchists actually spend more time organizing and systematizing than anybody else—certainly a good deal more than outsiders might suspect. And Savitri D, an avowed anarchist, is the Stop Shopping Church's great organizer. Without her work behind the scenes, several Choir members and Reverend Billy himself have assured me, the Reverend Billy project would never have evolved into anything beyond William Talen's quixotic if also brilliantly artful dissent.

Whether or not the Stop Shopping Church is a "real church" is another question the group often gets asked. For some of those asking the question, the idea that the community is a "Church" on Durkheimian grounds or according to Charles Long's understanding of religion as orientation is too academic and abstract. They want to know if the Stop Shopping Church is a "Church" in the ways they themselves might have experienced institutional religion at points in their own lives. On these mundane grounds, too, the Stop Shopping Church can sometimes look like the real deal.

An aspect of Western religious spaces is that they often assume that religious exclusiveness is a precondition of religion. For its part, I found that, as it is organized, the Stop Shopping Church reproduces tones and shades of this religious history. Members I interviewed identified themselves as Marxist atheists, "crystal-loving" New Ageists, cultural Jews, recovering Catholics, practicing Episcopalians, and "spiritual but not religious." Some members want the community to lean further into its religious composition. There are also members who admit to holding personal trauma around their experiences with traditional religion, so much so that the concept of "religion" in itself can sometimes serve as a "trigger." The Stop Shopping Church itself, however, is not formally ecumenical.[84] Members' old or other frameworks of religious value tend not to come up within the context of community life. Community life is, instead, like a brand, tightly organized around the Stop Shopping values and vision of the world to the public exclusion of competing religious biographies.[85]

As in any church community, people help each other out in the smallest but biggest of ways by, say, assisting with childcare or by offering to visit the sick and lonely. As previously mentioned, many church communities experience perennial tensions between the purity of ideals and the pressures of financial exigency. Anyone who has ever been a member of a religious community also knows that people will notice how committed you are. The same is true at the Stop Shopping Church.[86] Just like in a "real church," people can also inflate the smallest of perceived slights and leave the group in fits of resentment. Savitri D and Reverend Billy have also asked people to leave the community because they are deemed to be a bad fit or a possible distraction or danger to the Choir.[87] Choir members sometimes disagree with those decisions, sometimes quite bitterly so.

As in any American church, some members are more visible than others. There are the tireless activists who seem to make it to every rally and action across the City. There have also always been Choir members who are most interested in singing songs on Sundays and at performances and, conversely, have been less invested in the group's activism and communal orientations around "Earth Justice." Some members of the group remark in a consistent and public manner that the Choir is indeed their church and that they would be lost without it. If a member is in the hospital or laid out low, other members will bring them food and books to read. As we will return to in the conclusion, the Stop Shopping community is, sometimes by their own admission, increasingly legible as a "real" Church.[88]

In addition to the childcare, moving assistance, professional networking help, and clothing swaps I have seen the Choir perform and do for each other, Savitri D and Reverend Billy have also established a modest emergency fund to assist Choir members with the kinds of dire financial emergencies that can arise so easily living in New York. I have also heard of artistic jealousies and professional backstabbing. There are the love stories of people meeting "at church" and talk of secret hookups. There are self-appointed bossy church ladies and the people who have been coming back year after year since before the Twin Towers came down on 9/11, thrusting Reverend Billy into his pastoral role. There are uneasy and uncomfortable reunions and the warmest embraces.[89]

As Savitri D (Durkee and Talen 2013, 255) explains (implicitly giving voice to the Durkheimian perspective that the social is the sacred), even if one rejects the idea of an all-powerful God, "the best answer we have for sacred meaning in life is community." And, she adds, the "Earth" is our community of communities. Purposefully anchored betwixt and between society's understanding of religion, art, and politics, community life at the Stop Shopping Church is not always seamless. Sometimes the leadership may seem more focused on activism, singing, or community at the expense of everything else the group hopes to be or feels it needs to be. At the end of the day, the Stop Shopping Church is not a utopia. It is a heterotopia peopled by a group of humans oriented toward justice and, increasingly, the remembrance of Earth in all things.[90]

## Sung in the Key of Life

Especially through the iconic figure of Reverend Billy, the Stop Shopping Church is known for bringing attention to our multisensorial, phantasmagorical collectivization by consumer capitalism. Through sermon, what Savitri D (Durkee and Talen 2013, 245) conceives of as a communicative genre that exists in the space between speech and song, and through song itself, Reverend Billy and the Stop Shopping Choir have always called direct attention to consumer capitalism's enclosure of what they call the imagination. As we have already seen, there are strong conceptual correspondences between important methodological approaches to ritualization in religious studies, on the one hand, and North American discourses of advertising of the past three quarters of a century, on the other hand, that trap agents within self-perpetuating loops of power. At a basic, fundamental level, the Stop Shoppers look to disrupt the repetitive and preprogrammed cadence of this recursive, consumerist logic.

We are left with this important question: *How do the ritualizing performances of the Stop Shopping Church, today, given its critical and performative developments since the early Starbucks and Disney days, look to exploit cracks in the embodied rationality of consumer capitalism?* This question will preoccupy us for the remainder of the book. Towards this end, it is important to look further at the relationship between the "Stop Shopping Church," as a collective organization that has formed around the critique of consumerist collectivization, and the kinds of irreducible biographical histories that breathe life into social solidarity and provide it with its living stakes. For the Stop Shoppers, the "wildness" that simultaneously brings persons together and preserves their uniqueness is essential is the constitutive fabric of "Church" life.

\* \* \*

I wish to highlight the idea that purchase as practice is designed by the apparatus of marketing to attend to a problem that can bedevil all ritual—excessive conventionality. Since capitalist ritual celebrates individuated choice and obscures discipline, it might seem that scholars' talk of the creative agency of subjects can only play into the hands of the very kinds of dynamics academic critics of capitalism want to avoid. Without the likes of the Stop Shopping Church or Kathryn Lofton reminding us of the profound level of control that advertising discourse actually exercises, talk of the tactical appropriations of the weak can play right into the hands of global capitalist ad copy.

Accounts of "creative consumption" can mirror advertising's euphoric account of consumer freedom, in other words (Graeber 2004, 100). However, many of the methodological anxieties and quandaries that matter in scholarship can have little immediate significance in the daily life of the activist. As practice-oriented radicals, the Stop Shopping Church has never found the relationship between intentionality and the discursive formations that give rise to historically structured experiences as vexing as scholars sometimes have. Starbucks and Disney look to make and remake us, as in a Butlerian (or Foucauldian) account of power, but there are no hiccups or hesitations in the group's resolution to look to resist this formative power through creative means of active subversion.

Put another way, it is patently obvious (and politically pressing) to the Stop Shoppers that our experiences of freedom are not actually free but that, in the face of our ritualization by consumer capitalism, we also cannot but proceed to act as if we have freedom at the margins of history. Because these activists are not concerned in the same way with the question of how we can analytically describe the relationship between structure and action, their creative experiments in social action can provide critically unencumbered empirical insights for scholars.

In short, for the Stop Shopping Church, voluntarism is only a problem if we fail to recognize that we do not make meaning in a vacuum or really do believe that the speaking self is the singular font of its meaning. Taking their cues from musical experience, however, they do not conceive of the community and the individual in oppositional terms. To riff off Jason Bivin's (2015) study of religion and jazz, the group's sense of its own collective cohesiveness and the multisensorial agency it supports places the self within an ultimately inscrutable realm beyond the self that, in the end, also truly begs understanding at its limits. Life, as they perceive it, is far too musical to be captured by ad copy or as facsimile by analytical categories. As an ultimate matter, life, the Stop Shopping

Church suggests, is unexplained and its animating force is ultimately (fabulously) "Unknown" (Talen 2006, 212).

In contrast, in its attempt to psychically manage the individuated deviations of consumers, branding discourse would like nothing more than for us to act as if our lives simply reiterated corporate meaning or as if we were simply cultural exemplars of consumptive neoliberal cosmology. Difference, as we saw, is presumed to belong to the apparatus of branding discourse itself as a kind of standard deviation of performativity's selfsame logic. Of course, we must, I think, agree with Kathryn Lofton (2017) that our religious collectivization by consumer culture is ignored or disavowed at great cost. On the other hand, neither should we just collapse the existential into the discursive.

If we reduce every living moment to consumption, we risk dissolving anthropology into marketing (Graeber 2004, 100). Similarly, if we reduce biography to social function, we broadly risk strengthening the anti-humanistic logic of consumer performativity, which looks at persons as semiotic instances (citations) of discourse. Unless we are willing to surrender life to the coordinates of capital, the very strong degree to which capitalist technologies ensnare us does not relieve us of our responsibility to refuse corporate meaning and to speak back to it, in turn. This is the case even if the power that hails us can also can be said, as Judith Butler rightly argued, to constitute us.

The anthropologist Michael Jackson (2016, 9) importantly reminds us that Durkheim tended to focus on "collective representations" and to collectivize consciousness at the expense of individual, psychic states.[91] In short, Durkheim was less interested in the intersubjective spaces wherein what is shared is also taken up by persons negotiating their lifeworld. As they are lived, neither the religion of consumer capitalism, one easily amenable to functionalist, Durkheimian analysis (Lofton 2017), nor the community that the Stop Shopping Church strives to be has come to exist *in theory*, however.

Any attempt to place the Stop Shopping Church within the history of institutionalized ideas and practices about early twenty-first-century religion and economy must ultimately traverse the synesthetic, polymorphous, misty, and often uncanny nether regions of experience wherein subjectivity is both harmonized by history and subjects improvise the given score in their active performances of living. And, as in theater, sometimes forces "rudely" or "providentially" outside of one's control (depending) can dramatically conspire to change the course of existential history.

\* \* \*

For many music critics and aficionados alike, Stevie Wonder's crowning achievement is his 1976 double-album, *Songs in the Key of Life*. Structured, systematized life, as understood in *the key of life* rather than discourse, ends up seeming less oppressively dense and more inured with possibility even if it is also true that we must never forget that we are all played by convention as much as we might try to flout convention. For his part, Michael Jackson (1998, 97) has importantly suggested that ethnography can be understood as a mode of narrating history at the level of intersubjectivity, a framing that assumes the interminable dialectics of freedom and control.

We recall: Consumer performativity looks to processes of ritualization as a form of discursive management capable of domesticating bodily deviation and reshaping the self, the Ur-container of experience. It seeks to format human life and program social action in advance of conscious choice so that freedom is a riff on the corporate melodies of branded meaning. And the impact and importance of this sociological fact (of the religious conditioning of our subjectivity by capitalism) cannot be stressed strongly enough, the work of the Stop Shopping Church does affirm. Even in their unrelenting commitments to creative freedom, Reverend Billy, Savitri D, and members of the Stop Shopping Church are also the very first to remind us that corporate songs really, truly move us.

For would-be critics of capitalism, however, breathing room for the role of intentional resistance in social change is desperately needed. Performativity theory's formal, preconscious difference within an all-consuming sameness will never do. With the ever-present risk that we might rather too easily fall into undialectical descriptions of (consumerist) freedom, an ethnography of consumption framed as critique must acknowledge ad copy's religious collectivization of everyday life but also refuse to take ad copy's pronouncements about branded life at face value. It is vital that empirically minded scholars note the ways in which life as it is lived—even in a strongly consumerist society—can be resisted by the sheer existence of other kinds of social logics and practices, including those of activists like the Stop Shopping Church.

Put another way: Ethnography is, as a scholarly practice, well-suited to examine the ways in which advertising might be increasingly *everywhere* but is not, for this reason, *everything*. As I have suggested elsewhere (González 2012, 2015, 2016), applying Michael Jackson's (1998, 3) concept of existential deconstruction sociologically to the case of corporate management, ethnography is well-positioned to take up the dialectic between financialized "ways of knowing" and experience. Ethnographical details remind us that since collective representations (whether we mean a brand narrative or an activist group's manifesto) must always be lived, there are always and already potential wormholes into unforeseen and unconsumable paths.

In Kath Weston's (2017, 84) terms, tock does not invariably have to follow tick. Even the most collectivized existence can never be simply thetic and metronomic.[92] There is always more to social life than melody alone, whether the songs of life are sung by hegemonic discourse, the varieties of critical reason, or the quotidian negotiations of ordinary time. In other words, to sing one of the refrains of this book, confrontations with agency's historicity can only be avoided through dangerous forms of disavowal. To sing the contrapuntal refrain: We also needn't and sometimes actually don't move around the world in simple lockstep with consuming power.

Our collective psychic debts to the religion of consumer capitalism do not reduce any one of us to consumerist automata, simply predetermined to continuously reencode the sacralized mappings of late-stage capitalism. This is because a human *being* is not simply bundled information wearing a skin suit. Neither are activists simply cultural exemplars of their group association, reducible to its critical slogans and meanings. The collective representations of the Stop Shopping Church—say, the writings about themselves that they share through their social media accounts or the a/theology expressed in Reverend Billy's sermons—are, for the reasons above, always existentially mediated and biographically inflected.

An illustrative example of what I mean: At a sermon he delivered at a show at Starr Bar in Brooklyn in October 2018, Reverend Billy, referencing the contentious confirmation hearing of Brett Kavanaugh to the US

Supreme Court and the testimony delivered by Christine Blasey Ford of the sexual assault she suffered at his hands, suggested that "we all have memories of assaults to our bodies." The sentiment was certainly consonant with the group's core feminist sensibility and Reverend Billy's and Savitri D's concern for the body's relentless bombardments by industrial toxins and the inputs of corporate advertising. Moreover, standing in solidarity with Black Lives Matter and as someone who has been arrested as many times as he has been, Reverend Billy is always keen on pointing out the terror of police brutality in his sermons. The integrity of the body is a stock political theme of the group's own activist copy, in other words. In fact, the issue of bodily autonomy must always be of some personal interest, I suspect, for the Stop Shoppers who really get into the group's philosophical groove.

Earlier that summer, during a bus ride from Madison to Minneapolis, Reverend Billy told us the story of why he finally left home as a young man. Apparently, during a family gathering, some uncles, upset by his anti-war position and general "radical nature," had beaten him up. There was tension, grief, and evidence of trauma on his face as explained why "going home" has never been possible for him. Unbeknownst to most of those in the audience at Starr Bar, in addition to expressing support for Dr. Ford and "Me Too," Reverend Billy was also speaking of a bodily assault he had suffered at the hands of family. Once you have spent time with people, it becomes harder to sacrifice the particularities of their stories to the abstract cages in which they are enclosed by our discursive forms of understanding ("these are anti-consumerist activists") or even the discursive banners under which they themselves sometimes very happily march ("Stop Shopping!"). In other words, the gap between the "say-so" and "do-so," the bread and butter of ethnographers and historians, remains most fertile ground for scholars of religion and economy.

* * *

Walt Whitman ([1860] 1991) famously sings of rapidly industrializing "America" in terms of its internal diversity. He uses the metaphor of a singing choir of workers to express the "varied carols" he hears. Just as famously, however, Langston Hughes ([1926] 1994), clapped back at Whitman's vision of democracy, adding to America's democratic song the experiences of the forgotten darker brother, relegated to the kitchen but destined for beautiful recognition in the end.[93] As I tell my students, there are always victims and strangers of official history who are ready to make claims on society. Or, those who might be one day be in a position to do so.[94] For their part, Reverend Billy, Savitri D, and many of the members of the Stop Shopping Church I have come to know, speak of what they simply call "Extinction" on behalf of the proverbial children of their children.

It is nevertheless important to keep in mind that, for Savitri D and Reverend Billy, only the subject who chooses and commits to a radical politics can have an ethical hand in conjuring, through active performance, the spaces that bring us in intimate contact with our own earthliness, our own animality, and an abiding moral concern for those to come, like the "dead kid from 2044" they sing about in their song "Great Outdoors."[95] Together and with the community they lead, Savitri D and Reverend Billy refuse to traffic in abstract knowledge that is not always and already tied to the needs and use-value of somatic, activist labor. Savitri D, for her part, admits that while the group could be more intentional about cultivating its relationships with academic friends, her day-to-day needs are driven by immediate questions like how to get a particular woman who stands in front of her into sanctuary and, as such, theory can seem to have little to offer in the moment.[96]

The praxeological structure of the Stop Shopping Church's communal labors is very much expressed in their songs. One of the group's "hymns" that stresses Savitri D's view that singing simultaneously partakes of structure and anti-structure is "Love No Border," a traditional work song inspired by Branford Marsalis's "Berta Berta." As a work song, the singing mimics the repetitions of coordinated labor. Sonically replicating the movements of a chain gang, thereby tipping their hat at the collective sinews that allow the Choir to work together in concert, the song also amplifies, in its verse, the "beat of freedom" that loves "no border." The claim, if one listens carefully, is that borders (whether that of an individual self or a collective group), when reified as walls, become barriers to the musical movement of collective freedom.

In another song, "Unknowness," the Choir wishes the listener "vastness, vastness, vastness / I wish you un-knownness, knownness, knownness." If consumer performativity organizes us as ritualized consumers who cite brand narratives according to the logic of difference in sameness (e.g., the redemptive hegemonies of consumer freedoms), the Stop Shopping Church songfully conjures a *break* from the consumerist sign chain. "Knownness" is not just forever recited over there, at the next interval of the assembly line or at the Starbucks coffeehouse right next door, the next day. "Unknownness" rather than a new, non-identical citation of "knownness," arrests the never-ending proliferation of commoditized meanings in a branded and franchised world structured around the order of difference in sameness.

## Existential Archeology: Genealogies of Religion at the Stop Shopping Church

During an interview, Jeremiah, the group's musical director at the time, proposed that dogma is bad for religion because it "gets (us) further away from that human quality of experiencing it for oneself."[97] Fetishistic advertising and academic dogma can do the same to the cause of human understanding. At its most extreme, the ultra-nominalism in some contemporary accounts of embodied rationality like performativity theory fully confuses the movements of people with the abstract operations of language. Jeremiah's particular thoughts on the primacy of musical experience mirrored general sentiments present in the collective life of the Stop Shopping Church. His layered, musical-religious biography therefore proved broadly instructive. It forced me to further reflect on the ways in which bounded discourse can obscure the personal genealogies and histories that contribute to the layered consolidations of social history and the emergence of cultural dominants in particular places and times.[98]

Jeremiah was with the Choir for a decade before he left his position as musical director during the COVID-19 shutdown in order to pursue independent projects, including a musical depicting the life and times of a Baptist church in Alabama. In it, he musically explores the latently radical potential of a church dangerously ensconced in homophobia and conservative sexual politics. Jeremiah's own father, I learned, was a minister in the United Methodist Church.[99] In the past, Jeremiah has been on the board of Methodists in New Directions, a grassroots organization working to end the denomination's "doctrinal prejudice and institutional discrimination against lesbian, gay, bisexual and transgender people,"[100] from within. Although he told me that he considers himself decidedly post-Christian, Jeremiah readily admits that the Black Church is still an indelible part of who he is.

Jeremiah grew up in Jackson, Mississippi. In addition to his melancholic attempt as a young child to cope with the death of his family cat, Tiger, at the piano, which we discussed earlier, Jeremiah strongly attributes his lifelong passion for music to his involvement with the Church. John Wesley, he will remind you, was a hymnodist, and Christian theology has a tradition of understanding singing as an extra-efficacious form of prayer.

Jeremiah also developed his interests and talents for music at secular institutions. He attended the School for the Performing Arts in Jackson and sang with the Mississippi Children's Choir as a boy soprano. Although there were important artistic resources and opportunities at home, Jeremiah recalled that he had long dreamed of moving to New York City. Like William Talen before him, he had come to consider the City to be the American mecca of musical theater. He also appreciated the anonymity and the inexhaustible opportunities to meet people it offered. Jeremiah summarized the attraction: "I feel like at the end of the day, that's what makes New York. New York is the diverse voices all coming together and creating something new together."

Today, Jeremiah explains that taking stock of the homophobia he has faced, and the bellicose and patriarchal associations still associated with too much of the Christian tradition's monotheistic God, he is continuing to "disconnect from religion,"[101] preferring what he calls the connectivity of "spirituality" to the dogma of "religion." In addition to reproducing the common, modernist conceit that spirituality is divorced from religion and power,[102] Jeremiah pointed to some of the important dangers, as he sees it, of the political left's "disconnection from the Church." For one thing, he explains, progressive churches have historically been at the forefront of left social movements. The move away from traditional Christianity also means that there are even fewer opportunities in American society for people to "routinely sing together."

For Jeremiah, singing is an intersubjective practice that forces us to listen to the sounds others make while having to concurrently make our own sounds.[103] Singing is, thus, an important technology for working together in time. Singing structures agency as an experiential dialectic of push and pull and is guided by the intangibilities of feeling. Of the power of music, he explained: "when in a choir you have a group of people who are breathing together, and who are all working towards one common goal . . . music can speak to you regardless of the words that are being said or if there are words at all."[104] Making a case that Savitri D and others in the Choir often make, Jeremiah adds, "I think music can make you feel things without the layer of language." Music's emotional impact, he assured me, is quick and deep.

Jeremiah's account of singing together reflects the group's sense of the creative and pragmatic dynamism of social action. For their part, the members of the Stop Shopping Church do not work with any kind of analytical antinomy between the willful intentions of subjects and the antecedent signifying practices that make experience possible. The issue for them is never a matter of will *or* the discourse that constitutes the will but, rather, a musical agency that respects the ways in which agency is provisional, both constructed and interpretive, ad hoc, and implicated in the operations of the very power it might seek to overcome. Unlike scholars, they have not been tempted to overstate the ways in which we are *done* by social fields as a corrective to a previous generation's championing of the liberal humanist fiction of the autonomous will.

At least for now, the idea of musical rationality still conveys key experiential dimensions of interpretation and performance that social criticism must also work to preserve. Thankfully, as a general rule, we usually still balk at the idea of automatic, robotic musical performance,[105] even as some of us have, at the same time, become well-adjusted to the idea that selves are primarily the linguistic effects of discourse or that action is a hapless prisoner of structure.

\* \* \*

Social critique, at the level at which I practice it, turns to ethnography to attain a sharper understanding of how particular historical conditions shape social agents, including scholars, and how those same conditions are also re-shaped or even resisted by social agents. It is, of course, true that would-be rebels and resisters are generally situated within the same "truth games" and epistemic contexts as those and that which they seek to oppose. Today, niche consumer markets capitalize on this reality to great financial and social effect. Seen from this angle, we might stress all the ways in which the Stop Shopping Church actually reproduces some of the fundamentals of consumer capitalist discourse: through the group's interests in the pliability of the body, its strategy of desire, and its pious respect for the theatricality of power, for example.

While analyzing social grammar has its place, if criticism fails to also dialectically explore the ways in which human struggle is attempted and understood on the ground by living subjects, discourse can, surreptitiously, assume a uniformity and inevitability that plays out in ways not at all unlike an abstract (or sacred) law of history. If our movements in the world are necessarily textualized by the operations of language, this is the case only with this caveat in mind: we always bear and remold history; we are not flattened out by its collectivizing meanings. Generalizable knowledge alone cannot account for all the steps we take or the potentially unscripted experiences we might have with one another. In the most mundane kind of way, life must always remain a partial mystery.[106]

One way in which ethnography can begin to remediate the problem is to accent the personal stories and experiences that contribute to but are not reducible to discourse. Ethnography is well positioned to describe the ways in which we are creative actors, always pragmatically working with and within the conditions that life presents to us at any given moment. Action is always (interminably) dialectical since the inherited conditions of situations are not simply conserved but existentially overcome.[107] As it is lived, collectively organized or highly disciplined societies cannot but retain an open-ended quality that, for its part, the direct-action work of grassroots activist organizing seizes upon.

* * *

There are also other reasons history must always retain open-ended qualities, beyond the directions that human actors' movements can take it. There is, for example, as William James ([1897] 1979) explained it, the role chance plays in what he understands to be a radically plural universe. And the fact of chance can be a thorn in the side of systems theorists who desperately seek to control it. Whether it is global marketing's or the international security community's attempts to predict and control behavior, neoliberalism's account of freedom is very much one that considers chance a potentially unhappy risk to be managed.[108]

When they met more than twenty years ago, Reverend Billy and Savitri D arrived at their partnership with compatible life histories, visions for the world, and values behind them. However, it was not because they ran in the same intimate or professional circles that they ended up meeting. They met, in part, at the behest and provocation of chance. However closely placed they were within the social field at the millennium, this in itself was not enough to account for their actual meeting, which required the fortunate happenstance of their having worked in the same six-floor prewar building in Greenwich Village.

As it turns out, Savitri D and Reverend Billy met at 45 Bleeker Street, where Savitri D was working at the time and where Reverend Billy rehearsed. It is not only an account of agentive social action that is capable of reminding us that subjects are not merely effects of the closed relays of theoretical discourse, bound to coalesce and collide in particular ways. Experiences of fortune and kismet—those perennial poetic and religious obsessions—do much the same.

Another example of this type of experience is the arrival of Shirley Williams to the group. For the time I practiced with the Choir, she was known as the Deaconess of the Stop Shopping Church given her unique leadership role, and she has left a deep imprint on the group's work in the past decade. Her visibility front and center with the Choir, sometimes in a bright red wig, has often served as performative counterpoint to Reverend Billy.[109] When recounting the story of how she came to join the Stop Shopping Church, Shirley explained that she had first read about the good preacher in a media studies class. Broke and unsure she had made the correct decision to move from Texas to New York City in order to pursue art, she told the universe at a particularly low moment that that she needed to enter into a community of artists and, in particular, that she especially wanted a choir to sing with. With that, she sent her intentions into the universe. A week later, Shirley ran into Reverend Billy on the A train dressed in full regalia and he invited her to audition.

One could easily conclude that Shirley, Reverend Billy, and Savitri D shared important discursive space that made their eventual partnerships and friendships make good empirical sense.[110] Shirley herself, however, credits *fate* with her having come into the group. And Shirley is not the first or the last member of the Stop Shopping Church to suggest that a chance encounter led them to "Church."[111]

For his part, Paul Broussard, who was the musical director for much of the 2000s, had his own experience of unscripted coincidence worthy of a show-stopping Broadway show tune. At the very turn of the new millennium, Paul was desperately struggling to make a living in musical theater, having moved to New York City in 1999. One day, having seen Reverend Billy on public television just the night before, he ran into him at a Kinko's while making copies. Paul approached him and one thing led to another. In those days, Reverend Billy's vision was for a Gospel Choir to musically accompany and support his anti-consumerist preaching. Reverend Billy liked what he saw and, in Paul's words, immediately recruited him because, as the son of an African Methodist Episcopal (AME) pastor, he was "a real Gospel performer." The rest, as they say, was history. Paul Broussard became an influential leading member of the Stop Shopping Church for a decade.[112]

\* \* \*

The Stop Shopping Church strongly believes that consumer society ritualizes us into the pious gestures of a branded world. However, its community life also suggests that our ritualization by the proliferating brands is only one prong of living history. Even a consumer society must accommodate the provisional acts of creative resisters and allow for the unexpected scripts that the world sends our way or, rather, we help craft. Social criticism does well to attend to both our collectivization by a seemingly inescapable consumer society and the social practices and unscripted chance moments that reveal the limits of the consumerist management of biopolitical life.

What I call existential archeology (González 2016) is an approach to fieldwork and content analysis that channels the attention of scholars directly to the question of how historical knowledge and power are lived at the level of life history and intersubjectivity.[113] Existential archeology is an approach to empirical scholarship in religion that looks to simultaneously map and track the shifting coordinates of social power and the details of lived struggle with history. Like the members of the Stop Shopping Church, a practitioner of existential archeology appreciates the historicity of even the most intimate human matters and embodied experiences (including their own experiences and practices of scholarship) but does not thereby reduce these to the automatic, systematic expression of historical discourse. It shares with the Stop Shoppers an appreciation for the limits of human understanding and recognizes intellectual humility as absolutely necessary to the cause of life.

5

# Performing the Shopocalypse in the Age of Post-Secular Capitalism

We live in capitalism. Its power seems inescapable. So did the divine right of kings. Any human power can be resisted and changed by human beings.
—Ursula K. Le Guin

Blessed are you who see the Earth shining in an act of Justice.
—The Stop Shopping Church, "The Beatitudes of Buylessness"

## Mapping the Religious Coordinates of Post-Secular Capitalism

The 2007 documentary *What Would Jesus Buy?* opens with a stage performance of what, at that point in time, was known as Reverend Billy and the Stop Shopping Gospel Choir. A star diva of that era of the group is at the front of the stage singing, "We're going to put that Starbucks down and we'll stop shopping, shopping."[1] Directly behind her are the group's musical director, Paul Broussard, and the Gospel Choir in deep red robes. The Choir's movements are formally choreographed: Bodies turn together from one side to the other and arms are energetically raised in a unison of Hallelujahs. Accompanied by musical call and response in the background, Broussard, the preacher's kid who came to New York with dreams of performing on Broadway, sings sweet Gospel to introduce Reverend Billy.

A chorus of Amens accompanies the performance. Broussard shouts, "He will stop you, he will shock you, he will test you, he will bless you." The crowd goes wild, like the audiences at places like Joel Osteen's Lakewood Church. "*Our Reverend . . . Reverend Billy,*" enters the room from the back and makes his way down the aisle, the whole room either intentionally or subconsciously miming the passionate desire and embodied worship of late capitalist American megachurches. Looking toward the heavens and closing his eyes, Reverend Billy, adorned in a brilliant white preacher's suit and sporting a perfectly coiffed yellow pompadour, exclaims: "Help Us! Bless us, give us the power to . . . Stop Shopping!" Later in the performance the Choir will sing, "We will survive the fire . . . the Shopocalypse." From the perspective of the audience, the above is an example of American religion as set piece. It seems clear that Reverend Billy's stylized sermonic delivery and the Choir's exaggerated exaltation are performative shtick. On the public face of it, political theater and religion remain, here, at a comfortable, secular distance. In the subsequent fifteen years, the activist performances of the Stop Shopping Church will directly trouble the assumption that they merely play with religion or play at religion in the name of radical critique. Today, Reverend Billy's exaggerated delivery is no longer an indicator of parodic performance but is, rather, a signifier of his religious purpose and the affective intensity of his sincere critique.

* * *

For Max Weber, the most famous proponent of the ideas that were codified within the discourse of secularism, modern capitalism, as an ideal-type, did not stand alone. In Weber's estimation, it was the increasingly dominant system within a constellation of social systems in the Modern West. As Weber understood it ([1919a] 1946, 123), the modern world tended toward the rational differentiation of "various life-spheres, each of which is governed by different laws." Modern, progressive religion (or, in Robert Orsi's critical terms, so-called "good religion") was associated with the "rationalization of the irrational" ([1915b] 1946, 281) and a systemization of ethical conduct consonant with the "routinization of the economic cosmos" ([1915a] 1946, 332).

Ideally, for Weber ([1915a] 1946, 342), modern religion's grounding in ethical values stood as a bulwark against the inner-worldly indulgences of both mystical and artistic experience. As a constitutive matter, he added, the ideal form of modern religion did not interfere with politics as a vocation ([1915a] 1946, 355), economy's impersonal, value-neutral rationality, or scientific rationality's eschewal of "ultimate ends" ([1919b] 1946, 151) and its theoretically inexhaustible project of understanding how the world works. According to Weber, religion that is not sufficiently disciplined, however, especially the religion of the peasantry ([1915b] 1946, 281), fails to respect the borders of specialized knowledge, even though "the various value spheres of the world stand in irreconcilable conflict with one another" ([1919b] 1946, 147). Today, in a reversal of capitalist modernity's putative disenchantment of the world that demands the attention of religion scholars, contemporary "post-secular," neoliberal capitalism actively mines spaces wherein religion, art, and economics blend into one another in an effort to fuel capitalist growth and govern populations of citizen consumers.

Weber is clear about the historical momentum of the Modern West, as epitomized by the commercial culture of the United States. The spirit of capitalism, while historically grounded in the particular "economic ethic" of sixteenth-century Dutch Calvinism ([1904–1905] 2002), was, he thought, clearly moving in the direction of the bureaucratic separation of social action and the creative power of charisma ([1922a] 1946, 245–252) and proceeding in the direction of a thoroughgoing ([1919b] 1946, 138) "disenchantment" of the world. As a consequence, he anticipates that there would no longer remain any "mysterious incalculable forces" in the modern world since rationalization and intellectualization imply that human society can "master all things by calculation." There is, in Weber's thought, this important tension: On the one hand, Weber argues that capitalist society is marked by bureaucratic separation yet, on the other hand, he also suggests that capitalist reason is destined to become a kind of ur-rationality. The institutional and discursive displacements implied by this economization are, however, largely left unattended.

As students of religion begin our studies, Weber argues that the modern capitalist rationality of the early twentieth century was, in part, made possible by religious values from which it intellectually and institutionally separated itself. We learn that the Protestant ethic underwrote the emergence of a capitalist spirit that would eventually anathemize religion. As a related matter, we might learn, Weber argues that the psychic excesses of "enthusiasm" and "devotion" ([1922b] 1946, 254) are amenable to domestication by rational discipline. Weber metaphorically connects human and material "resources" to advance his argument: "the sociologically decisive points however, are, first, that everything, and especially these 'imponderable' and irrational emotional factors, are rationally calculated—in principle, at least, in the same manner one calculates the yields of coal and iron deposits." A question Weber elides is this: Does the rational calculation of the "irrational" necessarily imply its disappearance, or can the "imponderable" be put to rationalized use?

Stated another way, there is some ambiguity in Weber's take on the possible domestication of psychic power by economics. Much hinges on the question of what this rationalized, disenchanted world Max Weber outlines actually looks like. First, historiography has long strongly challenged the thesis that secularization is even the most accurate descriptor for the complex entanglements and co-implications of American religion, psychic life, and capitalist economy in the modern period. For our immediate purposes, let's focus on the question of economic subjectivity. What do the subjects of capitalism and capitalist social action look like for Weber?

There are two competing options one might be tempted to consider. Either the subject of capitalism is, for Weber, well-adjusted to the idea that economy is rational, impersonal, and ([1915a] 1946, 331) "a functional organization oriented to money-prices which originate in the interest-struggles of the market," or he means to suggest that economy disciplines extra-economic emotional experiences and aesthetic life at a distance, behind the scenes. Is the everyday subject of capitalism quintessentially rational, in other words, or does the instrumental reason of economic elites rationalize the conduct of the everyday subject through forms of aesthetic and affective control that remain in the background?[2]

In the end, the evidence strongly supports the view that Weber did not see the wholesale commercialization of religious, psychic, and aesthetic life coming. First of all, Weber, who takes the United States to be the paradigmatic exemplar of industrial capitalism, only visited the country once, at the turn of the twentieth century, as advertising and therapeutic consumption had begun to revolutionize the cultural landscape only a couple of decades earlier. Certainly, in terms of the historiography covered in this book, it would be a half century before Ernest Dichter's psychoanalytic motivation research methodology would reach its apogee and almost a full century before branding would become an everyday concept.

Second, Weber ([1922b] 1946, 261) writes very little about consumption and writes of workers in terms of the discourse of scientific management and the "rational conditioning and training of work performances." Weber even adds that capitalist discipline "increasingly restricts the importance of charisma and of individually differentiated conduct." Third, the rise of postindustrial capitalism required, in no small part, the singular historical influence of twentieth-century American Evangelicalism on the development of corporate culture.

Most important for our most immediate purposes, in the end, Weber ([1915a] 1946, 332) insists time and again on the systematic differentiation of religious, economic, political, erotic, and intellectual life.[3] Weber's account of modern capitalism assumes its ultimate grounding in impersonal reason. For all the reasons above, Reverend Billy's sermons about brands as lovers, Mickey Mouse as the Antichrist, and the "fundamentalist faith" of "Living Through Products" (Talen 2006, 28) would have been alien to this most iconic sociologist of religion and economy. For their part, while Reverend Billy and the Stop Shopping Church itself have always felt comfortable moving within the conceptual spaces that divide aesthetics, psychology, ethics, and politics, blurring the meaning of all of these in the process, their relationship with religion has always historically been more anxious and tortuous.

Within the history of this Weberian discourse, there are also tensions that directly implicate religious studies, as a field of endeavor. If the Stop Shoppers' relationship to religion has sometimes expressed elements of classic disavowal ("I know but don't want to know so I don't know"), religious studies, for its part, has, despite the felicitous turn to religion and economy in recent years, too often disavowed religion's relationship to capitalism, distorting the schema and tools with which it has proceeded to do its work in the process. I submit that Weber's furtive ghost still haunts the divisions of religion and economy that analytically underwrite the an-economic concepts of ritualization and performativity we covered in Act I.

Within the framing of Weberian secularism, modern religion became paired with values in direct contradistinction to the cold instrumentality of capitalist rationality. Weber himself has no doubt lost disciplinary authority within contemporary religious studies. However, the separations of sign and soma from capitalist economy he associated with the cosmology of the Modern West nevertheless implicitly live on through important accounts of embodied rationality and subjectivity that fueled the fantasy that soul-craft was inconsequential to (or even anathema to) capitalist rationality and vice versa.

* * *

A 2009 YouTube video in which Reverend Billy and Savitri D introduce the Stop Shopping Church's "anti-consumerist Gospel" is especially instructive when it comes to understanding the group's relationship to religion in the first phase of their work, before they firmly arrived at a focused environmental activism.[4] The video contains the usual references for that period of the group's work: ecstatic but choreographed performances of the Stop Shopping Gospel Choir in red robes, a focus on interiority as a site of political struggle, a nod to the "Great Unknown," Reverend Billy's exaggerated revivalist delivery, and Savitri D, behind the scenes, keeping the Choir focused and battle ready.

The short video also contains clips of Reverend Billy on the Fox News TV show, exhorting Americans to stop shopping during the upcoming retail holiday season, his performative exorcism of a cash register at Starbucks, and a clip, to end the video, of Reverend Billy triumphantly addressing an adoring crowd below from a prewar building's fire escape. Importantly, the group's desire to maintain some secular distance from religion, especially the Protestant Christianity they play with, is made clear in the conversation, before which the station flashed a proviso across the screen stating: "Reverend Billy is a performance character whose activist image and persona are not affiliated with any organized religion," and during which Reverend Billy himself explained that the Stop Shopping Church is "searching," but is "somewhere out there beyond organized religion."

During the course of my fieldwork, it became clear to me that there is always a worry among the leadership of the group that if the group comes across as too warm on religion, it runs the risk of alienating the old school activists who are the group's core, most devoted audience. There is also the matter of the board of trustees, who exercise influence behind the scenes. Thus, even if William Talen and Savitri D had, by 2009, already conceded that, like it or not, Talen had been thrust into a "sincere" pastoring role and that they were both leading a community that was beginning to look a lot like a "real" church, the public image of the Stop Shopping Church at this moment in their history kept American Christianity at some parodic distance.

In her study of the Sisters of Perpetual Indulgence, Melissa Wilcox (2018, 2) suggests that "serious parody simultaneously critiques and reclaims cultural traditions in the interest of supporting the lives and political objectives of marginalized groups." As discussed earlier, Wilcox (2018, 68) distinguishes between the Sisters and Reverend Billy, suggesting that whereas the Sisters "are quite serious they are nuns," Reverend Billy "does not claim to be a real Evangelical preacher." For Wilcox, the serious parody of religion implies an ethically superior performance of religion's own ethical practices and a superior inhabitation of its own norms. In Wilcox's terms, the Church of Stop Shopping could easily be said to parody "the dominant religion in support of progressive causes," but it is not looking to occupy and remake American Protestantism from the outside in. Although, as suggested earlier, the situation was from the start actually more porous and complicated at the Stop Shopping Church, it is still true that the group has never had any interest in rehabilitating or claiming American Protestantism as theological lineage or moral heritage. In its first phase, the group's avowed relationship to religion was much less sincerely and intimately held than Wilcox's definition of "serious parody" would seem to require.

However, if we reorient our focus away from the signifiers of American Protestantism to the embodied rationality of contemporary consumer society, precisely what Kathryn Lofton (2017) calls "consuming religion" and analyzes as a religious occupation of the economic (9), the Stop Shopping Church's early performances acquire a different kind of accent for the scholar of religion, apart from the issue of the parody of religion. William Talen, as we have seen, chose the character of the preacher for two primary reasons. First, he understood that, whether on television or on the street, preachers have a way of insisting they be heard. Second, coming into the character at the millennium, Talen (2006, 56) looked to, as he puts it, "grind together" what he believed were American society's strictest fundamentalisms: conservative, "apocalyptic Christianity" and consumer culture.

Both fundamentalist religion and consumption, Reverend Billy will readily explain, are premised in a fear of the "Unknown" and in their false resolutions to the limits of human understanding. The collectivization of human desire that consumerism proposes is for this reason akin to fundamentalist religion in the Stop Shopping worldview. The performances of the early Gospel Choir worked by figuring consumption in terms of religion. As stagings of the "post-secular" face of consumer capitalism, they suggested that we must find ways of critically accounting for consumerism's disavowed religious power if we are going to have any chance of loosening its grip over us.

"Religion," we recall, was never a free-standing concept but was set off by industrial modernism's charter to do its work as a coordinating concept within an interrelated social grammar. As the French sociologists Luc Boltanski and Eve Chiapello ([1999] 2007) tell the story, postindustrial capitalism is characterized by conceptual and institutionalized displacements that, together, warrant the epochal moniker, "the new spirit of capitalism." Fundamental to the shifts they track, displacements that, they argue, have accelerated since the 1970s and that found powerful expression in the management discourse of the 1990s (see also González 2012, 2015), was the incorporation of the "artistic critique" of the 1960s' New Left movements. A new, flexible paradigm of work emerged that emphasized worker freedom, creativity, disciplinary synergies, and aesthetic expression.[5] This, in turn, has blurred the border between the activities of work and practices of self-formation such that worker interiority is explicitly capitalized (Boltanski and Chiapello [1999] 2007, 457).

From the beginning, the character of Reverend Billy turned our attention to American neoliberal capitalism's sacred valences, whether the alliances with American Christianity or the changes in secularism's original charter institutionalized by the new spirit of capitalism. Reverend Billy, Savitri D, and the Stop Shopping Church not only suggest that American capitalism is sanctified by conservative American Evangelicalism—perhaps the more direct reading of what they do given the particular religious signifiers they play with—in their activist labors; they have also always marked postindustrial capitalism's interests in art, music, erotic attachment, and psychic interiority, all of which Max Weber believed to be proximate in nature to religion, potentially dangerous to the goals of rationalization, and extramural to the operations of capitalist rationality.

As we have seen, the Stop Shopping Church hones a musical form of agency. This makes good, critical sense since consumer capitalism is, itself, doused in musical sound effect. In the group's work, the remedy draws from rather than anathematizes the sickness. If Weber ([1915a] 1946, 342) considered music "the most 'inward' of all the arts," and in some forms "an irresponsible *Ersatz* for primary religious experience," and most certainly did not consider it relevant to the workings of capitalist rationality, the Church of Stop Shopping has long mapped "post-secular" capitalism's official enclosure of spheres of life considered by Weber to be intrinsically opposed to one another. Today, in an outgrowth of tendencies Weber seemed to sense but could not fully appreciate, American capitalism's calculative sights are squarely set on the penumbral experiences that music, art, ritual and, of course, religion (and magic) produce and convey. Accordingly, if they are to be effective, the eyes and ears of critics and activists must be squarely set on the same.

You need to marshal religious power to do battle with religious power, the work of the Stop Shopping Church ultimately suggests. Do not forget that the "demons" of consumerism are also inside us, having religiously formed us as persons, they will add. While the group continues to turn to the cultural resources, practices, and meanings of traditional religion as critical potentialities in their activist work, in the last decade, the Stop Shopping Church has importantly come to terms with the fact that they must actually seek to become a kind of (post)-religious community in order to meet the challenges of the Extinction event they know is upon us. The kind of transvaluation of values needed to undo the conceit of a human transcendence of and dominion over the natural world cuts right through religion and categories that religion was supposed to have overcome in the modern world.

## Performing Extinction

### The Billionaire's Pipeline

On a crisp, New England Saturday in April, we marched with activists and community organizers from the Boston Clean Energy Coalition (BCEC) in Copley Square to the site of the proposed "Billionaire's Pipeline" in Boston's Back Bay. The BCEC is committed to accelerating

Boston's transition to clean energy systems. On this day, the Stop Shopping Church had been invited to support the community's opposition to a proposed pipeline to carry gas to One Dalton, a luxury high rise in a neighborhood full of short, red-bricked nineteenth-century row homes. As we made our way, an African American man in a car honked his horn in a show of support. A sound that generally elicits a shudder from me proved to be a shot in the arm. Our purposes were immediately strengthened.

Although I had lived in the Boston area for almost a decade, my most formative memories are associated with the streets of New York City. But for many of the people we had come to support and inspire, these streets were "home." That nevertheless politically meaningful binary pair—*public and private space*—can sometimes confuse the fact that capitalism has enclosed the meaning of "private," as it also has the meanings of "freedom" and "choice."[6] The private is an existential category not reducible to the definitions of property law, however. For the denizens of the Back Bay, as for the denizens of any urban neighborhood, city streets are "haunted" by the furtive "spirits" of private experiences that normally blend into public life in only, shifty fragmentary ways (de Certeau ([1984] 1988, 108 ).[7]

The cityscape organizes individual and collective experience. Perhaps the primary reason that the street has been a particularly charged site of political struggle in American activism is that it is there, in public, where administrative discourse and personal experience can be so strongly felt in the very same instant. At any given moment, we can either "toe the line" or try to resist totalization as narrativizing selves. Memories etched into concrete and buildings can activate potentially transgressive connections to what the literary anthropologist Vincent Crapanzano (2004) refers to as our "imaginative horizons." Guided, as human beings, by much more than "cool reason,"[8] we can imaginatively wander beyond the pathways of the authorized social order in ways that (as the history of branding discourse makes abundantly clear)[9] either can shore up that order or, as performance activists like the Stop Shopping Church hope will be the case, might prove dangerous to that order, in the end.

Walking is always a form of retelling and restatement. In the form of prophetic denunciation, Reverend Billy has, for a quarter century, sounded the alarm with respect to the neoliberal erosion and religious enclosure of the commons—that is, the economic, legal, spatial, and aesthetic privatization of the cityscape by multinational capitalism and its iconic brands. The preacher's clarion call, one he has further refined in partnership with Savitri D, especially, as well as the Choir, has understood that social change is only possible if everyday people refuse the corporate scripts of capital and actively mine their own memories and the proverbial cracks in the sidewalk in order to reimagine new ways of inhabiting the world. This is why they have spent so much of their time in the past quarter century performing the reclaiming of public space. And while I was energized by our songful procession on this day, it is important to note that the stakes of activist struggle are always highest not only for those most directly affected, politically, but also for those most invested, as an existential matter.

As we approached our destination, we stopped at the steps of the Boston Public Library on Boylston Street and sang some songs from the Choir's Extinction repertoire. I picked out the feminist economist and sociologist of consumer culture Juliet Schor in the audience and thought about my graduate student days taking the Green Line to audit her seminar on consumer society. I knew some of the songs better than others and did a good amount of lip synching, thinking of *RuPaul's Drag Race* as I eked out some semblance of a performance. Choir members have suggested that the Stop Shopping Choir always prepares two versions of their songs: one for the stage and one for the street. Singing and chanting at street actions can be exceedingly dynamic, as the Choir responds to new inputs (and potential threats) in real time. This concert on the library steps was somewhere in between a formal stage and the messier (and often louder) realities of a charged street action, when you are really in the thick of things and music is not just communication but a form of defense.[10]

\* \* \*

After we had stopped singing, I went to find Juliet Schor but could not locate her in the crowd. Instead, a tall middle-aged, white woman named Monica dressed as a cartoonish billionaire with a bad mustache, a devious monocle, outrageous red, white, and blue top hat, and sign denouncing the logic of profit over people, introduced herself and asked me about the Choir. Noting my interest in what she was wearing, she suggested that costumes can "arrest people," making it "easier to organize them." What we wear externalizes who we wish to be and materializes the social order and, although one must be especially careful during these "cool," "hip" days of late-stage capitalism not to confuse dress and social action, how we adorn our bodies can also still be spun to temporarily unsettle power.

Across time and space, religious costume has always participated in the social construction of "authenticity" and the making of religiously special practices, spaces, and time. And dress has figured powerfully in the histories of religious minorities in places like North America.[11] We do well, however, not to limit the insight of costume's sacralizing power to the operations of traditional religion. So-called secular culture is strongly dependent on sartorial power as well. The imaginative and organizing power of dress is marshaled by the bland dress codes of office cultures, niche brands, and the stylings of subcultures alike. Even the fashion-ambivalent and -apathetic do not escape the social field of dress that they mean to ignore.[12]

Certainly, the politics of fashion can run the political gamut. Fashion, importantly, threads together the existential, cultural, political, and economic and, if analyzed beyond surface meanings, reminds us that personhood is material, political, psychological, linguistic, and always deeply social. Whatever cultural and political differences it can accommodate and accentuate through its charismatic power, fashion is also, today, at the center of an almost $2 trillion global industry. Fashion and clothing brands have also had their fair share of controversies regarding issues of cultural appropriation and the exploitation of both labor and the planet.

The business anthropologist Brian Moeran suggests that the contemporary fashion industry traffics in the mechanics of abstraction as a form of magical action. In short, much like stock valuations, it performatively makes things so by saying so. We are instructed about what is "in fashion" by an assemblage of persons and industries charged with the arbitration of taste in much the same way that money managers, financial advisors, and stock traders create value by proclaiming value. An assemblage of what Moeran calls "magicians" (designers, models, magazine editors, stylists, advertisers, and the corporate cultures and structures that stand behind them) conjure meanings of style and beauty that become detached "from the physical world of people and things" (Moeran 2015, 215).[13]

With her billionaire drag, Monica's dress, like Reverend Billy's, is unassimilable to even cool fashion and its voracious appetite for creative pastiche. Monica is able to parodically-yet-squarely re-join cultural production to the operations of political economy. Her costume, as she herself suggests, is indeed "arresting." It is so in the sense that it blocks and stops the interminable play of free-floating, linguistic appearances that can propel fashion as consumption. The live-action cartoon character deflects capitalist magic (the making so by simply saying so) by resisting the bifurcation of culture and economy in both what she says and does. Signification is returned to its existential valences as well as its contextual disciplining by the financialized world of corporate and social media.

\* \* \*

The Choir returned to the march and we finally reached our destination on the corner of Belvidere Street and Huntington Avenue. A speakers' podium stood, we were told, at the precise spot the pipeline would be going in. Whether this was true or not was beside the point since simply imagining the pipeline in a spot we could see, put our feet on, and panoramically relate to the surrounding area brought it and the dangers it poses into three-dimensional life. Street activists, I learned during the course of my fieldwork, are keenly aware of the power of physical crossroads and crucibles: Choose a place that somehow reflects the social problem, tensions, and contradictions you are most interested in, they will instruct you, and develop a stylized drama around it.

One speaker conjured the apocalyptic image of climate change forcing the whole Back Bay back into the sea. Another speaker spoke of American society "confusing lifestyle with life itself." Speakers made the point that justice for the environment and justice for people are inseparable, noting that capitalism is the fundamental problem since it damages both the "environment" and "human habitats." One speaker spoke of the wretched poetry and green-washing hypocrisy of Mayor Marty Walsh celebrating Earth Day while having approved the "Billionaire's Pipeline." Like advertising, public relations "magic," which was also historically forged through the American adoption of psychoanalysis, works by circulating discursive meanings that rise above material circumstance and the facts of lived experience. A young Latina mother punctuated the need to materialize the human stakes. She was present, she explained, to "keep her family and her community safe." The pipeline, she put it, is their "ground zero."

Reverend Billy asked the crowd to gather around him and to stand "on the Devil's church." Accompanied by the soft singing of the Choir around him, Reverend Billy, mournful and serious rather than parodic and playful, seized his gravitas as a "real" preacher of environmental justice and read the suicide note of David Buckel, a queer rights lawyer and environmental activist, who had set himself on fire in Brooklyn, New York's Prospect Park to sacrifice himself to the cause of ecological justice. Using the last tool at his disposal, his own body, Buckel's act of protest hinged on the transformation of human personality into political idea.

Buckel's annihilated body, a literal lightning rod, momentarily reintroduced into the social field the devastating realities of neoliberal extractivism's necropolitics. If bifurcating art and life is a basic error in the estimation of activists like the Stop Shopping Church, for some, like Buckel, their own martyrdom can become the site of political theater. Buckel's spectacularly tragic self-immolation made him,[14] Reverend Billy said, reiterating what Buckel had himself written, a victim of "climate change" and "climate injustice." Buckel, the preacher explained, had set himself on fire to bring our attention to the fact that we must "be nature" and "move with nature." Whatever else we might make of it, it made for a spectacular statement.

Famously, we are, according to Martin Heidegger ([1927] 1996), beings-toward-death. That is, awareness of our own finite nature, enclosed as we are in historical place and time, provides a certain kind of freedom since our awareness of death underscores the importance of living the kind of lives we want to, while we can. Even more famously, perhaps, Sigmund Freud ([1930] 2021) proposed that human civilization is the product of two opposing, human instincts: *eros*, which engenders cooperation, and *thanos*, or death, which engenders aggression and destruction, whether toward the outside world or inwardly, toward oneself, as in an act of suicide. We can understand David Buckel's self-immolation in terms of a merciless superego. However, his self-sacrifice brings immediate attention to a more sociologically embedded reality than either Heidegger's or Freud's historically abstracted considerations can, in of themselves, illuminate for us.

Climate change, as a consequence of carbon emissions, causes its financialized destruction even while relatively privileged (in a comparative, global sense) families sit down for steak dinners brought to them by big agriculture. Or, consuming fossil fuels to do so, those same families drive their SUVs down quiet country roads in an effort to escape the hustle and bustle of the nine-to-five workweek. Scenes of destruction are routinely masked by experiences of love, serenity, and connection. Even those of us aware of the inevitability of our own deaths might still readily disavow the deaths of honeybees, coral reefs, and tree frogs that our practices of "responsible," sociable life make necessary.[15]

One of the Stop Shopping Church's most arresting freedom songs, one they often sing at climate actions, is the "Digger's Song." It is a rearrangement of a seventeenth-century land rights protest song they learned several years ago while touring the United Kingdom. The group's version gives voice to mammalian "ancestors" buried as ice mummies in the permafrost, which, as a consequence of climate change, is melting at an accelerating rate, introducing infectious corpses into the environment. We must leave the oil in the ground, they sing, in order to leave "the souls in the ground."[16] One key aspect of contemporary consumption is, quite literally, the mechanical ingestion, consumption, and multiplication of death.

David Buckel's defiant act of martyrdom, one whose corporeal extremity flies in the face of the rationality of "good," rule-bound, Weberian political reason, is a testament to life's constitutive inseparability from death and to the political dangers of disavowing and denying that relationship.[17] In their new "Earth Riot" podcast, Reverend Billy and Savitri D have suggested that one thing consumer products do is interrupt our understanding of the ways in which, within the cycles of the natural world, there is always death at the center of life and life at the center of death (Durkee et al. 2022). How much energy guzzling consumption, we might wonder, is fueled by the midlife crises of the North American middle classes and our ritualized desire to outwit death or, at a grander scale, the phallic egoism of playboy billionaires intent on colonizing space in an effort to outmaneuver what the group calls "Extinction"?[18]

Driven by the reality of Extinction, an inventory of the climate actions the Stop Shopping Church has undertaken in the past almost decade and a half include, among others, the below: Small groups from the Choir have created small "mountains" of dirt inside bank branches, singing about the dangers of mountaintop removal. A large group of Stop Shoppers stormed the NYC headquarters of UBS dressed in white robes and singing against its financing of mountaintop removal. Flanked by the Choir, Reverend Billy has exorcised "the climate change demons" of ATM machines at Deutschebank, for the bank's participation in coal extraction. The group has also performed a public exorcism of British Petroleum's climate change demons from Tate Modern in London. This was during a protest at the world-famous museum in response to its having accepted dirty money used to finance tar-sand-oil extraction.[19]

More recently, chanting "we are the rivers, we are the sea," members of the Stop Shopping Choir entered a branch of Chase Bank in Manhattan with a blue tarp, spread it across the floor, and mimicked the movements of the ocean by moving it up and down. At this action, Reverend Billy, donning an orange suit nobody would now confuse for a conventional Protestant preacher's garb, excoriated Chase for financing climate change and killing the Earth. He exhorted all who would listen to understand that we are all "of the Earth, from the Earth." Customers recorded the moment on their phones while the bank employees, stock characters in the theater of financial officialdom, looked on in puzzlement and disbelief (Reverend Billy and the Stop Shopping Choir 2019). The spell of financial capitalism's routinized solemnity was, for at least the moment, pierced, letting in not only the figurative waters of the embattled sea but, also, the performative carnivalesque upon which the authority of capital actually rests but which it also at times strategically disavows.

### Performance in Action

As we have seen, performativity theory accents the ways in which social action is "locked into" a semiotic system, even unwittingly recirculating values and norms. The accent remains on discourse, the institutionalized symbolic values and norms that give rise to subjectivity. Performance theory, in turn, stresses the agency materialized in "the physical doing of something in the presence of others" (Shepherd 2016, 191).[20] Put another way, performance refers to the scripted activities of participants who come together to enact the social world.[21] Whereas performativity and performance are by no means mutually exclusive modalities of social action, for a grassroots activist group like the Stop Shopping Church, performance theory's stress on creative human agency within a structured and structuring environment is most to the point.[22]

We have already explored the Stop Shopping Church's weekly Sunday rehearsals,[23] where the Choir comes to embody the level of commitment that Savitri D and Reverend Billy believe is necessary to sustain the community and prepare Choir members for political assembly in public space under conditions of potential duress. Rehearsals are also where the Choir hones what I call its musical agency and readies itself to do artful battle with the musical machinations of "post-secular" capitalism.

When asked to participate in an online forum exploring choirs as specific forms of assembly, Savitri D produced a video in which she describes the activist work of the Stop Shopping Church through the lens of their musical performances (Durkee 2021). In the video, Savitri D proposes that choirs are at once organized by the collectivizing, repetitive force of "musical beats" and are invited to enter into "new spaces of possibility." A "spatial" practice, singing together, the Director of the Stop Shopping Church suggests, is "sacred" rather than "secular."

Rehearsals prepare the Stop Shopping Church to sing at street actions and the concerts they are regularly invited to perform. In the case of both, Extinction has become the group's central theme. Through acts of performance, musical agency at the Stop Shopping Church appreciates that we are organized by history but simultaneously looks to accomplish an unloosening of a historical form of power that the Stop Shopping Church knows to be destroying the planet.

Simon Shepherd (2016, 89) writes that performance aims to "make a practice of that which is possible [and to] use creativity in order to bring something new into being. The new thing on and by which creativity works is human action."[24] In the past decade, the Stop Shopping Church has deployed its creative agency less to directly conjure *away* the demons of capitalism through, say, strategic exorcisms of cash registers and the "spirit of Walmart," as they became famous for doing, and, increasingly, to conjure *forth* the "Earth" back into the imaginative horizons of a society who's dominant religio-economic system is financing the planet's ideological disappearance and broad and diverse kinds of ecological destruction. Today, the Stop Shopping Church looks to mimetically bring into being the truth of our own earthliness. In doing so, they apply a good dose of performative luminol to track our political hand in the acceleration of climate change and its financialized path of planetary destruction.

\* \* \*

In 2013, one of the Stop Shopping Church's "Extinction Resurrection" actions had the Choir enter into bank branches of J.P. Morgan Chase in Manhattan wearing golden toad heads made of papier mâché.[25] The toad heads were reminiscent of the costumes used in the much-maligned-by-Reverend Billy Broadway production of Disney's *Lion King*. The Choir wore them to represent the Golden Toad, a species of Costa Rican toad that had become extinct in 1989 and is considered by some scientists and environmentalists to be the first documented animal species whose extinction can be directly attributed to anthropogenic climate change.

How aggressively the Stop Shopping Church looks to unsettle public or privatized space depends on the situation. For example, at an action I attended, organized by the American Indian Community House, the goal was to create a compelling space within New York's iconic Grand Central Station that might draw in commuters and educate them about Chase Bank's dirty environmental practices. The action also reclaimed Native American lands, at least for the moment. Reverend Billy took to the sidelines, with the Choir, as we blended into the chanting and drumming, and observed the Haudenosaunee prayers and dances of the organizers. The beautiful art deco space of the world-famous rail station temporarily became a gilded cathedral and performance hall wherein communities that have been erased by the mythology of national "progress" could make themselves visible through song. For their part, certainly, the Golden Toad actions within bank branches had a more hard-nosed, disruptive agenda.

If one chooses to be observant and adopt something of Kathryn Lofton's Durkheimian approach to corporate culture, the events at a bank branch are high religious ritual. Patrons who line up for withdrawals and deposits must do so with a ritualized solemnity. As we have seen, one way in which religion operates at the Stop Shopping Church is that its signifiers are deployed by the group's activists to bring attention to our radical socialization by a "fundamentalist" consumer capitalism. Within the context of neoliberal capitalism figured as religion, marking our unfreedom is necessary critical work. Upending corporate culture's religious power, the Stop Shoppers know, means throwing the rhythms of its everyday rituals into disorder.

Even the act of ordering a chai latte at Starbucks involves ceremony: Both the performative emotional labor of the barista and the consumer's choreographed "thank you very much" are scripted. According to Erving Goffman, "interaction rituals" grease the wheels of social interaction, ensuring that it goes off smoothly. That has not changed in the intervening half-century since Goffman analyzed the situation. When the members of the Stop Shopping Church walked into bank branches for the Golden Toad actions wearing toad heads a decade ago, they routinely disturbed what they would think of as stock characters, wearing stock costumes, performing stock interaction rituals. Reverend Billy's exhortations and the Choir's sonic accompaniment upset the hushed tones of all the ritualized corporate quiet. When the Golden Toad-headed Stop Shoppers came through the doors, flustered tellers and branch managers in dark colors would work hard to maintain the self-control, decorum, and solemnity bank lobbies demand. Eyebrows would be raised and telephone calls made *sotto voce*, but the requisite composure was generally maintained by Chase's representatives on Earth. Not to do so would amount to its own kind of sacrilege.

Within this sanctuary wherein money is ritually exchanged and venerated through solemn practice, the intent of the Choir was specifically not to do special, prescribed things in the special, prescribed place, as ritual theory sometimes assumes,[26] but instead to do all the very wrong things in all the very right places, as Reverend Billy likes to say. The goal was to upset rather than to strengthen a sacred order. As the branch employees attempted to manage the situation, the Choir would sometimes stand in a line, potted plants in hand, and facing the preacher, ritually bow in front of him while he screamed loudly, urging the Church's unwitting congregants to research Chase's role as the top financer of $CO_2$ emissions. He would implore them to consider the question of what kind of world they want their children to inherit. Most basically, he sometimes urged them to "protect life!" Then and now, the Stop Shopping Church has been exhorting us to follow the money and find out who is financing the coal plants, gas pipelines, and mountaintop removal projects.

On one occasion that was recorded by onlookers and posted on YouTube for posterity, the Choir had set up a tent with a tree on top of it in the middle of the bank (Reverend Billy and the Stop Shopping Choir 2013). Reverend Billy entered his cozy wilderness abode in the bank and, when he reemerged, he and Savitri D gleefully offered the tree and the plants the Choir had placed around the tent, Savitri D adding, "a gift to Chase!"[27] Recognizing the genteel veneer of the social environment, Reverend Billy puckishly asked at the end of the disruptive reverie, "Are you alright? Nobody's angry?," grinning ear to ear. Some of the more pious customers went about their solemn business and ignored the event while others, taking to their camera phones, filmed the unexpected turn of events like tourists in their own lives. The Choir hopes that some of those present for an action like this will be inspired to challenge the values of Chase Bank from within or be moved to withdraw their deposits and transfer their money to a credit union instead.

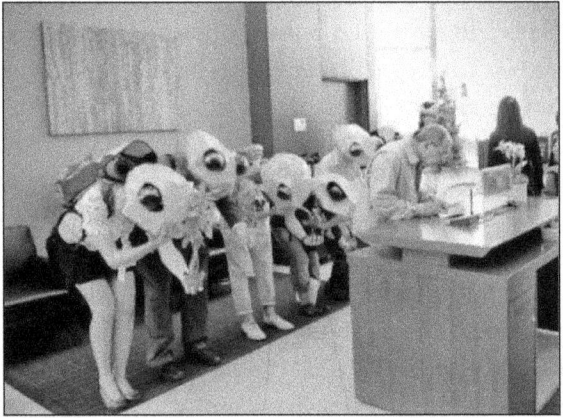

Figure 5.1. Resurrecting the Golden Toad at Chase Bank. ca. 2013. Photo by the Stop Shopping Church.

This was but one theatrical skirmish within the arc of a prolonged, collective, and individuated dramaturgical struggle.

* * *

Of course, actions like the ones described above enact a refusal of a status quo that the Stop Shopping Church knows to be unjust and destructive. The critical sociologist of grassroots social movements John Holloway ([2002] 2019) has suggested that social criticism always begins with the experience of dissonance—an affirmative negation of what presently is. Importantly, for Holloway, the structure of liberation is existential (experienced) rather than semiotic, discursive, or textual. Holloway's critical focus does not end with the fact of our socialization by history but, rather, moves into human attempts to remake the discursive conditions of our lives. Holloway frames revolutionary action within the metaphor of a scream that encapsulates the tension between "horror-and-hope." To reject the status quo is to scream:

> Our scream, then, is two-dimensional: the scream of rage that arises from present experience carries within itself a hope, a projection of possible otherness. The scream is ecstatic, in the literal sense of standing out ahead of itself towards an open future. We who scream exist ecstatically. We stand out beyond ourselves, we exist in two dimensions. The scream implies a tension between that which exists and that which might conceivably exist, between the indicative (that which is) and the subjunctive (that which might be). (Holloway [2002] 2019, 6)

For Holloway, the scream is "simply the recognition of the dual dimension of reality."

Holloway insists that the subjunctive wish is always as real as the negation announced in the indicative. The subjunctive mood scholars of religion are taught to associate with religious ritual is also endemic to the structure of what Holloway calls "anti-politics,"[28] a revolutionary, anarchist form of criticism grounded in the irresolvable tensions of life rather than the abstract resolutions of state agendas and party platforms. The musical street theater of the Stop Shopping Church is, in Holloway's terms, a form of evocative, alighting screaming meant to redirect the attention of our critical capacities back to the gritty textures of the Earth.

As Holloway's analysis would anticipate, the Stop Shopping Church does not consider the subjunctive "otherwise" of playful, creative, street theater less "real" than politics or an embellishment of politics but, rather, the very imaginative stuff of radical action in the world.[29] As theatrical projection, resurrecting the Golden Toad and reproducing a rainforest within a bank call capitalist rationality's bluff. The Golden Toad, a temporary totem, comes to haunt the abstractions of financialized logics, which would either convert mass death into the concepts of "externality" and the "cost of doing business" or altogether dismiss any responsibility for the acceleration of species Extinction. Recognizing that things could be otherwise deprives the status quo of its inevitability.

In short, the Extinction performances of the Stop Shopping Church call into question the closed epistemological universe of financial capitalism, with its self-corrections, hidden hands, shareholder profits, and beneficent greed. First, the performances call into being a new, noncapitalist world that *already could be* and, they feel, desperately *needs to be*. Second, the colorful costuming and sensory inputs of the performance mirror that of its adversary, consuming religion, but draw the implicit comparison within a sacred space of secularism wherein the vestiges of old school *Zwekrationalität* survive and are ritually affirmed.[30] Even in the days of NFTs,[31] the Gamestop circus,[32] millionaire influencers, and the Metaverse-world-to-come, our ritualized visits to bank lobbies are supposed to remind us that capitalism is measured and serious, fully worthy of the solemn respect some reserve for houses of worship and libraries.

Third, in light of all the above, the Golden Toad actions, much like the group's other actions, challenge the matter / spirit, culture / nature dualisms upon which religious capitalism grounds its authority: Creative spirit is material and human culture never independent of toad croaks, birdsong, and anthropogenic effects on the natural world. In terms we reviewed earlier, for the Stop Shopping Church, humanity's original sin in an age of ecological devastation is to disavow the violence we beget on the natural world in our ritual world-making and self-making. The group's resurrections of extinct animal species through performance are mournful avowals of the "rising dead" within us (and within our way of life) to whom we have moral responsibilities that we structurally disavow.

The Golden Toad, therefore, is not an allegory, of course; it was, until the late 1980s, alive in the flesh. "Consuming religion" abstracts meaning, divorcing the ideas of commodity things from the hands that have forged their material vesicles in place and time and from the natural world that is sacrificed by the processes of commoditization that make their appearances in the world possible. In fact, the Stop Shopping Church insists on the idea that the inexhaustible transformational possibilities (in the terms of the group, "the Fabulous Unknown") that litter our human experience of the world are always tactile and fleshy.[33] They experience these possibilities of what they also call "Unexplained Life" most keenly in relationship with the natural world. As Reverend Billy has posted on the group's text listserv, "the natural world supplies the beauty needed for human imagination."

\* \* \*

To celebrate its twentieth official year, in November 2021, the Stop Shopping Church performed at Joe's Pub, at the Public Theater in the East Village. To begin the show, Trina, a South Asian American civil rights attorney in her thirties and an alto singer with the Choir, walked onto the stage alone to sing "The Storm." The song, one I had rehearsed with the group in 2018, had been trimmed of the original baroque embellishments I had come to know. The song is as beautiful and raw as its subject matter, the apocalyptic effects of human-made climate change on precarious human communities, is catastrophic. The performance was a cappella and the audience's full attention was drawn to Trina, who, as a brown woman, physically looked like many of the politically dispossessed people most affected by the effects of anthropogenic climate change worldwide.

The haunting solo reinforced my thought that surrealist provocation and the tragic absurdism of a world ablaze and under water, rather than parodic shtick, is what really fuels the theatricality of the group's present performances.[34] The song began with a start: "Now it has begun / The Storm has finally come." Continuing, Trina plaintively wondered: "Water and the wind / Death makes its final speech / Did this storm come from me? / Drowning the dead?" The song then expressed the necessity of getting "to higher ground" as the "sea levels rise." At the end of the song, the singer, her voice wavering, made the sad confession that her "breath is out of reach." The waters prevented her from reaching higher ground: "When we gonna get to . . ." Submerged by the sea, Trina could sing no more.

Death puncturing and punctuating the performance with momentary silence, on the two sides of the stage small groups of Choir members then began to sing and chant, one side singing Violeta Parra's "Los Pueblos Americanos," a late sixties song denouncing American neo-imperialism in Chile, while on the other side of the stage, a second small group sang the Choir's own "Blessed Be the 1's," a song which calls for "Reparations Now!" in response to the "poison" of white supremacy, the racist police state,[35] and the extractive industries both of these protect. Performatively giving voice to the group's role as musical Cassandras wailing under darkening clouds, the whole Choir, wearing muted colors, then came forward on stage in unison, from the center, from the right, and from the left, chanting "Stop Shopping!"

"The Storm" having sonically burst through the borders that keep art removed from politics with its prophecy of the oncoming flood, Savitri D then invited the audience to engage with her in an Occupy Wall Street–like people's assembly, replete with a "people's mic," which she explained was a "technology for communicating and organizing." While Ruthie signed all the goings on in American Sign Language, Savitri D, who had made her way into the crowd, asked those gathered to share their experiences during the COVID-19 pandemic and to think of an everyday place where their imaginations are ignited.

While Savitri D and Reverend Billy are keenly aware that our subconscious functions as a dimension and facet of the "Fabulous Unknown" and agree with Freud on the general point that we are never fully knowable to ourselves, I have heard them worry that Freud's focus on the repetition of Oedipal drama encloses subjectivity within a loop of "dark interiority" (see also Durkee and Talen 2013, 25). Here, at the performance, Savitri D encouraged a practice of *active remembering* designed to break consumerism's psychic crowding out of "Earth." Responses to her question about places of deep imagination included a Metro-North commuter rail station and "mom's couch." After the audience members had chimed in, Reverend Billy stepped into the scene from the sidelines and offered a memory. He explained that, for him, that special place of imagination is the swamp behind a house he grew up in, where he would be surrounded by dragonflies and find himself up to his nose in water. He even recalled that when he saw a satellite in the sky while wading in his swamp as a boy, he thought of it as New York City. The flying city became his beacon.

After Reverend Billy finished telling his story, the Choir began a rendition of "Beautiful Earth," a popular song from their "Extinction" Song Cycle. The song asks, "Can you hear the Earth, she's crying? / What do we need to hear?" These questions also became the central focus of Reverend Billy's angry, plainspoken, and unfunny sermon about the Sixth Extinction. The Choir, wearing masks that temporarily hid their faces, undoing their individual personalities, laid on the ground, becoming one in the flesh with the Earth for the duration of the sermon. "How could we do this?," asked Reverend Billy angrily. COP 26, the twenty-sixth United Nations Climate Change Conference, was a disaster, he exclaimed with fiery contempt. It was, he said, just another example of the failure of the "big institutions" to address the climate catastrophe, Extinction, in any significant way.

Unlike the bourgeois, mainstream environmental movement, Reverend Billy suggested, we need to actually "become Earth and understand that death is a part of life." Calling upon the aid of his own teachers, Lenny (Bruce) and Duke (Ellington), Reverend Billy asked for guidance from the "Earth." If once upon a time he had implored his early audiences to reclaim their childhood memories from the parasitical attachments of brands like Disney, today he often implores his audience to positively recover their memories of the natural world. The post-consumer he has in mind has not just claimed critical distance from the power of consumerist fetish, but has also been resurrected as an earthly being. Transformation is inward remaking. Unlike most of the group's other formal stage performances, this event did not end with a musical bang. The show ended in quiet, sorrowful dispersal.

*\*\**

Towards the end of his sermon at the twentieth anniversary show, Reverend Billy made the interesting suggestion that "consumerism changes time," and that, in order to free ourselves from its tutorship, we need to "do something utterly strange . . . we need to do something we don't understand yet." His proposals reminded me of Kath Weston's (2002, 83) concept of the "zero," which she directly contrasts to the repetitions of consumerist performativity in this way: "The zero concept . . . concerns itself with the *interval* between signification and resignification, the fleeting instant after received wisdom begins to crumble and no convincing 'interpellation' has yet arisen to take its place." In a newer song, the Choir echoes the sentiment, singing about "walking through the night / Where no names are given" as precisely the moment wherein they are "filled with the Fabulous Unknown."

In other words, rather than focus on the "difference" that is constitutive of "sameness" which remains the focus of both academic accounts of performativity and consumer performativity, Weston, in this echoing Reverend Billy and the Stop Shopping Choir, in turn, wonders how these recursive cycles might be interrupted by radically new (and, hence, more politically disruptive) significations that upend rather than recite conventional, productized understanding. Weston's proposal is precisely not flight of fancy but, rather, like the musical scream of the activists, a refusal to simply assume consumer capitalism as social ontology.

If criticism seeks some kind of break with the status quo, the "difference that is constitutive of sameness" (the mere fact that this Adidas tennis shoe is not your Adidas tennis shoe or that this moment at Starbucks won't be identical to tomorrow's) will limit possibility and hitch it onto the "popularity of performativity itself, with its industrial rhythms of repetition" (Weston 2002, 135). For Weston, as an anthropologist, resources for loosening the hold of capitalism's contemporary regulatory regimes and orders of subjection can be found in archives and field sites that bear witness to noncapitalist ways of organizing society. Her discipline is, of course, especially well-suited to consider the variety of ways in which human beings can envision and structure the world, including the self's grounding in the social and humanity's relationships with the natural world.[36] The same no doubt holds true for the study of religion.

For the Stop Shopping Church, it is the resources of their imagination that serve as the possible countervailing force against the rhythmic and tireless loops and cycles of contemporary consumption. It allows them, in their melodic screams, to speak in the subjunctive mood—*and quite really so*. For our part as the scholars, however, the empirical archives of anthropologists, historians, and those who study religion can offer up careful, nuanced, and contextual understandings of noncapitalist and anti-capitalist "ways of knowing" as resources for challenging the consumptive deployment of otherness as a-historical talisman and commodity thing. An appreciation for religion's concrete materializations in specific times and places can undress the universalizing pretensions of religion as logo. In short, scholarly archives can keep and guard forms of difference that are not easily transformed into commodity sameness.

Returning directly to the activists, a comparison of the twentieth anniversary performance to those of the first decade of the millennium, the role of religion in the group's promiscuous imagination might, at first blush, seem diluted, especially in comparison to the unrelenting focus now on Extinction. Many of the signifiers of American Protestantism have melted away over the decades: the Gospel robes, the Choir's careful Gospel church choreography, Reverend Billy's white preacher's suit, and Reverend Billy's televangelist delivery. By the summer of 2022, Reverend Billy seemed to have even retired the collar for many of his public appearances.[37] These signifiers of American religion have served the Stop Shopping Church well as historical and cultural potentialities and as resources for engaging in a parodic criticism of consuming religion. But, as Savitri D and Reverend Billy alerted me early on into my fieldwork, they are increasingly less interested in ironic performance and more and more interested in doing "sincere" work around Climate Justice.

As noted earlier, Savitri D and Reverend Billy have explained to me that they suspect that this "turn" to sincerity has put off the academic world, which has found their performances less interesting as they have become less parodic. I admit that, at first, I had worried that the very thing I had come to study about the Stop Shopping Church, its interest in religion, was quickly drying up. Yet I ultimately suggest the opposite: *While the visual signifiers of American religion have been toned down, the Stop Shopping Church's engagements with religion have actually deepened and intensified.* The toned down, unplugged, undressed milestone performance was a coming out statement as a "post-religious religious" community that looks to move our imaginations beyond conceptual hierarchies that still haunt thought and underwrite the politically dangerous conceit of a human transcendence of nature. Put another way, the activists return the scholars to reconsiderations of deeper, supposedly progressive histories of animism, religion, and science long deemed settled.

Before turning to a direct consideration of what the history and present moment of the Stop Shopping Church can tell religion scholars about American religion in the neoliberal period, it is important to advance the point that, in their performances of "Earth," the Choir does not disavow the pragmatic humanism of their own immediate perspective.[38] The Choir's reality testing ability remains strong. They know that even if still unforeseen horizons might yet one day dissipate humanity into broader animality (or ecology and even physics) in ways that are inconceivable today, their own primary concerns in the present as activists demand their human action in the world: which is to call our attention to the anthropogenic causes of Extinction and to implore human institutions and persons to change course. They are well aware that they exist in a time before the Green *Parousia* in which they, like all of us, are and are not yet one with the Golden Toad.[39]

Certainly, one of the more popular forms of nonhumanist criticism in the study of religion falls under the umbrella of performativity, which, as we saw earlier, places the accent of social change squarely upon the constitutive mechanics of preconscious signification. Much has been critically accomplished in its name, including important avowals of our interdependencies, the deconstruction of naturalized categories, and the calling into question of the stability of the norm. I have argued, however, that performativity also mirrors the logic of consumer capitalism and delivers its promised change within the historical coordinates of "post-secular" neoliberalism itself and that, by the lights of the activism of the Stop Shopping Church, this is a decisive problem.

For the Stop Shopping Church, performativity's critiques of possessive individualism and normative subjectivity would seem important but also not sufficiently radical in intention and imagination. They strongly believe that the market cannot deliver us from our climate apocalypse. For them, there is no reason to limit ourselves to the cadence and repetitive beats of consumerism even as we certainly begin our songs of change from within its historical constraints. They strongly believe that the peril of our ecological situation demands that we seek a break from capitalism that does not simply lead us back to another instance of business as usual (the difference in yet more sameness). For the Choir, *performance in action* stresses our collective ensoulment (the subjective effects of ritualization) by consumer capitalism in capitalist time but also mimes an active undoing of our capitalization through imaginative recourse to an elsewhere and an otherwise that we can only now begin to see, hear, feel, or know.

## Love, Grief, and Hate at the Crossroads of American Religion and Economy

On city pavements and local stages, supported by the Choir, Reverend Billy has been playing with the entanglements and alliances between politically conservative morality and politically conservative economics for more than twenty years. He has exhorted us to stop shopping but has espoused a progressive sexual politics. The Stop Shopping Church has, from the start, identified itself as queer, feminist, and sex-positive. The group's formal commitments to libidinal antinomianism are precisely and explicitly not mediated by the brand rationalities of corporate feminism and rainbow capitalism. Rejecting the idea that lasting social justice is possible through commodity markets, the Choir has been a staple at the anti-corporate Queer Liberation March in New York City since 2019. They are never buttoned-up or unsexy in their criticisms. In contrast to Max Weber's sixteenth-century proto-capitalist, Calvinist saints, the worry has never been that consumption engenders passionate attachments.

The Stop Shopping Church's queer face was particularly visible during a time of public sorrow. In April 2020, at the height of the first wave of the COVID-19 pandemic in New York City, Reverend Billy made the news for being arrested while he protested Samaritan's Purse's emergency field hospital in Central Park.[40] Savitri D had reported to the Stop Shopping Church that Samaritan's Purse, headed by Reverend Billy Graham's son, Franklin, was homophobic and had been requiring volunteer doctors to affirm they were not homosexual. The arrest proved controversial among some members of the Choir, even among some of its queer members, because it put Reverend Billy at risk for infection, but stands as a testament to how tightly a resistance to conservative morality is woven into the core mission of the group.

The Samaritan's Purse action refused a bifurcation of sexual liberation and anti-capitalism into autonomous agendas. The Stop Shopping Church has never been tempted to de-libidinize economy in their pursuit of justice. They have never understood society in terms of separate spheres of life. They have always understood that, as Janet Jakobsen (2020, 24) puts it, "sexual politics is part of the set of patterns through which many powerful political forces run, including nationalism, race, and economics." Indeed, aided by this understanding and as I have heard Reverend Billy reflect on in his sermons, the Stop Shopping Church will tell you that they saw Trump's coalition coming ages ago.

\* \* \*

Capitalism is not disenchanted and passionless, as Max Weber had assumed. How we arrived at "post-secular" capitalism as our social ontology is, as an ethnographer, primarily a question that I strongly lean on the historians to help me consider. The co-implications and historical entanglements between American Protestant Christianity and neoliberalism are one important part of the story, even if one thing good historical analysis does is remind us that historical causality is never univocal or linear. Was secularism, from the start, a cover for the deep entanglements that always existed between religious and political power in the modern period? Or, if not, or in addition to that, what periods and places were most decisive in the development of the "soul of neoliberalism": the late nineteenth and early twentieth centuries, the industrial Midwest between the Depression and the end of World War II, the 1950s, or the Sunbelt of the 1970s and 1980s?[41]

And how might we characterize the relationship between consuming religion and Christianity? Are there good reasons, as Walter Benjamin ([1921] 2005, 259) suggests there are, for considering capitalism a religious cult in its own right, apart from its Protestant provenances?[42] One of the reasons I was drawn to the work of Stop Shopping Church is that their performative criticisms were not deterred by an impasse that can sometimes derail scholarship: the presentation of a false choice between genealogy *or* functionalism (or, put another way, the perceived need to be guided by either Foucault *or* Durkheim)? Reverend Billy's performances are amenable to the central insights of both kinds of approaches, suggesting the practical limits of our scholarly impasse. The preacher spoke of consumption in implicitly functionalist terms, noting the ways in which consumer capitalism's social organization is itself religiously endowed and conserved, while also drawing attention to its historical co-implications with conservative Protestantism, as a genealogist would.

In all cases, however, Reverend Billy has strongly drawn our attention to capitalism's libidinal attachments. He has written that in the consumer age, "we are surrounded by images of Love, unlike any other time in history" (Talen 2006, 15). One of the reasons we explored Ernest Dichter's consumerist Freudianism is that I believe that Reverend Billy, Savitri D, and the Stop Shopping Church have also intuited aspects of that history, engaging in a form of performative criticism that is rooted in an appreciation for the ways in which consumption's ritualized blind spots, which conspire to make us into persons who forget where and from whom we come, format the psyche.

Whereas I believe that their account of performativity problematically ontologizes social theory when criticism demands that we historicize it and pragmatically determine how it might aid our goals, Judith Butler, like the Stop Shopping Church, has come to understand that a libidinized break with prevailing regimes of power is necessary for any radical revolution to succeed. In their recent work, *The Force of Nonviolence* (2020), Butler returns to the role of melancholia in the constitution of the self in society. Since consumption is largely how we are constituted and governed under the rule of "post-secular" capitalism, and the rituals according to which those processes of self-making are accomplished have been strongly disciplined by psychoanalytic assumptions, the turn to melancholia is, I think, analytically and politically cogent because it can point clearly in the direction of historical subversion and immanent critique.

In their newer psychoanalytic work, Butler proposes that the lost others and ideals that have been incorporated by the ego through ambivalent forms of identification by the melancholic subject can lead not only to the "civilizing" self-beratement of the superego, but to forms of aggressive mania as well. This mania is outward facing, "unrealistic," and can, they caution, certainly move in murderous directions. Mania, like melancholia, "takes issues" (Butler 2020) with reality, but mania can turn the death drive outward against an unjust social order.[43] Butler returns to Freud to suggest a form of melancholia that has not only internalized the social discipline of society (the "civilizing" love of

*Civilization and Its Discontents* ([1930] 2021) but is also able to turn hatred of the law into a grab for freedom.

Mania can be potentially marshaled, Butler suggests, into the service of forms of aggressive but ultimately nonviolent resistance that have come to hate authority and the tyrannical rule that authorizes it, positioning us to upend (*not just re-signify*) the ruling order in the service of bonds of love (social solidarity and general flourishing). Mania seeks not to recite history in the style of the difference as an aspect of sameness; it looks to inaugurate something radically new. What will it take for us consumer melancholics to reject advertisement's exhortations to improve ourselves and achieve our "best lives" through our affiliations with brand products, stories, and experiences and, instead, to collectively channel our hatred of the ecologically destructive systems that sell us these tasks through forms of ritualization into nonviolent political struggle?

Importantly for my purposes, Butler (2020, 170) proposes that, as dangerous as it can become, mania's exuberant overestimation of the "power of the subject" might lead to the very kind of "unrealism" necessary for issuing the "psychic resources for taking leave of reality as it is currently established and naturalized." Unlike their account of performativity, which I argued encloses us in hermeneutic loops that finally mirror the cadence and rhythms of "post-secular" capitalism and reproduce the endless repetitions of the neoliberal order, Butler's more recent thinking on mania and melancholia is staunchly committed to the question of how subjects might collectively inaugurate new orders of justice, precisely the question that is very much always on the hearts, minds, and lips of the Stop Shopping Church. As Reverend Billy often puts it, the monoculture that is destroying the planet must be radically *interrupted*.

In writing about a famous Starbucks action in Barcelona at which the Choir went around licking a Starbuck's store clean, Savitri D (Durkee and Talen 2013, 65) offers that the goal of the action was to "induce a mass organ rejection." "Go to Starbucks. Lick and chew the Starbucks. Take it into your body. See if your body rejects it." The action mimed a rejection of the "exchange of money for goods or services," and, in its place, established new points of contact unrelated to the terms of retail scripts. As Savitri D adds to her own interpretation, "refusing to take into your body what the corporation wants you to take into your body and . . . forcing your body into the corporation's space" is not whimsy but a radical act that allows us "to expand that inside, that . . . interior." For the Stop Shopping Church, the internalized psychic power of the corporations must give way, in its place, to the remembrance of the self "as Earth."

Is the above something of what Butler means in their newer work, I wonder? When what we have repressed through historical forms of consumerist melancholia is brought to the light of political reason, is our potential repulsion—one that is felt in the body and not just the mind—a precursor to a wholesale rejection of the system and a renaissance of imagination? Can a hatred for what we once loved provide us with some of the needed psychic resources to enact politically dangerous and difficult social change that will require us to sing past the presently imaginable? Can historical melancholia, somehow re-tutored by nonviolent mania, actually help us begin to undo our historical ritualization by Freudian consumer performativity, in other words? Can the historical psychoanalytic power that compels consumption be redirected, subverted, and also shorn of its ontological pretensions?

Earlier, we discussed the story of Jeremiah's conversion to music as a child through the loss of his cat. Today, the Stop Shopping Church can often be found singing and sermonizing about the extinct creatures that haunt us from within. As we have seen, the current iteration of the Choir performatively resurrects dead fauna and reanimates dying ecosystems, reminding us that our most instrumentalized and rationalized economic behavior, finance, is actually tyrannous and cannibalistic. We *are* the Earth and we are consuming it to death, they plead all who will listen to understand. The intention is to produce a recoiling effect. If Descartes was so disturbed by the thought that he might not know with certainty if his hands were indeed his hands, inaugurating idealist Western perturbances and resolutions to the problem of knowledge throughout the ensuing centuries, the Stop Shoppers want us to recoil at the ethical question of what our hands have, in fact, done and what we have, in this, surreptitiously done to ourselves. Will our anger and horror finally compel us toward action?

From Reverend Billy's earliest street sermons that exhorted consumers to consider the alienated labor rendered invisible by consumer ritual,

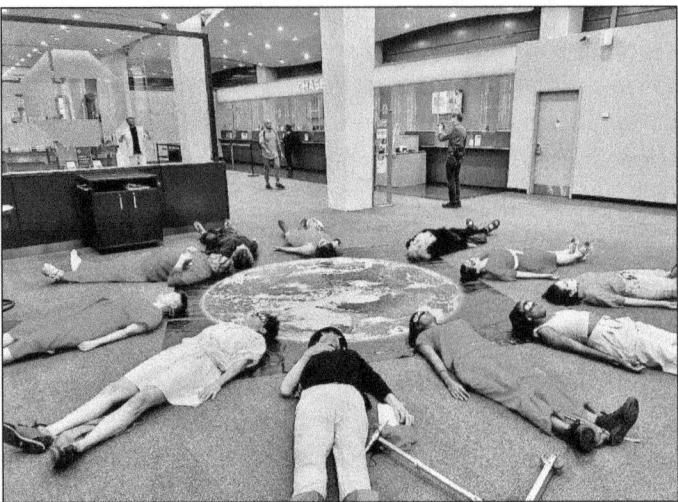

Figure 5.2. Remembering "Beautiful Earth" inside a Chase bank lobby. Manhattan. 2023. Photo by the Stop Shopping Church.

to the group's resurrection of the Golden Toad, to the more recent musical performances of the Stop Shopping Choir that conjure forth the extinct fauna cannibalized by Shopocalyptic capitalism, the Stop Shopping Church has always brought attention to the "rising dead" *within us* in an effort to produce a shuddering effect, forcing, as the essential perquisite of their hoped-for religious social change, our imaginations beyond human habits of thought and feeling that help reproduce death on a mass scale. In their suggestion that we need to actively mourn and grieve those who have given up their lives to enable our own, the Stop Shoppers express a critical melancholia in performative response to the consumerist variety. They make sorrowfully patent what consumer ritual anxiously looks to make latent. After an action at a Chase bank in the winter of 2023, in which a small group of the Choir performed a ritual wailing to mark all the financialized violence and to honor all the losses of its climate grief, Savitri D wrote on social media: "Sometimes we go right to the place doing the most damage and dispense with the normalization and rationalization and we lament and grieve."[44]

# Conclusion

## Scholars and Activists at the End of the World

Your network can become a living, breathing intelligent system that helps you rethink how you run your businesses.
—AT&T

Corporate capitalism is completely integrated into everyday life . . . we aren't just loyal to them, we are them.
—Savitri D

## Earth Chxrch

Picture it—a red brick Lower East Side storefront (a repurposed Capital One bank branch of all things) at East 3rd Street and Avenue C.[1] It's April 10, 2022. There's a sign above the storefront that reads *Earth Church* (later retired when the performance service was renamed Earth Chxrch).[2] A splendid papier mâché puppet of Marsha P. Johnson, the transgender activist and Stonewall rebel who is one of the group's key cultural references, is seated in the front window, all decked out in a bouquet of flowers, beckoning visitors to come to church. This puppet, a Durkheimian totem if you will, was designed by the Earth Chxrch's then new interim musical director, Judd,[3] a long-time member, who is seated at the piano inside. He has worked closely with Bread and Puppet, the political puppet theater, over the years. Marsha's puppet had led the way when the Choir marched with the Queer Liberation March in 2020.[4]

Inside, a multiracial and multigenerational choir in colorful but not costume-y attire stands at the front of the room, ready to break into song. A large print of planet Earth hangs on the front wall, behind them, where in another kind of church a cross might be placed.[5] Eight feet away, twenty or so people (generally middle-aged and white) are seated on folding chairs, waiting for the service to begin. The singing commences. It's familiar music—the "Hallelujah Chorus" from Handel's *Messiah*. But the words sound more like a Gaia-ist reinterpretation of the familiar message. This arrangement sings of Earth and of her everlasting glory. *And She is Change! And She is Change!* As is now standard for them, in the next forty-five minutes, other hymns sung by the Choir will conjure the ghosts of extinct animal species as a way of imaginatively haunting our collective complacency and introduce the audience to specters from the future, young victims of climate change who demand that we tell them what we have done to the "Great Outdoors."

In between the singing and the pizza and beer that followed the service, Reverend Billy, in a pink suit, sermonizes. He welcomes those gathered to the "inaugural event" of "Earth Church," what he calls a "post-religious religious service." Among other things, he exhorts us to feel gratitude for the Earth and to live in the material reality that we *are Earth*. He mourns the city's razing of old growth trees in East River Park on Manhattan's Lower East Side as well as the blooming cherry trees nearby.[6] In fact, just the previous week he was arrested for defending one of them from the buzz saws of so-called progress; the City's design for elevating downtown parks and making them less susceptible to rising sea levels called for the destruction of the trees, which Reverend Billy would call "forests."

The preacher continues: He explains that he and Savitri D (who is standing at the center right of the Choir), have been decrying the effects of consumerism for more than two decades. Along with the Choir and community that have stood by them, he adds that they have increasingly done so with the needs of "Earth Justice" at the forefront of their minds and hearts. In fact, Reverend Billy and Savitri D were just named "Climate Heroes" by the *Guardian* (see Yale Forum on Religion & Ecology 2020). Consumerism, Reverend Billy tells those gathered, is a problem not only because of its direct environmental effects (for example, having to do with our carbon footprint, the chemical poisoning of ecosystems and food chains, and water pollution) but because it keeps us paralyzed from doing anything that could help us save ourselves from the Sixth Extinction. For the members of this church, rising sea levels and consumer ritualization very strongly imply one another. To end his sermon,

Figure C.1. Venerating the iconoclastic spirit at Earth Chxrch. Honoring queer icon, Rollerina. East Village, Manhattan. 2023. Photo by the Stop Shopping Church.

Reverend Billy shares this secret about commodities: All of them sell change and transformation, which is precisely what is needed—we just do not need the kind of change that is mediated through and peddled by products. The primary grounding for radical change is rooted in our relationships with the "Earth," as Earth, he concludes. For this congregation, the Earth is the ultimate reality within which we must all finally learn to rest.[7] *Think Augustine but substitute the planet for God.*

\* \* \*

New Animisms, as a relational epistemology better equipped to explore human relationships with the natural world (Boughton 2020; Weston 2017), is emerging in cultural anthropology and beginning to influence religious studies as well. In their performances and orientation toward the world, the Stop Shopping Church has been anticipating these discursive shifts in their everyday grassroots labors. Today, in its current manifestation as the Earth Chxrch, The Stop Shopping Church is amenable to Bron Taylor's (2009, ix) definition of "dark green religion" since they certainly do consider "nature to be sacred, imbued with intrinsic value, and worthy of revenant care."⁸ The Earth Chxrch admits to a "quasi-semi-religious regard" for the Earth. "I'm a modern man stumbling toward what the old cultures always knew (about the Earth)," Reverend Billy has proposed.

Through their performances, which nevertheless remain ensconced within a human periphery (if only because epistemic modernity has not yet been overcome), they seek to undo our provincial idea of the human by introducing into it the realities of our animacies, our bio-intimacies, and our political hand in forms of ecological destruction that threaten us with extinction. As somewhat reticent humanists, they look to a different world that exists, for now, as present potentiality, future possibility, and subjunctive wish. The screaming, singing work of the Stop Shopping Church can be understood in the terms of *performance* since they try to create new possibilities out of the delimiting historical circumstances that they have inherited (Shepherd 2016, 89).

Religious studies theory would do well to continue to develop frameworks for the empirical study of our visceral relationships and experiences with the natural world not as a realm that transcends humanity but one that, instead, brings our political choices into intimate and devastating relief. Within the order of the given they poetically rage against, the natural world is, for the Stop Shopping Church, a "hyper-good" (Taylor 1989, 63) since it serves as the reference according to which their actions in the world are calibrated. While the group values radical instability in their work, their commitment to "being Earth" serves as an orienting force in their lives which, according to Charles Long, implies a grounding in "experiential modes that are material rather than conceptual" (Reid 2020, xv). We can say that when Savitri D, Reverend Billy, and many of the Choir members hug and speak with trees, they hope for a green analog of "real presence" (Orsi 2016), not a "Zwinglian" expression of solidarity with the cause of nature.⁹

The anthropologist Talal Asad (2018) has recently suggested that secular reason is inadequate to the task of nurturing a post-capitalist form of collective life capable of averting climate catastrophe. He explains that he is therefore open to forms of embodied discipline that can cultivate habits and dispositions that are not reducible to accounts of secularity and rational persuasion. As we have seen in this book, the Stop Shopping Church accomplishes their collective activist work through their primary investments in sensuous singing, rather than dispassionate reason, as a form of democratic pedagogy and, as Savitri D explains, as an "antidote to capitalism." The Stop Shopping Church has divined the need for a transformation of subjectivity not by reading the work of cultural anthropologists or scholars of secularism but, rather, through engagement with the contested streets of their beloved New York City and beyond. They have influenced others to follow suit. For example, their singing activism in the UK during their COP 26 tour inspired a group of London locals to form a spinoff of the Stop Shopping Choir across the pond.[10] It has been meeting, rehearsing, and performing since early 2022.

Just as Naomi Klein (2014, 61) has suggested we all must do, the Stop Shopping Church has long drawn connections between climate justice and disparate social struggles that challenge the basic assumptions of rapacious neoliberalism, from fights to save public parks to the provision of basic goods to all immigrants, regardless of legal status. Throughout this book, I have made the case that due in part to the an-economicism of some abstract social theory that became iconic in the field, the discipline of religious studies has, until relatively recently, had more difficulty than it otherwise might in tracing precisely the kinds of connections Klein proposes we need to make.

The linguistic turn in religious studies, as in allied fields, worked as a necessary corrective to philosophical foundationalism and the totalizing systems of previous generations of scholarship.[11] However, in our rejection of modernity's master narratives, we have sometimes confused our justified uneasiness with the overreach of philosophers and scholars,[12] in one sense, and the sociopolitical reality that global capitalism does, in actual fact, function as a totalizing, militarized system that is held in place by political, legal, cultural-linguistic, and economic structures and institutions, in the other. As Klein (2014) proposes, and Savitri D and Reverend Billy also echo in their activist provocations, the primacy and domination of market logic is, in fact, at the root of climate catastrophe. I hope that this point is clear to scholars: The fallacies of Marxian economism do not negate the fact that our extant form of neoliberal capitalism implies the growing collectivization of global society and the fact that this particular master narrative has actually achieved ontic status among its many faithful.[13]

There are, Klein writes, deep "cultural narratives" upon which "market fundamentalism" rests that "block critical, life-saving climate action on virtually every front" (2014, 63). Somewhat obviously, one area where religion scholars, theological ethicists,[14] and activists like the Stop Shopping Church might fruitfully converge is precisely around the ways in which Christian ideas about a human transcendence and dominion over nature have informed and shaped environmental policy (or the lack thereof) and have stretched into nominally "secular" thinking about ecology.

There are, however, other cultural narratives we must attend to as a field. Before religion scholars are able to put our best feet forward with respect to such collaborations with activists, we must reckon with and overcome any lingering disciplinary an-economicism as an expression of our own uninterrogated disciplinary fundamentals. The analytical chasm between religion and economy dug by the influence of leading accounts of ritualization and performativity has underwritten and given rise to our own "ecological amnesia" (Klein 2014, 4) as scholars.

While corporate culture was busy strutting its soulfulness, the religion academe largely remained too comfortable thinking of religion in terms of *Gemeinschaft* (community), as pertaining to intimate life, in opposition to *Gesellschaft* (society), as pertaining to impersonal relations and cold structures. The field's interests in lived religion, culture, language, affect, and aesthetics have too often kept issues of capitalism (and its relationship to power) at a comfortable arm's length. Since we are generally taught as scholars to value faceless writing, off-shoring aleatory dissonance onto texts and discourses and away from our own lives and performances as scholars, we are, in fact, ritualized to disavow our own religious ritualization by the religion of everyday life, a social process that routinely brings us into intimate (if also still largely disavowed) contact with political ecology. In other words, the intellectual refusal of our own consumption as scholars forecloses a religious archive with which we have an intimate relationship.

I do not think it practicable or wise for all scholars of religion to write in the first person, but I do mean to argue that our own ritualization by consumer capitalism must constitute an aspect of our field of study since the implication is that all scholars are participants in something of the scope of what they study, regardless of how historically and culturally distant their archives are or how not-religious we take ourselves to be. My suggestion is also ultimately not that all religion scholars should take up with the activists in street collaborations, although my sincere hope is that more than a few of us will want to. Finally, I also do not assume that every academic reader will agree with the Stop Shopping Church and Naomi Klein, as I do, that capitalism is the basic, unredeemable problem.[15] However, by even the most truncated lights of disciplinary aims and goals, the stealthy inhabitation of neoliberal logics in religion scholars' theories and methods represents an intellectual as well as political problem for the field.

Religion, as we well know, is transformative, and the horizons of even the most meticulous and scrupulous scholar in the North American academe will have been shaped by the very consumerist practices, icons, images, scents, and sounds that we regularly crop out of the scenes of our academic performances. The division between economy and "soul" that some secular accounts of embodied rationality and subjectivity implicitly assume can concomitantly make it difficult for scholars to appreciate the many other souls, both human and nonhuman, that make our labors possible—even in the mundane act of turning on our laptops, coffee in hand, to write emails or draft sentences about our religious organization by capitalism.[16] Framing these activities in terms of "consuming religion" will help us begin to recover a sense of some of the consequences of our own participation in the kinds of ritualizing phenomena we study. One basic insight that religion scholars should take away from an encounter with the Stop Shopping Church is the idea that neoliberal capitalism is "post-secular" (that is, no longer officially anathema to religion and its affective technologies) and that, rather than just analyzing religion at some safe, scholarly distance, we are actually religiously made over as a matter of soulful, consumerist course. Furthermore, possibilities for transforming the world as we know it must by very definition have at least one foot rooted and enmeshed in the very powers that the Stop Shopping Church looks to overcome and undo.

## Scholars and Activists in the Age of "Post-Secular" Capitalism

Although Reverend Billy's sermons have often shared a very dim view of the academe given its lack of political action around climate, I am not yet prepared to give up the ghost. While scholars must always respect activists' time and primary orientation toward direct-action work and there are potential class inequalities to navigate,[17] I agree with Janet Jakobsen (2020, 162) that possibilities for collaboration can be cultivated at university centers wherein social problems can receive a "kaleidoscopic" analysis that combines scholarly treatment and support for grassroots interventions.[18] Some scholars, like the Stop Shopping Church's one-time collaborator and "saint," David Graeber, will be equally adept at scholarship and activism. Most of us will not be since effective activism, like good scholarship, requires training and experience. Any collaborative work, whether at a university center or on the streets, must assume that activists *analyze* and scholars *act* even as some of us will spend more time immersed in either the world of grassroots organizing, or field sites, texts, and archives. The bourgeois privileging of conceptual thought over hands-on work, however, has absolutely no place in any radical social movement.

The purpose of this book has been a thinking through the project of religious studies, especially that of North American religion and economy, with activist interlocutors whose ongoing legacy has much to teach us about our "post-secular," neoliberal times. Nevertheless, there are also ways in which the work of the Stop Shopping Church can potentially benefit from engagements with religion scholars as we offer up thoughts on the broader implications of the group's almost quarter of a century of work.[19] The following is a non-exhaustive summary of areas where continued conversations between these activists and scholars could prove productive for both.[20]

In their orientation and their performances, the Stop Shopping Church upend the borders and hierarchies of (values-driven) religion, (animistic) magic, and (instrumental) science that still surreptitiously ground the study of religion. Shared, continued conversations around these deeper histories could prove generative for all concerned. A more intentional appreciation of their place within the history of religions as prophetic resisters of post-secular capitalism can intellectually support the Stop Shopping Church's activist work. Interrogations of these histories also have the potential for promoting greater self-reflexivity among religion scholars about the religious conditions of the work we do. These conversations might also even shake us loose from our inordinate perseveration as scholars on the social construction of "religion" in the past and toward the empirical questions of how persons in the world today use and deploy religion and related categories to reform, govern, and manage others (González 2015), make their own place in the world (Stewart 2017), and engage in critical struggle with the world (Goldstein et al. 2016).[21]

For their part, scholars who study activism, ritual, and performance will find the Stop Shopping Church of strong and continued interest.[22] Questions to pursue that could be of practical help to the activists include: *What kind of sustained ritual work will be needed to undo secularism's ritualized pretense of a transcendence of nature?*[23] *What are the future and performative limits of the Reverend Billy character given the group's interests in tackling global issues?* This question arises because the character can sometimes resonate in unintended ways outside of North America and its historical provenance might ultimately limit the reach of an Earth Church.[24] In all cases, the importance of ritualization to contemporary politics, in both its normalizing and critical guises, can be further considered.

I envision very fruitful conversations between the Stop Shopping Church and scholars who study the role of theologized economics in the development of sociopolitical technologies (Singh 2018) or the apocalyptic militarism, "generic evangelicalism," and "evangelical temporality" of contemporary lifestyle brands (Musselman 2019). These conversations can and should include religion scholars who are best prepared to explain the history and meaning of theological concepts, including Christian dominionism, and how these concepts have made their way into nominally "secular" ideologies, aesthetics, and affect. Moreover, in their criticisms of the overreach of capitalists and scientists and in their orienting principle that the world is not reducible to human understanding, the Stop Shopping Church challenge the completeness of secularism's "immanent frame" (Taylor 2007) and could benefit from a sustained engagement with scholars who study and theorize the secular age as well as what Edward Bailey (1997) calls implicit religion.[25] Given their critiques of consumerist fundamentalism and consumerism's fetishization of measurement, prediction, and classification, the activists have something to gain from an engagement with scholars regarding the religious character and the underlying scientific rationality of the secular.

Beyond the issues of Christian dominionism and the humanistic transcendence of nature, the group's central emphasis on the natural world provides powerful opportunities for associations with scholars. As any religion scholar will tell you, nature is a contested category. While Reverend Billy often sermonizes about communing with the flora and fauna in local New York City parks, especially Prospect Park, or in the out-of-state woods where actions sometimes take the Church, the state actively manages experiences of nature spirituality in ways that generally serve its own secular interests, often reproducing forms of social inequality in the process (Mitchell 2016). Sustained reflection on the relationships of power that undergird nature spirituality could provide added critical heft to the Stop Shopping Church's eco-activism.

Similarly, while the group's feminization of nature is in keeping with the standpoint of much second-wave feminist political ecology (e.g., See Radford Ruether 1995), some poststructuralist feminists in religion (e.g., see Hollywood 2002) have argued that the association with materiality and embodiment puts women at special patriarchal risk. Discussions around "nature," materiality, and sexual difference could prove pivotal to any encounters between the Stop Shopping Church and religion scholars who work on gender and sexuality.

For religion scholars, there should be great interest in the group's belief that the planet is not reducible to human classification and management. Very much in keeping with this book's pointed criticism of the hyper-nominal "linguistification" of social analysis, Jason Ananda Josephson-Storm (2021) has argued that otherwise important but overextended poststructuralist critique has, in fact, enclosed all understandings of the natural world within the question of human language and meaning, making it difficult for us to appreciate the forms of nonhuman communication that keep the world alive.[26] If all we can say about the natural world is that our ideas of nature are linguistically mediated and, hence, socially constructed, it becomes impossible to do the very thing Reverend Billy so often urges his congregants at Earth Chxrch to consider: that trees, flowers, grasses, animals, and fish communicate with each other (and us). In other words, despite surface appearances, the linguistic turn has actually further enclosed us in an anthropocentric loop.

Josephson-Storm (2021, 151) agrees with the activists that communication should not be reduced to issues of human meaning, as defined by conventional social theory, writing:

> I want to demonstrate the value of reorienting our notion of discourse to include a continuum of signs, including the chemical signals trees sense to each other through their roots, the scent trails of ants, the dances of bees, the hissing of snakes, and the roaring of lions. This will allow us to see human communication in a new way and to answer a number of puzzling conundrums around the nature of meaning.

It is almost uncanny how this philosopher of religion and the grassroots activists that this book journeys with come together around the idea that planetary "multispecies flourishing" (280) will require "cross-species communication" that assumes, as a basic principle, the functional limits of human discourse.

Josephson-Storm's work stands at the edge of religious studies today. However, the issue of humanity's relation to the natural world and our capacities to communicate with or somehow express "nature" is also long-standing and deep. Religion scholars will note that the theme of humanity's entanglements with the natural world (whether as a source of religious truth or as something to transcend) is strongly present in comparative religions, theological studies, biblical studies, philosophy of religion, anthropology of religion, and historical studies, among other subfields in religious studies. Within the study of the Modern West, including North America, the range of examples we might cite includes the natural law tradition, Spinoza's pantheism, Lockean empiricism, the philosophy of Jean-Jacques Rosseau, Kantian rationalism, European Romanticism, American transcendentalism,[27] the Völkish origins of Nazism, Hippie expressivism, and modern neo-Pagan ritual.

In short, even as we newly come to terms with the ecological intimacies and interdependencies of human embodiment, for religion scholars, due to the sheer historical, philosophical, and cultural diversity we attend to, there is, in the end, nothing self-explanatory, self-evident, or uncomplicated about the proposition that we are of the "Earth" and must communicate with, even channel, "Earth."[28] Earth religion can be no less of a challenge for scholars of religion than any other. As with any religion, scholars are often not privy to the same experiences of enchantment and religious relationship as the communities they study. While I might never have been able to speak to trees (or, if I am being honest, was ever truly motivated to try)[29] the way some of the Stop Shoppers have told me they do, their desire to expand our collective understanding of planetary community proved exceedingly instructive in terms of my attempt to understand where my interlocutors are coming from.

The relationships between people and the natural world are, no doubt, part of the sine qua non of what it means to study religion. In our investigations of our relationship to the natural world, Davíd Carrasco's (2007) work on a "borderlands lens" and the "asymmetrical hybridity" of religious experience would challenge the field to attend to the experiential livingness of history's relationship to "nature," histories in which the Western world's domination of peoples, geographies, and the planet go hand in hand and remain accessible to the human imagination.

I also suspect that generative questions and possibilities around the issue of humanity's relationship to the planet would only multiply if religion scholars committed to reading and gaining insights from the canon of public intellectuals and activists from whom the Stop Shoppers often seek their counsel, including: La Donna Brave Bull Allard, Wendell Berry, Josephine "Water Walker" Mandamin, Jess Worth, Wanghari Maathi, Maya Angelou, Judi Bonds, Gary Snyder, Larry Gibson, Berta Caceres, John Jordan, Vandana Shiva, and Edward Abbey. Religion scholars have opportunities to learn, revise our own assumptions, and offer cautionary advice regarding our planetary entanglements, as necessary. And, today, for reasons worth careful and continued disciplinary exploration, our preoccupations with the natural world seem to go hand in hand with a preoccupation with the organizing power of human technology. This point brings us back to issues we explored at the beginning of the book.

## Coda Digitalis

As we saw in Act I, one thing performativity theory does is purport to know, in advance, with psychic concessions made for ritual misfires and the constitutive vulnerabilities of the norm, more or less the direction in which human actors will move. This is why, in academic parlance, we speak of the generativity of power, the sameness in difference, and the hegemonic redemption of ritual in recursive terms. Any breaks (or points of possible dissonance and contradiction) are enclosed within the coordinates of the ruling regime itself, which accommodates, as in Ernest Dichter's account of consumer proto-performativity, the movement of difference.

What connects all of these ways of framing the relationship between self and society is that an autonomous symbolic realm formats subjectivity in advance of conscious willing. At the last Earth Chxrch service of its first season, Reverend Billy spoke of the urgent human need to resist being transformed into predictable and knowable "data." At a later moment in the performance service, community friend and partner-saint, media theorist Douglas Rushkoff, spoke with prophetic fire and rage about the Silicon Valley executives he met with in 2022 who fully understand that the way to make more money for themselves is to design technology that can know our consumer choices before we do but are also fully aware of the dangerous collective consequences of their machinations. He explained that these masters of the digitized universe understand that overconsumption is causing the world to become less and less habitable, and, astonishingly, actually asked him for advice about how to prepare futuristic bunkers that can protect them and theirs from the heat, the floods, and the suffering masses carrying pitchforks.[30]

Regarding the closed loops of performativity, David Graeber (2012) suggests the following:

> The phenomenon will attract a lively interest among future intellectual historians. The widespread assumption that no meaningful distinction could be made between the nature of reality (even scientific reality), the techniques of knowledge designed to analyze and interpret that reality, and the forms of institutional power within which knowledge is produced ensured that when social theorists did turn to economic matters, they would see things in the same light.

As we continue to transition from Weber's iron cage of work and the dominance of machine production to our semantic, networked, and still latently mechanical array of consumption, those intellectual historians to come, I suggest, might make much of the background influence of *cybernetic* discourse.[31] These histories bring scholars and activists into very intimate contact indeed.

\* \* \*

As we have seen, left social theory does well to dispense with the idea that contemporary power is intellectually grounded in (affectless) individualism. Individualism, as a second-order experience, is sold to consumers (and, hence, consumer citizens) as a virtue, but the power that ritualizes us *into that virtue* today is recursive and indebted to cybernetic theory, which, broadly defined, posits the basic, ontological reality of self-organizing processes that aim to achieve an optimal balance of systems by way of recursive, communicative feedback loops. For example, most to the point for this book, as brands accumulate information about us through our online activities and the fieldwork of corporate anthropologists, they hope to predict and anticipate our consumer choices before we even make them. As in the accounts of performativity and ritualization reviewed herein, experiences of individual consumer experience are thought to be recursively grounded in a flexible form of discursive objectivity.

Whenever social organization assumes the form of recursive intersubjectivity, whereby human nodes connect in concentric ways, this is not a departure from prevailing power but, rather, a historical mirroring of it. The suffusion of the networked form is the main reason that secular oppositions, including those of religion and economy and self and other, have institutionally unraveled. In a performative age, the fact that the group turns to dynamic performance to do its work is not in itself radical but, rather, a testament to its historical location and the smart, pragmatic decision to fight fire with fire, meet spectacle with spectacle. Performance, like performativity, is a kind of historical expression.[32]

The historical genealogy of performance includes the same Hippie expressivism of the 1960s that influenced the development of consumer ritualization (Shepherd 2016), and behind that, the cybernetic discourse that has come to define social metaphysics today (Turner 2006). In *From Counterculture to Cyberculture: Stewart Brand, the Whole Earth Network, and the Rise of Digital Utopianism*, Fred Turner (2006, 4) explains that cybernetic discourse was born in World War II–era research labs, which gave rise to "both computers and a new cybernetic rhetoric of systems and information." There, military scientists "began to imagine institutions as living organisms, social networks as webs of information, and the gathering and interpretation of information as keys to understanding not only the technical but also the natural and social worlds."

In cybernetic philosophies, the roles of information and communication in complex organizations are often said to link the computational and natural worlds. Biological systems have thus been reinterpreted through the computational metaphor (Turner 2006, 15). As John Johnston (2008, 29) puts it, "Cybernetic discourse ... tended to speak of machines in terms of living organisms and living organisms in terms of machines." The "computational" feedback loops of organic, nervous systems (293) are often explicitly compared to the operations of computer logic. For its devotees, cybernetics provides a language for understanding all kinds of organic, social, and organizational processes.

An inherent tension within cybernetic discourse, however, has always been that its seeming anti-humanism could leave potential adherents cold. The problem, especially early on, was that computers seemed to loom as technologies of rationalization and the dehumanization of social life. All the talk of communicative relays over and against any talk of persons initially inspired the suspicion of many of the baby boom generation.

By the 1990s, however, Turner writes, the advent of the Internet Age was couched in terms of personal transformation rather than social control. The New Economy was birthed, he proposes, through the marriage of Cold War technology and the counterculture. To summarize the history Turner traces: Through the singular historical influence of Stewart Brand, who founded the *Whole Earth Catalog* in 1968, and his network of scientific researchers, homesteaders, ecologists, and advertisers, "a series of encounters between bohemian San Francisco and the emerging technology hub of Silicon Valley to the south" (Turner 2006, 3) eventually brought these worlds together into one continuous community that has fully converged around cyberculture's expressivisim and creative play. Like Boltanski and Chiapello ([1999] 2007), crucial to the story Turner advances about the formation of contemporary ideology is the fusion of capitalism and the aesthetic expression of New Left critiques of the 1960s.[33]

The counterculture, which already appreciated the importance of language and culture in determining relationships of power, was taken by the cybernetic vision according to which "material reality could be imagined as an information system" (Turner 2006, 5). The still prevalent and still wishful discourse around cyberspace that lionizes its "decentralized control" and opportunities for immersive, playful experimentation is, in fact, indebted to the merging of military, countercultural, and consumerist horizons. One of the historical progenies of this epistemic estuary is the hypostatizing of analogous relationships between the self-organizing complexity of the natural world, the global economy, and that of the "liberated," "soulful" corporate form (see González 2015).

Of special interest to the existential archaeologies recounted in this book, Stewart Brand's *Whole Earth Catalog* (1968–1998), a pioneer in the establishment of countercultural consumption and in the selling of productized solutions to a network of enlightened consumers, sought to provide back-to-the-landers, communes, artists, and seekers with the tools they needed to establish their new communities. In fact, one of the communes with which he partnered was the Lama Foundation, the very commune founded by Savitri D's parents, which was her childhood home (Turner 2006, 75). Brand and Savitri's father, Stephen Durkee, who had yet to convert to Islam and adopt the name Shaykh Abdullah Nooruddeen, had established a friendship, and Brand was drawn to Durkee's work on immersive, multimedia art.

While Durkee himself moved in another direction, away from seeker consumerism and toward Sufism, some of Brand's affiliations (and Durkee's former associations) went on to join the faculty of the Harvard Business School and to found a for-profit company, Intermedia Systems Corporation, in 1969. Sounding like a Situationist manifesto for capitalism, Intermedia understood itself as being devoted to bridging business and art through the use of multimedia technology in order to build "environments that have particular kinds of psychological effects" (Scott 2015).

As a discourse, through the influence, in part, of the counterculture's fusion of capitalism, and expressive aesthetics, cybernetics shares strong parentage with branding. Branding, as we have seen, expresses the basic form of cybernetics in its concerns for unique and individuated expression within a totalizing information system. Performance theory, generally the tool of left scholars and activists, is actually branding's kissing cousin. It mirrors the humanistic cybernetic discourse that evolved through its productive encounters with New Left aesthetics in the 1960s. Therefore, while Reverend Billy likes to position "Dada vs. Data" in recent sermons, the history is actually more complicated since cyberculture, the mass fruit of cybernetic discourse, has actually blended the two.

Meanwhile, Judith Butler's account of performativity, in its focus on the recursive force of iterability itself, prior to issues of authorial intention, bears elemental traces of the earlier form of cybernetic discourse from the early twentieth century in which the MIT mathematician, Norbert Wiener analyzed the American military as a "self-directing (information) system," wherein control is dispersed (Turner 2006, 21–22). Moreover, one of Butler's closest influences and interlocutors, the psychoanalytic philosopher, Jacques Lacan, is said to have clearly participated in this "new discourse network, one that emerges in the aftermath of the Second World War and that has subsequently become our own" (Johnston 2008, 82). He did so in his use of "the term *cybernetics*, along with subsidiary notions like feedback, the circuit, and the message as information" (68).

Other scholars who engaged with and were influenced by cybernetics include Jacques Derrida,[34] Claude Lévi-Strauss, Roman Jakobson, Gregory Bateson, Margaret Mead,[35] Deleuze and Guattari, and Michel Foucault (August 2022; Geoghehan 2011; Krell 2020). In short, if we historicize our own iconic theories and theorists, it becomes clear that, to borrow a metaphor from cybernetic discourse itself, cybernetics might be in our disciplinary DNA as scholars. No doubt, more sustained and detailed historical analysis is warranted. Religion scholars would do very well to visit these histories of exchange between cybernetic theory and our chosen social theory as we set out to historicize our labors.

The activists, too, will want to historicize their own chosen theory. The Stop Shopping Church has come to speak of the Earth as a consciousness in its own right, a "living intelligence," with which humanity must learn to communicate. They have been strongly inspired in this view by chemist and environmentalist James Lovelock's critique of anthropocentricism. Following Lovelock's Gaia theory ([1979] 1995), the Earth Chxrchers consider the Earth a living, self-regulating organism of which we humans are only one constitutive but not timeless element. Recent scholarship, however, also reads Lovelock's Gaia theory as an expression of cybernetic philosophy (Johnston 2008, 435n15; Schrape 2014; Stolz 2016). And, to be clear, cybernetic theory no more "captures" the unvarnished "truth" of the world than any of its Newtonian predecessors did.[36] There is always a gap between world and word (Jackson 1996, 3). In enclosing human freedom within the self-adaptive coordinates it has itself announced, cybernetics' diffusion of the network form in society can actually be understood in terms of the neoliberal desire to end history (González 2015).

Max Weber's old concept of ideal-types might actually prove helpful here, as we seek to trace and track these unexpected correspondences. While the iconic theories and thinkers we tend to be drawn to as scholars differ in ways that matter a great deal to scholars, these intellectual and historical differences also bleed into pervasive patterns of thought that, while grounded in a plurality of genealogies, imply a general convergence *into* and *as* a cultural dominant.[37] We do well to look for the general shape of historical power even as we continue to split hairs when we are otherwise immersed in the weeds of our more specialized investigations.

That Judith Butler has not directly dealt with computational information systems or statistics in her academic writing, for example, does not negate their philosophy's seeming historical embeddedness in cybernetic discourse through the influence of the likes of Derrida, Lacan, and Foucault (and Freud, by way of consumer discourse) and her privileging of the semantic ordering of the world.[38] At one important level of social analysis what matters most is that, from Ernest Dichter's proto-performativity, to branding discourse, to Catherine Bell's account of ritualization, to religion scholars' Butlerian readings of citational bodies, to our own active participation in social networking, persons are now understood as (citational) nodes in recursive, dynamic, informational relays that stretch reason beyond its dispassionate, disembodied, secular costuming. If religion, as an idea and a problem, is often used by scholars to name what people do when we "interpret life," "name authority," and "harness immaterial power" (Lofton 2017), our networked consumption of branded ideas and forms of media implicates scholars of religion in the doing of religion and not just the study of religion.

* * *

After their twentieth anniversary performance at Joe's Pub, one longstanding member of the Choir lauded the fact that in its organic, self-adaptive improvisation the show was such a success because the dynamic rhythms of the performance, recursively taking its cues from audience feedback mirrored, in its self-organizing structure and form, the subject matter itself, which was the Earth. The thought was reminiscent of a comment Reverend Billy made at the St. John the Divine event, wherein he proposed that The Women's March was a "liquid ecosystem," in which there was "no Cartesian shape" and "no center," and in their place a network connecting a "million falcons and falconers."

While it is understandable anytime any denizen of the networked society will express its metaphysics in speech and thought, I have to respectfully disagree with the suggestion that the critical force and meaning of the twentieth anniversary performance was its cybernetic shape and form. The Stop Shopping Church is not radical because its contemporary performance style echoes mid-century cybernetics' interest in hypostasizing correspondences between biology and society.[39] The idea of human society learning to move and communicate with nature cannot be resolved by doubling down, without clear subversive intent, on the scripts of a historical discourse that, despite the metaphorical organicism, has always looked to supercharge capitalist rationalization and extend the reach of human systems into everything.[40] Instead, given the ways in which machine logic has infiltrated contemporary thought and speech, a much more radical diagnosis is assumed by the Choir's song "Machines," in which the Stop Shoppers sing of the dangers of having "Machines in the purpose / Machines in the goals / Machines in the feeling and the feeling."

The work of the Stop Shopping Church is radical because, rooted where they stand, the Choir looks to actively short-circuit consuming religion's cybernetic loops and to help us imagine another, more just world. The Stop Shopping Church is radical because it reintroduces natural ecosystems and human labor back into the imaginative horizons of contemporary society as (interrelated) moral goods, not because it has chosen an "organic" performance style. The Stop Shoppers are, in fact, radical precisely because, at their very best, they look to refuse a final identification with any discourse and force us instead to look, listen, do, and, they hope, change.[41]

Performance, like performativity, is anchored to the damaged thought of the dying world we live in. Unlike performativity, however, performance positions social agents within a space of creative freedom wherein we can begin to actively undo and remake history.[42] The imaginative leaps the Stop Shopping Church invite us to take *through performance* open up lived reality to other tenses, moods, neighbors, and souls. Performance's potential (but by no means empirically assured) radicality is the worldwise human spirit it can feed and support. The Stop Shopping Church's dogged insistence on the gap between life itself, on the one hand, and our human understanding of life, on the other, is radical because it posits what they call the "Fabulous Unknown" as a bulwark against the conceit of human power rather than envelop all living potentiality and difference within cybernetic coils (and markets) of our own making. The new prominence of general audience Artificial Intelligence (AI) Internet tools like ChatGPT only ups the ante for this kind of approach.

* * *

The deconstructive spirit of the Stop Shopping Church enhances its interest for religion scholars, for whom the example of the grassroots activists reminds us that our thinking about religion must, at a minimum, remain flexible, pragmatic, and nimble. Religion, as a non-necessary, historically mediated, classificatory term, can help us patiently and critically explore the multivalent and multisensorial shades, hues, and tones of social phenomena. It can be deployed to help us make sense of the situations and persons we encounter—especially of our relationships to them.

As we saw, for the Stop Shopping Church, religion marks the fundamentalism of consumerism (in ways amenable to both Marxist and Durkheimian analysis) as well as the historical entanglements between conservative Protestant American Christianity and neoliberalism (an example of always needed historical place-setting). I have also suggested that the performances of the Stop Shopping Church have historically marked the conceptual and institutional displacements of psyche and aesthetics whereby capitalism developed its neoliberal soul (in ways that are certainly amenable to genealogical elaboration). For the scholar, religion's specter is there in Reverend Billy's transformation into a "sincere" preacher and a Durkheimian perspective helps us appreciate how the Stop Shopping Church cum Earth Chxrch is held together via shared biophilic, social justice values that are organized by community rituals. For their part, however, members' own individual religious biographies, experiences, and anxieties press against too collective an understanding of religion at the Stop Shopping Church and remind us of the necessary limits of all categorical understanding.

I have suggested that the Stop Shoppers' Shopocalyptic exhortation that we understand ourselves as being "of Earth" echoes contemporary anthropological theory that examines the ways in which the borders of the self, the natural world, and political economy have been dissolved by the structured effects of our industrially sourced consumption. "New animisms" conjure the field's past for newly pressing kinds of scholarly reconsiderations. Reverend Billy still sometimes attempts his old right-wing televangelist delivery, but the schtick quickly devolves into earnest delivery. This is because the point of the performance is no longer to use parodic overidentification to bring attention to secular consumerism's disavowed religious fundamentalism but, instead, to exhort us to be transformed as "Earthly" beings who must bear witness to the traumas of ecological violence that dwell within us.

The group's commitment to the "Fabulous Unknown" means that they must continue to try to skirt the borders between religious ritual and performance and work toward a "post-religious religious" future wherein a heretofore unknown "Earthy religion" corrects what consumerism has distorted and destroyed, forces scholars to consider the future of phenomena that are transforming rather than disappearing and are, increasingly, capable of slipping past our labels for them. Social theory that is simply imposed from above and whose use-value does not arise from creative and pragmatic encounter with the lived world we share with nonscholars can very easily miss the mark. In the activists' terms, it becomes a label. Throughout the course of my fieldwork, it became viscerally clear to me that the Church of Stop Shopping, as Earth Chxrch, which began to serve as a warming and distribution center for homeless migrants in January 2024, upends an array of broadly accepted borders that thinking about religion (and nonreligion) generally finds comfort in.[43]

Scholars must resist collapsing the work we do into the stream of fashionable discourse. At their best, theories are helpful props in our academic performances. They should respond to empirical cases, not define them in advance. Theories certainly do not offer any escape from history. Our disciplinary overreliance on theory (and our reluctance to historicize social theory) has come at a significant analytical and political cost. Scholars problematically uncoupled performativity theory's main idea—that description does not simply read reality but, rather, engenders it—from the working context of our digital age wherein the accretion of "likes" and the sharing of social media posts analogously engenders plausibility.[44]

What if, instead of serving as a vehicle for claiming points of analytical purchase prior to empiricism or outside of our own historicity as scholars, we think of our theories as mirrors into our own socialization by history? Could these conceptual records not then become tools for creative and strategic inversions? Our core interests in everyday religion,[45] in the North American case, should be accompanied by ethnographic interests in cybernetics as epistemic history,[46] the historical entanglements between American religion and cybernetic discourse, the (shifting) role of religion across institutions,[47] and the "consuming religion" of neoliberal capitalism that social theory in religious studies has generally disavowed and, hence, enabled. We do well to reconsider Marx's view that capitalism's wholesale and unrelenting fetishism of capital itself has produced a kind of "religion of everyday life" (Boer 2011). The Church of Stop Shopping would urge haste in our reckoning with the religion of everyday life, for this apocalyptic religion has ensnared and ensouled us all, threatening the end of the world (as we know it).

ACKNOWLEDGMENTS

All books are profoundly social artifacts. This one feels especially so. The work of ethnography is necessarily beholden to the hospitality of others. When I sang with them, the members of the Stop Shopping Choir went out of their way to make sure I felt at home. My rough singing was forgiven with generous smiles and invitations to go get beer after rehearsal. Savitri D and William Talen graciously answered questions they've been asked a thousand and one times. Savitri D and Reverend Billy are as incisive as the social theorists we consult with ritualized regularity in the study of religion. As I suggest in the book, they are also distinguished by their uncanny prescience. As one says in show business, you need good material to work with. A scholar of contemporary North American religion and economy can do no better than the Stop Shopping Church, and I need to thank my former Dean at Monmouth University, Ken Womack, for putting in a good word for me back when I began the process of conceptualizing the fieldwork. I felt a great burden of responsibility to do some justice to the precious legacy with which the Church entrusted me. At this point, I can only hope the community finds that their lives are accurately reflected by what is written on these pages and that this book can add some useful academic notes to the Choir's evolving activist hymnody. My book, of course, represents only one scholar's engagement with and reflections on the work and life of the Stop Shopping Church. I encourage interested academic readers to begin to further explore the community at www.revbilly.com.

For sharing their time, their rehearsal space, their hard-earned know-how, their inspiring vision, their stories, their archive, their incredible music, their art, and sometimes even their snacks, thank you Danny Valdes, James ("Mother") Benn, Charlene Ruscalleda, David Yap, Debbie Ciraolo, Dixie Estes, Robin Laverne Wilson (aka Dragonfly), Francisca Benítez, Gina Figueroa, Jess Beck, Mark Read, Michele Smith, Molly Chanoff, Nehemiah Luckett, Pat Hornak, John Quilty, John Carlin,

Shilpa Narayan, Mayfield Brooks, Dawn Stewart-Lookkin, Susannah Pryce, Gregory Corbino, Donald Gallagher, Al Smith, Colista Turner, Max Andrucki, Graham Garlington, Sylver Pondolfino, Barbara Lee, Lena Talen, Sundar Ganglani, Katie Hogan, Mink, Wesley Garlington, Denice Kondick, Travis Tench, Nate Stevens, Anclaudys Rivas, Ashni Sunder, Amber Gray, Jessica Wiscovitch, Alice O'Malley, Gaylen Hamilton, Vera Kahn, Marnie Glickman, Eva Jiménez, Killian Sundermann, Kai Pelton, Katie Degentesh, and Christopher Fleck. I am immensely grateful to Tewodros Tamirat and Carol Porteous, members of the Choir that welcomed me, whose memories liven and inform the pages of this book. Like university departments, one can speak of the Stop Shopping Choir in terms of cohorts. Most of the people I have named sang with the Choir when I was a regular participant. A special thank you to Deborah Talen for hosting us during our midwestern tour and for regaling us with childhood stories of her brother William. There are so many talented singers, activists, and community organizers in the Stop Shopping orbit at any given time that it can be hard for even a meticulous ethnographer to keep track. Please very kindly excuse any unintentional oversights on my part.

The work we do as scholars to come to a new or refined understanding of the world is always the fruit of an ensemble cast. As a scholar, I have greatly benefited from the work and example of extraordinary mentors. Michael Jackson's approach to fieldwork as a practice of radical empiricism and negative dialectics is foundational both to my ethnographic approach and to my approach to the life of the mind even more generally. Nobody has had a deeper and more profound influence on my thinking and, in the end, on my sense of vocation. The storytelling fluency of his prose and his openness to the world remain the gold standard many of us aspire to. In the end, however, Michael's extraordinary gifts and talents as an ethnographer and a thinker are only surpassed by his signature intellectual honesty and humility as a person.

Bethany Moreton has taught me all the most important things about the historical ins and outs of neoliberal capitalism. And she taught me to aspire to be both red and feminist in my approach. My work is also deeply indebted to her primary lesson that within this radicalized milieu, no bright line can be struck between economy and culture. Over the years, she has also become my academic big sister, a cherished confidant, and a dear friend. I often find myself asking WWBD? Bethany's unwavering support of me not just as a student and fellow academic worker but as a whole person has made all the intellectual *and* practical difference, and I can only hope to one day pay forward my sizable debt to her.

If I am honest, I must admit that Profe Carrasco recognized my potential as a student of religion well before I did. A little more than a decade removed from the completion of my doctoral work, he remains a stalwart champion and guide. Profe's influence abides most deeply within those intellectually liminal spaces where my scholarly analysis must reckon with the dynamic religious powers that inhabit and enchant the worlds of the persons I learn from on the ground, including members of my own Latin American immigrant family and Latino/a/x lifeworld. I very much look forward to continuing to learn from him and from his work as I engage future projects in Latino/a/x religion and economy.

If you are fortunate, you sometimes encounter people in life who have absolutely no reason to be as good to you as they end up being, and their generosity ends up potentially changing the course of your life. Angela Zito has been one such angel for me. She has become my benchmark and first point of reference for what smart, humane, and in all ways elegant academic citizenship looks like. In equal measure, Carol Duncan is a scholar's scholar and teacher's teacher whose humane and artful mentorship has enabled me to thrive professionally and to grow into my sense of vocation as a scholar-teacher of color. Even at age fifty, it is no exaggeration to say that I want to be just like them when I grow up.

Elayne Oliphant and Dan Vaca invited me to serve on the inaugural steering committee of the Religion and Economy Unit at the American Academy of Religion (AAR), which I loved doing and which provided the backdrop for so many intellectually and professionally satisfying moments. Within that capacity, I have thoroughly enjoyed working with and learning from Devin Singh, Rebecca Bartel, and Kati Curts, among others. I miss the camaraderie of serving on the steering committee and our ritualized frenzy around the call for papers and reviewing paper and panel proposals. I feel fortunate and honored to be building this conversation with such a smart, thoughtful, and collegial group. Dan also read the manuscript of this book with immense care and with such a friendly spirit. Not only did he help me improve the book, but his gift of time and expertise also confirmed how strongly committed he is to collaborative ways of being in the world.

As graduate students, Deonnie Moodie and I played tennis together, sang karaoke together, and drank more pitchers of Molson Golden than anyone probably should. And we talked shop and shared our hopes for the future. Today we're all grown up and Deonnie's exacting read of a draft of the manuscript proved critical and helped me to turn the corner with it. As a department chair, I know that the time she spent with the manuscript was especially precious. I am forever grateful to her.

Ever since I met him twenty years ago, Wallace Best has had an uncanny way of saying or doing the right thing at just the right time. I won't soon forget a now ancient conversation we had walking through a campus courtyard at Harvard that convinced me to keep at it and to keep going. Fast forwarding into the present, his invitation to workshop a chapter of this manuscript at the Religion in the Americas doctoral colloquium at Princeton was exactly what I and this book needed at the time. The day I spent with the faculty and graduate students Wallace introduced me to was magical. I was exceedingly impressed by the intellectual climate at RAC and the young scholars I met. A very special thanks to William Stell and Lauren Kerby for taking the lead and for their sharp and powerfully perceptive comments and suggestions.

Beyond ensuring that I engaged with all the right literature on music, sound, and religion in chapter 4, Francis Stewart is my partner in academic crime—or in the making of "good trouble" as she might say. She makes responsible look and feel so very fun. The time we spend together is always a shot in the arm and reminds me of what I value most about what we get to do for a living. Francis is a gem of a person, one of the best I know, and very graciously, consistently, and quietly invests in young scholars behind the scenes. That work of social reproduction at the level of our discipline is among the most important professional work that we get to do, and at the risk of embarrassing a fellow introvert, I want to shine a spotlight on Francis's careful and caring cultivation of our disciplinary futures. She does the field a great service with the Implicit Religion networks she makes available to students and early career scholars. In a similar vein, Ipsita Chatterjea does much the same for marginalized scholars as the Executive Director of SORAAD (Study of Religion as an Analytical Discipline).

I was fortunate to learn from brilliant teachers of theories and methods at Harvard Divinity School, most notably Robert Orsi. Classes and conversations with him, Anne Monius, and Parimal Patil productively haunt the pages of this book. The afterlives of conversations we had with Bob in seminar regarding the relationship of the discursive and the existential have proven especially resplendent over the years. Chapter 1 and the foundational questions and considerations that would lead directly to the research and writing of this book had their first ruminations in the form of stray thoughts that distracted me during theories and methods class as well as a short seminar paper I wrote for Parimal and Anne, whom I used to enjoy running into while checking out the books at the AAR. She is missed. I won't soon forget Anne's matter-of-fact materializing of the conditions of our work when she quipped in seminar that one of the most pressing questions that preoccupied her as a poor graduate student had to do with how much cheap ramen one should possibly consume.

Amy Hollywood and Hille Haker expertly taught me how to read Judith Butler, which as we all know is no small feat. Rigorously working out that exegesis helped me become a more capable reader and interpreter of difficult social theory, more generally. At this same time that I was relearning how to read social theory, I had the enormous privilege to audit Juliet Schor's graduate seminar on consumer society at Boston College. That class provided me with a basic vocabulary and toolkit that strongly enabled the writing of this book, more than fifteen years later. While at Harvard, I also met Warren Goldstein, whose work with the Center for Critical Research on Religion and the journal, *Critical Research on Religion*, I value and respect immensely. Finally, I also want to thank Atalia Omer, who was someone I greatly looked up to at Harvard, for inviting me to contribute some thoughts on religion and branding to the Contending Modernities blog at the Kroc Center (University of Notre Dame).

My colleague and friend at Monmouth University, Katie Parkin, a social historian and Americanist, introduced me to the thought and history of Ernest Dichter, a discovery that proved key to the progression of this book. Through Katie's work, I came across Laurence Samuel's social histories of cultural Freudianism and learned of its influence on American marketing history. As an ethnographer, I lean heavily on Samuel's important historiography in chapter 2. The analysis in this book is also strongly indebted to Kath Weston's groundbreaking work on capitalism and new animisms, the evergreen social commentary of Naomi Klein, and, even where there is disagreement, Judith Butler's social philosophy.

In the end, however, in addition to the Stop Shopping Church, my strongest and deepest intellectual debt in this book is to Kathryn Lofton, without whom it would never have been written. Katie's brave reformations of the field have given voice to a generation of scholars who have long suffered from behind the reified walls of academic silos. Her work, *Consuming Religion*, asks us to consider consumption in terms of religion, to appreciate the depth of our ritualization by neoliberal capitalism, and to begin to take social responsibility for reimagining a better future from within the very historical coordinates that have collectivized us. As the book argues, the Stop Shopping Church, which has informed my thinking about religion since the millennium, has long been engaged in practices of world-remaking that absolutely fulfill the exhortation to better understand our predicament so that we might have a hand in dreaming about and building an elsewhere. The chance to conduct an intellectual duet of sorts between the complementary brilliance of the scholar and the activists has helped me unleash my own academic voice. Katie also made the practical introduction to the series editors, knowing it would be a match made in publishing heaven. Her artisanal care of our vocations as scholars of religion reverberates well beyond New Haven and is felt widely in the discipline.

Working with New York University Press on this book has been a dream. Jennifer Hammer's professionalism and stalwart support of the project kept me steady. Whenever my own faith faltered, hers pushed me forward. The production phase of this book went along so smoothly thanks to Alexia Traganas, who kept me on task and in the loop, the meticulous copyediting prowess and deep care of Karen Verde, and the general thoughtfulness of their whole team. My brilliant disciplinary colleagues, Laura Levitt, David Harrington Watt, and Tracy Fessenden, provided just the right levels of encouragement to see me through an extensive and sometimes painful revision process. I am exceedingly honored to contribute to their influential and venerable book series. Finally, even when they sometimes delivered bad news and medicine in the form of a bitter pill, the anonymous reviewers vastly improved this book. In fact, I shudder at the thought of what would have become of this book without their help, especially with regard to issues of organization, readability, and clarity of argument. In this case, peer review worked out exactly as it is designed to and, that arduous process now behind me, I can only feel immense gratitude for the experience.

These acknowledgments might read as a long list of all the people without whom I could not have written this book. To the degree that this is the case, I must circle Kali Handelman's name. For reasons of personality, background, commitments, and interests, Kali is very simply the perfect editor of my work. She read versions of these pages more than a handful of times and her feedback was always incisive and fresh. As an editor, Kali does it all with panache and aplomb. Her feedback is written with such care and sensitivity that it becomes immediately intelligible and useful. Beyond her editorial precision, she also played the role of therapist and coach, as needed. Kali knows my thinking and writing as well as anybody at this point and she has become not just a valued interlocuter but a cherished friend.

At Baruch College, I am enjoying working with Carla Bellamy and Ken Guest on growing the program in Religion and Culture. I also want to thank Ken for putting in his own good word with NYU Press when I was ready to pitch the project to editors. Barbara Katz Rothman read and responded to the manuscript from a sunny beach during a well-earned vacation, an act of solidarity that speaks for itself. Barbara, who is a friend of the Stop Shopping community, has been a great support to me and to this project and I am forever grateful.

Support for the project was provided by multiple PSC-CUNY Awards, jointly funded by the Professional Staff Congress and the City University of New York. I am also very grateful to the Eugene M. Lang Foundation for their generous support. Their dedication to faculty research has been instrumental in bringing this work to fruition. A big thank you to the Dean's Office of the Weissman School of Arts and Sciences at Baruch, for providing additional support that allowed me to hire the masterful Josh Rutner to complete the index. Josh crafted an invaluable map for the reader and also caught more than a couple of stray typographical issues along the way. Finally, I also want to thank Omri Elisha and Alex Bauer at the CUNY Graduate Center for their many expressions of support and encouragement.

For conversations about central themes in this book that provided insight, constructive criticism, and encouragement over the years, thank you to some very wonderful friends: Jamil Thomas, Jorge de la Rosa, Jay Youngdahl, Jen Greenberg, Lisa Kavanaugh, Katherine Peil Kauffman, Nan Hutton, Julie Pederson, Ned Boyajian, Chris Ashley, Shil Sengupta, Kathy Dawson, and Mara Block. In particular, Jay's support of me as a scholar extends beyond the call of duty and reflects his lifelong professional commitments and personal values. For the head scratches, licks, and belly rubs that always make the worst moments somehow surmountable, I am deeply grateful for my beloved fur babies, Cricket, Clover, and Parker. Clover was my tenure-track pup and she crossed the rainbow bridge in the middle of the writing of this book. I cannot help but regret the extra walks and daytrip adventures she missed out on because I was so consumed with work.

It would be impossible to do anything more than scratch the surface of enormity of the debt I owe my family—without whom nothing. Scholarship too easily reifies the ideas that scholars present in our books, articles, and talks. However, if we are lucky, behind these academic performances stand the love, sacrifices, difficult choices, steady encouragement, material support, and hard work of loved ones. For everything they have done to make the work I do possible, my deepest love and gratitude to *los González*, my *muy querida madre*, Ana, the bedrock and anchor of our family, my sister and best friend, Laura, and the loving (and living) memory of our father, Héctor. Much love to my aunt Tere, my uncle Teo, and to *the Phelans*: my beloved nieces, Beca and Miranda, and my brother-in-law, Michael. I have truly wonderful in-laws, and my mother-in-law, Barbara, is one of the most engaging storytellers I have ever had the good fortune to spend time with. My partner Gary is my heart. I have never met a more caring soul in my life. His abiding sociality and the constancy and depth of his interest in the welfare of others do not cease to teach and inspire me.

# NOTES

## INTRODUCTION

1 Following ethnographic convention and protocols, I use pseudonyms for all members of the Stop Shopping Church with the exception of William Talen, also known as Reverend Billy, and Savitri Durkee, the group's director, who are public figures.
2 An oft-puzzling term that one frequently comes across on the nightly news, the "real economy" refers to our active relationships with capital through modes of production and consumption (to which we must also add social reproduction) while the "financial economy" refers to exchange rates, interest rates, and the world of economic speculation.
3 The classic Marxist account of political economy (e.g., Marx ([1857] 1983), 375–394) suggests that human cultural and political life, including the historical appearance of European individuality, is a unilinear production of the organic laws of economy. This fully structuralist approach to society and economy has proven much too coarse for religious studies given the former's reduction of diverse religious expression to superstructural efflux. While the unapologetic rejection of economism is necessary, an aspect of my argument here is that some of our chosen theories and methods have lost a sense of religion and economy's important co-implications as well as their own participation in these.
4 A new documentary, *In Bed with the Rev*, by artist and filmmaker Richard DeDomenici, is currently in production.
5 The group has also gone by the names Reverend Billy and the Church of Stop Shopping, Reverend Billy and the Stop Shopping Gospel Choir, The Church of Not Bombing, and the Church of Life After Shopping.
6 See Related Companies (2020). Given a spate of suicides in which visitors threw themselves off the new landmark, the Vessel temporarily closed in January 2021 and reopened in May 2021, with new protocols and an admissions fee in place. See Yakas (2021).
7 According to the urban anthropologist Julian Brash (2011), practices of urban branding greatly expanded under the Bloomberg administration. Brash (102) explains that urban branding entails the active development of images and meanings of a city in order to influence the perceptions of target markets that might invest in it as businesses, tourists, and residents, recursively bringing it in line with the desired brand. Aided by the conclusions of McKinsey consultants (107), Bloomberg's strategy was to enhance New York City's global competitiveness by

238 | NOTES

rebranding it as a luxury city populated by a diverse, well-educated, postindustrial workforce. Urban branding takes our comprehensive self-reflexive economies of signs to their logical extension.

8  On the central importance of consumption to American belonging and citizenship in the postwar period, see Cohen (2004).

9  For example, Davíd Carrasco (2013) argues that in pre-Colombian Mesoamerica, ceremonial centers like Teotihuacan dramatized and ritualized the Aztecs' interrelated terrestrial and cosmic orientations. Or we might think of the role of religious iconography and architecture in the imperial Hindu kingship of the Rashtrakutas, who were overlords of large swaths of the Indian subcontinent between the sixth and tenth centuries BCE (Inden 1990).

10  I had joined members of the Stop Shopping Church at an action four months earlier at the Statue of Liberty at which, each of us carrying a letter, we unfurled a banner that spelled out SANCTUARY. There was some talk among members of the group about whether Okoumou, who was associated with the group Rise and Resist, was inspired by their action. See Aguilera (2019). Reverend Billy sometimes speaks of the Stop Shopping Church as the proverbial canary in the coal mine of New York City–based activism, starting trends that other more visible groups take and run with. He admits to some perennial annoyance with the fact that Reverend Billy and the Church of Stop Shopping are not often fully credited for the work they do.

Some in the grassroots activist communities that surround the Stop Shopping Church have taken umbrage with Okoumou's online requests for donations and have accused her of using her activism to brand *herself* as an icon. In my view, a more helpful perspective would be to recognize that all social action, including social activism, is existentially inflected and materially structured. Self-interest and social interest are by no means mutually exclusive, although our continued disavowal of genius and nobility's economic mediations can be distorting and analytically telling.

11  The marketing professor Douglas Holt (2004, 4) suggests that iconic brands have "become consensus expressions of particular values held dear by some members of a society."

12  On the production of *cultural objects* through consumption and the concomitant construction of consumer identities through repositories of meaning, see Brash (2011, 105–106).

13  In designing the Woolworth building in 1931, Frank W. Woolworth was inspired by his visits to Europe and the Gothic architecture he encountered there. The Reverend Parkes Cadman (1916) christened the Woolworth Building a "Cathedral of Commerce." In the early twentieth century, John Wanamaker, a Presbyterian builder with strong connections to the Young Men's Christian Association (YMCA), would convert his flagship department store in Philadelphia, Wanamaker's, into a Christmas cathedral replete with the world's grandest pipe organ (Schmidt 1995, 162).

14  Amusingly, pointing to power's linguistic qualities and vulnerabilities, a theme this book takes up in more than one guise, the Vessel has also been mockingly compared to a giant shawarma. See Alburger (2019).

15  For Walter Benjamin ([1982] 1999), the *flâneur* moving about through nineteenth-century mercantile arcades was an exemplar of the new modern bourgeois subject. According to Fredric Jameson (1991), Baudelaire and his poetic allegorizing of the city are, for Benjamin, indicative of the emergence of a new experience of urban modernism, one that demands the development of new habits of bodily perception.

16  For example, Jamil, one of my oldest friends and a college roommate, has explained it this way: "Popular music is popular for a reason; it articulates feelings and sells." Along with our friend and classmate, Jorge, Jamil and I have often reflected on the ways in which the music we listened to in college in the 1990s simultaneously offered resources for self-expression and also fueled the (historically mediated) consumer markets of the day.

17  Today, processes of hypergentrification are front and center. Specifically, the corporate aestheticization and narrativization of whole neighborhoods as brand stories written by and for real estate developers, their brokers, and their well-heeled consumers threaten to displace the largely immigrant communities that make New York City, as a global city, so vibrant in the first place. See also Harvey (2013).

18  Members of the Church of Stop Shopping often cite the urbanist Jane Jacobs as an influence. Indeed, the preservation of local economies and neighborhoods gained special prominence in the group's activism in the post–9/11 period and in the leadup to Mike Bloomberg's third term as mayor of New York City in 2009, most especially. One can read some of the work the group has done and continues to do through the lens of Marshall Berman's (1982) analysis of "shout in the street" critics of urban modernism, a kind of organic howling at the encroaching expressway. Now it would be the creep of postmodern branding rather than Robert Moses's expressways that would play the role of villain. This villain is exceedingly more semiotic, immaterial, psychic, and patently aesthetizing in its presentation of self. As we will see, in order to advance their critique as effectively as possible, the Stop Shopping Church dons the postmodern and postindustrial trappings of the historical form of capitalism they look to oppose.

19  For Debord, the society of the spectacle is a negation of life masquerading as life in that life's immediacy is somehow kidnapped by marketing and commercial media. After the discursive turn and its general devaluation of ideas of essence and authenticity, it is difficult, I think, for scholarship to sustain any kind of bright line between noncommercial and commercial experience on ontological grounds. Outside of theological analyses, however, *political* contrasts have become the critical terrain upon which analyses of commodity fetishism have generally come to stand.

20 Savitri D suggests to a Church member in an interview he did with her and William Talen that music and song are human beings' earliest social technologies. With their deep roots within the human condition, she finds reason for some optimism. Music and song are "way more ancient than shopping and police states." See Valdes (2020).
21 On philanthropy's unpaid and unpayable debts see Lucia Hulsether (2019).
22 The turn to volunteerism and charity (an appeal to "caring individuals") often goes hand in hand with a diminution of the roles of social solidarity and of the state apparatus in the provision of welfare (see Weston 2018). As such, the abstract issue social scientists tend to spend time considering—*how does human agency relate to forms of collective organization?*—is, from the start, *political*, not merely methodological. As the Stop Shopping Church understands it, the work of creating structures of care starts with local, small-scale pursuits.
23 The historian Leigh Eric Schmidt (1995, 159) reminds us that the commercialization of Christmas is nothing new. In the late nineteenth century, "Middle-class Victorian women regularly integrated Christian piety into the quite material world of the home and into holiday rituals that revolved around shopping and family."
24 The reference is to Peter Jackson's cinematic interpretation of J.R.R. Tolkien's *The Lord of the Rings*.
25 For an influential publication examining the "proper" role of traditional religion in public debate, see Mendieta and VanAntwerpen (2011).
26 We might be tempted to understand Reverend Billy's concerns in terms of the economization of the political, or what Wendy Brown (2015, 44) calls "the conversion of basic principles of democracy from a political to economic semantic order." Following Melinda Cooper (2017), Bethany Moreton (2009), and others, Brown (2019), however, has since nuanced and revised this materialist argument in order to better grasp the ways in which markets and morals alike are released by neoliberal rationality and to bring into clearer view the ways in which "patriarchal family norms" are deeply embedded within neoliberal reform. That is, the economic semantic order that neoliberal reason seeks to extend is also, as Brown now puts it, grounded in the "activation of traditional morality in place of legislated social justice." The Stop Shopping Church has also understood the strong relationship between markets and morals. As I will reference in chapter 5, one of the group's most significant and internally contested actions in the era of COVID-19 was to challenge the place of Franklin Graham's Samaritan's Purse at Mount Sinai's field hospital on the grounds that Samaritan's Purse's anti-homosexual policies should disqualify it from playing a role in the collective healing of New York City, prima facie.
27 On a secular dance parade as an opportunity for neo-Pentecostals to engage in spiritual warfare, see Elisha (2017).
28 Reverend Billy sometimes speaks of performatively resignifying The Passion, the essential narrative structure of the Christian drama (already noted by the

midcentury French Marxist, Henri Lefebvre ([1947] 2008), for its alienating effects). According to Reverend Billy, the Passion play is structured in conflict, sacrifice, and return. In his case, Talen has been arrested around sixty times, a sacrifice that allows him to return to his fold with renewed authority and purpose, that is, iconic stature. "We sing to the tombs . . . only to rise again," Reverend Billy has explained. Jesus and his disciplines, Talen believes (2006, 84), knew well how to turn nonviolent performance into effective activism that displays conviction and courage to street audiences.

Sometimes, as Chase Bank did in the summer of 2023, Reverend Billy's opponents, understanding the performative power of his acts of martyrdom, refuse to call for his arrest even when his provocations would otherwise statutorily warrant a return to the tombs (i.e., the New York City jail system).

29 The history of social movements teaches us that alienation, when politically activated, can be a powerful impetus to collective action of all sort. On the left, this is why so much critical theory on consumerism takes direct aim at mechanisms (unities) for positively smoothing over the lived negativity of social contradictions. As György Lukács ([1923] 1972), Theodor Adorno and Max Horkheimer ([1947] 2002), Guy Debord ([1967] 1994), and others have suggested in their own way, one of the elemental powers of capitalism is its ability to deliver, through the media and practices of consumption, smoothing unities of the world remade in its own image. Marx, their shared progenitor, was, for this very reason among others, so spooked by what he considered to be Hegel's patently bourgeois philosophical and dialectical reconciliation of spirit and matter.

30 One of the group's central concerns, from its inception, has been the abuse of police power, especially as this militarizes corporate efforts to gentrify the City and has disproportionately targeted and terrorized Black and brown communities. In the summer of 2020, the group surrounded the residence of Patrick Lynch, the head of the patrolmen's union, and protested his role in legitimizing the murders of unarmed Black and brown New Yorkers.

31 However, it is important to also keep in mind that, depending on where we have been—*that is made*—and where we want to go—the stage directions we follow in our self-remaking will differ. Based in an ethnography of two sister organizations engaged in the "spiritual" reform of business management, my first book (2015) offers a revision of Jean-Paul Sartre's existential Marxism for a postindustrial, digital age. While it draws strongly from Michel Foucault's theorizations of *episteme* and power, it preserves Sartre's original interest in the intersubjective dialectics and biographical inflections of freedom and control.

32 In his classic theory of value, Thorstein Veblen ([1899] 2005) proposes that consumption is driven by the desire to elevate one's position in the social hierarchy through the public display of wealth. Naomi Klein ([1999] 2009) and Thomas Frank (1997), among others, have described the ways in which critiques of capitalism have today come to compel consumption. In all cases, existential energies are socialized within the parameters of structured ends, begging the pressing

question of what it would take for us to *choose* to actually break with the law of consumption. As I will argue, the poststructuralist emphasis on the instabilities of language is insufficient to the critique of political economy and the fight for climate justice.

33 The Stop Shopping Church often avoids organizing strategies that anathematize or alienate their political opponents. Their desire to "save souls" generally implies futures of solidarity rather than the rude overcoming of adversaries. However, in the summer of 2023, the group participated in New York City's Drag March, which received some negative global attention, some of it within queer organizing, when a video clip emerged on Twitter that captured a group of participants, including some members of the Choir, chanting, "We're Here / We're Queer / We're Coming for Your Children!"

34 The latently Protestant ethical architecture of this kind of framing and approach is clear enough. A red thread that runs through this book is the idea that the example of the Stop Shopping Church reminds us that human life implies a dialectic of freedom and control in which the very same power that we might want to banish has also, in fact, made us.

35 In 2014, dressed as queen bees and singing an homage to the endangered honeybee, the Stop Shopping Church invaded the microrobotics lab at Harvard's School of Engineering to point out the absurdity of prioritizing research on the manufacture of robotic pollinators rather than research into the ways in which human activity can lessen its negative impact on honeybee populations. "It doesn't pass the guffaw test!" exclaimed the Reverend.

36 Almost 9,000 New Yorkers cast their ballots for Reverend Billy.

37 The anti-capitalist Occupy Wall Street movement of 2011 against wealth inequality and money in politics came on the heels of the housing crash and Great Recession of 2008 and was characterized by a populist reclaiming of public space in the form of overnight encampments, most notably in Wall Street's Zuccotti Park. In the summer of 2014, a grassroots mobilization in Ferguson, Missouri, protested the police murder of Michael Brown, an eighteen-year-old African American man, which sparked local and national conversations around police racial terror. In 2016, a national coalition gathered in support around Native American protests of the Dakota Access Pipeline near the Standing Rock Indian Reservation, the construction of which threatened the reservation's water supply. The anti-racist Black Lives Matter movement began in 2013 with the acquittal of the Hispanic man who had murdered an African American teen, Trayvon Martin, as he walked through a residential community on his way back from running an errand. As a loose grassroots network, it has, in part, organized public protests in response to subsequent cases of police racial terror, most recently the 2020 extrajudicial murder of an African American man, George Floyd, by a white police officer in Minneapolis, Minnesota.

38 The group rightly takes some of the credit for a New York State statute signed into law by Governor Cuomo in December 2020 banning the use of Glysophate on state grounds.

39 The group argues that, having suffered through prior mass Extinction events, the Earth will adjust, with or without human beings in its fold. The future of life itself, not to be confused with human life or human flourishing, is, they believe, secured. Like the environmental activists Extinction Rebellion, the Stop Shopping Church capitalizes the word Extinction to stress its central explanatory and political importance.

40 Their most recent album, *change without us*, was published online in August 2022.

41 A Church ritual that is written into their formal, theatrical performances involves the conferral of "sainthood" on activists, artists, and intellectuals whom the group believes have done life-caring work. During the ritual, Reverend Billy likes to add that, unlike the Christian Church, the Church of Stop Shopping prefers that their saints stay alive.

42 In 2004, they did not teach you about capital in religious education at Harvard Divinity School for reasons that are shrouded in important and instructive national and institutional histories (see Hulsether 2018).

43 To elaborate on the critical dangers: If students are not introduced to literature that examines the postindustrial turn, they might well assume that power continues to look like the industrial modernism that much of religious studies considers most closely given our interests in the development of the category of religion in the nineteenth century. That misrecognition could lead beginning students to believe that simply reintroducing repressed affect and the disappeared body back into the human situation is, in itself, a critical move. What's needed, instead, is for students of religion to understand that consuming religion is highly ritualized, affective, and anchored in the semiotic management of bodies.

44 On the grounding assumptions according to which American religious studies was established as an academic discipline, see Orsi (2005, 183–198). Orsi's discussion emphasizes the ways in which the scientific study of religion, an object of study framed within the evaluative coordinates of nondenominational, domesticated Christianity, worked to establish and promote the contours of supposedly "good," democratically necessary religion over and against the affective and ethical "madness" of religious "others." Orsi's cultural history of the discipline importantly reminds us, in a broader sense, that secularism's separation of spheres was never actually strict and that the prominence it gives to scientific method was never value-neutral. To Orsi's discussion of the origin of American religious studies, I want to add that a precondition for the disciplinary arrangements he calls on scholars of religion to self-reflexively reckon with was the Weberian conceit that capitalism had transcended and overcome religion. This ruse allowed capitalism to disappear from the study of religion to the degree that a return to the study of religion and capitalism became necessary.

As religion scholars reengage with necessary critiques of capitalism, I strongly believe that we must be vigilant to avoid reinscribing updated versions of the good / bad religion dichotomies Orsi brings to our attention. It will be important not to give the scholarly short end of the stick to religious expressions that we might correctly understand to participate in, invest in, and help reproduce socially and ecologically destructive systems. Religion can do many things in the world and can take on many kinds of dance partners. Otherwise urgent condemnations of racial capitalism's destructive effects on communities and the planet do not absolve scholars of religion of our primary disciplinary mandate to do justice to the human and historical messiness of religion's life in the world (including its co-implications with economy). This mandate arises from the polyvalent character of religious phenomena themselves, which do not admit of any final political, historical, or experiential synthesis. The demands of critique are complex, plural, and enter into the fray of lived worlds at different levels of analysis and from different vantage points. As Orsi (2012) argues, "everyday religion" is not amenable to "either / or" analysis, in which either liberation or social control is stressed to the direct exclusion of the other. If we understand "consuming religion" as an expression of "everyday religion," neither is an "either / or" framing the most useful. This is because a complex understanding of how religious ideologies *and* forms of therapeutic consumption make economic frameworks and systems attractive on the ground can only improve the quality and precision of critique in the end.

45 Weber toured the United States in 1904, a visit that greatly influenced his thoughts about the future directions of industrial capitalism and the decline of religious sects.

46 Of course, there have been notable early exceptions, of which Liston Pope's (1942) classic study of Gastonia, North Carolina, is one of the most important and best known.

47 Lofton's student, Lucia Hulsether (2023), has asked important questions about Lofton's intervention. First, Hulsether observes that social theory has its own historical "baggage." Second, in the case of Durkheim's functionalist sociology and its focus on social organization as the primary marker of the religious, Hulsether reminds that Durkheim's theory was the result of a lifelong commitment to liberal reform over class revolution. Those commitments and those histories accompany the Durkheimian return that Lofton facilitates, Hulsether suggests. I strongly agree with Hulsether that social theory must be historicized and materialized. The suggestion that conjuring Durkheim is no innocent affair is well taken. In fact, I suggest in chapter 2 that the thought of a celebrated left social theorist, Judith Butler, has, in certain articulations, reproduced the performative logic of consumer capitalism in ways that her many readers in left religious studies generally miss.

In my own view, historicizing social theory is necessary, but it is important to consider that social theories are tools that scholars can creatively and actively deploy to redirect original or authoritative meanings or can employ in efforts at immanent critique. Culture jamming is not just for the activists, in other words. As historical artifacts, social theories can be strategically hotwired and realigned once we understand where they come from, how they come to us, their ideological pressure points, and the work that they do. As a practical matter, Lofton's Durkheimian turn has cleared intellectual terrain by arresting the closed loop of genealogical treatment that has proliferated within the academe. This will enable the more radical thinkers and theory Hulsether is eager to summon to the field (Marx most urgently and obviously) to achieve a fairer hearing within the discipline.

48 Lake Lambert (2009) has suggested that today's retail therapy is a form of what Weber would have called *this-worldly* mysticism, had this particular combination been intelligible to Weber and his specific account of capitalism. On the role of corporate constructions of mysticism in contemporary business management, see my first book, *Shape-Shifting Capital—Spiritual Management, Critical Theory, and the Ethnographic Project* (2015).

49 Stanley Tambiah ([1990] 2004) has brilliantly analyzed these hierarchies within the context of Enlightenment culture and the modern West.

50 While I had not read the 2006 book by Talen, having come across them in my hometown of New York City, I had been following the Stop Shopping Church since the early 2000s, before I began graduate school at Harvard Divinity School. Inspired by their example, I wanted to write on consumption for my dissertation project but was not able to convince the committee that approves dissertation topics. Instead, I researched and wrote on workplace spirituality, although taking steps even back then to begin a fieldwork-based follow-up research project on the Stop Shopping Church.

51 In short, as a methodological matter, my first book (see González 2015), taking the work and worlds of management reformers of capitalism as its empirical case, dwells on the question of how we might think the critique of capitalism through the co-constituting valences of existence and structure. The present book asks how the labors of grassroots activist interlocuters might help scholars with interests in religion and power better understand the relationship of our theories and methods to wider consumerist culture and better appreciate the stakes for our scholarly accounts of subjectivity and embodied rationality.

52 On the sympathetic magic that dwells between biography and ethnography, see Weston (2018).

53 Bartel and Hulsether call on the field to combine analyses of secularism and capitalism, which they suggest have tended to run along separate tracks. They also suggest that, due to a weak and unconvincing aversion to Marx, scholars of religion have tended to underexplore and undertheorize what it is that capitalism actually does—that is, capital's extractions, its alienations, and its world-making effects. I strongly appreciate and agree with the suggestion that Marxist framings have more to offer religious studies than the field itself tends to admit. At the same time, as an existential Marxist, I hold out hope that scholars can simultaneously take our subjects' intentions and experiences of the world seriously while

also investing in a robustly normative critique of contemporary capitalism's constitutive excesses.

54 My academic interests in "post-secular" capitalism have long been guided by Bethany Moreton's (2007) groundbreaking suggestion that scholarship must attend to the "soul of neoliberalism," which, she suggests, experientially bridges what we might call (religious) culture and (economic) system (or, in her own terms, the software and the hardware of the neoliberal consensus).

55 The networks and practices of capitalist humanitarian reform Hulsether covers and decries in the spirit of relentless critique and a "pessimism" meant to oppose theologically mediated capitalist optimisms, include fair trade, microfinance, and Christian philanthropy.

56 On the struggles of socially engaged churchgoers in Tennessee to move their Evangelical communities toward a focus on progressive social issues like urban poverty and race relations, see Elisha (2011).

57 Kathryn Lofton's (2017, 13) suggestion that "consuming religion" might "incite the beginning of a new self-consciousness to liberate us from the very obsessions it compels" is an expression of the logic of subversion that I argue the Stop Shopping Church also follows and that scholars must more clearly adopt since our social action cannot but derive from the social contexts in which we are shaped and disciplined as certain kinds of (differentially rewarded) late capitalist academic workers and (differentially empowered) postindustrial consumers.

Before Lofton, Henri Lefebvre ([1947] 2008, 195), and, after him, Michel de Certeau (1984), also drew direct analogies between religion and consumption in the context of "everyday life." For Lefebvre, consumption is a form of religious media that inverts reality and breeds false consciousness. For his part, de Certeau (xiii), turning to the example of religious syncretism of the Spanish empire to draw the analogy, highlights the ways in which consumers of media (the "weak") tactically subvert and transform the meanings of those who claim to own and dictate culture. In practice, it is important to recognize both the agency that is produced by consumer power and ways in which our pursuit of freedom within consumerism can work to strengthen the chains of consumerism as the primary system wherein we fashion selves (Halter 2000; McGee 2006) and make and sell culture in a consumer society (Ohmann 1996). On the general need for a dialectic of consumption that moves between agency and control, see Holt and Schor (2000).

58 For a fulsome explication of what I understand the explanatory and critical power of existential Marxism to be within the context of contemporary shape-shifting capitalism, see González (2015).

59 I mean this in a specific and limited way that has much to do with my interdisciplinary training within the already interdisciplinary field of religious studies. I was trained in ethnographic method by Michael Jackson, who introduced me to existential Marxism. He is a formally trained cultural anthropologist (not—like me—a religious studies scholar who works ethnographically) who found that

both the doing of and the analysis of his fieldwork were sharpened and productively focused through his intellectual engagements with certain philosophical currents in phenomenology, critical theory, and Jean-Paul Sartre's mid-twentieth-century synthesis of existential philosophy and Marxism. Jackson's eclectic approach, which mediates between storytelling and analytical exposition, has greatly influenced my own.

On the general coordinates and concerns of philosophical anthropology today, see Das et al. (2014).

60 The book's (along with its ethnographic interlocuters') interests in challenging the reduction of social action to an abstract account of (consumer, scholarly, or activist) habit, and its interests in bringing empiricism to bear on theory, place it in line with some of the interests of recent articulations of philosophical anthropology (see, e.g., Das et al. 2014). The argument that scholars' own socializations by social theory are part of the ethnographic field presses in the direction of Michael Jackson's (1996) understanding of ethnography as a practice of radical empiricism.

61 What ethnographers can learn is strongly delimited by what their interlocuters wish to talk about. When I began my fieldwork with the Stop Shopping Church in late 2016, Reverend Billy and Savitri D made it very clear they thought my focus should remain firmly planted in the group's present, not its past. Some of the questions I had coming into the fieldwork, questions that in some important ways were largely replaced by the ones I grapple with in this book, had to do with the original conceiving of the parodic Reverend Billy character and the religious histories, biographies, and encounters that grounded the performance. I wanted to know more about Talen's relationship, in particular, to the "fool for Christ" theology he seemed to have refashioned and reframed as anti-consumerist drama. When I met my new friends, however, they had largely stepped out of the ironic distance of that iteration of Reverend Billy and were stepping into the "sincerity" of the Earth Justice advocacy they are increasingly known for. While I have been able to glean information to satisfy some aspects of my initial questions, questions I had not anticipated became both more compelling and accessible.

62 An argument that tracks throughout the book, consumer capitalism is "post-secular" in the sense that it actively and systematically defies the anathematized relationship between libidinized religious values and pure capitalist rationality that, at least in theory, underwrote secularism's original charter. What I do not mean by "post-secular" here are the debates that arose within Continental philosophy, political theory, and religious studies in the first decade of the new century regarding the "proper" role of religion in the democratic public square.

63 The argument is this: Performativity theory, which is often deployed by scholars to press in the direction of methodological anti-foundationalism, in fact expresses the fundamentals of neoliberal consumption, but this relationship generally has been disavowed by its academic acolytes. One of the necessary means by which our disciplinary sidestepping of our own formatting by capitalist discipline has been accomplished is as a consequence of the general elision of the intersubjective

(and, as a structural matter, consumptive) contexts of scholarship. The disciplinary focus on the scholarly mastery of discursive knowledge (that importantly tends toward hyper-nominalism and an evasion of its own relationship to advertising semiosis) has allowed scholarship in religion to generally position itself in terms of an "outside" interrogation of religion rather than as a participant in religious history, as this book argues we must actually ultimately understand the doing of religious studies.

64 I have argued (González 2015) that Foucauldian genealogy, with its interest in geographies of power (what Wendy Brown [2001] analyzes as a recasting of the weight of history in "heterogenous layers" of "spatial accretion") can be understood as a practice of what Sartre ([1960] 2004) would call analytical reason since the focus remains squarely on conceptual entities. According to Sartre after his Marxist turn, while necessary, analytical reason must be complemented by dialectical reason's interest in "living interrelatedness" (see Poster 1975). As activists, my suggestion is that the Stop Shopping Church engages in and relates forms of, in Sartrian terms, analytical and dialectical reason, in ways that also speak to the critical necessity of actively mapping geographies of power.

65 Weber proposed that a cold instrumental rationality grounded in the accounting of externalized economic price rather than an appreciation for internalized cultural value defined capitalism's historical apogee. He directly opposed the formal secularity of capitalist value-neutral rationality to the value systems of religion. As I begin to suggest in chapter 3 and further develop in chapter 5, the work of the Stop Shopping Church over the past quarter-century marks and traces neoliberal capitalism's metabolizations of art, music, psychology, and, of course, religion in ways that force a reconsideration of the reduction of capitalism to economic terms.

## CHAPTER 1. RITUALIZATION IN THE AGE OF STARBUCKS

1 During an interview, one long-standing member of the Church was horrified to see that her parents, who had come to observe one of the group's street actions, were sipping Starbucks lattes. Marly Genovese, Interview with the author, October 30, 2020.
2 Savitri Durkee, Interview with the author, February 8, 2019.
3 Savitri Durkee, Interview with the author, February 8, 2019.
4 Savitri Durkee, Interview with the author, February 8, 2019.
5 During rehearsal, Savitri D once remarked that the socialist conference the Left Forum, housed at the CUNY Graduate Center, was the only place she had ever seen "Marxists drinking Starbucks."
6 Pan Leif-Thompson, Interview with the author, February 12, 2021.
7 Turning to direct selling organizations like Mary Kay as her case studies and to Weber in her analysis, Nicole Biggart (1989) argues that (brand) devotion, personal networks, and charismatic leadership rather than strict bureaucratic rationalization increasingly drive the contemporary sale.

8  In the social historian T. J. Jackson Lears's view, the "decentered self" had already begun to make an appearance in the nineteenth century, within the context of a Victorian antimodernism (1994, 34). And, as we will see in chapter 2, the Freudian revolution of mid-twentieth-century American marketing opened up the psyche to intimate forms of capitalist discipline. Today, the vision of the consumer as "fragile self" is, in fact, quite dominant. The use of neuroscientific techniques to target pre-conscious metaphorical associations is one increasingly common method by which marketing elites attempt to communicate with the "decentered consumer" (Zaltman 2003, 71).

9  Indeed, a romantic ethos was constitutive of the Industrial Revolution and, hence, of the development of capitalism (Campbell 1987). We should resist speaking of the calculating logic of a rationalist capitalism as making use of romantic tropes in advertising and instead appreciate, as a historical matter, that capitalism was, from the start, already born of and expressive of romantic passions and longings.

10  I suggest in the conclusion of this book that scholars could learn from reading more broadly and engaging with the public writers and public intellectuals that the activists read and take their counsel from. As is true of academic scholarship, scholars might not always agree with what is written or might quarrel with aspects of what they read. Active reading and discernment are what matter. While the vetting of peer review is necessary, the charismatic authority that guards the sanctity of the "properly" academic can work against our purposes as scholars if it keeps us from the archives we should consult, as an empirical matter. In my estimation, Naomi Klein's public-facing writing as a cultural critic is more than worthy of generous reference and citation in a scholarly book like mine.

11  This approach differs in a striking way from nineteenth- and even some mid-twentieth-century printed advertisements, which spoke to consumers by way of pictures ("visual clichés"), accompanied by a relatively lengthy text which provided advice and instructed them how to make their way through the world of proliferating goods (Marchand 1985). Branding, for its part, is meant to construct and reconstruct consumer subjectivity, psychically, from the inside out, such that an anthropomorphism of brands is accomplished by consumers whose performances, both within and outside of the immediate brand context, automatically express the values and qualities associated with the brand, in circular, tautological fashion.

However, key aspects of modern Western consumer culture had already been developing since the seventeenth century (Stearns 2001, 6–9). Certain dimensions of consumer practice are also perhaps better approached in phenomenological terms. Thus, we cannot speak of consumer society in simply homogenous ways, or with reference to clear lines of periodization. If history is, as Robert Orsi (2005, 9) claims, *braided*, then at best we are here talking about ideal-types in the Weberian sense, even if, as I strongly believe, Weber overstated his conviction of secularization as one such type. The history of consumerism is nothing if not complex. It is marked by dissent and, seemingly, cross-purposes.

12  A central theme in the anticonsumerism of the Stop Shopping Church is the suggestion that a key danger of consumerism is that it metabolizes artful dissent, the impulses of activism, and even childhood memories. Gilles Fauconnier and Mark Turner's (2002, 37) cognitive linguistics suggests that creativity is the product of "conceptual blending" that "brings together elements from different domains" and integrates meanings that are at once social and personal. An aspect of the argument in this chapter is that branding has an implicit awareness of these dynamics and achieves cognitive blending through the ritualization of consumption.

13  There are important similarities between the ways in which scholars understand gender, sexuality, disability, and race in terms of "regimes of truth," and the ways in which marketers understand the objectivity of brands. The brand form strongly echoes the academic concept of a discursive regime that constitutes and produces subjects and "incites" their desires (Butler 1997a) in advance of individuals' conscious acts of choosing.

14  See also Aggarwal and McGill (2012, 307–323) for a discussion of the ways in which branded consumers take on the traits associated with their beloved brands, even in nonbrand contexts. I argue that ritualization is another way to account for the branding of selves, time, and space.

15  See Thurston (2007).

16  There are intentional echoes, here, of Peter Berger's ([1967] 1990) *The Sacred Canopy*. Berger argues that religious meanings are overlaid onto everyday life, providing a protective sacred canopy for the religious, who would otherwise have to confront the possibilities of nihilism and meaninglessness in the universe. In Berger's account, secularization threatened to disintegrate the sacred's protective covering. Klein's quip suggests something different: The raw materials of meaning-making, and, hence, person-making, are increasingly controlled by economic power, which reenchants its own world.

17  Reframing Pierre Bourdieu's interests in the subjective consequences of "structuring structures," *social body* in Catherine Bell's thought refers to the structures of authority and hierarchies of value that imprint onto the body in action, ritualizing asymmetrical relationships and hypothesizing dynamic correspondences between self and society. As Angela Zito explains (1997, 210), "the human body has functioned, generally, and continues to function, as a powerful organizing metaphor for nature, society, and self in many social contexts all over the world." This insight speaks to a central impulse of this book: to outline the shape of the body that ritualizes relationships between realms of experience in the globalizing, consumerist context. As the activists understood in their own terms, this ritualizing and consuming body is dynamic and iterative, both substantial and immaterial, like a dynamic node within a network.

18  The second aspect of Bell's idea of misrecognition is also important to branding. Following Bourdieu, she explains, gift-giving involves a "deliberate oversight"

of the obligations and demands of the gift. Misrecognition thus "enables the gift or counter-gift to be seen and experienced as an inaugural act of generosity" (1992, 82). If the act of gift-giving demands the misrecognition of the economy of exchange (the power dynamics of gift and counter-gift), consumption can demand the misrecognition of the motivations of corporate actors. Bryant Simon writes that Starbucks customers certainly understand that Starbucks sells its hospitality and rents out its clean, comforting spaces for money. Oftentimes, however, consumers deliberately choose not to dwell on issues of economic exchange in deference to the experience. Of the "corporate generated recognition and banter" taken from scripts delivered to baristas in training manuals, one consumer put it this way: "maybe it's part of the 'sell' but I don't care. A kind word goes a long way" (2011, 96). In this way, Starbucks charges its employees to deliver coffee and to create, through their tone, faces, and moods, "a particular emotional state in others," in what it hopes will be experienced in an organic fashion (95).

19  In Bell's account, religionists will similarly misrecognize the ways in which liturgies generate integrated experiences of God or of tradition.

20  Simon's extended treatment confirms much of Naomi Klein's diagnoses of brand power even if he differs with Klein on prescriptive grounds. The group Adbusters, which was one of the organizers of the Occupy Wall Street protests of 2011, has long argued that one of the ways in which ideology is reproduced is in the seats of economics and business school classrooms. In particular, they point out that while these classes construct economy, in abstract, numerical terms, capitalism is actually highly invested in commodifying everything, including the psyche, nature and, increasingly, life itself. The orthodox curriculum deflects attention away from this fact and keeps interested parties from engaging in interdisciplinary analysis of economy, ceding critical territory to economics. See Adbusters (2009, 85). One of the group's traditional strategies has been to redirect and subvert corporate signs. So, for example, an ad-busting poster replaced the image of a white woman runner below Nike's "Just Do It!" slogan with the image of a brown *maquilladora* in an effort to call into question the associations with feminism and women's rights that the Nike brand evokes and manages as cultural capital. Naomi Klein, writing a decade earlier, vests more hope in these strategies than does Bryant Simon (2011, 9), who argues that brands can absorb and redirect critique more effectively than even Klein had thought possible.

21  Bobo is an implied reference to David Brooks's (2000) "comic sociology" of the new cultural elites of the information age. Bobo is a neologistic combination of *bourgeois* and *bohemian*.

22  It is important to note that none of this excludes the thoroughgoing standardization of important areas of the North American labor economy, especially with respect to some of the economy's most devalued and invisible workers. On the "McDonaldization" of society, see Ritzer (1993).

23  Something that neoliberal capitalism very much does is metabolize difference and dissent. Consumer performativity and branding as ritualization is largely how this accomplished at the level of consumer subjectivity.
24  Michel Foucault (1994, 357) isolates the question of space in the reproduction of power in an essay reproduced in English as "Space, Knowledge, and Power."
25  Greg Dickinson (2002, 43). Importantly for the present conversation, Dickinson argues that "we cannot expect nor hope that the rituals of Starbucks serve as practices of resistance to dominant modes and relations in postmodernity. Rather, Starbucks is a place in which visitors can come to better accept those modes." Ritualizing strategies that disrupt the epistemological structure for the postmodern consumer self would somehow need to break or escape from the logic of the brand and its cybernetic and managed absorption of citational difference. This is what the actions of the Stop Shopping Church in retail spaces hope to achieve.
26  In keeping with the basic coordinates of neoliberal capitalism, Starbucks has been strongly opposed to union power. As of January 2023, however, more than 250 Starbucks stores across the United States have voted to unionize (see Sbworkersunited.org). The corporation, for its part, continues to fight this unbranded expression of internal "difference" (see Durbin 2021).

See Ecotubereview (2009). Reverend Billy also looked to discredit Starbucks as "Libertarian" and "Zionist." Former Starbucks CEO Howard Schultz has been targeted by pro-Palestinian activists for, in their estimation, tacitly supporting the Occupation (see Dolsten 2019). During the time I rehearsed with the group, it seemed that, while the Israeli Occupation of Palestine sometimes came up in the everyday discourse of the group, it did so much less frequently than other global social justice issues do and it was very rarely mentioned in Reverend Billy's sermons. Savitri D once explained to me that her father, who converted to Islam and whose relationship to Savitri D will be discussed in a later chapter, asked her why the group hasn't made more of the Occupation as an activist issue. She responded that she believed that governments learning to take their own violence against the planet seriously would necessarily create political openings for issues like the suffering of the Palestinian people.

After the eruption of new violence in Israel and Palestine in October 2023, however, several long-standing members of the group advertised and attended rallies organized by Jewish Voices for Peace. Post-Zionist and Anti-Zionist Jewish members of the group have communicated with sadness over the text listserv about how difficult it is to be fundamentally at odds with parents and grandparents around the politics of Occupation. Reverend Billy, Savitri D, and members of the Stop Shopping Church drove down to Washington, DC, to attend the mass rally on November 4, 2023, calling for an immediate ceasefire in Gaza. The Choir has also developed and performed a simple "Ceasefire Now!" chant.

In January 2024, the Stop Shopping Church participated along with the activist performance collective Bread and Puppet in an "Emergency Mass for Palestine."

27 Sidamo is a regional Ethiopian coffee. On the Ethiopian government's attempt "to control the value chain and to protect the names of its high-quality coffees," see Arslan and Reicher (2011). Simon (2011, 234) frames Starbucks' efforts to block this attempt as its pursuit of the "path of controlling words."
28 While making a "to do" out of an initiative to help the people of Rwanda recover from the aftermath of the horrific violence of the 1990s, in actual practice the company purchases its coffee not from cooperatives of small farmers, but, instead, from the plantations of local elites (Simon 2011, 216).
29 Starbucks regulars who might not have otherwise heard of them were introduced to artists such as Cuba's Buena Vista Social Club and Brazil's Sergio Mendes (Simon 2011, 151).
30 Starbucks went public in 1992. As it happens, this was also the year that Catherine Bell's *Ritual Theory, Ritual Practice* was published and two years after Judith Butler's *Gender Trouble* revolutionized left social theory.
31 Importantly for histories I address in the conclusion of this book, the historical roots for this conceptual framework, Lury suggests, can be found in "developments in computing" and the mechanized circuits of detection and response around which military and state surveillance are formed (2004, 9). Branding means to function as our consumerist operating system.
32 Performativity is often conjured forth scholarly readings that look to denaturalize gender and other kinds of cultural identity and is especially prominent in the methodologies of contemporary queer theory. As we will see, because it is pegged to capitalist "spacetime," the anthropologist Kath Weston finds it to be an ultimately conservative approach to the deconstruction of normative gender. In chapter 5, I analyze the performances of the Stop Shopping Church, which is an explicitly trans-inclusive community, in tandem with Weston's critiques of performativity. To signal what is to come: For the Stop Shoppers, the cadences of performativity, to the degree that they express and mirror those of consumption, would not be sufficiently radical to underwrite the aims of queer justice or trans-inclusion. Inclusion, for the group, is grounded in the ethics of intersubjectivity (what they call "living in community") rather than the mechanics of signification.
33 In their readings of performativity, Judith Butler and their readers borrow heavily from the linguistics of J. L. Austin (1962), John Searle (1969), and Jacques Derrida (1988, 1978), in addition to the psychology of Freud. Central to Butler's formulation of their account of performativity is a troubling of the analytical bifurcation of statements that are themselves kinds of actions (the wedding officiant's "I pronounce you married"), illocutionary speech acts, and statements that are descriptive ("the wedding cake is delicious"), or perlocutionary speech acts.

Butler theorizes that supposedly descriptive speech acts meant to suggest reality ("that is obviously a man"), as they accrue, reveal that they make it so. Focusing their analysis on the case of gender, they (Butler 2024, 281 n. 11) argue that what Austin considers illocutionary performatives "bring about the situation they name" (e.g., "you are now legally married") while perlocutionary performatives that supposedly simply name reality importantly lead "to a set of circumstances" (e.g., "as legally married persons you are entitled to these state benefits") and, as they accrue citational power, also enact and make so.

Butler's related interests in drag inform their theorization of gender performativity (1990, 1993). Revisiting those early analyses of drag and of drag ball culture in New York City, I am struck by how muted issues of capitalist intensification are in their discussions. As the first season of the recent hit television show, *Pose,* does a good job of capturing, the intersectional context for the emergence of drag ball culture is neoliberalism's birth pangs and the racialized and gendered inequalities it deepened through the cultural ascendancy of mediatized forms of conspicuous consumption.

Judith Butler's newer work on a pandemic phenomenology (2022) is their most materialist in a Marxist sense (they have even referred to it as an articulation of a Marxist ontology) but given that their iconic work on performativity has influenced a discourse that now far exceeds the scope of Butler's own writings, it still remains important to draw out the lacunae in her earlier, less Marxist work, in my view. Indeed, Butler (2024, 23) themself has recently intimated that the theory of gender performativity that they offered "nearly thirty-five years ago" should be reassessed and reevaluated in light of "trans and materialist criticisms."

34 Although subsequent social theory has sometimes taken issue with Butler's hyper-nominalist account of embodiment (see Cooper and McFall 2017), what is important to understand is that in Butler's account of gender performativity, bodies are signs whose acts and gestures reproduce norms of gender through their social accretion and, hence, constitute rather than simply express gender. Amy Hollywood (2006) rightly recognizes the limits of Butler's tendency to reduce bodies to signs but, in my view, misrecognizes the ways in which the somatic account of iterative processes Catherine Bell proposes mirrors the mechanics and logic of postindustrial consumption.

35 Celia Lury (2004, 13) understands logos as "markers of the *multiple temporalities* that characterize the global economy (Appadurai 1986). They are markers of the multiple logics of global forms."

36 Lury (2004) explains that brand interactivity implicates the brand form as a *cultural* rather than purely economic medium through which a sensuous rationality resists the reduction of value to issues of price alone. Brands organize the broader market in ways that far exceed the parameters of the classic model of capitalist economy, which assume the conceit of calculating self-interest and price valuation, rather than meaning and values, as the driver of capitalist economy. In Lury's account of the brand form, its "truth" is always reproduced through our iterative practices of consumption. Brands acquire a discursive objectivity that we can liken to regimes of truth, wherein social accretion (citationality) strengthens the force and authority of social norms.

37  If branding is ritualization and is grounded in the cadences of performativity, scholars with interests in religion do not just analyze and work with performativity; we have actually been ritualized by its consumerist logic. Even if the religious contexts we study are pre-capitalist or non-capitalist, our embodiment (language, institutionalized labor, field of vision, sense of time, values, and desires) as scholars disciplined and organized by capitalism is, by very definition, neither of these.

It is incumbent on historians and ethnographers who are guided by the concept of performativity to frame their analyses in terms of a pragmatic encounter between contexts, their own and that of their archive, rather than as a neutral uncovering of the semantic dimensions of their subject.

38  The philosophical anthropologist Michael Jackson (2018, 259) writes, "The same tension lies at the heart of anthropology and history, for while both disciplines have evolved sophisticated methods for understanding the lives of others at other times or in other places, all intellectuals possess preunderstandings and prejudices, born of the time and place from whence they came."

39  Cooper argues that neoliberalism's architects and institutions understood that it was politically necessary to domesticate the Fordist liberation movements of the 1960s. They did so, in part, by extending credit to antinormative consumers, including queer consumers.

This broadening of credit to the nonstandard risk was a disciplinary measure that privatized risk through family values and implicated performativity's constitutive tensions. Even though "the aspirational promise of credit" can seem "infinitely elastic" (2017, 162) (and, hence, what we might, linguistically speaking, call *deconstructive*), Cooper explains that credit-backed freedoms are always tenuous because as asset prices take a downward turn, creditors will "call in" their debts and "demand the immediate materialization of assets" (162). The burdens of debt also explain why visible queer organizing took a conservative turn toward the politics of marriage as households, including queer ones, have assumed responsibilities for the provision of welfare from the state. In the context of Cooper's reading, reducing performativity to the mechanics of signification alone distorts context. Performativity's freedoms (its constitutive "difference"), Cooper suggests, do not, in the end, escape the historical sameness of political economy. Language does not free-float above economy even if it is surely true that, as is also the case with other social institutions, our organization and experience of economy is always mediated by language.

40  On performativity and capitalist culture, see also Hennessy (2000).

41  On Michel Foucault's "odd neglect" of capitalist domination, see Brown (2015, 73).

42  Consumption's self-making capacities and effects and its powers of symbolic production and manipulation are, however, precisely the reason some queer organizing in the neoliberal period, for example, turned to consumer markets as technologies to affect social change (Chasain 2001). While Judith Butler (1997a, 148) offered up the activism of Queer Nation and its AIDS-era "die-ins" in the 1990s as exemplary of the kind of performative work of ritually resignifying social

norms that she finds politically encouraging, more recent feminist and queer scholarship has taken critical issue with Queer Nation's reduction of queer politics to the realm of consumption (see Hennessy 2000, 127–128); see also Berlant and Freeman 1993, 164). Though the important, life-saving work accomplished by queer organizing during the first decades of the AIDS epidemic can certainly not be underestimated, and the Stop Shopping Church place ACT UP within their own genealogy, for the Stop Shoppers, unlike Queer Nation, the goal always is to ritually *undo* rather than *resignify* capitalism and queer consumption. When the Stop Shopping Church shout, "We're here, We're Queer, We're not shopping!," as they did to start their Fall and Winter shows at Joe's Pub in 2019, they do so as a statement of their wholesale rejection of the politics of consumerist liberation, or what Jasbir Puar (2007) has called "homonationalism." They reject the notion that activism can only be accomplished from within the coordinates of consumer capitalism itself. For other important and relevant critiques of and from queer and feminist theory, see Cooper (2017) and Schulmann (2021).

In 2022, Disney publicly denounced Florida's Parents Rights in Education ("Don't Say Gay") law. The move was lauded by many, adding to its brand appeal, and also led to a consumer boycott by proponents of the law and the critics of "Woke" capitalism. Disney filed a First Amendment suit in Federal Court alleging that Governor Ron DeSantis had stripped the company of its "self-governing powers" in retaliation for its free political expression (see Burga 2023). In 2023, Bud Light received sharp criticism when a transgender influencer, Dylan Mulvaney, tweeted about her partnership with the brand. A conservative boycott ensued. For their part, LGBTQIA activists have been critical of what they consider a walking back of the brand's commitment to LGBTQIA rights (see Caruso 2023). In response to a similar conservative boycott and backlash, Target pulled pride merchandise from some of its stores, citing safety concerns. Target has also received criticism from LGBTQIA organizers for what they consider a pulling back of political support for queer issues (see Stewart 2023).

Social media, with its ability to harness citational power, has facilitated the conservative campaigns against brands that have exercised their own performative power to enter into the fray of the culture wars (see Hartmans and Musumeci 2023). These three cases of brand speech and political backlash in a networked age speak to the contemporary preeminence of brands in mediating cultural fissures and controversies and to the important political limitations of rainbow capitalism as queer activism.

43  Again, the Stop Shopping Church is strongly queer-and-trans-inclusive. As anarchists, however, Savitri D and Reverend Billy strongly resist the reduction of gender and sexual politics to consumerist terms.

44  Kati Curts (2015) argues that the industrial logic of the Fordist assembly line underwrote twentieth-century American secularism's religious futures.

45  Kath Weston (2002) offers that the cultural politics of consumer performativity is always much less liberating for poor lesbians, who simply don't have the cash

resources to mix and match gender through practices of commodity fetishism. On the erasure of poverty in mainstream queer organizing, see Maskovsky (2002).
46 Act II of this book explores the ways in which the Stop Shopping Church seeks to break these self-promulgating consumptive loops through performance.
47 The iconic green Starbucks cup with the mermaid logo has always been an ambulant vehicle for the branding of bodies and of space. However, more recently, the company has promoted a policy that allows customers to bring and use their own mugs and thermoses. Couched by Starbucks as an attempt to reduce waste, the practice has been panned as untenable by the company's newly organized national union, Starbucks Workers United. From an advertising perspective, a policy allowing personal drinkware to be brought into and used at the store further strengthens the bond between consumers' home worlds and Starbucks as a "third place" between home and work.
48 See Equalexchange (2008).
49 Experience is itself a linguistic event (see Scott 1991). By the same token, language is a human experience, meaning that it is lived out by creative, culturally knowledgeable human actors.

## CHAPTER 2. PRIVATIZING THE CONSUMER SOUL

1 On Ravi Ragir's case and settlement see Pinto (2022).
2 For example, Tom Kiefer (2019), a former janitor for US Customs and Border Patrol, published a photographic essay of objects seized and discarded by Border Patrol entitled *El Sueño Americano*.
3 In the American context, issues of subjectivity and racial capitalism cannot be divorced from the history of the Fourteenth Amendment, which was passed to protect the rights of formerly enslaved Black Americans but became the basis for the legal fiction of corporate personhood.

   To speak of the social body is to suggest that cosmographic hierarchies and relationships that are collectivized in place are also patterned within the microworlds of bodies existing together and ritually moving about in space and time, reinforcing and transgressing socially productive boundaries (see Zito 1997; see also Carrasco 2013). As we saw, Catherine Bell (1992) argues that ritualization allows subjects to experience the naturalization of distinctions that are, in fact, a kind of necessary artifice. The Stop Shopping Church intuited the importance of consumer bodily activity in the religious cosmography of neoliberal capitalism and importantly grounded this insight within the Protestant capitalism that naturalizes our own ostensibly secular North American social body, and which ritualizes relationships between both consumers and producers and human beings and the natural world. Contemporary branding is of strong ritual consequence precisely because it organizes asymmetrical relationships through embodied practices (see Lury 2004).
4 When I had the occasion to participate in the roll call as a performer with Choir, I generally called out Eleanor Bumper's name.

5 In Michel Foucault's later work (see Foucault 2007), governmentality refers to the ways in which the security and surveillance state classifies and calculates populations, thereby giving rise to new kinds of subjectivities.
6 On the central importance of consumption to American belonging and citizenship in the postwar period, see Cohen (2004).
7 Rose's analysis of contemporary governmentality extends to the workplace, the family, and the military.
8 While Freud's welcome reception by sexually permissive Greenwich Village bohemians is one important part of the story, Freud's ideas were also, by the 1920s, being interpreted and redeployed to promote state and corporate propaganda. Edward Bernays, Freud's nephew, applied Freudian principles to sell World War I on behalf of the US Committee of Public Information (CPI). Among his corporate clients was the United Fruit Company, which played a critical role in the 1954 CIA-led military coup of the democratically elected socialist government of Guatemala. In *Propaganda* (1928), his most famous tract on the engineering of consent, Bernays (2005, 37) suggests that propaganda is necessary to the essential functioning of democracy.
9 See Jackson Lears ([1981] 1994, 47–58).
10 Against the rationalist view that markets simply provide for existing social needs in the most efficient ways, the economist John Kenneth Galbraith ([1958] 2000, 22) argued in 1958 that markets create demand through advertising. If demand must be engineered, desire is clearly an economic category (*even if that is never all that it is*). Before Galbraith, in a 1925 speech before the Associated Advertising Clubs, Herbert Hoover had already lauded marketers for having "*taken over the job of creating desire*" (Taylor 2012, 12). Like the "self," desire is a conceptual crossroads at which religion and economy directly meet.
11 Unsurprisingly, critiques of Dichter's sampling method abounded given his racially and economically homogenous sample set, a testament to the ways in which psychoanalytic categories liquidate sociological categories in Dichter's work.
12 In *Beyond the Pleasure Principle*, Freud ([1920] 1990) explores the reasons why, through the machinations of the superego, we will sometimes forgo pleasure, defer gratification, or even endure pain. He suggests that in the interest of promoting future possibilities of pleasure (since the sex drive proves so basic), the reality principle modifies but does not replace the pleasure principle as it works to preserve the organism. The neurotic effects of the suppression of our pursuits of pleasure strongly interested Freud.

Dichter associates the reality principle with the rationalized account of consumer behavior that fails to consider consumer behavior in its full preconscious libidinality.
13 Adjusting for inflation, the per diem cost in 2023 dollars would be $4,943 and the cost of a full-blown study, almost $600,000.
14 Of consumer society as anthropological culture, Dichter ([1960] 2012, 41) writes, "Almost every day we go out and buy something. We do hundreds of things in our

daily lives which have meaning only because we are members of a special tribe, because we live in a special society and culture."

15  In Dichter's archive, everyday rituals run the gamut from the consumption of Westerns as morality plays to brushing one's teeth. These rituals organize time and organize experience. This midcentury marketing account of embodied activity in the making and remaking of collective organization and Dichter's focus on the psychic dimensions of what Kathryn Lofton (2017) indexes in terms of "consuming religion" and its practices of ritualization warrant a place in the genealogy of ritual.

While outside of the scope of this book, the task ahead for disciplines such as religious studies and cultural anthropology in the age of corporate culture, industrial chaplains, and military religion is to track the movement of disciplinary ideas and sentiments into non-academic institutional contexts by way of ambulant agents who have been ritualized by our fields but professionally settle elsewhere. This implies a return to issues of biography and the concrete operations of labor markets in addition to the genealogy of ideas.

16  In a letter to Dichter, Mead compared her own interests in the personified objects of the peoples of Samoa and New Guinea to Dichter's fascinations with the consumption of "the natives of New York" (Schwarzkopf and Gries 2010).

17  Bartel's (2021) excellent ethnography explores the ways in which financialization and deregulation in the contemporary Colombian context are reproduced at the level of aspiration and practice. On the internalization of economic cosmology see also González (2015).

18  Italics are mine.

19  In *Madness and Civilization* (1961), *The Birth of the Clinic* (1963), *The Order of Things* (1966), and the *Archaeology of Knowledge* (1969), Foucault's interests lay with the conceptions that constitute knowledge at different epistemic periods and the necessity of an archaeological method for unearthing and understanding them.

20  Butler makes it clear that they aim to distinguish their account from a romantic deployment of the "unconscious" as a primal force somehow existing outside of regulatory power. While I appreciate this move, I want to insist on the thoroughgoing *capitalization* of desire in historical terms. The Freudian unconscious was, *in the American context*, from the start imbricated in the history of capitalism.

21  Linking the Oedipal complex to the socializations of civilization, Freud also comes to argue that this adoption of the father's authority prepares us for our ambivalent identifications with social norms in the main ([1930] 2021).

The authority that scolds, disciplines, even berates from the outside is internalized as an aspect of the psychic self. In a consumer society, there is no doubt that this psychic power is enmeshed with the operations of capital.

22  Similarly, a putatively gay man will also have foreclosed heterosexual cathexes that destabilize the assumption that sexual identities are closed. To the case of

sexuality, we can add the messiness of racial and class histories and identifications wherein excess also can also unsettle social categories as they are actually lived.
23 Specifically, Butler turns to Freud's discussion of these in the *Ego and the Id* ([1989] 1923).
24 This is the case for Butler because we are haunted by desires we cannot know and objects of affection we never knew we "had" (never had). Butler's paradigmatic examples of psychic foreclosure revolve around the regulatory power (and its fissures) of their own society's regnant gender regime. They find critical power in the fact that gender is ultimately depthless and its accomplishment is never complete.
25 On the religious history of contemporary fitness brands, see Musselman (2023).
26 The norms that come to govern our psyches have everything to do with our socialization and where we are placed within social fields in the sense proposed by Pierre Bourdieu ([1979] 1984). Experiences of resocialization (such as those experienced by immigrants or the upwardly mobile) can alter the force and hold of specific norms but, as Judith Butler insists, subjective experiences of freedom are always fundamentally social.
27 For his part, in *Writing and Difference* (1978, 230), Jacques Derrida further radicalizes Freud's concept of the unconscious via the concept of the *trace* which, he writes, "is the erasure of selfhood, of one's own presence, and is constituted by the threat or anguish of its irremediable disappearance, of the disappearance of the disappearance."
28 Connecting the discussions in chapter 1 and chapter 2 of this book, what I mean to suggest is that, in order for consumer markets to grow, contemporary consumption capitalizes on the disquiet of the consumer self, for whom a perfect coincidence with the dictates of social norms is unobtainable and unsustainable but still drives much consumer activity, as a regulatory matter. In order for consumption to psychically work in this way, it needs to be flexible enough to accommodate the movement of difference, or what Catherine Bell refers to as "redemptive hegemony." Consumer performativity is in this way indebted to capitalism's metabolization of Freudian concepts.
29 Kevin Floyd (2009, 96) argues that Judith Butler's reading of Althusserian interpellation in chapter 4 of *The Psychic Life of Power* (1997a) untenably frames "labor without capital" despite Althusser's own Marxist designs. While a detailed analysis would be beyond the scope here, I believe that in their discussion of the intersubjective struggle between the lord and the bondsman, Butler reproduces a scene of consumption divorced from capital.

While I strongly admire Judith Butler's anti-capitalist work as a public intellectual (for example, their work with Occupy Wall Street), their written work on capitalism is uneven. For example, their famous worries about unnamed "neoconservative Marxists" whom they argued were intent on trivializing sexuality and queer critique as superstructural (1997b) seem, in retrospect, off the mark given the clear political ascendency, some twenty-seven years later, of queer homonationalisms (Puar 2007) rather than a sexually dour, orthodox Marxist left. Similarly, as she acknowledges the importance of the attention Butler brings to contingency and the messiness of social categories, Melinda Cooper also takes issue with Butler's queer deconstruction of class (2017, 159).

30  For their part, one hidden psychological motivation for mothers that incites consumption, Dichter surmised, is that they take pride in the growth of their children's bodies.

31  The popular idea that neoliberalism is grounded in the concept of the autonomous individual chooser is empirically false. Individuality might be sold as a virtue but, in a networked age, neoliberal social institutions are keenly aware of the affective mechanics of social imbrication. On the consumer end, a psychic disavowal of the interdependencies capitalism exploits is, in fact, ritualized. Rather than simply counterpose an abstract account of ontological sociality to the straw man of robust individuality, we must draw contrasts between *competing historical accounts of sociality*.

32  Walter Benjamin ([1921] 2005) offers that capitalism, as "a pure religious cult," is perhaps the first case of a "blaming" rather than "repenting" cult and hammers "guilt" into "consciousness."

33  The more our consumer souls are disquieted, the more money there is to be made. In 2017, American consumer spending was worth $15 trillion.

Rainbow capitalism, like all consumption, traffics in the logic of identity, which implies a strengthening rather than an undoing of regulatory mechanisms and regimes of sexuality and gender.

34  Savitri Durkee, Interview with the author, February 8, 2019.

35  For Reverend Billy and Savitri D, recalling early experiences with special places in the natural world, like a park, a forest, or a lake, can help adults reconnect with "the Earth."

36  Daniel Vaca (2023) reminds us that capitalism's commitments to efficiency have implied the routine sacrifice of possible ways of knowing and of being in the world to the ruthless discipline of normative economic logic. For its part, the Stop Shopping Church ritually refuses the transfiguration of loss into economic abstractions (e.g., talk of externalities, shareholder value, and growth).

37  Lauren Berlant (2011) has argued powerfully that neoliberalism depends on aspirations for the "good life" that, as effects of what she calls capitalism's "cruel optimism," become the affects of self-administered shackles.

38  Judith Butler's (2005) work on ethics, which foregrounds the responsibility we have for the social effects of our actions, could be concretized and made amenable to the activists' purposes.

39  We might hear in the activists' suggestion that persons are not separate from "nature" echoes of Bruno Latour's ([1991] 1993) influential suggestion that "hybrid" social systems (for example, biomedicine) and practices in the West (for example, the practice of pasteurization) or social problems (like global warming) blur and force recombinations of modern dichotomies such as

nature-culture and person-thing. More like Kath Weston (2017), I suggest in this book, the activists stress the ways in which our embodied intimacies with and within a world in which the natural world *acts* and technologies deconstruct the borders of the human cannot be considered without directly attending to the role of capitalism in dissolving conceptual borders as a consequence of its deterritorializing effects and its role in unevenly distributing the attendant and associated risks and costs to more precarious populations around the world, including communities of color, persons in the global South, the working poor, and women.

40 Scholarship in media studies and consumer society has noted striking similarities between brand management and Foucault's analyses of governmentality (Arvidsson 2006, 74) and consumerism and Foucault's account of ethics (Slater 2005, 5). The late American philosopher and historian, Mark Poster, has argued that the general coordinates of Foucault's thought are consonant with the priorities of the digital age because Foucault foregrounds the role of language in the "self-constitution" of the subject. Poster writes: "The individual wrestles with self-constitution through the manipulation of symbols, through carefully elaborated and systematized rules of formation, enunciative statements, and so forth" (1989, 68). In today's society, he explains, "Power is exercised through networks, and individuals do not simply circulate in those networks; they are in a position to both submit to and exercise this power [...] they are its relays [...] power passes through individuals. It is not applied to them" (2006, 37).

In our digital age, Poster explains that Foucault's approach is indispensable because it can help scholars "account for the line of new languages that stretches from body signals, grunts, spoken language, and writing to print, the telegraph, radio, film, television, computers and other new linguistic technologies" (2006, 110). In the end, then, Foucault's work is useful to the critique of capitalism, not because it denaturalizes the modern liberal construction of an autonomous, rational, and superintending "self" (a construction of subjectivity that is no longer economically "productive" or desirable to capitalism) but, rather, because it provides a fairly good description of the cultural form of contemporary institutions. Foucault is very much caught up in the "power" of his (and our) own time and, as such, can help map the epistemic context he, other scholars, and activists share.

On Foucault and neoliberalism, more generally, see Zamora (2016).

41 Theoretical frameworks are revisable pragmatic tools that should guide, not determine, social analysis.

42 As a phenomenological matter, we can say that social theory springs from scholars' active engagement with the world (see Jackson 1996). To this I want to add a more materialist twist: Given how power is structured and given how behavior is institutionally incentivized by the rule of capital, we will do well to assume that the going ideas of the bourgeois academe can easily reflect the interests of the ruling classes. In the end, as is also true of the activists, what ultimately matters for social change

is how we creatively respond, in turn, to our socialization by history. The politics of subversion and immanent critique can serve our critical purposes well.

43 Perhaps unsurprisingly, Judith Butler (2008, 111) makes the opposite suggestion regarding the relationship between theory and empiricism in her published conversation with Axel Honneth on the concept of reification.

## CHAPTER 3. CRUCIFYING MICKEY MOUSE TO SAVE THE EARTH

1 As a genealogical matter, the retail calendar is based on what Geeta Patel (2008) calls "secular-Christian" time.
2 William Talen (2023) has written on the cavernous New York City subway system as a "cruel psychic experiment" characterized by militarized surveillance, advertising glut, and racial terror. What he calls the "over-saturated sonic world" of the subway is an important aspect of this urban experiment.
3 Adorno and Horkheimer ([1944] 2002) famously associate Hollywood film with the rise of the culture industry and of a particularly American-style brand of magic: the statistically produced "incantations" of marketers.
4 Eventually, the group will drop the term "Hallelujah!" and substitute it with Earthalujah! Peacealujah!, Strangealujah! (and other riffs organically concocted to fit the occasion) that they believe are more consonant with their post-Christian constitution.
5 We must be careful not to reify the scene with the eager brushes of social criticism, however. As a counterpoint, see Paul Stoller (2002) for descriptions and analyses of the life of West African street vendors on the very city blocks upon which Reverend Billy preaches against the storytelling of multinational corporations. Even commodity practice and capitalist exchange are always vitally lived, as a phenomenological matter.
6 The Atlantic slave trade would become the apotheosis of these Enlightenment currents.
7 On the cultural privilege that attaches to and is reproduced by that which is religiously unmarked, see Oliphant (2021). The relative invisibility of masculine consumption reproduces heteronormative and patriarchal power.
8 According to Adorno (and his chief collaborator Max Horkheimer) our bureaucratization by the culture industry, what we call consumer culture today, so distorts our understanding of capitalism that popular culture is unable to provide for dialectical possibilities ([1947] 2002). For example, (in)famously, while he later walked some of his critiques back, Adorno ([1936] 1990) dismissed jazz as an expression of romantic capitalist rationality. In contrast, modern avant-garde art and music, he believed, preserved some autonomy from capitalism and could help audiences develop their capacities for the very kind of non-identity thinking that consumer culture looks to supplant with its closed meanings.
9 The Situationist International (1957–1971), a largely French collective of critics, artists, and writers, advocated for critical praxes that would expose the ideology of capitalism within the sphere of everyday life.

Talen's work finds common cause, here, with the anthropologies that trace out the social life of commodities. For example, see Appadurai (1986).

10  I am in this analysis strongly influenced by conversations and study with Davíd Carrasco, who insisted I read Pietz for my competency exams in graduate school. I remember my teacher trying to help me see that any object today that someone with the interests I have in critical theory would be tempted to consider in terms of "commodity fetishism" actually has a deep religious history of politically asymmetrical encounter. He also wanted me to understand that even the most mundane object can have multiple valences that might be finally irreconcilable and even somewhat inscrutable to the coordinates of social science.

11  A situationist tactic, *détournement*, refers to the fault lines in the ideology of the society of the spectacle brought into relief by critical praxis in the realm of everyday life.

12  At the level of cultural representation, Disney has also long been accused of perpetuating racism and misogyny through its strategic trafficking in racial, ethnic, and gender stereotypes.

13  However, Asad is oddly silent on the cultural arms of capitalism such as marketing and management. For it to work as ideology, neoliberal mathematization must be translated into the kind of corporate storytelling Reverend Billy takes aim at. Secular reason, as the Stop Shopping Church knows full well, is not only abstract and numerical; it is also highly somatic and affective.

14  In recent sermons, Reverend Billy counterposes "living in the question" and the green mysticism of the "Fabulous Unknown," on the one hand, to advertising's "neoliberal naming" and the measurements and quantitative predictabilities of Earth science, on the other. Our "measuring trap" is, he argues, human-centric and an expression of our fundamental habit of trying to control the Earth. See Reverend Billy and the Church of Stop Shopping (2023).

15  Talen's understanding of marketing as religion is reminiscent of Henri Lefebvre ([1947] 2008). Like the later Situationists he influenced, Lefebvre argues that both capitalism and religion accumulate human alienation and feed it back to consumers of "religious" (that is, organizing) media.

16  Although not all the members of the group share this affinity, William Talen identifies with the early twentieth-century artful anarchism of the Industrial Workers of the World (aka the Wobblies).

17  While this admonition might sound harsh, it should be noted that Talen and Savitri D position the workers and police officers who often stand in their way at actions as being like them in other shoes. As they sing in one of their songs, cops and bankers love their children, too.

18  This is the name of a catchy Culture Club song from childhood that came to my mind when writing these sentences.

19  On religion and negative dialectics, see Mendieta (2005).

20  William Talen, Interview with the author, June 11, 2019.

21  Reverend Billy does not talk very often in public about his childhood family, for reasons that will become clearer in chapter 4. Nevertheless, he does tell audiences how his father's constant job changes turned him into a wanderer. During a trip to Wisconsin and Minnesota, I also learned that Reverend Billy's mother, June, had fought a Walmart opening in their Northfield, Minnesota, hometown.
22  William Talen, Conversation with the author, November 11, 2018.
23  Paul Broussard, Interview with the author, March 18, 2020.
24  Shirley Williams, Interview with the author, March 11, 2018. In this, the Reverend Billy Project mirrors marketing strategies for mining authenticity from Black and brown bodies. In order for the tactic to not backfire, the life and the activism of the group have to sustain an ongoing interest in the actual needs of communities of color.
25  Paul Broussard, Interview with the author, March 18, 2020. Another long-standing Choir member relayed a story of the time when Reverend Billy's bombast and boisterous shtick landed horribly in Germany, where, he came to learn, the character had an unintended resonance with twentieth-century fascistic performance.
26  William Talen, Interview with the author, June 11, 2019.
27  William Talen, Interview with the author, June 11, 2019.
28  In fact, Reverend Billy met and married a gay couple at Burning Man who have gone on to become long-standing members of the group. Today, he admits that Burning Man, with its connections to Silicon Valley venture capital, is no longer an expression of the rebellious spirit he believes it once was. In my view, one can understand the yearly festival as an expression of the artistic appetites of neoliberal capitalism.
29  Savitri Durkee, Interview with the author, February 8, 2019.
30  For an extended treatment of this history, see Wenger (2009).
31  "Sheikh Abdullah Nooruddeen Durkee," *The Muslim 500*. https://themuslim500.com (Accessed June 3, 2022).
32  Byerly (1996).
33  On these historical relationships see Shepherd (2016, 68–75). In a future article, I will place the biography of the poet and entrepreneur, Gerd Stern, a friend of Stephen Durkee's, within the development of contemporary North American "post-secular" capitalism.
34  See Shepherd (2016, 70).
35  William H. Whyte's (1956) emotionally truncated "organizational man" is considered unproductive by contemporary creative and cultural labor. One of the corollary arguments of this book is that, today, ritualized as we are by a branded consumer capitalism that seeks to, in Catherine Bell's terms, produce ritual agents through the interaction of a body within a structured and structuring environment, affective and aesthetic antinomianism, in itself, is insufficient to the critique of capitalism.
36  This moment is described in Cobb (2018).

37 Savitri D veiled as a child and even as a young woman when she was with her father. On the group's listserv she has suggested that while the decision to veil is a very personal one made within a "religious framework," this was a source of some conflict with her father growing up. At a couple of the rehearsals I attended, one of Savitri's nieces who veils sang with the Choir. A comment that serves as a testament to the impossibility of fully extracting oneself, under present historical conditions, from the naming conventions and quantifying labels of the very consuming power that Reverend Billy condemns, the preacher remarked to me that Savitri's niece was the Choir's "first Hijab."
38 See "Lama Foundation," www.lamafoundation.org/ (Accessed June 3, 2022).
39 Savitri D's comment can also be usefully interpreted through the lens of Levinasian ethics.
40 Savitri Durkee, Interview with the author, February 8, 2019.
41 Jeremiah Drake, Interview with the author, April 12, 2019.
42 Talal Asad (2018) suggests that secular reason is inadequate to the task of creating a post-capitalist form of collective life able to avert climate catastrophe. As such, he is open to forms of embodied discipline that cultivate habits and dispositions that are not reducible to accounts of secularity and rational persuasion.
43 According to Savitri D, her basic spiritual values were taught to her by Native American lifeways (Savitri Durkee, Interview with the author, February 8, 2019). The anthropologist, Kath Weston, suggests that indigenous cultures less indebted to the rise of capitalism tend "not to value change or originality for its own sake, the better to sell them on" (2018, 195).
44 Paul Broussard, Interview with the author, March 18, 2020.
45 Paul Broussard, Interview with the author, March 18, 2020.
46 For a religious studies audience, the group works with a too untroubled ideal of a "natural" world that has not been despoiled by human activity. Our experience of "nature" is actually socially mediated and managed (Mitchell 2016). The group also feminizes nature. Some feminist scholarship asks whether and how the nature / culture binary is always and already gendered and, as such, can only but perpetuate essentialist gender hierarchies (e.g., see Donna Haraway 1991). According to Michael Jackson (2005), however, taking into account the lifeworlds of non-Western societies necessarily complicates the generalizability of this kind of critique. I briefly return to these issues in the conclusion.
47 William Talen, Interview with the author, June 11, 2019.
48 There are echoes in this of the discursive form of the "new management" of contemporary business (see González 2015). There are critical dangers to the degree that the group fails to acknowledge the emergent strategies of late-stage capitalism itself. I return, in a direct way, to these concerns in the conclusion.
49 This truism (*Der Mensch ist was er isst*) is attributed to the materialist philosopher of religion, Ludwig Feuerbach ([1863] 2020, X (5)).

## CHAPTER 4. BECOMING THE BELOVED COMMUNITY OF MUSICAL EARTH

1 On the complex and blurry relationships between music and sound, see Laack (2015). Both sound and music have proven essential to the ritualization of consumer capitalism.
2 King (2020).
3 Hanlon (2022).
4 The jingle featured in this commercial was especially memorable to me and my grammar school friends. "I'm a Pepper" TV Commercial (2008).

The most canned jingle can help us recollect deep-seated experiences, relationships, and feelings that have been buried under the furtive and fugitive psychic surfaces of time's accretions. Personal timbres are thusly woven into economic transformation, market segmentation, and technological revolution. Under the conditions of consumer capitalism, sentimental nostalgia can be powerfully political, in the end.

5 Since as the sociologist Tia DeNora (2000, 163) suggests, "music can be seen to get into subjectivity and action, then the issue of aesthetic control and its relationship to the constitution of agency is serious."
6 Spanish-language television at the time, like Spanish-language radio, was rife with easily memorized commercial jingles for personal injury lawyers, plastic surgeons, and car service agencies that would "drone sing" a phone number for consumers to call. These commercials became shared generational touchstones for Latino/a/x New Yorkers who grew up in the New York City metropolitan area at more or less the same time I did in the late 1970s and the 1980s.
7 Jean and John Comaroff (2001) have argued that, under neoliberalism, the ascendency of consumption as a driver of market economy and culture has implied the attendant ascendency of identity as a social marker.
8 As Martin Jay (2005, 343–348) analyzes it, Adorno's idea of "damaged life" has to do with both the commodification of experience and the growing impossibility, as a consequence, of narrating life stories that possess an internal continuity. According to Adorno, even the existentialists' and phenomenologists' attention to lived experience remained a reification. In terms of my own argument in this book, I mean to suggest that while it is certainly vital to the project of criticism to analyze how capitalist power transforms experience, we will want to avoid any prelapsarian account of "undamaged life." Capitalism's vulnerabilities are in its political and environmental effects, not its experiential poverty. The reality is that consumer culture serves as the foundation for intensities of affective experience, as Kathryn Lofton (2017) suggests. Adorno, I believe, is analytically blinded by his aesthetic and not just political disdain for "low culture."
9 This is to also say that, although academic work can prove vital to the fortunes of political possibility, politics cannot be reduced to the textual and ethnographic activities with which scholars are most engaged.

10 Saba Mahmood (2005) provides one of the most influential treatments of this quandary in religious studies. On secularism and the binary opposition of freedom and religion, see Jakobsen and Pellegrini (2008).
11 See Seigworth and Gregg (2010).
12 Or, for example, we might recall Scott Gac's (2007) history of the Baptist revivalist Hutchinson Family Singers' role in the development of the nineteenth-century protest song.
13 On the religious dimensions of twentieth-century African American aesthetics and literary movements, see Sorett (2016).
14 Carrasco's case study is the "Deadhead" subculture that has emerged around the music and mythology of the American rock band the Grateful Dead.
15 On the existential and political origins of hip-hop, see Tricia Rose (1994) and her follow-up treatment (2008) of the commercialization of hip-hop and the capitalist disciplining of the genre's critical potential.
16 The leading thinkers of the Frankfurt School questioned the possibilities for experience itself. See Jay (2005). Later poststructuralist theories radicalized the academic critique of experience by framing it as a linguistic event (Scott 1991) and by, in a Foucauldian sense, inverting the Kantian question and exploring the historical conditions that give rise to the possibilities for particular kinds of self-knowledge. However, there can be in certain academic circles a problematic tendency to confine critical reason to the work of scholars alone. This, in turn, can reproduce closed hermeneutic loops. A suggestion of the present book is that we do well as academics to spend time at field sites and in archives that are not as invested in the kinds of methodological and analytical questions that can preoccupy us. Indeed, as I have suggested, the Stop Shopping Church's non-academic critique of consumer ritualization brings into relief the ways in which some leading *academic* accounts of embodied subjectivity have been dangerously uncritical about their own relationship to the power of consuming religion.
17 For a now classic fusion of Marxist and psychoanalytic theory, see Marcuse ([1955] 1974).
18 On the critical limits of the cultural turn to visuality (especially at the expense of temporality), see Weston (2002).
19 Weber writes that music contains an "inescapable irrationality" that musical notation attempts to bypass or cover up. Both religious and musical rationalization cannot finally overcome what we might consider the penumbral borders and limits of experience.
20 Elayne Oliphant (2021) explores the ways in which cultural Catholicism continues to nostalgically confer explicit and implicit privileges under the guise of contemporary French secularism. Her study is a leading text in the growing subfield of religion and economy.
21 What Jackson refers to as the penumbral, suprarational dimensions of experience are precisely the aspects of embodiment that Celia Lury (2004) argues the brand form allows the market to better predict and control. This is why I will argue more

fully in chapter 5 that we must conceive of contemporary consumer culture in terms of "post-secular" capitalism.

22   Our concepts and ideals, like our re-membered pasts and our hoped-for futures, embed us as *beings-in-time*. As Michael Jackson (2018, 216) explains, while these touchstones participate in our subjectivity and must therefore be, by definition, intelligible to us, they are also importantly *not us*. It is precisely *through* their otherness, he adds, that our ownness becomes thinkable. This existential logic is at play in the aspirations of someone training to improve a skill (like a backhand), someone seeking to therapeutically redeem and overcome problems (by, say, taking Oprah's consumer advice), or in the fandom of devotees of celebrity icons who simultaneously exist as unreachable ideas and also come to hold the key to our very hearts (as we consume their transcendent meanings). Drenched and wrapped up in poetic association and metaphor, brand stories and their commodity goods and experiences, it must be admitted, are instruments of transformation. In understanding that commodities must engage the dialectics of self and other, thereby deepening our connections to ourselves, others, and the world, "post-secular" capitalism has developed a much more precise anthropological sense than Max Weber, as we will see, could have ever known to imagine.

23   Michael Jackson (2016, 186) makes this point about what he calls the "arts of life," which, for him, includes ritual, artistic, and religious technologies. To this list we can add consumer ritual as well.

24   According to Orsi, the practitioners of everyday religion do not simply parrot the authorized doctrines of religious elites. Nor do their improvised movements perfectly coincide with the abstractions of ritual instruction. In fact, since the strictures of religious elites can only ever serve as guides but never foolproof blueprints for living, religious actors are often deft in their abilities to outmaneuver religious officialdom in their creative responses to life's existential challenges.

25   If Feuerbach ([1841] 1989) insisted that religious alterity must be finally overcome by a philosophical humanism that recognizes religion to be enervating projection, Orsi understands the "gods" to be akin to real, living powers in the life of the devoted for whom they fundamentally matter.

26   I am alluding here to Theodor Adorno's (1966) account of negative dialectics, which refuses the final syntheses of Hegelian and Marxist dialectic and all conceptual thought, and, when applied ethnographically as Michael Jackson does (1998), reminds scholars to always mind the gap between word and world.

27   To be clear: "Consuming religion," if we are serious about attending to its sacred valences, ups the ante on the limits of ethnographic *epoché* (suspension of judgment). To limit ourselves as scholars to phenomenological questions regarding *What is?* would be to abrogate the goals of criticism in the face of consumer capitalism's role in global ecological catastrophe. I follow Bartel and Hulsether (2019) in their suggestion that the work of religious studies is not just to describe the world but, wherever possible, to assist in changing it. What needs to be avoided, however, is a game of essences in which "consuming religion" is found wanting

because it is "inauthentic." Unless one is explicitly working theologically, scholarly critiques of capitalism must be grounded in sociology, not metaphysics.

The questions that must be asked are pragmatic: *What are the effects of consumerism on individuals, communities, societies, and the planet, and how might scholars play their part in the critique of religion while doing justice to the prismatic irreducibility of religion?*

28  This is Karl Marx's ([1852] 1983) refrain in the "18th Brumaire of Louis Bonaparte."
29  All academic research involving human subjects, even ethnographies that present minimal risk to research subjects, must be approved by Institutional Review Boards (IRBs), which are university committees made up of faculty the core of which are expert researchers and whose review of research proposals is coordinated by specialized administrators. IRB committees are charged with making sure that research involving human subjects is performed in an ethical manner and look to protect the rights and welfare of human subjects, especially members of vulnerable populations. IRBs consider the conditions of all research involving human subjects, including the method and manner of data collection, how to keep and file research data, and how to protect the privacy and welfare of human subjects in publications that result from sponsored research.
30  I mean the related tendencies to confuse social struggle and discursive analysis, to disavow the "magic" in our own scholarly practices (see Weston 2018), and to enclose ourselves within closed, self-reinforcing hermeneutical circles.
31  Savitri Durkee, Interview with the author, February 8, 2019.
32  As we saw, American advertising has long appreciated the social imbrications of consumption.
33  Also see Cornel West (1989, 225) on Edward Said's indirect relationship to pragmatic thought.
34  Graeber stresses the artistic, creative ways in which human beings and communities resist power (including Marxist alienation) and engage in the convivial practices that human beings have engaged in across space and time. In short, anarchist struggle, for him, implies highlighting and participating in social action that is not reducible to systems of power.
35  While I was practicing with the Choir, the requirement for remaining in good standing as an active member was to attend three out of four monthly Sunday rehearsals.
36  Jeremiah left his position during the COVID-19 pandemic, when the group was forced to meet online. I have heard from other community members that one reason he did so was that it was increasingly difficult to practice music as a choir remotely and that he decided to move on for, at least in part, artistic reasons.
37  A small detail one might miss that is illustrative of Savitri D's unique role in maintaining the Stop Shopping Church community is this: When the group rehearsed at the Lower Eastside Girls Club in Manhattan, there was a glass door that needed to be opened from the inside whenever someone showed up for rehearsal. Savitri D tended to open the door for Choir members on a regular basis.

Reverend Billy would do so much less frequently. As in academic departments, one might wonder if what is at play, here, is the often uncredited and invisible labor women tend to perform in areas of social reproduction and what Rosemary Hennessy (2020) calls an "ecology of life-making."

38  This was part of the group's "Radical Ritual" events at the time. These actions were low-risk for arrest and stressed creative expression (like automatic writing) and the occupation of public space.

39  Savitri Durkee, Interview with the author, February 8, 2019.

40  Certainly, Savitri D's feminist politics are decidedly not libertarian. Since it is the case that consumption is generally coded as "feminine" in contemporary North Atlantic societies, some might be tempted to take on the defense of consumption as a feminist issue, lionizing consumption's patent privileging of desire, embodiment, and play. Instead, Savitri D's anarchistic sensibilities privilege all of these but refuse to peg them onto ecologically destructive forms of capitalist discipline.

41  This refusal to reify identity shares similarities with Michael Jackson's (2019) critique of identity thinking.

42  On the Covington High School controversy, see Mervosh and Rueb (2019).

43  Broussard hoped the Choir would continue to focus on recording polished albums and look to make their way onto television.

44  In other words, the Stop Shopping Church has often engaged in practices designed to resist their own professional reification.

45  There are performative resonances with the character of the holy fool in Orthodox Christian history. On this history see Ivanov (2010).

46  An amusing moment: I was on my way to an action with the group at the Statue of Liberty but had missed the ferry. Upon witnessing my frustrations, Reverend Billy noted that he had only ever seen me as an unflappable academic. I believe he thought my having let others see me sweat was a good thing.

47  While limit situations in which an actor feels uncertain and even torn (see Jaspers [1932] 1970) are facts of life, as such, we can run the risk of depoliticizing these experiences in societies structured by capitalism. For example, I have elsewhere described the ways in which sacralized experiences of worker displacement are marshaled by contemporary business management to its own end. See González (2012, 2015, 2016). The plight of workers figuring out how to reinvent themselves in the face of downsizing and competition by machines or that of young academic workers navigating a broken labor market in fields like religion, for example, cannot be reduced to issues of existential psychology and charged experiences with liminality.

48  David Graeber passed away unexpectedly in 2020. Savitri D was deeply involved in organizing the local New York City satellite event of a worldwide "Carnival 4 David" to live out his ideas and embody them rather than just passively remember his life of pleasurable, anarchist anti-capitalist activism.

49  According to David Graeber (2004, 71–72), it would not take academics too long to remember the realities of brute force ("a man with a big stick") that complement the forms of reversible, generative Foucauldian power academics are drawn

to were we to lose the institutional privileges, like ID cards, that shield us from less genteel mechanisms of exclusion and control that most of the world must contend with every day.

50 Like many academics, I have unfortunately too often sacrificed physical health to the sedimentary work we do.

51 On the importance of refusing a theoretical disappearance of working-class bodies in American religious history, see Orsi (2010).

52 Within ethnographic approaches to the study of religion, Michael Jackson's phenomenological anthropology stands as an important contemporary corrective to the tendency of much social theory to bifurcate soma and logos.

53 In their everyday language, the community stresses the personal uniqueness of human beings.

54 See Sprinkle et al. (2021) on "ecosex" practices and adopting the Earth as lover.

55 Savitri Durkee, Interview with the author, February 8, 2019.

56 I am alluding here to William James's ([1912], 1976, 35) concept of a "more" that outstrips conscious experience.

57 Micky, a basso who, not counting Savitri D, is one of two remaining singer activists who has been with Reverend Billy since the founding of the Stop Shopping Church at the turn of the century, taught me to watch for the ways in which my voice tends to go "under the note." In other words, I am often "flat."

58 The Stop Shopping Church has a board and a network of donors they must remain responsive to and continue to engage and inspire.

59 Tracy Fessenden (2018, 107) incorporates Kathryn Lofton's analysis of the ways in which in American cultural production the signifiers of the Black Church speak to "authenticity" and "struggle." Associations with "authenticity" are fetishized and circulated through advertising discourse. See Goldman and Papson (1996).

60 Recruitment at the Stop Shopping Church usually happens through word of mouth and comes from members' extant networks. Savitri D and Reverend Billy have the final word regarding who is invited to join the Choir.

61 The experiences of deaf communities should remind us that an inordinate privileging of aurality is not more inclusive than an inordinate privileging of visuality. My references to musical agency should not be understood too literally. I mean to stress the penumbral dimensions of experience, complexities I see very valued in the life and work of the Stop Shopping Church and which can also be indexed through poetic writing, for example.

62 For the hearing, music and sound are "felt," not just "heard."

63 The First Amendment, though, has been used, of course, to support corporate political speech.

64 Cornel West (2022) has suggested that white supremacy is "as American as apple pie."

65 "Rhythm is a ritual," Shirley once quipped.

66 For his part, very much expressing the rationalist conceits of his day, Hegel ([1807] 1977, 131) equated religious devotion with a lack of philosophical rigor and

expressed the dangers, as he understood them, in terms of "a musical thinking." Importantly, however, the *postindustrial* capitalist system that the Stop Shopping Church has spent the past quarter-century calling into question and looking to undo is by no means invested in the conceit of unmusical reason, as an anthropological matter. Judith Butler's (1997a, 47) reading of the *Phenomenology of Spirit* emphasizes Hegel's disavowal of the body as an instrument of reason.

67 The line is from the Robert Creeley poem, "The Plan is the Body."

68 Bethany Moreton details the ways in which, in the early 1990s, the Walton International Scholarship Program, which sponsored scholarship students from Central America to study in places like Bentonville, Arkansas, created transnational networks that were made possible not simply by the sheer intellectual force of the new economic orthodoxy but by more fully human and embodied activities such as shared Evangelical worship. The ideological loyalty won "singing in chapel" is, Moreton suggests, one of the "quiet backstories of free trade in the Americas."

69 Reverend Billy rattled off to me a list of some of the temporary and long-term couples who had met through the Choir, including two, one same-sex and the other not, that he had married.

70 We might wonder whether the un-avowed specter of Golden Rule Christianity haunts Reverend Billy's account of loving service, even if, like Feuerbach, the group does not think the responsibility to love and meet others in a stance of critical nonviolence requires godly sanction or that it has its necessary origins in any kind of godly condescension. On "Golden Rule Christianity" see Ammerman (1997). Even if she and Reverend Billy cannot themselves keep from grappling with American religious power in their work, Savitri D once recounted to me how pleased they were when their then grammar school–aged daughter referred to the Cross as "Jesus's stand."

71 The term is Henri Bergson's ([1907] 1998) and marks the vital and finally inscrutable force that drives and organizes life.

72 More than once during the course of my fieldwork, I found myself remembering Cornel West discuss the importance of the dance party on the beleaguered Zion, the last human city, in the film, *The Matrix Reloaded* (2003). Much like it is for the citizens of Zion, the struggle for justice, the Stop Shopping Church suggests, should be tactile and pleasurable by very definition.

73 The Guardian Angels, hardly associated with left-wing New York City politics, was founded by Curtis Sliwa in 1979 to support citizen-led, anti-crime activities like street patrols. Charges of racism and vigilantism have dogged the group since its inception.

74 See Westboro Baptist Church. www.splcenter.org (Accessed June 2, 2022).

75 In order to gain access to power around drug trials and treatments, important currents of ACT UP relied on an "insider" strategy that leveraged cultural capital and class privilege. This, in turn, deepened internal racial and class divisions within ACT UP and also helped mainstream visible gay politics as a whole. See Schulman (2021).

76  According to their Facebook page, "the NYC (dis)Order of Sisters was founded during the famous ACT UP 'Stop the Church' direct action demonstration at Saint Patrick's Cathedral in 1989." www.facebook.com/nycsisters/.

77  After his Marxist turn, Jean-Paul Sartre (1968, 174) proposes that the "questioner, the question, and the questioned are one." If experiences of loss are, as I have argued, central to our experiences of capitalism and under capitalism, this is just as true for academics as it is for artists and activists. Lucia Hulsether (2023, xiii) grounds her study's endless meditation on the losses which comprise neoliberalism's "architecture of everyday life" in a personal story of her brother's suicide and victimization by a service economy that had sold them "the barest physical subsistence at the cost of your incandescent perception."

78  In this vein, the ethnographer is also always caught up in the webs of associations of fieldwork subjects.

79  To be clear: My argument in this book is not that performativity, as a concept, fails to capture something central about the mechanics of signification but, rather, that the fact that many scholars have performativity on the collective mind is related to shifts in technology and the organization of neoliberal capitalism. *Performativity jumps out to us in part due to its heightened importance in a digital age.*

80  On "left" spirituality and the exclusionary politics of enlightened capitalism, see Martin (2014). On the case of business management and corporate culture, in particular, see LoRusso (2017) and González (2015). On the uses and abuses of social gospel and liberation theology within neoliberal institution-building, see Hulsether (2023).

81  According to Jan Rehman (2015, 113), Weber believed that the entrepreneur was uniquely able to resist their own bureaucratization. Contemporary efforts to teach and sell enlightened entrepreneurship at storied centers for religious studies like Harvard Divinity School redouble this evocation of entrepreneurship as a site of spiritual potential.

82  Savitri D has suggested to me that even though she and Reverend Billy lack the security and benefits that can accompany other kinds of work, they have a privileged quality of life because they are able to focus on labors of love and live off the clock. She also credits their landlady for making it possible for them to afford their Brooklyn rent.

83  Festivals can pay the group, which Savitri and Reverend Billy divide among the singers. The group also receives donations (including monthly donations) through the virtual platform Patreon, which allows content creators to receive payment and donations through digital subscriptions.

84  Savitri D once remarked over the Choir text thread that she has had enough religious ecumenicism to last a lifetime. I assumed that she was speaking, at least in part, of her family's experiences at the Lama Foundation.

85  Members' outside political affiliations with groups like the Democratic Socialists of American (DSA) can sometimes come up in the meetings that follow rehearsal or in the group's internal text and email exchanges, but the borders between activist community and political party associations are generally respected.

86  Strong levels of participation at monthly rehearsals and actions generally elevates standing within the community (although talent and experience can sometimes override commitment when invitations are made regarding participation in major public performances, especially those outside of New York City). Sometimes members who struggle to keep up with the time commitment due to childcare responsibilities and/or work try to reassure the community of their interest by presenting excuses over the text listserv and by publicly affirming the importance of the group to their lives.

87  For example, members have been asked to leave because they proved homophobic or because Reverend Billy and / or Savitri D thought they were somehow undermining their authority or the community's mission.

88  As the conclusion will make clearer, future research within religious studies on the Stop Shopping Church might track whether or not the community develops robustly into the kind of "secular congregation" that is increasingly of interest to sociologists of religion (e.g., see Frost 2024). While I have argued that the Stop Shopping Church functions as a religious community (in a Durkheimian sense) that does activist battle with the forces of religious capitalism, it remains to be seen how the community itself might settle into an explicit understanding of itself as a religion. At the present moment of the community there is a concerted effort to skirt the borders between art and religion, and the adjective "religion" or "religious" is not one that the Stop Shoppers generally embrace without some creative tension. Reverend Billy still hedges his bets by calling the Church of Stop Shopping a "post-religious" religious community. It seems important to him, Savitri D, and some of the members of the group to simultaneously conjure forth and maintain some distance from "religion."

89  In the summer of 2019, the Choir hosted a reunion in which it invited past members to come and sing old songs during Sunday rehearsal. A prominent ex-member from the *What Would Jesus Buy?* and Occupy Wall Street days whom others have described to me as a "former protégé" who left the group on difficult terms attended the reunion. During the community dialogue, she publicly doubled-down on the importance of her charting her own course as an artist and did not hug Reverend Billy and Savitri D, as other returning members did. The tension between the three was palpable.

90  Michel Foucault ([1966] 1994, xviii), writing in his archeological phase, describes heterotopias as sociocultural spaces that press up against, disturb, and unsettle dominant social grammar.

91  Durkheim's thought, which is itself grounded in its own particular genealogy (Nielson 1999) and is, thus, amenable to historicization, has a tendency to collapse the existential and the social into a singular field. I agree with Kathryn Lofton (2017) that the religious hold of consumer culture on society is so pervasive that it is constitutive. In this vein, I argued in chapter 1 that Judith Butler's account of *subjectivization* strongly applies to the case of consumer ritualization. As an ethnographer, however, I am strongly committed to the practice of empirically

exposing and analytically exploiting the unbridgeable gaps between official discourse and lived experience.
92  For Julia Kristeva ([1974], 1984), the semiotic refers to the pre-logical, sound effects that words have before they are endowed with meaning. The semiotic is potentially disruptive of language's thetic, that is, "thesis-making," capacities.
93  For a brilliant study of the religious horizons of Hughes's ostensibly "secular" writing, see Best (2017). The Chicano biblical studies professor Roberto Mata reminded me in a talk I heard him deliver in 2023 that Walt Whitman also supported American manifest destiny to Mexican territory and did so in explicitly racist terms, remarking upon Mexico's "superstition" and framing it, along with its Latin American neighbors, as "weak and imbecile."
94  In my view, Jacques Derrida (1993) was very right to call for an ethics that accounts for the needs of those still to come.
95  The Stop Shopping Church greatly values the ethical and political value of spaces of "radical instability." At first blush, this commitment bears a strong resemblance to Derridian deconstruction. However, as Kenneth Surin (2009, 167) puts it, within the Derridian system, "there is no way of (actually) inserting the subject into the domain of the political." Given its textual emphasis, Derridian deconstruction would not be the Stop Shopping Church's most obvious theoretical traveling companion.
96  Savitri Durkee, Interview with the author, February 8, 2019.
97  Jeremiah Drake, Interview with the author, April 12, 2019.
98  Robert Orsi (2005, 9) suggests the metaphor of braiding as a correction to modernity's penchant for neat, linear, progressive historical narratives in which a clearly demarcated "past" is superseded and transcended by the "present." Orsi's is an important reminder that even more contemporary methodological talk of *episteme* or the performative accretion of emergent meaning must remain attentive to the supposed "pasts" that never actually leave us.
99  Jeremiah Drake, Interview with the author, April 12, 2019.
100  Methodists in New Directions. www.mindny.org/ (Accessed June 3, 2022).
101  Jeremiah recounted a diverse religious biography. For example, in addition to his experiences in the United Methodist Church, he explained that his ex-boyfriend is a Rabbi with whom he enjoyed keeping a Kosher home and that he had considered converting to Judaism.
   Jeremiah Drake, Interview with the author, April 12, 2019.
102  See especially Carrette and King (2004) and Lofton (2011).
103  Jeremiah Drake, Interview with the author, April 12, 2019.
104  Jeremiah Drake, Interview with the author, April 12, 2019.
105  For example, Tracy Fessenden's (2018) brilliant study of the great jazz and blues singer Billie Holiday presents her performances as a vocalist as anything but rote.
106  According to the pragmatic philosopher Cornel West (1989, 225), Michel Foucault's interventions, while indispensable, also had the effect of trapping human

agents within the closed loops of "anonymous and autonomous discourses, disciplines, and techniques."

107  This concept of existential transcendence should not be confused with the overcoming of capital or other organizing structures like gender and race. The everyday cadences of creative living and human survival within conditions of dispossession, deprivation, and injustice will not, in and of themselves, overturn the rule of capital or its socially and ecologically destructive systems. However, the political transcending of those structures will require the coordinated and collective human action of persons who know how to live to see another day (see Sartre [1957] 1960).

108  The never-ending "war on terror" has only heightened this predictive dimension of governmentality in the first decades of the twenty-first century.

109  As her alter ego, Lady Fortuna, Shirley often wore a bright red wig at actions, making her one of the most visible members of the group. A brilliant performance artist in her own right, she has, at least for now, left the Choir to return home to Texas to care for her elderly mother and to focus on her own political and performance art projects.

110  We might well think of Reverend Billy and Savitri D as being structured by the same *habitus* in the sense Pierre Bourdieu ([1972] 1977) uses the term. Bourdieu's framing, however, can tell us little about the chance encounters that also bring people together.

111  I experienced the attractions of a concept like fate when I unexpectedly ran into Judith Butler in November 2023 on a New York City sidewalk on my way from campus to my commuter train at Penn Station. I had never met them in person, and they had no idea who I was. Statistical probability felt more like mystery when I pondered all the minute decisions (e.g., when I left the building, how quickly I walked) that I needed to have made in order to surreptitiously run into one particularly iconic person (with whose thought I had spent so much time!) in a city of over eight million.

112  Paul Broussard explained that his departure from the group as the salaried choir director was not by choice and initially proved very painful. Recently, however, he has attended virtual reunions of the Stop Shopping Church and often promotes *What Would Jesus Buy?* on his social media feeds. In early 2023, he starred in a vaudeville show, giving voice to the music of singers and songwriters from the Harlem Renaissance who are today being spotlighted by queer historiography.

113  This approach follows Michael Jackson (1998, 3), who has long argued that the situations and social relationships of everyday life necessarily expose the incompleteness of analytical categories, although my particular interests in the interstices between history and biography are also indebted to C. W. Mills's ([1959] 2000) account of the "sociological imagination" and his more Weberian influence. In my interests in the practical dialectics of history, I am also strongly influenced by Jean-Paul Sartre's existential Marxism, Robert Orsi's work on lived religion,

278 | NOTES

Davíd Carrasco's borderlands hermeneutic, American pragmatism, and am influenced but also productively challenged by Michel Foucault's archeology.

## CHAPTER 5. PERFORMING THE SHOPOCALYPSE IN THE AGE OF POST-SECULAR CAPITALISM

1   Reverend Billy and the Stop Shopping Choir (2007). "What Would Jesus Buy?" YouTube. Video, 1:31:07. www.youtube.com/watch?v=mAxuNdtZt7c.
2   Another way of outlining the stakes is to ask whether Weber fully appreciated the ways in which the penumbral realms of psychic attachment and immersive aesthetic experience could be channeled into and made useful to the efficiencies of capitalist, instrumental reason. Daniel Vaca (2023) explains that "efficiency ideology," which has its roots in the Progressive era but has a strong afterlife under contemporary conditions, produces distinctions that deem some priorities, practices, and people as wasteful and beyond the pale of the system. Did Weber finally understand emotions and values as external to capitalist efficiency, or did he have a clear sense and conviction that the imponderable was amenable to efficient management by capitalism? And if he did, did he jettison the masculinist idea that "economic man" himself is quintessentially rational?
3   According to David Graeber (2011), the concept of debt emerges in the Axial Age (800 BCE–600 CE) out of cosmological and moral considerations but, once it becomes "economic" and subsumed by systems of coinage, comes into abstract form and severs social relations.
4   Reverend Billy and the Stop Shopping Choir (2011).
5   As I discuss more fully in the conclusion, the cybernetic form of flexible and creative neoliberal discipline is still latently mechanical. It is the case, however, that society's most precarious workers, such as the people who work the line at a meat processing plant or fire up burgers and fries at fast food chains, are often not even afforded the niceties of romantic appeal.
6   The slippages between existential and economic concepts of "choice" can allow capitalist choice to assume an ontological status in a consumer society.
7   These private experiences are not just individual but also always mediated by communal and family memories, attachments, and responsibilities.
8   See Lakoff and Turner (1989) for an analysis of our poetic reason that is grounded in cognitive linguistics.
9   An example of consumer subversions of meaning that strengthened brand capital, in the end, would be the appropriation and resignification of Tommy Hilfiger's original preppy apparel by young, urban consumers of color in the 1980s and 1990s. While the designer himself originally balked at the urbanization of his apparel in ways that conveyed and expressed racist undertones, once the Tommy Hilfiger brand realized the amount of profit it could make from this turn of events, it came to think of it as an "opportunity." The political limits of brand representation are clear.
10  According to a long-standing member of the group who has been with the Stop Shopping Choir since the millennium, police can find it more difficult to arrest singers who are singing beautifully.

11  The *NYU Revealer* published an excellent special edition on religion and fashion. For an introduction to that edition of the web magazine, see Krutzsch (2020).
12  Miranda Priestly makes this point in the David Frankel film *The Devil Wears Prada* (2006) when Andrea Sachs naïvely suggests that her own proud apathy with respect to high fashion is an indication of how little she has been influenced by the standards and tastes of the fashion industry.
13  As Fredric Jameson (1991) explains, late-stage capitalism is itself characterized by the prominence of the pure image, unmoored from the semiotic pull of the thing signified.

Adorno and Horkheimer ([1944] 2002) argue that the statistically produced "incantations" of marketers allow them to "magically" instrumentalize and manipulate meaning.
14  On the practice of self-immolation within the context of Buddhist philosophy and the concept of Bodhisatvva vows, see Benn (2013). It is clear from David Buckel's note that he understood his own self-immolation as an act of protest and a consequence of his desire to serve others by bringing attention to climate inaction.
15  Similarly, as Savitri D and Reverend Billy like to point out, ecological destruction also occurs any time we use neonicotinoid pesticides to tend to our gardens.
16  As Naomi Klein (2014, 176) reminds us, Jean-Paul Sartre, after his Marxist turn, referred to fossil fuels as "capital bequeathed to mankind by other living beings."
17  For a classic study of our denial of death, see Becker ([1973] 1997).
18  On Jeff Bezos's phallic space rocket, see Dessem (2021). We might also consider, here, Elon Musk's stated desire to colonize Mars (see Torchinsky 2022).
19  In June 2023, Savitri D and Reverend Billy expressed how happy they were with the decision of the British museum system to cut ties with British Petroleum. Reverend Billy called it a hard-earned activist victory.
20  According to the ritual theorist Ronald Grimes (2011), *acting* is the genus to which different species of action such as ritual, sport, dance, music, and (dramaturgical) performance are all related. Grimes is critical of performance theory's tendency to collapse these separate domains into an account of scripted and coordinated action in the presence of others. Grimes also importantly concedes that performance, like ritual, is a non-necessary historically embedded and mediated classificatory term. In the conclusion, I will suggest that performance is as historically embedded as branding and performativity and is, in fact, their historical kissing cousin.

In this book, I pragmatically turn to performance to make sense of the social action of the Stop Shopping Church for the following reasons. First, while Reverend Billy and Savitri D sometimes speak of what they do in terms of radical ritual, more often than not they speak of what they do in terms of performance. As a phenomenological matter, it makes sense to work with concepts that are already empirically extant in the fieldwork. Second, Schechner (1977) argues that performances exist along a continuum that can either stress entertainment (e.g., like a night out at the theater) or efficacy (e.g., like a ritual cleansing).

From the start, the Stop Shopping Church has insisted that political efficacy is dependent on imaginatively compelling social action. Performance theory's capaciousness does relative justice to the group's ritualized singing and dancing activism and political vaudeville. In chapter 1, I argued that this impulse to inhabit the space between art and activism mirrors the mechanics of branding, in which aesthetic power is illocutionary and does capital's bidding through semiotic means. In this sense, performance, as a potentially subversive reflection and redirection of the very problem the group means to address, captures something important about the ways in which neoliberal consumption blends enjoyment, even entertainment, and world-making. No doubt, corporate television news media is an obvious example of this kind of synesthetic brew.

The intervention of the present book is not to directly involve itself in a full-scale genealogy of social action. Its argument is grounded in ethnography and is necessarily delimited by that encounter. Instead, I have suggested that the Stop Shopping Church has long turned to performance to mime and resist the power of consumerism, which they understand in ways that are strongly evocative of the ways in which religion scholars of the past thirty-plus years understand and deploy ritualization and performativity to analyze religious phenomena. My argument has been that while the Stop Shopping Church understood, from the start, consumerism in religious terms, religion scholars have, until relatively recently, misrecognized the ways in which consumption (to which I add the specific layer of branding) is everything many of us claim religious ritualization to be and that this, of course, is not surprising and makes full epistemic sense since the cultural production of academics does not escape the forces of religious collectivization and capitalization.

21 According to the performance theorist Erika Fischer-Lichte "a performance is any event in which all the participants find themselves in the same place at the same time, partaking in a prescribed set of activities" (Shepherd 2016, 206).

22 For a thorough genealogy of performance studies, see Shepherd (2016).

23 Performance studies scholars sometimes make room for everyday processes of rehearsal as a type of performance. On Richard Schechner's view on the matter, see Shepherd (2016, 155).

24 Shepherd (2016, 89) adds, "the creation of the possible, of the unforeseen, aleatory, and playful may be said to be one of the bases of performance."

25 On my first day of rehearsal, Jane, who refers to herself as a middle-aged suburban mom from New Jersey who never imagined she'd end up a long-standing member of a grassroots anarchist performance community full of New York City creatives, gave me a golden toad pin that was left over from those earlier actions.

26 Secular society is still suffused with what Roy Rappaport (1999) calls "liturgical orders."

27 One way to understand why Savitri D and Reverend Billy insist on leaving a gift for Chase Bank is that, like David Graeber (2001), they understand gifts as emblems and tokens of social relations that might serve as a contrast to the

commodity coin, which dissolves social relations and social action into the mystification of the thing itself. Their performative gifting to a bank upends the commodity chain of financialized futures.
28  On the subjunctive mood of ritual, see Seligman et al. (2008).
29  On "An Anthropology Otherwise," see Raschig and McTighe (2019). Society for Cultural Anthropology. https://culanth.org.
30  *Zweckrationalität* is Max Weber's term for industrial capitalism's value-neutral, procedural, and affectless rationality.
31  Non-Fungible Tokens (NFT) are a form of digitized financial security that contain unique identifying codes. They have entered the public consciousness especially around the selling of digital art. Their uniqueness, which embeds scarcity in the "thing," can be understood, I think, as an expression of societal exhaustion with the sameness in difference of traditional commodity production and consumption. In late 2022, former US president Donald Trump announced an online store selling $99 digital trading cards depicting him in the likeness of a pantheon of superheroes (Bender and Haberman 2022).
32  On the Gamestock scandal that "upended Wall Street," see Thorbecke (2021).
33  This approach is reminiscent of Davíd Carrasco's (2019, 118) understanding of Toni Morrison's literary imagination.
34  These days, Reverend Billy sometimes does solo performances in places like Times Square that are decidedly more absurdist than the performances of the Choir. For example, he has writhed dramatically on the ground in a plastic bag to bring attention to the ways in which these plastics pollute the seas and pose grave dangers to marine fauna.
35  Savitri D served as a "class rep" for a lawsuit filed by activists victimized by police violence during the Black Lives Matter protests in Mott Haven, Bronx, in 2020. As a result of that lawsuit, which settled for $13 million, each of 1,300 mostly Brown and Black young protestors and activists that were manhandled will receive $10,000. Savitri D was interviewed about the case and her role (see Tarleton 2023). With characteristic political soberness, she assesses the situation this way: "The settlement doesn't address the injustice but it does address our right to protest the injustice."
36  An excellent example of cultural anthropology's ability to introduce readers to the sensuous dimensions of diverse lifeways is Keith Basso's (1996) study of the Apache people.
37  The retirement of a parodic Christian collar speaks to Reverend Billy's transformation into a "sincere" post-religious preacher.
38  In other words, despite their posthuman aspirations, the performance theory and praxis of the group does not disavow "its (own) humanist subjectivity of the human" in the ways some posthumanist scholars can assume that methodology itself is somehow capable of overcoming scholarly anthropomorphism (Weston 2017, 30).
39  *Parousia* is the Christian theological term of Greek provenance, for the second coming of Christ.

282 | NOTES

40 Central Park was also the location of a recent act of spatial resignification performed by the Choir. Following the murder of Jordan Neely, an African American street performer in a New York City subway, by a white train passenger who felt threatened by Neely's request for food and water, the group put up an official-looking "Jordan Neely Memorial Grove" sign in the park. The act also speaks to the importance of memorialization in the politics of the group. Reverend Billy has forcefully and powerfully written on Neely's murder (Talen 2023).
41 As an ethnographer, primarily though not exclusively, I am most interested in the ways historical genealogies can, as lived, converge to reproduce the epistemic authority of a cultural dominant.
42 While he does not dispute the Christian genealogy of secularism, Talal Asad (2018) problematizes the idea of an "essential continuity" between Christianity and secularism.
43 While subsequent queer historiography has exhorted readers not to overestimate the role the situation played in the Stonewall riot, Martin Duberman's (1994) social history of the Stonewall uprising suggests that the loss and funeral of queer icon Judy Garland, played an affective role in igniting passions of resistance in the trans-activist Sylvia Rivera on the night of the riot.
44 Behind these actions stand the activist influences of ACT UP's political funerals. For a recent treatment of religion, race, and the politics of martyrdom in queer memorialization, see Krutzsch (2019).

In the summer of 2023, members of the Choir dressed for a wake and went to the US District Court in Manhattan to wail and mourn the Supreme Court's obliteration of affirmative action in college admissions (*Students for Fair Admissions, Inc. v. President and Fellows of Harvard College* and *Students for Fair Admissions, Inc. v. University of North Carolina*), its rolling back of the authority of the federal government to regulate and protect wetlands under the Clean Water Act (*Sackett v. Environmental Protection Agency et al.*), its limiting of LGBTQIA protections in the name of religious freedom (*303 Creative LLC v. Elenis*), and its overturning of *Roe v. Wade* and the constitutionally guaranteed right to an abortion (*Dobbs v. Jackson Women's Health Organization*), among others.

CONCLUSION

1 A wealthy friend of the community loaned the space to the Stop Shopping Church rent-free for a year and a half.
2 In early 2023, the sign was changed to read "Earth Chxrch," and that has become how Savitri D addresses it in emails and communications.

Earth Chxrch, which the community spoke of as an experiment between performance and (religious) service, originally ran for sixty-nine Sundays. Its first run ended on July 30, 2023, when they lost access to the space. In his sermon at the time, Reverend Billy vowed that the experiment was only the beginning. To commemorate the moment, the Choir held a prayer circle, which some members greatly appreciated, while others felt anxious about it. Some members confessed that they are made uneasy by anything that so clearly evokes the form of organized religious worship. To other, more latently mystical members of the Choir, too formal a liturgical prescription threatens to suffocate precisely that which they hold sacred. For them, the tension had everything to do with the paradox Reverend Billy pointed out in his sermon: "Worshipping the Fabulous Unknown" poses a conundrum because worship demands pointing out what also cannot be named. In any event, it is important to note how far removed the Stop Shopping Church is today from the secularly safe parody of religion. For her part, Shirley Williams came as a visitor and in her own short performance spoke of the need to consider the Anthropocene the *Plantationocene*, since extraction and the exploitation of the natural world are based in histories and systems of racial capitalism.

In December 2023, it was announced that the community would be able to remain in the space at what Savitri D described to me as a "greatly reduced price," and weekly Earth Chxrch services resumed. In June 2024, however, it was announced that the group would lose access to the space in October 2024, when a retail cannabis store is scheduled to assume the lease.

3   Separately from the Stop Shopping Choir, Judd, who has called himself a "harborsexual artist," has designed an interactive public performance in which icons of marine life are constructed from single-use plastics collected from New York harbor. The intent is to draw attention to the ecological crisis of the plastics pollution of the oceans, to "acknowledge our non-human neighbors," and to ritualize participants to see themselves as being "part of the harbor."
4   The daily Google Doodle ran a very similar Doodle of Marsha P. Johnson decked out in a crown of flowers to celebrate queer liberation two days after the parade and the group's iconic display. There was talk of Google lifting the concept and its aesthetic from the Stop Shoppers' papier mâché icon.
5   In recent sermons, Reverend Billy is keen to suggest that the "Earth is the only celebrity that matters."
6   The neighborhood, which has been strongly pressured by the forces of gentrification since the 1990s, has been traditionally Puerto Rican and working class.
7   Importantly, as I have already suggested, political ecology, for the Stop Shopping Church, necessarily includes issues of social violence and human need. For example, since late 2023, Earth Chxrch has housed and run a "free store for newly arrived immigrants," which Savitri D has called an experiment in "mutual aid."
8   Tellingly, given the overall argument of this book, Taylor, a religion scholar, almost fully omits capitalism from his analysis. The term does not appear in the book's index.
9   In his Eucharistic theology, the Swiss Reformer Ulrich Zwingli (1484–1531) argues that the Eucharist wafer is a sign of the holy body of Christ, not the body of Christ itself, and considers the act of communion an expression of allegiance to the cause of Christ and membership in his church body.

10  A short film, *Earth Riot,* musically chronicles the group's activism at COP 26 (Reverend Billy and the Stop Shopping Choir 2022a).
11  On the methodological opportunities and excesses of the linguistic turn in historical analysis and writing, see Spiegel (2004).
12  Ironically, the social theory we have turned to in order to resist the master narratives of previous generations has sometimes surreptitiously made our labors conduits of emergent power. The central lesson to digest in this is that theories and methods do not, in of themselves, offer an escape from historical power but cannot but reflect it. What we creatively do with theory, how, and why in our scholarly performances are the key pragmatic considerations we must make as scholars.
13  Importantly, scholars of religion like Deonnie Moodie (2018) and Daromir Rudnyckyj (2010, 2018) have made vital interventions in the area of globalization and its growing entanglements with world religious traditions such as Hinduism and Islam.
14  On Christianity's animistic inheritance and possibilities, see Wallace (2018).
15  Implicit in my agreement with the activists that capitalism is incompatible with ecological well-being is the suggestion that the traditional cultural relativism and descriptive biases of the social scientific study of religion cannot extend in the same way to capitalist formations that threaten the very marginalized communities that scholars often look to humanize. We must, no doubt, remain decidedly empirical and ask why and how capitalist rationalities end up being so compelling, but also reject the conceit that the task of the scholar is to remain neutral on questions of ecological justice.
16  This is the logic of the argument: Many religion scholars take it as their task to analyze and study religion but assume critical distance between themselves and religion. If consumerism is understood according to the terms of religion, as both the Stop Shopping Church and scholars like Kathryn Lofton propose, it becomes harder for the consequences of capitalism to be analytically off-shored onto the impersonal structures of "economy" (as "externalities") at the expense of the somatic and psychic intimacies of "religion" (which speak to "who we are").
17  The Paterson Silk Strike of 1913 is a good example of these dangers. Middle-class IWW (Industrial Workers of the World) artists and anarchists in New York City hoped to support striking textile workers in nearby Paterson, New Jersey, by performatively recreating Wobbly Hall in Madison Square Garden and charging for tickets. The production was bloated and costly. In the end, the striking workers never received the promised monies and, embarrassed and exhausted, some of the artists simply departed for European vacations. In terms of more recent and proximate experience, as Judith Butler (2021) argues, the ranks of contingent academic labor serve as a first line of possible solidarity between academic workers and precarious populations.
18  Other examples of public collaborations include Laura McTighe's collective authorship and research partnership with the community-based, nonprofit out of New Orleans, Women with a Vision (2024), and Freedom University, a Georgia-based nonprofit that provides college-level instruction to undocumented students

and serves as an advocacy group for education access. It was founded by, among others, the religion scholars Bethany Moreton and Pamela Voekel.
19  Academics are trained to relish our expertise. Any collaborations with grassroots organizations demand the scholar's prolonged suspension of judgment and a commitment to listening and learning from organic intellectuals. Ethnography is especially well-suited to the goals of this kind of trust-building.
20  To start: By no means is religion and economy, as a subfield of religious studies, reducible to business ethics and the ways in which scholarship on religion can improve business practices. That suggestion is a disciplinary non-starter. As an archive and field site, the Stop Shopping Church offers a veritable smorgasbord for religion scholars, especially for those of us who work on capitalism. The most interesting and, I would argue, urgent points of convergence do not assume normative economics and business philosophy as their hermeneutical ground rules, by any means.
21  I am partial to the approach taken by scholars of critical theory of religion, who distinguish their approach from critical religion. The latter emphasizes the political genealogy of "religion" while the former emphasizes the lived consequences of religion and the ways in which religion not only buttresses the status quo but can also become the vehicle for the delivery of values-driven critiques of the world.
22  In February 2024, Reverend Billy and Savitri D were invited to participate in a public series on "Reverent Irreverence: Parody, Religion, and Contemporary Politics" at the John C. Danforth Center for Religion and Politics at Washington University–St. Louis.
23  On the sustained ritual work that makes transcendent experience possible, see Luhrmann (2020).
24  The Stop Shopping Church has long resisted the framing of Reverend Billy as a messianic hero. Nevertheless, Reverend Billy has also become iconic in certain progressive organizing circles, and the group has marshaled this iconicity to its strategic benefit. I wonder, however, if, in a very general way, Elizabeth Castelli's (2013) analysis of the limiting factor of historicity (including the cultural and political production of race) in Continental philosophy's recent interests in the figure of Paul can offer some guidance around the necessary limits of the Reverend Billy character, as a product of early neoliberal, North American times.
25  Attributed to the foundational studies of Edward Bailey (1997), Francis Stewart, a scholar of punk rock and anarchist communities and the present director of the Edward Bailey Centre for the study of Implicit Religion, boils down the work of implicit religion to this question: "Would our understanding of the secular and everyday life benefit from asking if it has a religion of its own?" www.implicitreligion.co.uk.
26  The ecological philosopher, David Abram (1996, 71–71), argues that non-Western and Western cultures differently use language to either bind humanity to participation in the nonhuman world, as in the *general* case of the former, or to deaden the nonhuman world for human perspective, as in the case of the latter.

27 Of particular influence would be the nature spirituality of Henry David Thoreau ([1854] 2012), whose "life in the woods" impulse is today packaged by simple living brands such as *Martha Stewart Living*.
28 At the start of the COVID-19 pandemic, some of the members of Stop Shopping Church seriously balked at Reverend Billy's suggestion that the pandemic was a communication and warning from the Earth, with one member suggesting that the thought could easily veer in the direction of "eco-fascism."
29 What is required for a transformation of social consciousness around the relationship of humanity to the non-human world is beyond the matter of intellectual assent. As the Stop Shopping Church knows, ritualized meanings must be undone and redone through ritual means.
30 For the masses, Reverend Billy has suggested, situations of disaster can sometimes lead to the emergence of barter economies that cut past neoliberal commoditization.
31 The term is most directly attributed to the mathematician and philosopher of science, Norbert Wiener (1954), who looked to capture and contain his interests in the incomplete determinism of the world, its prerational, semantic organization, and the relationship between human nervous systems and computational machines. He writes, "I derived from the Greek word *kubernētēs* or 'steersman' the same Greek word from which we eventually derive our word 'governor.'"
32 Some business theory has argued that, today, "all work is theater" and "every business is a stage." B. Joseph Pine II and James H. Gilmore (1999) turn to the work of Richard Schechner and Erving Goffman to understand what they call "the experience economy" in terms of *performance*.
33 I think that contemporary eco-activism has assumed tactics that hold the high art that hangs in museums hostage for a specific reason. The surface reading is that the activism brings attention to the complacent pretensions of our "civilizational" assumptions of the long-standing relevance of cultural heritage. But is it also an acknowledgment of the fact that neoliberalism's gains have been fueled, in part, by its aesthetic appetites and metabolizations?
34 Scholarship has explored the "seriousness with which Derrida read Wiener," and places Derridian linguistics, which is foundational to performativity theory, within the genealogy of cybernetics (Geoghegan 2011).
35 Margaret Mead also corresponded with and influenced Ernest Dichter, as we saw in chapter 2.
36 Reverend Billy's sermons often connect Darwinist evolution to the principles of Gaia theory. The historical metabolism of evolutionary frameworks by racist forms of social Darwinism, however, is left unattended to.
37 The argument is not one of pure origins, suggesting somehow that cybernetic history can explain all we need to know about the emergence of performativity theory. Instead, I mean to suggest that cybernetic history is an important genealogical register in the emergence of performativity theory (in part through the labors of theorists that were documented to have been influenced by cybernetics)

and that at some point genealogical questions must give way to sociological questions that focus on the pervasive present-day patterns in society and the ways in which histories converge.

38   While Judith Butler has not published any kind of extensive academic discussion of artificial intelligence, they are quoted in a recent popular article on the dangers of collapsing the difference between contextual human language and the probabilistic speech of language technologies like chatbots (Weil 2023). Therein, Butler worries that an elision between the two obscures "the question of what's living in my speech, what's living in my emotion, in my love, in my language, (which) gets eclipsed."

As I have argued all along, the thought of even icons like Judith Butler must be allowed to develop over time. Butler's concern is one I share and one that their earlier work on performativity was importantly inattentive to, given the ways in which it seemed to suggest that, as the automatic mechanism of signification, "performativity itself never falters" (Cooper and McFall 2017) and given the ways in which Butler turned to it to present signifiers as being "capable of circulating in an autonomous semiotic realm, like money." Since thinkers like Freud, Foucault, Lacan, and Derrida have strongly influenced Butler's thought, their account of performativity cannot be divorced from the influence of the very cybernetic discourse that has given rise to today's conceptual slippages between human language and the semantic dynamism of information systems. Even if Butler themself now seems increasingly interested in the interpretive dimensions of language, the iconic account of performativity they helped popularize remains in need of historicization and reformation.

39   Judith Butler (2024, 260) has recently suggested that embodied critique must "ally the struggle for gender freedoms and rights with a critique of capitalism" and should ground itself in an understanding of the ways in which "the individual body (bears) the trace of the social in its relations with others, both actual and implied—a body at once porous and interdependent." This outline of a broader collective struggle for freedom and against precarity applies very well to the example of the Church of Stop Shopping. Although Butler imagines the possibility of a form of collective struggle that is not premised in a human transcendence of the natural world (206) but in a kind of solidarity that "includes and exceeds human life to include other living being and processes" (251), it must be noted that this turn to political ecology was anticipated and enacted as a way of life by the Stop Shoppers two decades ago. This juxtaposition and gap between the time and place of academic theory, on the one hand, and grassroots practice, on the other, again leads us to the conclusion that social theory would very often do well to ground itself in empirical circumstance and everyday cases.

40   Recent public conversation around the predictive and suggestive power of generative AI (e.g., see Klein 2023), especially as applicable to marketing and political advertising, strongly echoes the postwar subliminal advertising controversy referenced in chapter 2 and returns us to a key consideration of the activists tracked by

this book, a set of concerns that scholars must also take up: *the ways in which the formatting of choice in advance of conscious intentionality through signifying practices that shape subjectivity is central to the form contemporary cybernetic power has taken.*

41  For her part, my friend Kathy, who is in her early seventies, cheekily suggested this after a Stop Shopping Church performance at Joe's Pub: If the end is nigh, then shouldn't we all adopt a devil-may-care, even cavalier, attitude and prioritize having a good time here and now? Her nihilistic suggestion is precisely why a "quasi-religious" revolution of our social values that prompt concern for the planet that our children's children will inherit is required, according to the Stop Shopping Church. Time, as such, becomes a key arena of moral and ethical reflection and reform.

42  In other words, while performance theory is as historically embedded as performativity theory in the strands of cybernetic, "post-secular" capitalism from which branding also emerged, I believe, like the activists, that coordinated and intentional social action, rather than faith in the automatic slippages of signification, is most pressing in our Shopocalyptic age. This is because performance can position social actors to engage in acts of creative subversion. In response to our assured collectivization by "consuming religion," we must proceed as if it were possible to change what must be changed. As the activists remind us, our lives depend on an appreciation for the fact that while rising sea levels and consumer ritualization go hand in hand, we do not have to actually assume a perspective of hopeless inevitability in the face of boiling oceans and smoky skies.

43  In addition to serving as a warming and distribution center, Earth Chxrch hosts English as a Second Language (ESL) classes for new migrants. Reverend Billy was also asked to say a few words at a memorial for an infant who died at a motel that houses whom he calls our "unhoused newest New Yorkers." Within the context of the Earth Chxrch's new role in the community, Reverend Billy has expressed the sentiment that "Earth justice is human justice."

Simultaneously, the Choir is also ascendant as a performance group, having been invited to tour the country with Neil Young in April and May 2024.

44  In other words, social media's citationality is directly linked to processes of capitalist accumulation in a branded world, wherein brands traffic in iconic power. Digital technologies allow consumers' perlocutionary statements (say, a review of a product or a political analysis) to much more easily acquire citational (and illocutionary) power, today. The power of influencers and Reddit conspiracies are different in degree and effect, not kind. Language's productive power is newly privileged because material culture allows it to come at (and through) us in repetitive waves and organizing cycles.

45  I mean, by "everyday religion," what Robert Orsi (2012) does: the politically unassuming religious practices and meanings of communities and religious actors who are grounded in local forms of allegiance and identification, flexible in terms of doctrine, and yet still engaged with the (post)modern world. "Everyday

religion" is not inconsequential to the structures and consequences of political economy (see, e.g., Moreton 2009), but practitioners themselves tend to remain squarely focused on "life's existential challenges." None of this precludes the need for content analyses of popularized and institutionalized discourses as a form of empirical analysis, especially as this kind of mapping can suggest to us the ways in which religion's revisions are central to understanding who we are becoming.

46 Cybernetics is, I mean to suggest, an Ur-discourse of postmodern North Atlantic societies (and beyond). Heather Melquist's (2017) investigations of "screen Christianity" in transnational, multisite churches based in South Korea are precisely the example of the kind of encounters between digital technologies and ideologies and traditional religion that religious studies must study and analyze today.

47 Religion is increasingly of interest to a plethora of nominally secular institutions, not just business management and marketing, and comparative analyses of these interests that can help us take stock of the shifting post-secular landscape are needed.

# BIBLIOGRAPHY

Abram, David. 1996. *The Spell of the Sensuous—Perception and Language in a More-Than-Human World*. New York: Vintage Books.
Adams, Susan. 2012. "Obama Voters Are From Starbucks, Romney Voters Are From McDonald's, and Other Political Breakout Brands." *Forbes*, October 11. www.forbes.com/.
Adbusters. 2009. *Journal of the Mental Environment* 17:85.
Adorno, Theodor [1966] 2007. *Negative Dialectics*. New York: Continuum.
———. [1936] 1990. "On Jazz." *Discourse* 12(1): 45–69.
Adorno, Theodor and Max Horkheimer. [1947] 2002. *Dialectic of Enlightenment—Philosophical Fragments*. Palo Alto, CA: Stanford University Press.
———. [1944] 2002. "The Culture Industry: Enlightenment as Mass Deception." In *The Dialectic of Enlightenment*, edited by Gunzelin Schmid Noerr, 94–136. Palo Alto, CA: Stanford University Press.
Aggarwal, Pankaj and Ann McGill. 2012. "When Brands Seem Human, Do Humans Act Like Brands? Automatic Behavioral Priming Effects of Brand Anthropomorphism." *Journal of Consumer Research* 39(2): 307–323.
Aguilera, Jasmine. 2019. "This Woman Climbed the Statue of Liberty to Protest Family Separation. One Year Later, She's Wondering What's Really Changed." *Time*, July 2. https://time.com (Accessed October 28, 2020).
Alburger, Carolyn. 2019. "Hudson Yards $200M Art Piece Looks Like a Giant Schawarma." Eater, March 15. https://ny.eater.com/.
Alderson, Wroe. 1952. "*Psychology* for *Marketing* and Economics." *Journal of Marketing* 17(2): 119–135.
Ammerman, Nancy. 1997. "Golden Rule Christianity: Lived Religion in the American Mainstream." In *Lived Religion in America*, edited by David Hall, 196–216. Princeton, NJ: Princeton University Press.
Appadurai, Arjun, ed. 1986. *The Social Life of Things—Commodities in Cultural Perspective*. Cambridge, UK: Cambridge University Press.
Armour, Ellen T. and Susan M. St. Ville, eds. 2006. "Introduction." In *Bodily Citations—Religion and Judith Butler*, edited by Ellen T. Armour and Susan M. St. Ville, 1–12. New York: Columbia University Press.
Arslan, Aslihan and Christopher P. Reicher. 2011. "The Effects of the Coffee Trademarking Initiative and Starbucks Publicity on Export Prices of Ethiopian Coffee." *Journal of African Economies* 20(5): 704–736.
Arvidsson, Adam. 2006. *Brands: Meaning and Value in Media Culture*. London: Routledge.

Asad, Talal. 2018. *Secular Translations—Nation State, Modern Self, and Calculative Reason*. New York: Columbia University Press.

———. 2003. *Formations of the Secular—Christianity, Islam, Modernity*. Palo Alto, CA: Stanford University Press.

———. 1993. *Genealogies of Religion—Discipline and Reasons of Power in Christianity and Islam*. Baltimore, MD: Johns Hopkins University Press.

Askegaard, Soren. 2006. "Brands as Global Ideoscape." In *Brand Culture*, edited by Jonathan Schroeder and Miriam Salzer-Mörling, 91–117. London: Routledge.

August, Vincent. 2022. "Network Concepts in Social Theory: Foucault and Cybernetics." *European Journal of Social Theory* 25(2): 271–291.

Austin, J. L. 1962. *How to Do Things With Words*. Cambridge, MA: Harvard University Press.

Bailey, Edward. 1997. *Implicit Religion in Contemporary Society*. Kampen, Netherdlands: Kok Pharos.

Balmer, John. 2006. "Corporate Brand Cultures and Communities." In *Brand Culture*, edited by Jonathan Schroeder and Miriam Salzer-Mörling, 34–49. London: Routledge.

Bartel, Rebecca. 2021. *Card-Carrying Christians: Debt and the Making of Free-Market Spirituality in Colombia*. Oakland: University of California Press.

Bartel, Rebecca and Lucia Hulsether. 2019. "Classifying Capital—A Roundtable." *Journal of the American Academy of Religion* 87(3): 581–595.

Basso, Keith. 1996. *Wisdom Sits in Places: Landscape and Language Among the Western Apache*. Albuquerque: University of New Mexico Press.

Bates, Colin. 2014. "What Is a Brand?" www.sideroad.com (Accessed July 3, 2018).

Becker, Ernest. [1973] 1997. *The Denial of Death*. New York: Simon & Schuster.

Bekkering, Denis J. 2016. "Fake Religions, Politics and Ironic Fandom: The Church of the SubGenius, *Zontar*, and American Televangelism." *Culture and Religion* 17(2): 129–147.

Belk, Russell and Gülner Tumbat. 2005. "The Cult of Macintosh." *Consumption, Markets and Culture* 8(3): 205–217.

Bell, Catherine. 1998. "Performance." In *Critical Terms for Religious Studies*, edited by Mark C. Taylor, 205–225. Chicago: University of Chicago Press.

———. 1997. *Ritual Perspectives and Dimensions*. London: Oxford University Press.

———. 1992. *Ritual Theory, Ritual Practice*. London: Oxford University Press.

Bell, Daniel. [1976] 1996. *The Cultural Contradictions of Capitalism*. New York: Basic Books.

Bender, Courtney. 2003. *Heaven's Kitchen—Living Religion at God's Love We Deliver*. Chicago: University of Chicago Press.

Bender, Michael and Maggie Haberman. 2022. "Trump Sells a New Image as the Hero of $99 Trading Cards." *New York Times*, December 15. www.nytimes.com.

Benjamin, Walter. [1982] 1999. *Arcades Project*. Cambridge, MA: Harvard University Press.

———. [1921] 2005. "Capitalism as Religion." In *The Frankfurt School on Religion—Key Writings by Major Thinkers*, edited by Eduardo Mendieta, 259–262. New York: Routledge.

Benn, James. 2013. "Burning for the Buddha." *Tricycle*, Winter. https://tricycle.org.

Berger, Peter. [1967] 1990. *The Sacred Canopy: Elements of a Sociological Theory of Religion*. New York: Anchor Books.

Bergson, Henri. [1907] 1998. *Creative Evolution*. New York: Dover Publications.

Berlant, Lauren. 2011. *Cruel Optimism*. Durham, NC: Duke University Press.

Berlant, Lauren and Elizabeth Freeman. 1993. "Queer Nationality." In *Fear of a Queer Planet*, edited by Michael Warner, 193–229. Minneapolis: University of Minnesota Press.

Berman, Marshall. 1982. *All That Is Solid Melts Into Air*. New York: Penguin Books.

Bernays, Edward. 2005. *Propaganda*. Brooklyn, NY: IG Publishing.

Berthon, Pierre, Katrin Fischer, and Philip DesAutels. 2011. "From Mummers to New Media: Captivity, Liberation, and the Church of Life after Shopping." *Journal of Public Affairs* 11(3): 181–187.

Bessem, Matthew. 2021. "Why Does Jeff Bezos' Rocket Look So Much Like a Penis? We Asked a Rocket Scientist." *Slate*, July 21. https://slate.com.

Best, Wallace D. 2017. *Langston's Salvation: American Religion and the Bard of Harlem*. New York: New York University Press.

Bielo, James S. 2017. "Literalism as Creativity—Making a Creationist Theme Park, Reassessing a Scriptural Ideology." In *The Bible in American Life*, edited by Philip Goff, Arthur E. Farnsley II, and Peter J. Thusen, 292–304. New York: Oxford University Press.

Biggart, Nicole. 1989. *Charismatic Capitalism—Direct Selling Organizations in America*. Chicago: University of Chicago Press.

Bivins, Jason. 2015. *Spirits Rejoice! Jazz and American Religion*. New York: Oxford University Press.

Blazenhoff, Rusty. 2014. "Brandalism Rampage Leaves Subversive Damage in Its Wake." CNET, May 21. www.cnet.com/.

Blondie. 1979. "Dreaming." Track 1 on *Eat to the Beat*. Capitol Records, CD.

Boer, Roland. 2011. "*Kapitalfetisch*: 'The Religion of Everyday Life.'" *International Critical Thought* 1(4): 416–426.

Boltanski, Luc and Eve Chiapello. [1999] 2007. *The New Spirit of Capitalism*. London: Verso.

Booker, Vaughn. 2020. *Lift Every Voice and Swing: Black Musicians and Religious Culture in the Jazz Century*. New York: New York University Press.

Boughton, Josh. 2020. "New Animism: Relational Epistemologies and Expanding Western Ontologies." *Student Anthropologist* 7(1): 56–59.

Bourdieu, Pierre. [1979] 1984. *Distinction*. London: Routledge.

———. [1972] 1977. *Outline of a Theory of Practice*. Cambridge: Cambridge University Press.

Bourdieu, Pierre and Jean-Claude Passeron. [1970] 2000. *Reproduction in Education, Society, and Culture*. London: Sage.
Boym, Svetlana. 2001. *The Future of Nostalgia*. New York: Basic Books.
Blankenship, Kim, Amy B. Smoyer, Sarah J. Bray, and Kristin Mattocks et al. 2005. "Black-White Disparities in HIV/AIDS: The Role of Drug Policy and the Corrections System." *Journal of Health Care for the Poor and Underserved* 16(4): 140–146.
Brash, Julian. 2011. *Bloomberg's New York: Class and Governance in the Luxury City*. Athens: University of Georgia Press.
Brintnall, Kent. 2013. "Queer Studies and Religion." *Critical Research on Religion* 1(1): 51–61.
Brooks, David. 2000. *Bobos in Paradise—The New Upper Class and How They Got There*. New York: Simon & Schuster.
Brown, Wendy. 2019. *In the Ruins of Neoliberalism: The Rise of Antidemocratic Politics in the West*. New York: Columbia University Press.
———. 2015. *Undoing the Demos—Neoliberalism's Stealth Revolution*. New York: Zone Books.
———. 2001. *Politics Out of History*. Princeton, NJ: Princeton University Press.
Burga, Solcyre. 2023. "Where the Disney v. DeSantis Case Stands—and How It Unfolded." *Time*, May 21. https://time.com.
Butler, Judith. 2024. *Who's Afraid of Gender?*. New York: Farrar, Straus and Giroux.
———. 2022. *What World Is This?: A Pandemic Phenomenology*. New York: Columbia University Press.
———. 2020. *The Force of Nonviolence: An Ethico-Political Bind*. Brooklyn, NY: Verso.
———. 2019a. "Anti-Gender Ideology and Mahmood's Critique of the Secular Age." *Journal of the American Academy of Religion* 87(4): 955–967.
———. 2019b. "The Backlash Against Gender Ideology Must Stop." *New Statesman*, January 21. www.newstatesman.com.
———. 2019c. "We Are Wordless Without One Another." *The Other Journal—An Intersection of Theology and Culture* 27. https://theotherjournal.com/.
———. 2014. "Bodily Vulnerability, Coalitions, and Street Politics." *Critical Studies* 37: 99–117.
———. 2013. *Parting Ways: Jewishness and the Critique of Zionism*. New York: Columbia University Press.
———. 2010. "Performative Agency." *Journal of Cultural Economy* 3(2): 147–161.
———. 2009a. "Performativity, Precarity, and Sexual Politics." *AIBR: Rivista de Antropologia Iberoamericana* 4(3): x–xiii.
———. 2009b. *Frames of War: When Is Life Grievable?* Brooklyn, NY: Verso.
———. 2008. "Taking Another's View." In *Reification, A New Look at an Old Idea*, edited by Martin Jay, 97–199. Oxford: Oxford University Press.
———. 2006. *Precarious Life—The Powers of Violence and Mourning*. Brooklyn, NY: Verso.
———. 2005. *Giving an Account of Oneself*. New York: Fordham University Press.
———. 2004. *Undoing Gender*. New York: Routledge.

———. 1997a. *The Psychic Life of Power: Theories in Subjection.* Palo Alto, CA: Stanford University Press.
———. 1997b. "Merely Cultural." *Social Text* 52/53: 265–277.
———. 1993. *Bodies That Matter: On the Discursive Limits of "Sex."* New York: Routledge.
———. 1990. *Gender Trouble: Feminism and the Subversion of Identity.* New York: Routledge.
Butler, Judith and Athena Athanasiou. 2013. *Dispossession: The Performative in the Political.* Malden, MA: Polity Press.
Byerly, Victoria. 1996. "From Beat Scene Poet to Psychedelic Multimedia Artist in San Francisco and Beyond, 1948–1978." Regional Oral History Office, University of California, Berkeley. https://oac.cdlib.org.
Byrne, Melissa. 2014. "Don't Drink Starbucks Free College PR Stunt." *Medium* (blog), June 16. https://medium.com.
Callahan, Richard. 2009. *Work and Faith in the Kentucky Coal Fields.* Bloomington: University of Indiana Press.
Campbell, Colin. 1987. *The Romantic Ethic and the Spirit of Modern Consumerism.* London: Basil Blackwell.
Cantwell, Christopher, Heath Carter, and Giordano Drake, eds. 2016. *The Pew and the Picket Line: Christianity and the American Working Class.* Champaign: University of Illinois Press.
Carrasco, Davíd. 2019. "The Ghost of Love and Goodness." In *Toni Morrison: Goodness and the Literary Imagination*, edited by Davíd Carrasco, Stephanie Paulsell, and Mara Willard, 116–137. Charlottesville: University of Virginia Press.
———. 2007. "Cuando Dios y Usted Quiere: Latino/a Studies Between Religious Powers and Social Thought." In *A Companion to Latino/a Studies*, edited by Juan Flores and Renato Rosaldo, 60–76. Malden, MA: Blackwell Publishing.
———. 2013. *Religions of Mesoamerica.* Long Grove, IL: Waveland Press.
Carrasco, Octavio. 2022. "Restive Spirits Seeking Release: The Implicit Religion of the Grateful Dead." *Journal of Belief and Values* 43(1): 29–39.
Carrette, Jeremy and Richard King. 2004. *Selling Spirituality.* London: Routledge.
Carter, Heath. 2015. *Union Made: Working People and the Rise of Social Christianity in Chicago.* Oxford: Oxford University Press.
Caruso, Skyler. 2023. "Everything to Know About the Bud Light Controversy." *People*, July 19. https://people.com.
Castelli, Elizabeth. 2013. "The Philosopher's Paul in the Frame of the Global: Some Reflections." In *Paul and the Philosophers*, edited by Ward Blanton and Hent de Vries, 143–158. New York: Fordham University Press.
Chasain, Alexandra. 2001. *Selling Out: The Gay and Lesbian Movement Goes to Market.* New York: Palgrave Macmillan.
Chatelier, Stephen. 2018. "Beyond the Humanism/Posthumanism Debate: The Educational Implications of Said's Critical, Humane Praxis." *Educational Theory* 67(6): 657–672.

Cobb, Ahad. 2018. *Life Unfolding: Memoirs of a Spiritual Hippie*. Albuquerque, NM: Night Sky Books.
Cohen, Lizbeth. 2004. *A Consumer's Republic—The Politics of Consumption in Postwar America*. New York: Vintage Books.
Coleman, Charly. 2021. *The Spirit of French Capitalism: Economic Theology in the Age of Enlightenment*. Palo Alto, CA: Stanford University Press.
Comaroff, Jean and John Comaroff. 2001. "Millennial Capitalism: First Thoughts on a Second Coming." In *Millennial Capitalism and the Culture of Neoliberalism*, edited by Jean and John Comaroff, 1–56. Durham, NC: Duke University Press.
Cooper, Melinda. 2017. *Family Values—Between Neoliberalism and the New Social Conservativism*. New York: Zone Books.
Cooper, Melinda and Liz McFall. 2017. "10 Years After: It's the Economy and Culture, Stupid!" *Journal of Cultural Economy* 10(1): 1–7.
Cox, Harvey. [1965] 2014. *The Secular City*. Princeton, NJ: Princeton University Press.
———. 1999. "The Market as God." *The Atlantic*, March.
Crapanzano, Vincent. 2004. *Imaginative Horizons: An Essay in Literary-Philosophical Anthropology*. Chicago: University of Chicago Press.
Curts, Kati. 2015. "Temples and Turnpikes in 'The World of Tomorrow': Religious Assemblage and Automobility at the 1939 New York World's Fair." *Journal of the American Academy of Religion* 83: 722–749.
Danesi, Marcel. 2006. *Brands*. London: Routledge.
Das, Veena. 2014. "Action, Expression, and Everyday Life: Recounting Household Events." In *The Ground Between—Anthropologists Engage Philosophy*, edited by Veena Das, Michael Jackson, Arthur Kleinman, and Bhrigupati Singh, 279–305. Durham, NC: Duke University Press.
Das, Veena, Michael Jackson, Arthur Kleinman, and Bhrigupati Singh, eds. 2014. "Introduction." In *The Ground Between—Anthropologists Engage Philosophy*, edited by Veena Das, Michael Jackson, Arthur Kleinman, and Bhrigupati Singh, 1–26. Durham, NC: Duke University Press.
Dávila, Arlene. [2001] 2012. *Latinos, Inc.—The Marketing and Making of a People*. Berkeley: University of California Press.
Dean, Jodi. 2012. *The Communist Horizon*. London: Verso.
Debord, Guy. [1967] 1994. *The Society of the Spectacle*. New York: Zone Books.
De Certeau, Michel. [1984] 1988. *The Practice of Everyday Life*. Berkeley: University of California Press.
DeNora, Tia. [2000] 2009. *Music in Everyday Life*. Cambridge: Cambridge University Press.
Derrida, Jacques. [1993] 2006. Specters of Marx. *The State of the Debt, the Work of Mourning, and the New International*. New York: Routledge.
———. 1988. *Limited Inc*. Evanston: Northwestern University Press.
———. 1981. *Positions*. Chicago: University of Chicago Press.
———. 1978. *Writing and Difference*. Chicago: University of Chicago Press.
Diamond, Elin, ed. 1996. *Performance and Cultural Politics*. New York: Routledge.

Dichter, Ernest. [1960] 2012. *The Strategy of Desire*. Eastford, CT: Martino Books.
———. 1971. *Motivating Human Behavior*. New York: McGraw-Hill.
———. 1964. *The Handbook of Consumer Motivations: The Psychology of the World of Objects*. New York: McGraw-Hill.
———. 1960. "A Small-Scale Pilot and Review of Literature on Attitudes to Dieting and Obesity." Report. Delaware: Hagley Museum and Library.
———. 1947a. "A Psychological Study of [[Thom]] McAn's Boys' [[Market]]." Report. Delaware: Hagley Museum and Library.
———. 1947b. *The Psychology of Everyday Living*. New York: Barnes and Noble.
Dickinson, Greg. 2002. "Joe's Rhetotic: Finding Authenticity at Starbucks." *Rhetoric Society Quarterly* 43(4): 5–27.
Dochuk, Darren. 2019. *Anointed with Oil: How Christianity and Crude Made Modern Religion*. New York: Basic Books.
Dolsten, Josefin. 2019. "7 Jewish Things to Know About Possible 2020 Candidate Howard Schultz." *Times of Israel*, February 1. www.timesofisrael.com.
Domhoff, G. William. 2013. *Who Rules America?: The Triumph of the Corporate Rich*. New York: McGraw-Hill.
Duberman, Martin. 1994. *Stonewall*. New York: Plume.
Dubuisson, Daniel. 2003. *The Western Construction of Religion—Myths, Knowledge, and Ideology*. Baltimore, MD: Johns Hopkins University Press.
Durbin, Dee-Ann. 2021. "Starbucks Fights Expanding Unionization Effort at Its Stores." PBS News Hour, December 2. www.pbs.org/.
Durkee, Savitri. 2021. "Singing Towards Assembly." Vimeo, 15:10. https://art-of-assembly.net.
Durkee, Savitri and Bill Talen. 2022. "Episode 16: Rewind 3 Months, Johnny and Amber are About to Swallow the Culture." *Earth Riot Radio*, May 27. Podcast, Audio, 29:00. https://podcasts.apple.com.
———. 2013. *The Reverend Billy Project: From Rehearsal to Super Mall with the Church of Life After Shopping*, edited by Alisa Solomon. United States of America: Stop Shopping Publishing.
Ecotubereview. 2009. "Reverend Billy Confronts Police at Starbucks." Video. June 6. https://www.youtube.com/watch?v=H7NuoJLVwoU.
Einstein, Mara. 2008. *Brands of Faith: Marketing Religion in a Commercial Age*. London: Routledge.
Eliade, Mircea [1957] 1959. *The Sacred and the Profane: The Nature of Religion*. London: Harcourt Brace Jovanovich.
Elisha, Omri. 2017. "Proximations of Public Religion: Worship, Spiritual Warfare, and the Ritualization of Christian Dance." *American Anthropologist* 119(1): 73–85.
———. 2011. *Moral Ambition: Mobilization and Outreach in Evangelical Megachurches*. Berkeley: University of California Press.
Engelhardt, Jeffers. 2012. "Music, Sound, and Religion." In *The Cultural Study of Music—A Critical Introduction*, edited by Martin Clayton, Trevor Herbert, and Richard Middleton, 299–307. London: Routledge.

Equalexchange. 2008. "Reverend Billy on the Disconnect Between Consumers and Food." Video, October 21. www.youtube.com/watch?v=1aTPT1xIiko.
Fauconnier, Gilles and Mark Turner. 2002. *The Way We Think: Conceptual Blending and the Mind's Hidden Complexities*. New York: Basic Books.
Feltmate, David. 2017. *Drawn of the Gods—Religion and Humor in the Simpsons, South Park, and Family Guy*. New York: New York University Press.
Fessenden, Tracy. 2018. *Religion Around Billie Holiday*. University Park: Pennsylvania State University Press.
Feuerbach, Ludwig. [1863] 2020. *Ludwig Feuerbach's Samtliche Werke*. Los Angeles: Hardpress Publishing.
———. [1841] 1989. *The Essence of Christianity*. Lanham, MD: Prometheus Books.
Fiske, John. 1991 [1989]. *Reading the Popular*. London: Routledge.
Foucault, Michel. 2007. *Security, Territory, Populations—Lectures at the Collège de France, 1977-1978*, edited by Michel Sennelart. New York: Picador.
———. [1977] 1995. *Discipline and Punish*. New York: Vintage Books.
———. [1966] 1994. *The Order of Things—An Archaeology of the Human Sciences*. New York: Vintage Books.
———. 1994. "Space, Knowledge and Power." In *The Essential Works of Michel Foucault Vol. 3: Power*, edited by James Faubion and Translated by Robert Hurley, 349-364. New York: New Press.
———. [1984] 1990. *The History of Sexuality Vol. 3: The Care of the Self*. New York: Vintage Books.
Floyd, Kevin. 2009. *The Reification of Desire—Towards a Queer Marxism*. Minneapolis: University of Minnesota Press.
Frank, Thomas. 2016. *Listen Liberal: Or, What Ever Happened to the Party of the People?* New York: Metropolitan Books.
———. 1997. *The Conquest of Cool—Business Culture, Counterculture, and the Rise of Hip Consumerism*. Chicago: University of Chicago Press.
Frank, Thomas and Matt Weiland. 1997. *The Business of Culture in the New Gilded Age: Commodify Your Dissent*. New York: Norton.
Frankel, David. 2006. *The Devil Wears Prada*. Fox 2000 Pictures. DVD.
Fraser, Nancy. 2022. *Cannibal Capitalism: How Our System Is Devouring Democracy, Care, and the Planet—and What We Can Do About It*. Brooklyn, NY: Verso.
———. 2013. *Fortunes of Feminism—From State Managed Capitalism to Neoliberal Crisis*. London: Verso.
Freud, Sigmund. [1930] 2021. *Civilization and Its Discontents*. New York: Norton.
———. [1923] 1989. *The Ego and the Id*. New York: Norton.
———. [1920] 1990. *Beyond the Pleasure Principle*. New York: Norton.
Freyenhagen, Fabien. 2014. "Adorno's Politics: Theory and Praxis in Germany's 1960s." *Philosophy and Social Criticism* 40(9): 867-893.
Frost, Jacqui. 2024. "Inside the 'Secular Churches' that Fill the Need for Some Nonreligious Americans." CBS News, January 11. www.cbsnews.com.
Fukuyama, Francis 1992. *The End of History and the Last Man*. New York: Free Press.

Gac, Scott. 2007. *Singing for Freedom: The Hutchison Family Singers and the Nineteenth-Century Culture of Reform*. New Haven, CT: Yale University Press.

Galbraith, John K. [1958] 2000. "The Dependence Effect." In *The Consumer Society Reader*, edited by Juliet Schor and Douglas Holt, 20–25. New York: New Press.

———. *The Affluent Society* [1958] *1998*. Boston: Mariner Books.

Geoghegan, Bernard Dionysius. 2011. "From Information Theory to French Theory: Jakobson, Lévi-Strauss, and the Cybernetic Apparatus." *Critical Inquiry* 38 (Autumn): 96–126.

Giddens, Anthony. 1982. *Profiles and Critiques in Social Theory*. Berkeley: University of California Press.

Glaude, Eddie. 2008. *In a Shade of Blue—Pragmatism and the Politics of Black America*. Chicago: University of Chicago Press.

Goffman. Erving. [1967] 1982. *Interaction Ritual—Essays on Face-to-Face Behavior*. New York, NY: Pantheon Books.

———. [1956] 1959. *The Presentation of Life in Everyday Life*. New York: Anchor.

Goldman, Emma. 1934. *Living My Life*. New York: Knopf.

Goldman, Robert and Stephen Papson. 1996. *Sign Wars: The Cluttered Landscape of Advertising*. New York: Guilford Press.

Goldstein, Warren, Rebekka King, and Jonathan Boyarin. 2016. "Critical Theory of Religion vs. Critical Religion." *Critical Research on Religion* 4(1): 3–7.

González, George. 2017. "Shopping for Salvation in a Brand New World." *NYU Revealer*, March 8. https://therevealer.org/.

———. 2016. "Towards an Existential Archeology of Capitalist Spirituality." *Religions* 7(85), available online.

———. 2015. *Shape-Shifting Capital: Spiritual Management, Critical Theory, and the Ethnographic Project*. Lanham, MD: Lexington Books.

———. 2012. "Shape Shifting Capital: New Management and the Bodily Metaphors of Spiritual Capitalism." *Journal for the Theory of Social Behaviour* 42(3): 325–344.

Gorski, Philip, David Kyuman Kim, John Torpey, and Jonatahn VanAntwerpen, eds. 2012. *The Post-Secular in Question: Religion in Contemporary Society*. New York: New York University Press.

Goux, Jean-Joseph. 1990. "General Economics and Postmodern Capitalism." *Yale French Studies* 78: 206–224.

Graeber, David. 2012. "The Sword, the Sponge, and the Paradox of Performativity—Some Observations on Fate, Luck, Financial Chicanery, and the Limits of Human Knowledge." *Social Analysis* 56(1): 25–42.

———. 2011. *Debt—The First 5,000 Years*. Brooklyn, NY: Melville House Publishing.

———. 2004. *Fragments of an Anarchist Anthropology*. Chicago: Prickly Paradigm Press.

———. 2001. *Towards an Anthropological Theory of Value: The False Coin of Our Own Dreams*. New York: Palgrave.

Granfield, Robert. 1992. *Making Elite Lawyers—Visions of Law at Harvard and Beyond*. New York: Routledge.

Grimes, Ronald. 2011. "Religion, Theater, and Performance." In *Religion, Theater, and Performance: Acts of Faith*, edited by Lance Gharavi, 27–41. London: Routledge.

———. 2008. "Consuming Ritual: A&E's Sacred Rites and Rituals." In *Contemporary Consumption Rituals—A Research Anthology*, edited by Cele Otnes and Tina Lowrey, 21–36. New York: Psychology Press.

———. 1996. "Introduction." In *Readings in Ritual Studies*, edited by Ronald Grimes. Saddle River, NJ: Prentice-Hall.

Hall, Stewart. 1968. *The Hippies: An American "Moment."* Birmingham: Centre for Contemporary Cultural Studies. www.birmingham.ac.uk.

Halperin, David. 1995. *Saint Foucault: Towards a Gay Hagiography*. New York: Oxford University Press.

Halter, Marilyn. 2000. *Shopping for Identity—The Making of Ethnicity*. New York: Schocken Books.

Hammond, Sara. 2017. *God's Businessmen: Entrepreneurial Evangelicals in Depression and War*, edited by Darren Dochuk. Chicago: University of Chicago Press.

Hanlon, Keara. 2022. "The (Unofficial) Pope Francis Playlist." *America—The Jesuit Review*, January 14. www.americamagazine.org (Accessed June 1, 2022).

Haraway, Donna. 1991. *Simians, Cyborgs, and Women—The Reinvention of Nature*. London: Routledge.

Hardt, Michael and Antonio Negri. 2017. *Assembly*. Oxford: Oxford University Press.

———. 2004. *Multitude: War and Democracy in the Age of Empire*. New York: Penguin Books.

Hardwick, M. Jeffrey. 2010. *Mall Maker—Victor Gruen, Architect of an American Dream*. Philadelphia: University of Pennsylvania Press.

Hartman, Saidiya. 1997. *Scenes of Subjection—Terror, Slavery, and Self-Making in Nineteenth-Century America*. New York: Oxford University Press.

Hartmans, Avery and Natalie Musumeci. 2023. "Conservative Boycotts against Target and Bud Light Are Working Thanks to a 'Perfect Storm' of Social Media and Culture Wars, Experts Say." *Business Insider*, June 3. www.businessinsider.com/.

Harvey, David. 2013. *Rebel Cities: From the Right to the City to the Urban Revolution*. London: Verso.

———. 2005. *A Brief History of Neoliberalism*. Oxford: Oxford University Press.

———. 1982. *All That Is Solid Melts into Air*. New York: Penguin Books.

Hegel, Georg Wilhelm. [1807] 1977. *The Phenomenology of Spirit*. Oxford: Clarendon Press.

Heidegger, Martin. [1927] 1996. *Being and Time*. Albany: State University of New York Press.

Hennessy, Rosemary. 2020. "Toward an Ecology of Life-Making: The Re-membering of Meridel Le Sueur." *Comparative Literature and Culture* 22(2). https://doi.org/10.7771/1481-4374.3841

———. 2000. *Profit and Pleasure—Sexual Identities in Late Capitalism*. New York: Routledge.

Ho, Karen. 2009. *Liquidated—An Ethnography of Wall Street*. Durham, NC: Duke University Press.

Holloway, John. [2002] 2019. *Change the World Without Taking Power*. New York: Pluto Books.

Hollywood, Amy. 2016. *Acute Melancholia and Other Essays*. New York: Columbia University Press.

———. 2006. "Performativity, Citationality, Ritualization." In *Bodily Citations—Religion and Judith Butler*, edited by Ellen T. Armour and Susan M. St. Ville, 252–275. New York: Columbia University Press.

———. 2002. *Sensible Ecstasy: Mysticism, Sexual Difference, and the Demands of History*. Chicago: University of Chicago Press.

Holt, Douglas. 2004. *How Brands Become Icons—The Principles of Cultural Branding*. Cambridge, MA: Harvard Business School Press.

Holt, Douglas and Juliet Schor. 2000. "Introduction." In *The Consumer Society Reader*, edited by Douglas Holt and Juliet Schor, vii–xxiii. New York: New Press.

Honneth, Axel. 2012. *Reification—A New Look at an Old Idea*, edited by Martin Jay. Oxford: Oxford University Press.

Hughes, Langston. [1926] 1994. "I, Too." In *Collected Poems by Langston Hughes*, 46. New York: Alfred A. Knopf.

Hulsether, Lucia. 2023. *Capitalist Humanitarianism*. Durham, NC: Duke University Press.

———. 2019. "Reparative Capitalism." Gospels of Giving (blog forum), The Immanent Frame, July 31, 2020, https://tif.ssrc.org.

———. 2018. "The Grammar of Racism: Religious Pluralism and the Birth of the Interdisciplines." *Journal of the American Academy of Religion* 86(1): 1–41.

Hume, David. [1748] 1993. *An Enquiry into Human Understanding: With Hume's Abstract of a Treatise of Human Nature and a Letter from a Gentleman to His Friend in Edinburgh*.

"I'm a Pepper." " 'I'm a Pepper' TV Commercial 70s." 2008. YouTube. 0:37. www.youtube.com/watch?v=jvCTaccEkMI.

Inden, Ronald. 1990. *Imagining India*. Bloomington: University of Indiana Press.

Ivanov, Sergey. 2010. *Holy Fools in Byzantium and Beyond*. Oxford: Oxford University Press.

Jackson Lears, T. J. [1981] 1995. *Fables of Abundance: A Cultural History of Advertising in America*. New York: Basic Books.

———. 1994. *No Place of Grace: Antimodernism and the Transformation of American Culture 1880–1920*. Chicago: University of Chicago Press.

Jackson, Michael. 2019. *Critique of Identity Thinking*. New York: Berghahn Books.

———. 2018. *The Varieties of Temporal Experience—Travels in Philosophical, Historical, and Ethnographic Time*. New York: Columbia University Press.

———. 2016. *The Work of Art: Rethinking the Elementary Forms of Religious Life*. New York: Columbia University Press.

———. 2009. *The Palm at the End of the Mind—Relatedness, Religiosity, and the Real*. Durham, NC: Duke University Press.
———. 2005. *Existential Anthropology—Events, Exigencies and Effects*. New York: Berghahn Books.
———. 1998. *Minima Ethnographica*. Chicago: University of Chicago Press.
———. 1996. "Introduction." In *Things As They Are: New Directions in Phenomenological Anthropology*, edited by Michael Jackson, 1–50. Bloomington: University of Indiana Press.
Jaffe, Steven. 2018. *Activist New York: A History of People, Protest, and Politics*. New York: New York University Press.
Jakobsen, Janet A. 2020. *The Sex Obsession: Perversity and Possibility in American Politics*. New York: New York University Press.
Jakobsen, Janet A. and Ann Pellegrini. 2008. "Introduction: Times Like These." In *Secularisms*, edited by Janet Jakobsen and Ann Pellegrini. Durham, NC: Duke University Press.
James, William. [1912] 1976. *Essays in Radical Empiricism*. Cambridge, MA: Harvard University Press.
———. [1897] 1979. "The Will to Believe." In *The Will to Believe and Other Essays in Popular Philosophy*. Cambridge, MA: Harvard University Press.
Jameson, Fredric. 1991. *Postmodernism, Or the Cultural Logic of Late-Capitalism*. Durham, NC: Duke University Press.
———. 1982. *The Political Unconscious—Narrative as a Socially Symbolic Act*. Ithaca, NY: Cornell University Press.
Jaspers, Karl. [1932] 1970. *Philosophy Vol. 2: Existential Elucidation*. Chicago: University of Chicago Press.
Jay, Martin. 2005. *Songs of Experience—Modern American and European Variations on a Universal Theme*. Berkeley: University of California Press.
Johnston, John. 2008. *The Allure of Machinic Life: Cybernetics, Artificial Life, and the New AI*. Cambridge, MA: MIT Press.
Josephson-Storm, Jason. 2021. *Metamodernism: The Future of Theory*. Chicago: University of Chicago Press.
Kaylor, Brian. 2013. "Earth-a-lujah!: The Prophetic Environmental Discourse of Reverend Billy." *Environmental Communications* 7(3): 391–408.
Kelman, Ari. 2018. *Shout to the Lord: Making Worship Music in Evangelical America*. New York: New York University Press.
Kiefer, Tom. 2019. *El Sueño Americano*, online exhibition. https://librarygallery.umbc.edu.
King, Daniel. 2020. "Barack Obama Drops a Playlist of 20 Memorable Songs From His Presidency." *Mother Jones*, November 20. www.motherjones.com/.
Klein, Ezra. 2023. "The Imminent Danger of AI Is One We're Not Talking About." *New York Times*, February 26.
Klein, Naomi. 2014. *This Changes Everything: Capitalism vs. The Climate*. New York: Simon & Schuster.
———. [1999] 2009. *No Logo—No Space, No Choice, No Jobs*. New York: Picador.

Krell, Jacob. 2020. "What Is the 'Cybernetics' in the History of Cybernetics, A French Case, 1968 to the Present." *History of Human Sciences* 33(1): 188–211.
Kristeva, Julia. [1974] 1984. *Revolution in Poetic Language*. New York: Columbia University Press.
Kruse, Kevin. 2015. *One Nation Under God—How Corporate America Invented Christian America*. New York: Basic Books.
Krutzsch, Brett. 2020. "Special Issue: Religion and Fashion." *NYU Revealer*, September. https://therevealer.org.
———. 2019. *Dying to Be Normal: Gay Martyrs and the Transformation of American Sexual Politics*. Oxford: Oxford University Press.
Kyuman Kim, David. 2007. *Melancholic Freedom—Agency and the Spirit of Politics*. Oxford: Oxford University Press.
Laack, Isabel. 2015. "Sound, Music and Religion: a Preliminary Cartography of a Transdisciplinary Research Field." *Method and Theory in the Study of Religion* 27 (2015): 220–246.
Lakoff, George and Mark Turner. 1989. *More than Cool Reason: A Field Guide to Poetic Metaphor*. Chicago: University of Chicago Press.
Lambert, Lake III. 2009. *Spirituality Inc.: Religion in the American Workplace*. New York: New York University Press.
Lamberth, David. 1997. "Intimations of the Finite: Thinking Pragmatically at the End of Modernity." *Harvard Theological Review* 90(2): 205–223.
Lane, Jill. 2002. "Reverend Billy: Preaching, Protest and, Postindustrial Flanerie." *Drama Review* 46(1): 60–84.
Lash, Scott and John Urry. 1994. *Economies of Signs and Space*. London: Sage.
Lasn, Kalle. 1999. *Culture Jam: How to Reverse America's Suicidal Consumer Binge—And Why We Must*. New York: HarperCollins.
Latour, Bruno. [1991] 1993. *We Have Never Been Modern*. Cambridge, MA: Harvard University Press.
Leach, William. [1993] 1994. *Land of Desire: Merchants, Power, and the Rise of a New American Culture*. New York: Vintage.
Lechaux, Bleuwenn. 2010. "Non-Preaching Activism in New York: The Theatrical Militancy of Billionaires for Bush and Reverend Billy." *International Journal of Politics, Culture, and Society* 23(2/3): 175–190.
Lefebvre, Henri. [1947] 2008. *The Critique of Everyday Life*. New York: Verso.
LeVasseur, Todd. 2020. "Reverend Billy and the Church of Stop Shopping: Contemporary Religious Production on a Planet Passing Tipping Points." *Novo Religio* 23(3): 86–109.
Levitt, Laura. 2020. *The Objects that Remain*. University Park: Pennsylvania State University Press.
Lindquist, Galina. [2006] 2009. *Conjuring Hope: Healing and Magic in Contemporary Russia*. New York: Berghahn Books.
Linn, Susan. 2004. *Consuming Kids—The Hostile Takeover of Childhood*. New York: New Press.

Locke, John. [1695] 1958. *The Reasonableness of Christianity*. Palo Alto, CA: Stanford University Press.
Löfgren, Orvar and Robert Willim. 2005. *Magic, Culture, and the New Economy*. Oxford: Berg Publishers.
Lofton, Kathryn. 2019. "Our Political Economy." *Journal of the American Academy of Religion* 87(3): 655–661.
———. 2017. *Consuming Religion*. Chicago: University of Chicago Press.
———. 2011. *Oprah—Gospel of an Icon*. Berkeley: University of California Press.
Long, Charles. 2018. "Introduction." In *Ellipsis: The Collected Writings of Charles H. Long*, edited by Charles Long, 1–10. New York: Bloomsbury Academic.
———. 1986. *Significations—Signs, Symbols, and Images in the Interpretation of Religion*. New York: Fortress Press.
LoRusso, Dennis. 2017. *Spirituality, Corporate Culture, and American Business: The Neoliberal Ethic and the Spirit of Global Capital*. New York: Bloomsbury Academic.
Lovelock, James. [1979] 1995. *Gaia: A New Look at Life on Earth*. Oxford: Oxford University Press.
Luhrman, Tanya. 2020. *How God Becomes Real: Kindling the Presence of Invisible Others*. Princeton, NJ: Princeton University Press.
Lukács, György. [1923] 1972. *History and Class Consciousness: Studies in Marxist Dialectics*. Cambridge, MA: MIT Press.
Lury, Celia. 2004. *Brands: The Logos of the Global Economy*. London: Routledge.
Mahmood, Saba. 2004. *Politics of Piety—The Islamic Revival and the Feminist Subject*. Princeton, NJ: Princeton University Press.
Malherek, Joseph. 2014. "Ernest Dichter and American Market Research, 1946–77." *Market Research & American Business, 1935–1965*. Accessed April 2, 2018. www.marketresearch.amdigital.co.uk/.
Malinowski, Bronislaw. 1954. *Magic, Science, and Religion and Other Essays*. New York: Doubleday.
Manovich, Lev. 2001. *The Language of New Media*. Cambridge, MA: MIT Press.
Marchand, Roland. 1985. *Advertising the American Dream: Making Way for Modernity, 1920–1940*. Berkeley: University of California Press.
Marcus, George, ed. 1998. *Corporate Futures: The Diffusion of the Culturally Sensitive Corporate Form—Late Editions*. Vol. 5. Chicago: University of Chicago Press.
Marcus, George and Douglas Holmes. 2006. "Fast Capitalism: Para-Ethnography and the Rise of the Symbolic Analyst." In *Frontiers of Capital—Ethnographic Reflections on the New Economy*, edited by Melissa Fisher and Greg Downey. Durham, NC: Duke University Press.
Marcuse, Herbert. [1937] 2009. "The Affirmative Character of Culture." In *Negations: Essays in Critical Theory*, 65–98. London: Mayflybooks.
———. [1955] 1974. *Eros and Civilization*. New York: Beacon Press.
Market Research and American Business, 1935–1965. Adam Matthew Digital Collections and Archives. Wiltshire, UK. www.marketresearch.amdigital.co.uk/.

Martin, Craig. 2014. *Capitalizing Religion: Ideology and the Opiate of the Bourgeoisie*. New York: Bloomsbury Academic.

Marx, Karl. [1843] 1983. "Contribution to the Critique of Hegel's Philosophy of Right: Introduction." In *The Portable Karl Marx*, edited and translated by Eugene Kamenka, 115–124. New York: Penguin Books.

———. [1846] 1983. "The German Ideology: Volume 1." In *The Portable Karl Marx*, edited and translated by Eugene Kamenka, 162–195. New York: Penguin Books.

———. [1852] 1983. "From the Eighteenth Brumaire of Louis Bonaparte." In *The Portable Karl Marx*, edited and translated by Eugene Kamenka, 287–323. New York: Penguin Books.

———. [1857] 1983. "From *Grundisse*, Introduction." In *The Portable Karl Marx*, edited by Eugene Kamenka, 375–394. New York: Penguin Books.

———. [1867] 1983. "Chapter 1: Commodities (Capital: Vol. 1)." In *The Portable Karl Marx*, edited by Eugene Kamenka, 437–461. New York: Penguin Books.

Maskovsky, Jeffrey. 2002. "Do We All 'Reek' of the Commodity?: Consumption and the Erasure of Poverty in Lesbian/Gay Studies." In *Out in Theory*, edited by Ellen Lewin and William Leap, 264–286. Urbana and Chicago: University of Illinois Press.

Masuzawa, Tomoko. 2005. *The Invention of World Religions—Or, How European Universalism Was Preserved in the Language of Pluralism*. Chicago: University of Chicago Press.

May, Elaine and Reinhold Wagnleitner. 2000. *"Here There and Everywhere": The Foreign Politics of American Popular Culture*. Lebanon, NH: University Press of New England.

McDannell, Colleen. 1995. *Material Christianity—Religion and Popular Culture in America*. New Haven, CT: Yale University Press.

McGee, Micki. 2005. *Self-Help, Inc.—Makeover Culture in American Life*. New York: Oxford University Press.

McKelway, St. Clair. 1958. "Meaningful Patterns." *New Yorker*, January 3.

McClish, Carmen L. 2009. "Activism Based in Embarrassment: The Anti-Consumption Spirituality of the Reverend Billy." *Liminalities—A Journal of Performance Studies* 5(2):1–20.

McTighe, Laura and Women with a Vision. 2024. *Fire Dreams—Making Black Feminist Liberation in the South*. Durham, NC: Duke University Press.

Melquist, Heather. 2017. "Screen Christianity: Video Sermons in the Creation of Transnational Korean Churches." *Acta Koreana* 20(2): 395–421.

Mendieta, Eduardo. 2005. "Religion as Critique: Theology as Social Critique and Enlightened Reason." In *The Frankfurt School on Religion—Key Writings by Major Thinkers*, edited by Eduardo Mendieta, 1–17. New York: Routledge.

Mendieta, Eduardo and Jonathan VanAntwerpen, eds. 2011. *The Power of Religion in the Public Square*. New York: Columbia University Press.

Mervosh, Sarah and Emily Rueb. 2019. "Fuller Picture Emerges of Viral Video of Native American Man and Catholic Students." *New York Times*, January 20. www.nytimes.com (Accessed June 2, 2022).

Miller, Vincent. 2005. *Consuming Religion—Christian Faith and Practice in a Consumer Culture*. New York: Continuum.
Mills, C. W. [1959] 2000. *The Sociological Imagination*. New York: Oxford University Press.
Mitchell, Kerry. 2016. *Spirituality and the State: Making Nature and Experience in America's National Parks*. New York: New York University Press.
Moeran, Brian. 2015. *The Magic of Fashion—Ritual, Commodity, Glamour*. New York: Routledge.
Moodie, Deonnie. 2018. *The Making of a Modern Temple and a Hindu City: Kālīghāt and Kolkata*. Oxford: Oxford University Press.
Moore, R. Laurence. 1994. *Selling God—American Religion in the Marketplace of Culture*. Oxford: Oxford University Press.
Moreton, Bethany. 2009. *To Serve God and Wal-Mart—the Making of Christian Free Enterprise*. Cambridge, MA: Harvard University Press.
———. 2007. "The Soul of Neoliberalism." *Social Text* 25, 3(92): 103–123.
Morton, Donald, ed. 1996. *The Material Queer—A LesBiGay Reader*. Boulder, CO: Westview Press.
Murtola, Anna-Maria. 2012. "Materialist Theology and Anti-Capitalist Resistance, or, 'What Would Jesus Buy?'" *Organization* 19(3): 325–344.
Musselman, Cody. 2023. "Making Sweat Feel Spiritual Didn't Start with SoulCycle—a Religion Scholar Explains." *The Conversation*, January 5. https://theconversation.com.
———. 2019. "Training for the 'Unknown' and 'Unknowable': CrossFit and Evangelical Temporality." *Religions* 10: 624.
Neal, Judith. 2006. *Edgewalkers: People and Organizations That Take Risks, Build Bridges and Break New Ground*. Westport, CT: Praeger Press.
Negri, Antonio. 1999. "The Specter's Smile." In *Ghostly Demarcations—A Symposium on Jacques Derrida's Specters of Marx*, 5–16. London: Verso.
Nielson, Donald. 1999. *Three Faces of God: Society, Religion, the Categories of Totality in the Philosophy of Émile Durkheim*. Albany: State University of New York Press.
Nietzsche, Friedrich. [1887] 1989. *On the Genealogy of Morals and Ecce Homo*. New York: Vintage Books.
Ohmann, Richard, ed. 1996. *Making and Selling Culture*. Hanover, NH: Wesleyan University Press.
Oliphant, Elayne. 2021. *The Privilege of Being Banal: Art, Secularism, and Catholicism in Paris*. Chicago: University of Chicago Press.
Orsi, Robert. 2016. *History and Presence*. Cambridge, MA: Harvard University Press.
———. 2012. "Afterword: Everyday Religion and the Contemporary World." In *Ordinary Lives and Grand Schemes*, edited by Samuli Schielke and Liza Debevec, 146–161. New York: Berghahn Books.
———. 2010. "Theorizing Closer to Home." In *Harvard Divinity School Bulletin*, Winter/Spring, available online.

———. 2005. *Between Heaven and Earth—The Religious Worlds People Make and the Scholars Who Study Them*. Princeton, NJ: Princeton University Press.

Otnes, Cele and Tine Lowrey, eds. 2004. *Contemporary Consumption Rituals—A Research Anthology*. Mahwah, NJ: Lawrence Erlbaum Associates.

Otto, Rudolph. [1917] 1958. *The Idea of the Holy: An Inquiry into the Non-Rational Factor in the Idea of the Divine and Its Relation to the Rational*. London: Oxford University Press.

Outka, Gene. 1977. *Agape: An Ethical Analysis*. New Haven, CT: Yale University Press.

Packard, Packard. 1957. *The Hidden Persuaders*. Brooklyn, NY: IG Publishing.

Parkes Cadman, Samuel. 1916. *The Cathedral of Commerce*. New York: Broadway Park Place.

Parkin, Katherine. 2006. *Food Is Love: Advertising and Gender Roles in Modern America*. Philadelphia: University of Pennsylvania Press.

Patel, Geeta. 2008. "Ghostly Appearances." In *Secularisms*, edited by Janet Jakobsen and Ann Pellegrini, 226–246. Durham, NC: Duke University Press.

Pavitt, Jane. 2000. *Brand New*. Princeton, NJ: Princeton University Press.

Peirce, Charles Sanders. 1932. *Collected Papers. V. 1–6*. Cambridge, MA: Harvard University Press.

Pellegrini, Ann. 2007. "'Signaling Through the Flames': Hell House Performance and Structures of Religious Feeling." *American Quarterly* 59(3): 911–935.

Pérez-Peña, Richard. 2014. "Starbucks to Provide Free College Education to Thousands of Workers." *New York Times*, June 15. www.nytimes.com/.

Perucci, Tony. 2008. "Guilty as Sin: The Trial of Reverend Billy and the Exorcism of the Sacred Cash Register." *Text and Performance Quarterly* 28(3): 315–329.

Pietz, William. 1988. "The Problem of the Fetish, IIIa: Bosman's Guinea and the Enlightenment Theory of Fetishism." *RES: Anthropology and Aesthetics* 16: 105–124.

———. 1987. "The Problem of the Fetish, II: The Origin of the Fetish." *RES: Anthropology and Aesthetics* 13: 23–45.

———.1985. "The Problem of the Fetish, I." *RES: Anthropology and Aesthetics* 9: 5–17.

Pine, Joseph B and James H. Gilmore. 1999. *The Experience Economy: Work Is Theater and Every Business a Stage*. Cambridge, MA: Harvard Business Review Press.

Pinto, Nick. 2022. "ICE Settles with Immigrant Rights Leader Who Sued Over First Amendment Rights Violations." *The Intercept*, February 24. https://theintercept.com/.

Pope, Liston. 1942. *Millhands and Preachers—A Study of Gastonia*. New Haven, CT: Yale University Press.

Post, Dietmar and Lucía Palacios, dir. 2002. *Reverend Billy and the Church of Stop Shopping*. New York: Docurama Films. DVD.

Poster, Mark. 2006. *Information Please—Culture and Politics in the Age of Digital Machines*. Durham, NC: Duke University Press.

———. 1989. *Critical Theory and Poststructuralism—In Search of Context*. Ithaca, NY: Cornell University Press.

———. 1984. *Foucault, Marxism & History—Mode of Production Versus Mode of Information.* Cambridge: Polity Press.

———. 1975. *Existential Marxism in Postwar France—From Sartre to Althusser.* Princeton, NJ: Princeton University Press.

Puar, Jasbir. 2007. *Terrorist Assemblages—Homonationalism in Queer Times.* Durham, NC: Duke University Press.

Quart, Alissa. 2008. *Branded: The Buying and Selling of Teenagers.* New York: Basic Books.

Raboteau, Albert. [1978] 2004. *Slave Religion—The "Invisible Institution" of the American South.* New York: Oxford University Press.

Radford Ruther, Rosemary. 1995. *New Woman, New Earth: Sexist Ideologies and Human Liberation.* Boston: Beacon Press.

Radway, Janice. [1984] 1991. *Reading the Romance—Women, Patriarchy, and Popular Literature.* Chapel Hill: University of North Carolina Press.

Rappaport, Roy. 1999. *Ritual and Religion in the Making of Humanity.* Cambridge: Cambridge University Press.

Raschig, Megan and Laura McTighe. 2019. "An Anthropology Otherwise." Society for Cultural Anthropology. https://culanth.org/.

Reed, T. V. 2006. *The Art of Protest: Culture and Activism from the Civil Rights Movement to the Streets of Seattle.* Minneapolis: University of Minnesota Press.

Rehman, Jan. 2015. *Max Weber—Modernisation as Passive Revolution, a Gramscian Analysis.* Chicago: Haymarket Books.

Reid, Jennifer. 2020. "Introduction." In *With This Root About My Person: Charles H. Long and New Directions in the Study of Religion*, edited by Jennifer Reid and David Carrasco, ix–xxii. Albuquerque: University of New Mexico Press.

Related Companies. 2020. "The Vessel: Public Square and Gardens." www.hudsonyardsnewyork.com/ (Accessed November 12).

Reverend Billy and the Stop Shopping Choir. 2023. "Earth Chxrch." Instagram, 57:27. www.instagram.com.

———. 2022a. "Earth Riot: Edit 17 StereoNF." YouTube, 21:55. www.youtube.com/watch?v=y8GP_inTNlI.

———. 2022b. Podcast. *Earth Riot Radio.* https://open.spotify.com/show/17Lx8CLiPIiR6Ig8uPo6yJ.

———. 2019. "Rising Sea Levels in Chase Bank." YouTube, 1:36. www.youtube.com/watch?v=F4ROzsZoMkI.

———. 2018. "#32. California Fires, Orcas in Pain, Trump Depression Hotline," narrated by Savitri D and Reverend Billy, The Earth Wants You Podcast, *Soundcloud*, August 7. https://soundcloud.com.

———. 2013. "Reverend Billy & the Golden Toads @ Chase Bank in Manhattan." YouTube, 2:22. www.youtube.com/watch?v=d2kZ2fxy91g.

———. 2011. "Reverend Billy's Freakstorm: Life After Shopping." YouTube, 7:10. www.youtube.com/watch?v=Xw3LoKfiNWY.

———. 2007. "What Would Jesus Buy?" YouTube. Video, 1:31:07. www.youtube.com/watch?v=mAxuNdtZt7c.
Rifkin, Jeremy. 2000. *The Age of Access: The New Culture of Hypercapitalism—Where All of Life Is a Paid-For Experience*. New York: Tarcher.
Rinallo, Diego, Linda Scott, and Pauline Maclaran, eds. 2013. *Consumption and Spirituality*. London: Routledge.
Ritzer, George. 1993. *The McDonaldization of Society*. Los Angeles: Sage.
Robin, Corey. 2018. "The Erotic Professor—Money and the Murky Boundary of Teaching and Sex." *Chronicle of Higher Education*, May 13. www.chronicle.com/.
Robinson, Brett T. 2013. *Appletopia: Media Technology and the Religious Imagination of Steve Jobs*. Waco, TX: Baylor University Press.
Rolex. 2013. "The Role of Rolex with Roger Federer." February 20. Video, 3:39. www.youtube.com/watch?v=TW6Sp7lzDww.
Rose, Nicholas. [1989] 1999. *Governing the Soul—The Shaping of the Private Self*. London: Free Association Press.
Rose, Tricia. 2008. *The Hip Hop Wars: What We Talk About When We Talk About Hip Hop And Why It Matters*. New York: Basic Books.
———.1994. *Black Noise: Rap Music and Black Culture in Contemporary America*. Hanover, NH: Wesleyan University Press.
Rudnyckyj, Daromir. 2018. *Beyond Debt: Islamic Experiments in Global Finance*. Chicago: University of Chicago Press.
———. 2010. *Spiritual Economies: Islam, Globalization, and the Afterlife of Development*. Ithaca, NY: Cornell University Press.
Said, Edward. 2004. *Humanism and Democratic Criticism*. New York: Columbia University Books.
———. 1983. *The World, the Text, and the Critic*. Cambridge, MA: Harvard University Press.
Saint Clement's Episcopal Church, n.d. www.stclementsnyc.org/.
Samuel, Lawrence. 2013. *Shrink: A Cultural History of Psychoanalysis in America*. Lincoln: University of Nebraska Press.
———. 2010. *Freud on Madison Avenue—Motivation Research and Subliminal Advertising in America*. Philadelphia: University of Pennsylvania Press.
Sánchez, Abel and Andrés Alegría. 2021. Song for Cesar. Video Project: San Francisco.
Sandlin, Jennifer A. 2010. "Learning to Survive the 'Shopocalypse': Reverend Billy's Anti-Consumption 'pedagogy of the unknown.'" *Critical Studies in Education* (51)3: 295–311.
Sandlin, Jennifer A. and Jennifer L. Milam. 2008. "'Mixing Pop (Culture) and Politics': Cultural Resistance, Culture Jamming, and Anti-Activism as Critical Public Pedagogy." *Curriculum Inquiry* 38(3): 323–350.
Sartre, Jean-Paul. [1960] 2004. *The Critique of Dialectical Reason*, Vol. 1. London: Verso.
———. [1957] 1968. *Search for a Method*. New York: Vintage Books.

Schechner, Richard. 1977. *Essays in Performance Theory*. New York: Drama Book Specialists.
Scheffield, Tricia. 2006. *The Religious Dimensions of Advertising*. New York: Palgrave-McMillan.
Schleiermacher, Friedrich. [1799] 1996. *On Religion: Speeches to Its Cultured Despisers*. Cambridge: Cambridge University Press.
Schmidt, Leigh Eric. 1995. *Consumer Rites—The Buying and Selling of American Holidays*. Princeton, NJ: Princeton University Press.
Schneider, Rebecca. 2006. " 'Judith Butler' in My Hands." In *Bodily Citations—Religion and Judith Butler*, edited by Ellen T. Armour and Susan M. St. Ville, 225-251. New York: Columbia University Press.
Schor, Juliet. 2008. *Born to Buy: The Commercialized Child and the New Consumer Culture*. New York: Scribner.
———. 1999. "The New Politics of Consumption." In *Boston Review: A Political and Literary Forum*. www.bostonreview.net/.
Schrape, Niklas. 2014. "Gaia's Game." In *Communcation +1* 3(1): 1-24.
Schulman, Sarah. 2021. *Let the Record Show: A Political History of ACT UP New York, 1987-1993*. New York: Farrar, Straus, and Giroux.
Schwarzkopf, Stefan. 2014. "Introduction to Ernest Dichter and Motivation Research." *Market Research & American Business, 1935-1965*. Accessed May 7, 2020. www.marketresearch.amdigital.co.uk/.
Schwarzkopf, Stefan and Rainer Gries. 2010. "Motivation Research—Episode or Paradigm Shift? From Ernest Dichter to Consumer Ethnography, Neuromarketing and Bio-power." In *Ernest Dichter and Motivation Research: New Perspectives on the Making of Post-war Consumer Culture*, edited by Stefan Schwartzkopf and Ranier Gries, 269-290. London: Palgrave UK.
Scott, Felicity D. 2015. "Vanguards." In *E-Flux Journal* 64. https://oac.cdlib.org.
Scott, Joan W. 1991. "The Evidence of Experience." *Critical Inquiry* 17(4): 773-797.
Seales, Chad E. 2013. *The Secular Spectacle—Performing Religion in a Southern Town*. New York: Oxford University Press.
Searle, John. 1969. *Speech Acts*. Cambridge: Cambridge University Press.
Seigworth, Gregory and Melissa Gregg. 2010. "An Inventory of Shimmers." In *The Affect Theory Reader*, edited by Melissa Gregg and Gregory Seigworth, 1-25. Durham, NC: Duke University Press.
Seligman, Adam, Robert Weller, Michael Puett, and Bennett Simon. 2008. *Ritual and Its Consequences: An Essay on the Limits of Sincerity*. Oxford: Oxford University Press.
Shell, Marc. 1982. *Money, Language and Thought—Literary and Philosophical Economies from the Medieval to the Modern Era*. Berkeley: University of California Press.
Shepherd, Simon. 2016. *The Cambridge Introduction to Performance Theory*. Cambridge: Cambridge University Press.
Shirazi, Faeghah. 2016. *Brand Islam: The Marketing and Commodification of Piety*. Austin: University of Texas Press.

Simon, Bryant. 2011. *Everything but the Coffee: Learning about America from Starbucks*. Berkeley: University of California Press.

Simpson, Scott. 2011. "Joke Religions: Make-Believe in the Sandbox of the Gods." *Ex Nihilo* 2(6): 91–118.

Singh, Bhrigupati. 2014. "How Concepts Make the World Look Different: Affirmative and Negative Genealogies of Thought." In *The Ground Between—Anthropologists Engage Philosophy*, edited by Veena Das, Michael Jackson, Arthur Kleinman, and Bhrigupati Singh, 159–187. Durham, NC: Duke University Press.

Singh, Devin. 2018. *Divine Currency: The Theological Power of Money in the West*. Palo Alto, CA: Stanford University Press.

Slater, Don. 2005. *Consumer Culture & Modernity*. Cambridge: Polity Press.

Smith, Adam. [1749] 2002. *A Theory of Moral Sentiments*. Cambridge: Cambridge University Press.

Smith, J. Z. 1982. *Imagining Religion: From Babylon to Jonestown*. Chicago: University of Chicago Press.

Solomon, Alisa. 2013. "Introduction." In Savitri Durkee and Bill Talen, *The Reverend Billy Project*, edited by Alisa Solomon, 1–18. United States of America: Stop Shopping Publishing.

Sorett, Josef. 2016. *Spirit in the Dark: A Religious History of Racial Aesthetics*. New York: Oxford University Press.

Sorgo, Gabriele. 2010. "Ernest Dichter, Religion, and the Spirit of Capitalism: An Exegete of Pure Consumer Religion Serves Society." In *Ernest Dichter and Motivation Research: New Perspectives on the the Making of Post-war Consumer Culture*, edited by Stefan Schwartzkopf and Ranier Gries, 75–90. London: Palgrave.

Spiegel, Gabrielle. 2004. "Introduction." In *Practicing History—New Directions in Historical Writing After the Linguistic Turn*, edited by Gabrielle Spiegel, 1–31. London: Routledge.

Sprinkle, Annie, Beth Stephens, and Jennie Klein. 2021. *Assuming the Ecosexual Position: The Earth as Lover*. Minneapolis: University of Minnesota Press.

Stearns, Peter. 2001. *Consumerism in World History*. London: Routledge.

Stewart, Emily. 2023. "Target Giving in to Conservative Pressure on Pride Is Not a Great Sign." Vox, May 25. www.vox.com.

Stewart, Francis. 2017. *Punk Rock Is My Religion: Straight Edge Punk and "Religious" Identity*. London: Routledge.

Stoller, Paul. 2002. *Money Has No Smell: The Africanization of New York City*. Chicago: University of Chicago Press.

Stolz, John. 2016. "Gaia and Her Microbiome." *FEMS Microbiology Ecology* 93(2).

Surin, Kenneth. 2009. *Freedom Not Yet—Liberation and the Next World Order*. Durham, NC: Duke University Press.

Sweet, Elizabeth. 2014. "Toys Are More Divided by Gender Now Than They Were 50 years Ago." *The Atlantic* (Accessed June 16, 2019). www.theatlantic.com/.

Talen, William. 2023. "Saving the Earth Up the Street From Racist Murder." *The Revelator*, July 21. https://therevelator.org/.

———. 2012. *The End of the World*. New York: O/R Books.

———. 2006. *What Would Jesus Buy?—Fabulous Prayers in the Face of the Shopocalypse*. New York: Public Affairs.

———. 2003. *What Should I Do If Reverend Billy Is in My Store?*. New York: New Press.

Tambiah, Stanley. [1990] 2004. *Magic, Science, Religion, and the Scope of Rationality*. Cambridge, UK: Cambridge University Press.

Tarleton, John. 2023. "NYC's $13 Million Settlement with BLM Protestors 'Not a Victory But Something to Hold Onto.'" *The Indypendent*, July 25. https://indypendent.org/.

Taylor, Bron. 2009. *Dark Green Religion: Nature Religion and the Planetary Future*. Berkeley: University of California Press.

Taylor, Charles. 2007. *A Secular Age*. Cambridge, MA: Harvard University Press.

———. 1989. *Sources of the Self*. Cambridge, MA: Harvard University Press.

Taylor, Diana. 2007. "Afterward: Place-a-lujah!! Reverend Billy Claims a Democratic Public Space." In *Performing Religion in the Americas: Media, Politics, and Devotional Practices of the 21st Century*, edited by Alyshia Gálvez. Kolkata, India: Seagull Books.

Taylor, Timothy D. 2012. *Sounds of Capitalism: Advertising, Music, and the Conquest of Culture*. Chicago: University of Chicago Press.

Thompson, Craig and Arsel Zaynep. 2004. "The Starbucks Brandscape and Consumers' (Anticorporate) Experiences of Globalization." *Journal of Consumer Research* 31(3): 631–642.

Thorbecke, Catherine. 2021. "Gamestop Timeline: A Closer Look at the Saga that Upended Wall Street." ABC News, February 13. https://abcnews.go.com.

Thoreau, Henry David. [1854] 2012. *Walden and Civil Disobedience*. New York: Signet Classics.

Thornton, Daniel. 2019. "Star Wars Soundtracks: The Worship Music of John Williams." *Journal of Religion and Popular Culture* 31(1): 87–100.

Thrift, Nigel. 2010. "Understanding the Material Practices of Glamour." In *The Affect Theory Reader*, edited by Melissa Gregg and Gregory Seigworth, 289–308. Durham, NC: Duke University Press.

Thurston, Baratunde. 2007. "What Would Jesus Buy? (SXSW Starbucks Protest)." March 11, video. www.youtube.com/watch?v=zMQetYjbH5s.

Tönnies, Ferdinand. [1887] 2002. *Community and Society*. Mineola, NY: Dover.

Torchinsky, Rina. 2022. "Elon Musk Hints at a Crewed Mission to Mars in 2029." NPR, March 17. www.npr.org/.

Traub, James. 2004. *The Devil's Playground—A Century of Pleasure and Profit in Times Square*. New York: Random House.

Turner, Fred. 2006. *From Counterculture to Cyberculture: Stewart Brand, the Whole Earth Network, and the Rise of Digital Utopianism*. Chicago: University of Chicago Press.

Twitchell, James B. 2007. *Shopping for God: How Christianity Went from In Your Heart to In Your Face*. New York: Simon & Schuster.

Tylor, Edward Burnett (E.B.). [1871] 2016. *Primitive Culture: Research into the Development, Mythology, Philosophy, Religion, Language, Art, and Custom*. Mineola, NY: Dover.

Vaca, Daniel. 2023. "Reimagining the Gospel of Efficiency." *American Religion* 5(1): 33–65.

———. 2019. *Evangelicals Incorporated: Books and the Business of Religion in America*. Cambridge, MA: Harvard University Press.

Valdes, Danny. 2020. "Taking the Vac-Screen: How Community, Art and Getting Offline Can Fuel Movements." Through (Blog), December 12. https://through.blog/.

VanAlkemade, Rob, dir. 2007. *What Would Jesus Buy?* New York: Arts Alliance Films, DVD.

Veblen, Thorstein [1899] 2005. *Theory of the Leisure Class: An Economic Study of Institutions*. Delhi: Aakar Books.

Vitello, Paul. 2013. "Sidney Lanier, 90, Experimental Stage Producer, Is Dead." *New York Times*, October 5. www.nytimes.com.

Wallace, Mark. 2018. *When God Was a Bird: Christianity, Animism, and the Re-Enchantment of the World*. New York: Fordham University Press.

Walton, Jonathan. 2009. *Watch This!—The Ethics and Aesthetics of Black Televangelism*. New York: New York University Press.

Weber, Max. [1922b] 1946. "The Meaning of Discipline." In *From Max Weber—Essays in Sociology*, edited by H. H. Gerth and C. W. Mills, 253–264. London: Oxford University Press.

———. [1922a] 1946. "The Sociology of Charismatic Authority." In *From Max Weber—Essays in Sociology*, edited by H. H. Gerth and C. W. Mills, 245–252. London: Oxford University Press.

———. [1919a] 1946. "Politics as a Vocation." In *From Max Weber—Essays in Sociology*, edited by H. H. Gerth and C. W. Mills, 77–128. London: Oxford University Press.

———. [1919b] 1946. "Science as a Vocation." In *From Max Weber—Essays in Sociology*, edited by H. H. Gerth and C. W. Mills, 129–156. London: Oxford University Press.

———. [1915a] 1946. "Religious Rejections of the World and their Directions." In *From Max Weber—Essays in Sociology*, edited by H. H. Gerth and C. W. Mills, 323–359. London: Oxford University Press.

———. [1915b] 1946. "The Social Psychology of the World Religions." In *From Max Weber—Essays in Sociology*, edited by H. H. Gerth and C. W. Mills, 267–301. London: Oxford University Press.

———. [1904–1905] 2002. *The Protestant Ethic and the Spirit of Capitalism*. New York: Penguin Classics.

Weil, Elizabeth. 2023. "You Are Not a Parrot and a Chatbot Is Not a Human." *New York Magazine*, March 1.

Weiner, Isaac. 2014. *Religion Out Loud: Religious Sounds, Public Space, and American Pluralism*. New York: New York University Press.

Weisgram, Erica and Lisa Dinella, eds. 2018. *Gender Typing of Children's Toys: How Early Play Experiences Impact Development*. Washington, DC: American Psychological Association Books.

Wenger, Tisa. 2009. *We Have Religion: The 1920s Pueblo Indian Dance Controversy and American Religious Freedom*. Chapel Hill: University of North Carolina Press.

West, Cornel. 2022. "Trump Isn't Out There with a Gun, but He's Enabled This War against Black People." *The Guardian*, May 21. www.theguardian.com/.

———. 1999. "On My Intellectual Vocation." In *The Cornel West Reader*, 19–33. New York: Basic Books.

———. 1989. *The American Evasion of Philosophy—A Genealogy of Pragmatism*. Madison: University of Wisconsin Press.

Weston, Kath. 2019. "The Ethnographer's Magic as Sympathetic Magic." *Social Anthropology* 26(1): 15–29.

———. 2017. *Animate Planet*. Durham, NC: Duke University Press.

———. 2002. *Gender in Real Time—Power and Transience in a Virtual Age*. London: Routledge.

Whitman, Walt. [1860] 1991. "I Hear America Singing." In *Selected Poems*, 1. New York: Dover Publications.

Whyte, William. 1956. *The Organization Man*. New York: Simon & Schuster.

Wiener, Norbert. 1954. *The Human Use of Human Beings: Cybernetics and Society*. Boston: Da Capo Press.

Wilcox, Melissa M. 2018. *Queer Nuns—Religion, Activism, and Serious Parody*. New York: New York University Press.

Wilkinson, Darryl. 2017. "Is There Such a Thing as Animism?" *Journal of the American Academy of Religion* 85(2): 289–311.

Wilson, Mark. 2018. "The Starbucks Logo Has a Secret You've Never Noticed." January 18. www.fastcompany.com/.

Winters, Joseph. 2011. "Unstrange Bedfellows: Religion and Hip Hop." *Religion Compass* 5/6: 260–270.

Yakas, Ben. 2021. "Vessel at Hudson Yards Will Reopen With Big Changes." *Gothamist*, May 26. https://gothamist.com.

Yale Forum on Religion & Ecology. 2020. "Climate Heroes: Reverend Billy and Savitri D." https://fore.yale.edu/news (Accessed March 31, 2022).

Zaloom, Caitlin. 2006. *Out of the Pits—Traders and Technology from Chicago to London*. Chicago: University of Chicago Press.

Zaltman, Gerald. 2003. *How Customers Think: Essential Insights into the Mind of the Market*. Cambridge, MA: Harvard Business School Press.

Zamora, Daniel. 2016. "Foucault, the Excluded, and the Neoliberal Erosion of the State." In *Foucault and Neoliberalism*, edited by Daniel Zamora and Michael C. Behrent, 63–84. Cambridge: Polity Press.

Zaretsky, Eli. 2017. *Political Freud: A History*. New York: Columbia University Press.

———. 2005. *Secrets of the Soul: A Social and Cultural History of Psychoanalysis*. New York: Vintage Books.

Zito, Angela. 2008. "Secularizing the Pain of Foot Binding in China: Missionary and Medical Stagings of the Universal Body." In *Secularisms*, edited by Janet Jakobsen and Ann Pellegrini, 205–225. Durham, NC: Duke University Press.
———. 1997. *Of Body & Brush: Grand Sacrifice as Text/Performance in Eighteenth-Century China*. Chicago: University of Chicago Press.

# INDEX

Abbey, Edward, 218
Abram, David, on humanity and the nonhuman world, 285n26
abstraction, 88–90; of the debt concept, 278n3; and the fashion industry, 184–85; and marketing, 62; refusal of, 165; and secular reason, 101, 264n13
acting, 279n20; and agency, 106; as if, 160, 288n42
activism, 122; eco- (and high art), 286n33; and love, 152; and performance, 240n28; and place, 185; and political affiliation, 274n85; religious, 120; and scholarship, 213–18, 245n51, 249n10, 287n39; and singing, 7–9, 132, 146–47, 278n10
ACT UP, 34, 108, 255n42, 274n76, 282n44; insider strategy of, 273n75
Adbusters, on ideological reproduction in business schools, 251n20
Adorno, Theodor, 101, 241n29, 267n8, 269n26; on the culture industry, 133, 263n3, 263n8; on experience and capital, 131, 133, 267n8; on intelligence, 1; on marketers and meaning, 279n13; on music, 263n8
advertising, 162–63, 185–85; and agency, 11, 69–70; and "best lives," 204; and the body, 164; and children, 77, 82–83, 86; and choice/freedom, 11, 69–70, 137; and control, 160; and Freud, 90; for iPods, 15–19; and memory/nostalgia, 86; and music, 130–31; resistance to, 42; and subjectivity, 75; subliminal, 51, 72,

287n40; as ubiquitous, 163; and visual clichés, 249n11. *See also* marketing
*Advertising Age*, on Starbucks' success, 47
agency, 136; and acting, 106; and activism, 189; and advertising, 11, 69–70; and the Church of Stop Shopping, 134–37; and collective organization, 240n22; and the commodity fetish, 122; and community, 160; consumer, 246n57; and control, 154; creative, 137, 159–60; critical, 80, 111; historicity of, 163; and loss, 87; moral, 139; and performativity, 59; political, 120; and singing, 167–68; and subjectivity, 51. *See also* choice; freedom
Alegría, Andrés, 132
alienation: of (old-school) activists, 178; as avoided by the Church of Stop Shopping, 242n33; of Black audiences, 109; capitalist, 88–89, 245n53, 264n15; and collective action, 241n29; Marxist, 270n34; and the Passion, 240n28; self-, 143
Allard, La Donna Brave Bull, 218
Amazon, 121; and actions by the Church of Stop Shopping, 3, 12–13. *See also* Bezos, Jeff
American Place Theater, 106
anarchism, 11, 139, 142, 146, 193, 270n34; and gender, 256n43; neo-, 104; and organization, 156
Angelou, Maya, 218
anger: as leading to action, 205–6; of Reverend Billy, 35, 197

animisms, 117, 124–26, 199, 209–10, 227, 234
archeology, existential, 171–72
archive: as critical resource, 198–99, 255n37, 268n16
Armour, Ellen T.: on performativity, 57
Artificial Intelligence, 226, 287n38; and marketing, 287n40
Asad, Talal, 16, 264n13; on post-capitalist life, 210; on secular reason, 101–2, 266n42; on secularism, 282n42
attachment, affective, 65, 77, 79, 82–83
Austin, J. L., 57, 253n33
authenticity, 239n19; and the Black Church, 108–9, 148, 171, 265n24, 272n59; consumer, 53; and consuming religion, 269n27; and religious costumes, 184; and roughness, 142

Baez, Joan: and the Church of Stop Shopping, 3
Bailey, Edward: and implicit religion, 215, 285n25
Balmer, John: on corporate brands, 44
Bartel, Rebecca, 19–20, 245n53, 259n17; on neoliberal economy, 76; on the work of religious studies, 269n27
Basso, Keith, 281n36
Bateson, Gregory: and cybernetics, 223. See also cybernetics
Bekkering, Denis, 108
Bell, Catherine, 16, 91, 253n30, 254n34; on misrecognition, 50, 250n18, 251n19; on redemptive hegemony, 52–54, 90, 113, 260n28; on ritualization, 26, 39–41, 44, 47–54, 57–59, 76, 90, 224, 257n3, 265n35
Bell, Daniel, 113
Bell, Sean, 65
belonging: and consumption, 258n6; and shopping, 8; and the "Starbucks Experience," 47
Benjamin, Walter: on capitalism as religious, 99, 202, 261n32; on the *flâneur*, 239n15

Berger, Peter: on the "sacred canopy," 250n16
Bergson, Henri, 273n71
Berlant, Lauren: on capitalism's "cruel optimism," 261n37
Berman, Marshall: on capitalism, 6–7; on critics of urban modernism, 239n18. See also capitalism
Bernays, Edward: on propaganda, 258n8; and public relations, 68–69. See also marketing; public relations
Berry, Wendell, 218
Best, Wallace, 276n93
Bezos, Jeff, 121, 279n18. See also Amazon
Biden, Joe: musical playlist of, 129–30. See also music
Biggart, Nicole: on direct selling organizations, 248n7
Bivins, Jason, 134, 160. See also music
Black Church: and authenticity, 108–9, 148, 171, 265n24, 272n59; and the Civil Rights movement, 22, 108
Black Friday, 100
Black Lives Matter, 13, 121, 141, 164, 242n37, 281n35
Bland, Sandra, 65
Bloomberg, Mike, 10, 13, 36, 237n7, 239n18; and Hudson Yards, 4. See also Hudson Yards; New York City
body, the: and advertising, 164; and capital, 10; and citation, 76, 80, 224; and consuming religion, 243n43; corporatization of, 18–19; and cosmology, 145; and desire, 79; and the environment, 48; and habits, 2, 48; and ingestion, 204–5; and memory, 36, 57; as metaphor, 250n17; and music, 135, 151; and narrative, 9; and perception, 239n15; as the plan, 122; and rationality, 177–78, 272n66; and resistance, 151; and ritualization, 47; as sign, 254n34; and the social, 287n39; vs. soul, 17; vs. thought, 145; and the voice, 145; warming up of, 10

Boltanski, Luc: on postindustrial capitalism, 180, 221
Bonds, Judi, 218
Booker, Vaughn, 132
Boston Clean Energy Coalition (BCEC), 181–82
Bourdieu, Pierre, 260n26, 277n110; on capital and social life, 10
boycott: as requested by the Church of Stop Shopping, 98; of Disney, 255n42
Brand, Stewart: *Whole Earth Catalog*, 112–13, 220–22
brand: and consumer choice, 219–20; devotion, 248n7; flexibility of, 52; as lifestyle, 47, 52; as lover, 11, 97, 177; management, 262n40; prestige of, 50, 53, 72; representation, 278n9; "speech" of, 255n42; values of, 42, 52–53, 90, 249n11
branding, 4–6, 41–44, 57, 161–62, 176, 239n18, 253n31, 254nn35–36, 268n21, 279n20; brand anthropologists, 34, 43; and citation, 38–39, 138, 165, 252n25, 254n36; corporate, 35, 42–43; of consumers, 250n14; and cybernetics, 222–23; and desire, 250n13; and difference, 161, 165, 252n25; and narrative, 52, 269n22; and New York City, 96, 239n17; and performativity, 76, 102, 134, 161–62, 252n23, 255n37; and religion, 22, 35; and repetition, 40, 53, 161; and ritualization, 15, 26, 38–40, 54–57, 90, 115, 137, 140, 250n12, 252n23, 255n37, 257n3; self-, 41, 238n10; as social act, 43–44, 47–48, 113; and transformation, 44, 269n22; urban 6, 237n7
Brash, Julian: on urban branding, 237n7. *See also* branding
Bread and Puppet, 207, 252n26
British Petroleum, 12, 279n19; and climate change, 188. *See also* climate change/catastrophe
Brooks, David, 251n21

Brown, Michael, 242n37. *See also* police brutality
Brown, Wendy, 240n26, 248n64, 255n40
Bruce, Lenny, 107, 197
Buckel, David: protest suicide of, 186–87, 279n14. *See also* climate change; suicide
Bumpers, Eleanor, 65, 257n4
Burning Man, 111–12, 265n28
Butler, Judith, 91, 244n47, 253n30, 260nn23–24, 277n111; on capitalism, 260n29; on chatbots, 287n38; on contingent academic labor, 284n17; and cybernetic discourse, 224, 287n38; on embodied critique, 287n39; on ethics, 261n38; on experiences of freedom, 260n26; on gender, 82, 92, 253n33, 254n34, 260n24, 287n39; on mania and critique, 203–4; on melancholia, 79, 203–5; on performativity, 57–60, 76, 82–83, 134, 204, 223, 253n32, 254n34, 255n42, 287n38; on power, 26–27, 77–85, 88, 90, 160–61, 203, 259n20; and religious studies, 57; on subjectivization, 77–78, 82, 275n91; on theory and empiricism, 263n43

Caceres, Berta, 218
Cadman, Parkes: on the Woolworth Building, 238n13. *See also* Woolworth Building
Callahan, Richard: on Holiness Pentecostalism and union organizing, 21
call-out culture, 142
capitalism, 6–7, 16–17, 34–39, 279n12, 180, 207; vs. ecological well-being, 284n15; and efficiency, 261n36, 278n2; fast, 2; and feeling, 6; and freedom, 182; and libido, 201–6; and loss, 76, 85, 274n77; and music, 263n8; as not indexed (elsewhere), 283n8; and power, 3; and Protestantism, 119–20; and race, 257n3, 287n2; rainbow, 255n42, 261n33;

capitalism (*cont.*)
    and religion, 16–22, 40, 68, 174–77, 180, 191; as religious, 99; and repetition, 34, 36–39, 80, 204; and the romantic, 249n9; and scholarship, 14–23, 212; and soul-craft, 3–4, 9, 56, 66, 76, 85, 120, 178; and subjectivity, 91, 162; and the unconscious, 259n20. *See also* post-secular capitalism
capitalism, new spirit of, 180
Carrasco, Davíd, 264n10, 277n113, 281n33; on religious experience, 218, 238n9
Carrasco, Octavio: on popular music, 132, 268n14. *See also* music
Carter, Heath: and social Christianity, 21
Castelli, Elizabeth, 285n24. *See also* history; race
Catholic Mass, 48–50, and experience, 50; and familiarity 52
chain stores, 34, 46. *See also* Starbucks
chance, 169–71, 277n110
charisma: and capitalism, 175, 177, 248n7
charity, 240n22; and class, 8. *See also* gift-giving
Chase Bank, 7; and actions by the Church of Stop Shopping, 3, 12–13, 121, 188, 190–95, 205–6, 240n28, 280n24, 280n27; and climate change, 13, 121, 188, 190, 192, 206. *See also* climate change/catastrophe
Chiapello, Eve: on postindustrial capitalism, 180, 221
Chino, Kobun: on spiritual health and business, 18
choice: and advertising/marketing, 11, 69–70, 137; consumer (anticipated), 219–20; existential vs. economic, 278n6; false, 202; and neoliberalism, 261n31. *See also* agency; freedom
choreography: of the Church of Stop Shopping Choir, 173, 178, 199; of consumer capitalism, 12, 56–57. *See also* gestures

Church of Stop Shopping, 12–14, 92–126, 237n5, 279n20; and Amazon, 3, 12–13; as award-winning, 3; "Beautiful Earth," 197; "Beatitudes of Buylessness," 66, 101, 173; "Blessed Be the 1's," 196; cell phone opera, 38, 53, 58; *change without us*, 243n40; and Chase Bank, 3, 12–13, 121, 188, 190–95, 205–6, 240n28, 280n24, 280n27; Choir, 7–9, 11, 27–28, 35, 115, 121, 123, 131–32, 137–52, 173–74, 178, 180, 183, 189, 195–200, 206, 225, 270n37, 272n57, 274n84, 275n89; and community, 56, 89–90, 114, 116, 118–19, 123, 141, 143, 146–48, 150–52, 157–58, 160, 181, 189, 218, 227, 253n33; and (taking) credit, 242n38; delegation within, 156; "Digger's Song," 187; and Disney, 12, 27, 33, 95–100, 102–4, 115, 121, 159; diversity of, 141, 146–49, 256n43; and Earth Justice, 3, 13, 22, 27–28, 65, 85, 111–18, 122–23, 141, 158, 178, 181–201, 208, 216, 223–25, 247n61, 283n7, 288n43; and the "Fabulous Unknown," 45, 122, 195–96, 198, 226–27, 264n14, 282n2; "First Amendment," 149; funding of, 155–56, 158, 272n58, 274n83; gatekeeping, 157, 270n35, 272n60, 275nn86–87; governance of, 272n58; "Great Outdoors," 165; and Harvard University, 12, 242n35; "Imagination," 147; "Machines," 225; and memorialization, 282n40, 282n44; as "post-religious," 7, 27–28, 199, 208, 227, 275n88, 281n37, 263n4, 275n88; radicalness of, 225–26; Radical Ritual events of, 271n38, 279n21; as "real" church, 118, 157–58, 275n88, 282n2; recruitment, 272n60; as safe space, 149; and sainthood, 243n41; and Samaritan's Purse, 201, 240n26; sexual politics of, 201; as social project, 156; and Starbucks, 3, 26, 33–62, 73–74, 86, 159, 173, 178, 204–5; Statue of Liberty

INDEX | 321

action, 238n10; "The Storm," 195–96; suitcase event, 63–64; Supreme Court decision actions, 282n44 tension within, 149–50, 155–58, 201, 275n89, 282n2; and Trump Tower, 34, 140–41, 145; twentieth anniversary celebration, 195–99, 225; "Unknowness," 165–66; and Walmart, 3, 12. *See also* Earth Chxrch; Savitri D; Reverend Billy

citation: bodily, 76, 80, 224; and branding, 38–39, 138, 165, 252n25, 254n36; and consumerism, 161; and consumption, 90; gestures as, 34, 38–39; and performativity, 61; and power, 90; and ritual, 58, 61; and social media, 288n44

civilization, 203–4, 186, 259n21, 286n33

climate change/catastrophe, 122–23, 141, 181–201, 208–13, 266n42; and capitalism, 211–12; and race, 195; and shopping, 9, 15

Code Pink: and the Church of Stop Shopping, 13

collectivity: and authorship, 284n18; and choirs, 165, 167–68, 189

Comaroff, Jean and John: on consumption and identity, 267n7. *See also* consumption; identity

commodity fetishism, 50, 61, 75–76, 99–100, 121–22, 239n19, 256n45, 264n10. *See also* fetish

communication: between advertiser and consumers, 70, 249n8; between consumer and workers, 56–57, 104; between human and non-human, 210, 216–18, 223; feedback loops, 220

community: and agency, 160; and the Church of Stop Shopping, 56, 89–90, 114, 116, 118–19, 123, 141, 143, 146–48, 150–52, 157–58, 160, 181, 189, 218, 227, 253n33; Earth as, 158; and justice, 151–52; and loss, 88; and music, 87–88, 129, 132–33, 138–39; and religion, 137, 212; and singing, 129, 138–39, 165, 167–68

Company of US (USCO), 112–13

consuming religion, 4–6, 52, 59, 84, 161, 179, 195, 213, 225, 228, 243n43, 259n15, 268n16, 269n27, 284n16, 288n42. *See also* Lofton, Kathryn; religion

consumption: and belonging, 258n6; and childhood development, 83; as citational, 90; creative, 160; and death, 187; and forgetting, 203; and lack, 81; as loss, 88–89; and freedom, 68, 113, 159–60, 162, 246n57; as gendered, 100, 263n7, 271n40; and identity, 84, 267n7; imagination vs. 198, 201; as iterative, 81, 90; and mediation, 83; and memory, 36, 203; and mothers, 261n30; as motivational theater, 70; and norms, 260n26; and religion, 246n57; vs. resistance, 10; and ritual, 5, 59, 65, 74–76, 250n12; and self-making, 203, 255n42; and the social, 241n32, 270n32; as ubiquitous, 78

control: and advertising, 160; and character, 110; decentralized, 222; of the Earth (attempted), 264n15; and freedom, 23, 51–52, 136–37, 139, 154, 162, 242n34; iterative, 74–77. *See also* freedom

convention, 58, 83, 90, 159, 162, 237n1. *See also* sameness

conversion, 113–14, 222, 276n101

Cooper, Melinda, 260n29; on neoliberalism, 60, 240n26, 255n39; on performativity and neoliberalism, 60

COP 26, 197, 211, 283n10. *See also* climate change/catastrophe

costumes: as arresting, 183–84; and authenticity, 184; and the Church of Stop Shopping, 190–94, 197, 242n35, 277n109; and Reverend Billy, 11, 22, 45, 117, 188. *See also* fashion; drag; masks

Cox, Harvey, 20; on music and the market, 130. *See also* music

Crapanzano, Vincent, 182

critical theory of religion: vs. critical religion, 285n21

Crossan, John Dominic, 107
Cuomo, Andrew, 242n38
Curts, Kati: on secularism's religious features, 256n44
cybernetics, 287n38, 287n40, 289n46; and branding, 222–23, 252n25; and Derrida, 223–24, 286n34; and performativity, 220–28, 286n37, 288n42. *See also* performativity

Dada, 145; and data, 223
Danesi, Marcel: on branding as social act, 43–44. *See also* branding
Dar al-Islam, 113. *See also* Durkee, Stephen
data collection, 51, 70, 219; "depth interview," 71; and IRBs, 270n29
Dávila, Arlene: on "Latinos Inc.," 130
deafness, 272n61; and sound, 149
death: "die-ins," 255n42; drive, 186–87; as part of life, 197; of a pet, 167; "rising dead" within, 24, 29, 86, 101, 194, 206; and silence, 196. *See also* suicide
Debord, Guy: on capitalism, 241n29; on the society of the spectacle, 7, 239n19. *See also* spectacle
decentering: of the consumer, 249n8; of humanity, 146; of the subject, 41, 249n8
de Certeau, Michel, 131; on religion and consumption, 246n57
DeDomenici, Richard: *In Bed with the Rev*, 237n4. *See also* Reverend Billy
Deleuze, Gilles: and cybernetics, 223. *See also* cybernetics
DeNora, Tia: on music and agency, 267. *See also* agency; music
Derrida, Jacques, 253n33, 276nn94–95, 287n38; and cybernetics, 223–24, 286n34; ethics of, 276n94; on the trace, 260n27. *See also* cybernetics
DeSantis, Ron: and Disney, 255n42. *See also* Disney
description: and social reality, 57–58

desire, 260n24; antinormative, 85; to avoid death, 187; to *be*, 78; and branding, 250n13; capitalization of, 259n20; consumer, 41, 53, 55, 59, 63, 68–73, 83, 180, 258n10; embodied, 79; formation of, 82, 258n10; for God, 84; and homophobia, 79; and music, 131; redirection of, 65, 69; repressed, 70; strategy of (for the Church of Stop Shopping), 140
*détournement*, 101, 264n11
devotion, 129, 272n66; brand, 248n7; to the Church of Stop Shopping, 275n86; domestication of, 175; and the iPod, 18
Diallo, Amadou, 65
Dichter, Ernest, 26, 81–85, 88, 113, 219, 258nn11–12, 259n15, 286n35; clients of, 72; on consumer society, 258n14; on desire, 63; and marketing, 68–77, 80–85, 122, 176, 203, 224; on melancholia, 84; on mothers and consumption, 261n30; on motivation, 82; protoperformativity of, 76; on ritualization, 74–77, 134. *See also* Freud, Sigmund; marketing; ritualization
Dickinson, Greg: on Starbucks and ritual, 54, 252n25. *See also* ritualization; Starbucks
difference: and branding, 161, 165, 252n25; and consumption, 260n28; internal, 252n26; melancholy and, 79–80; metabolized, 252n23; and performativity, 80, 162, 255n39; and sameness, 51–54, 58, 61, 138, 198–200, 204, 219, 255n39
Dimon, Jamie, 121. *See also* Chase Bank
Disney, 125, 160, 197; and actions by the Church of Stop Shopping, 12, 27, 33, 95–100, 102–4, 115, 121, 159; and exploitation, 97–98, 101–4; and LGBT issues, 255n42; and stereotyping, 264n12
disruption, 190–91, 198, 204–5. *See also* Church of Stop Shopping

diversity: of the Church of Stop Shopping Choir, 141, 146–49, 256n43; and marketability, 148; of New York City, 167
Dochuck, Darren, 21
dogma, 166–67
drag, 253n33; Drag March, 242n33; *Pose*, 253n33; religious, 22; *RuPaul's Drag Race*, 183. *See also* costumes
Duberman, Martin: on the Stonewall riot, 282n43
Dubuisson, Daniel, 16
Durkee, Barbara, 112–14. *See also* Lama Foundation
Durkee, Savitri. *See* Savitri D
Durkee, Stephen, 266n37; conversion of, 113–14, 222; and USCO, 112–13. *See also* Lama Foundation
Durkheim, Émile, 17, 161, 244n47, 275n91

Earth: as celebrity, 283n5; as consciousness, 223–24; humanity as one with, 86, 115–16, 121, 123–24, 146, 188, 197, 205, 208, 217, 227; as lover, 272n54
Earth Church. *See* Earth Chxrch
Earth Chxrch, 207–13, 216, 219, 223–24, 227–28, 282nn1–2, 283n7, 288n43, 288n43. *See also* Church of Stop Shopping
Earth Justice, 3, 13, 22, 27–28, 65, 85, 111–18, 122–23, 141, 158, 178, 181–201, 208, 216, 223–25, 247n61, 283n7, 288n43. *See also* Church of Stop Shopping
economy: and culture, 41, 44; and language, 255n39; and mediation, 255n39; political, 237n3; real vs. financial, 237n2; and religion, 18, 111, 212
ecumenism, 114–15, 157, 274n84
Eisner, Michael, 98; and labor exploitation, 101. *See also* Disney
Eliade, Mircea: 16
embarrassment, 142–43
end of the world, 125–26; as we know it, 228; and feeling fine, 288n41. *See also* climate change/catastrophe; Extinction

ethnography, 19, 162–64, 169, 247nn60–61, 274n78; and intersubjectivity, 162; and narrative, 162. *See also* scholarship
everyday, 40; artefacts, 64; gestures, 10, 36, 38, 54, 56–57; movements (of the body), 2; and performance, 280n21; practices (of capitalism), 9, 51; religion, 228, 243n44; 269n24; 288n45
exorcism, 47, 104, 115, 122; of cash registers, 38–40, 45, 178, 189; of climate change demons, 188
experience, 268n16, 272n56; and capital, 131, 133, 267n8; and the Catholic Mass, 50; economy, 120, 286n32; as linguistic event, 257n49; and power, 59; rediscovering, 62; religious, 218; sonic, 132; the Starbucks, 45–50, 55–56, 250n18; suprarational dimensions of, 268n21
exploitation, 205: of children, 78; by Disney, 97–98, 101–4; in the coffee industry, 54–56, 73; in the fashion industry, 184. *See also* labor
Extinction, 90, 123, 181–201, 208, 243n39. *See also* end of the world
extraction, resource, 84, 196. *See also* climate change/catastrophe

familiarity, 51–52
fashion, 184–85, 279n12. *See also* drag; costumes
Fauconnier, Gilles: on creativity, 250n12
Federer, Roger: brand partnership with Rolex, 43. *See also* branding
feeling: and capitalism, 6; and markets, 46; vs. understanding, 1
Feltmate, David, on religious satire, 118
Ferguson protests, 13, 121, 242n37
Fessenden, Tracy, 136, 276n105; on authenticity and the Black Church, 272n59. *See also* authenticity; Black Church; music
fetish, 99–104, 111, 115, 124, 126, 197; and race, 99–100. *See also* commodity fetishism

Feuerbach, Ludwig, 269n25, 273n70; we are what we eat, 123, 266n49
Finney, Charles, 14
Fischer-Lichte, Erika: on performance, 280n21
*flâneur*, 239n15. *See also* walking
Floyd, George, 242n37. *See also* police brutality
Floyd, Kevin, 260n29
Fogo Azul, 64
Ford, Christine Blasey, 164
Ford, Henry, 76
Foucault, Michel, 60, 68, 91, 125, 160, 241n31, 248n64, 252n24, 259n19, 276n106, 277n113, 287n38; and cybernetics, 223–24; on governmentality, 258n5, 262n40; on heterotopias, 275n90; on norms, 78–79. *See also* cybernetics; norms; power
Frank, Thomas: on critiques of capitalism, 241
Fraser, Nancy, 59; on capitalism, 89; and the Church of Stop Shopping, 141
freedom, 107; and advertising, 11, 69–70, 83; and capitalism, 182; and chance, 169; and consumption, 68, 113, 159–60, 162, 246n57; and control, 23, 51–52, 136–37, 139, 154, 162, 242n34; and finitude, 186; and history, 150; and labor, 180; and music, 132, 151; as physical, 134; and the secular/religious, 119, 131, 136–37; and the social, 260n26; worker, 180. *See also* agency; choice; control
Freedom Tower, 4
Freedom University, 284n18
Freud, Sigmund, 67–68, 74, 76, 79, 90–91, 100, 196, 203, 224, 249n8, 253n33, 258n8, 259nn20–21, 260n23, 260n27, 287n38; on the death drive, 82–83; on melancholia, 203–4; on the Oedipal complex, 259n21; on the pleasure principle, 258n12. *See also* Butler, Judith; Dichter, Ernest; marketing; psychoanalysis
Fukuyama, Francis, 73

Gac, Scott, 268n12
Gaia theory, 223–24, 286n36; cybernetic aspects of, 224
Galbraith, John K.: on markets and desire, 69, 258n10. *See also* desire: consumer
Garland, Judy, 282n43
gender: and anarchism, 256n43; and consumption, 100, 263n7, 271n40; criminalization of, 64; and labor, 270n37; and nature, 266n46; and performativity, 60–61, 253n32; and socialization, 82
gentrification, 34, 39, 239n17, 241n30, 283n6
gestures: and the body, 151; as citation, 34, 38–39; consumerist, 10, 36, 38, 54; everyday, 10, 36, 38, 54, 56–57; of a preacher, 148
Gibson, Larry, 218
gift-giving, 280n27; and misrecognition, 250n18. *See also* charity
Gilmore, James H., 286n32
Giuliani, Rudy, 96, 104
Glaude, Eddie: on Butler's account of performativity, 134. *See also* Butler, Judith
gods, 136–37. *See also* idolatry
Goffman, Ervin, 286n32; on interaction rituals, 103, 191
Golden Rule Christianity, 273n70
Goldman, Emma, 108; on love, 151
Gómez-Peña, Guillermo: and the Church of Stop Shopping, 13
governmentality, 258n5, 258n7, 262n40, 277n108
Graeber, David, 139; on anarchist struggle, 270n34; and the Church of Stop Shopping, 13, 24, 60; on contemporary left academic thinking, 144; death of, 271n48; on the debt concept, 278n3; on gifts, 280n27; on performativity, 60,

219; on scholars and activists, 24–25, 214, 271n49
Graham, Billy, 154, 201
Graham, Franklin, 201, 240n26
Great Recession, 111, 242n37
Greer, Asha. *See* Durkee, Barbara
Grimes, Ronald: on acting, 279n20
Guardian Angels, 273n73
Guattari, Félix: and cybernetics, 223. *See also* cybernetics

habits: of the body, 2, 48; of the heart, 68
Hall, Stuart: on Hippie expressivism, 113. *See also* Hippie expressivism
Hammond, Sara, 20–21
Handman, Wynn, 106–7
Hardt, Michael, 138
Hartman, Saidiya, 149–50
Harvard University: and actions by the Church of Stop Shopping, 12, 242n35; Divinity School, 243n42, 245n50, 274n81
Harvey, David: on neoliberalism, 67–68
Hegel, G. F. W., 241n29; on devotion, 129, 272n66
Heidegger, Martin: on being-toward-death, 186–87. *See also* death
Hennessy, Rosemary, 270n37; on desire in bourgeois ideologies, 82. *See also* desire
Henry, Bill, 108
Hippie expressivism, 113, 217, 220
history, 136; braided, 249n11, 276n98; collective meanings of, 169; and freedom, 150; *historicize!*, 60, 66–67, 81, 85, 91–92, 133, 154, 168, 171, 202–3, 223–24, 226–27, 244n47, 275n91, 287n38; and nature, 218; and open-endedness, 169; and performativity, 60–61
Holloway, John: on capitalism, 34; on the indicative and subjunctive moods of social criticism, 193; on social criticism and dissonance, 193–94

Hollywood, Amy: on melancholy, 89; on ritual and performativity, 58–59, 61
Holmes, Douglas: on fast capitalism, 2. *See also* capitalism
Holt, Douglas: on brands and identity, 52, 238n11
homophobia, 87–88, 148; and the church, 109, 153–54, 166–67, 201, 240n26; and popular music, 133; and sexual desire, 79
Hoover, Herbert: on marketers, 258n10
Horkheimer, Max, 241n29; on the culture industry, 133, 263n3, 263n8; on marketers and meaning, 279n13
Hudson Yards, 1–2, 4–7, 12, 34, 131. *See also* New York City; Vessel
Hughes, Langston, 276n93; on race and American democracy, 164–65, 277n107
Hulsether, Lucia, 19–22, 245n53, 246n55; on the architecture of everyday life, 274n77; on neoliberal institution-building, 21–22; on social theory, 244n47; on the work of religious studies, 269n27
Hutchinson Family Singers, 268n12

identity: and brands, 52; and consumption, 84, 267n7; deflections of (by Reverend Billy), 117; and marketing, 75; national (and psychoanalysis), 68; and rainbow capitalism, 261n33; sexual, 259n22; as social marker, 267n7. *See also* subjectivity
idolatry, 100–102. *See also* gods
Immediate Life, Inc., 156. *See also* Church of Stop Shopping
immigration: and Earth Chxrch, 283n7; and marketing, 130; and Trump, 5, 63. *See also* Immigration and Customs Enforcement (ICE)
Immigration and Customs Enforcement (ICE), 63–64, 149. *See also* immigration

Industrial Workers of the World. *See* Wobblies, the
institutionalization, 154–58
Institutional Review Boards, 270n29
intelligence: as a moral category, 1
interdisciplinarity, 246n59
interiority: expanding, 205; and music, 181; worker, 180
Intermedia Systems Corporation, 112, 222
intersubjectivity, 18, 62, 65, 85, 101, 122, 241n31, 247n63, 253m32; ecological, 28; and ethnography, 162; excessive, 100; and historical knowledge/power, 171; and music, 135, 138, 167; psychic, 85, 88; recursive, 220; and religion, 136. *See also* community; subjectivity

Jackson, Michael, 135, 161–63, 255n38, 266n46, 269n26, 271n41, 272n52, 277n113; on the arts of life, 269n23; eclectic approach of, 246n59; on ethnography, 162, 247n60; on the limits of human understanding, 122; on one's ownness, 269n22; and radical empiricism, 247n60
Jacobs, Jane, 34, 239n18; on scholars and activism, 214
Jakobsen, Janet: on secularism, 119; on sexual politics, 202
Jakobson, Roman: and cybernetics, 223. *See also* cybernetics
James, William, 272n56; on chance, 169
Jameson, Fredric, 239n15; on the consumer system (and desire), 63; and the injunction to always historicize(!), 60; on late-stage capitalism, 279n12. *See also* history
Jay, Martin: on Adorno's idea of "damaged life," 267n8. *See also* Adorno, Theodor
Jobs, Steve, 18
Johnson, Marsha P., 207, 283n4
Johnston, John: on cybernetic discourse, 221. *See also* cybernetics

Jordan, John, 218
Josephson-Storm, Jason Ananda: on nonhuman communication, 216–17. *See also* communication
J.P. Morgan Chase Bank. *See* Chase Bank

Kavanaugh, Brett, 163–64
Kaylor, Brian: on Talen's rhetorical strategies, 116. *See also* Reverend Billy; Talen, William
Kelman, Ari: on music and American Protestantism, 132. *See also* music
Kiefer, Tom: *El Sueño Americano*, 257n2
Kim, David Kyuman: on the melancholy of difference, 79. *See also* difference; melancholy
Klein, Naomi, 46–48, 249n10, 279n16; on brands, 42, 47, 50, 251n20; on capitalism, 211–13; on consumerism, 250n16; on critiques of capitalism, 241; on Starbucks, 46, 48
Koch Foundation, 13
Kristeva, Julia: on the semiotic, 276n92
Kruse, Kevin: on commercial Christianity, 21

labor: as absent (in Dichter's ideology), 75, 88; academic, 144–45, 272n50, 284n17; and freedom, 180; and gender, 270n37; and health, 272n50; and reinvention, 271n47; and religion, 21; and standardization, 251n22, 278n5; and Starbucks, 34, 73. *See also* unions
Lacan, Jacques, 287n38; and cybernetics, 223–24. *See also* cybernetics
lack: and consumption, 81, 89
Lama Foundation, 112–14, 222, 274n84. *See also* Durkee, Barbara; Durkee, Stephen
Lambert, Lake: on retail therapy, 245n48
Lane, Jill: on Reverend Billy and the Church of Stop Shopping, 117; on Times Square, 96

language: and Earth Chxrch, 288n43; and economy, 255n39; and experience, 257n49; vs. music, 139, 168; and participation in the non-human world, 285n26; and power, 222, 288n44; and the subject, 262n40

Lanier, Sidney: and Talen, 106-7. See also Talen, William

Latour, Bruno, 261n39

Leach, William: on American commercial capitalism, 41

Lears, T. J. Jackson: on American commercial capitalism, 41; on the decentered self, 249n8

Lefebvre, Henri: on consumer capitalism, 131, 135, 246n57, 264n15; on the Passion, 240n28

Le Guin, Ursula K., on resistance to capitalism, 173

Lévi-Strauss, Claude: and cybernetics, 223. See also cybernetics

Levitt, Laura: on the living presence of objects, 64

libidinality: and consumer behavior, 258n12; and repression, 78

Life on the Water, 106

lifestyle: brand as, 47, 52; vs. life itself, 185; and marketing, 41

listening: of academics, 285n19; to the Earth, 197; and singing, 167

Litwin, George: on USCO, 112. See also USCO

Lofton, Kathryn, 17–18, 160, 244n47, 246n57; on consumer practice, 97, 267n8, 275n91; "consuming religion," 4–6, 52, 59, 84, 161, 179, 195, 213, 225, 228, 243n43, 259n15, 268n16, 269n27, 284n16, 288n42; on consumption as loss, 88; on corporate capitalism, 67–68, 190; on religion and economy, 18, 111; on religion and materiality, 99; on the sacred and the profane, 119; on scholarship and world-making ritual, 20

logo, 41, 59, 254n35; as lover, 11, 97, 177; Starbucks, 7, 35–36, 38–39, 45, 55, 257n47

Long, Charles: on religion, 150–51, 157, 210; on Schleiermacher's thought, 147

loss, 101; and agency, 87; and consumerism/capitalism, 76, 85, 274n77; and community, 88; and melancholia, 84; and music (as balm/outlet), 86–88, 167, 205; and normativity, 80; and subjectivity, 80, 84–85. See also death

love: and the Church of Stop Shopping, 158; images of (in the consumer age), 203; and life, 151–52; as masking destruction, 187

Lovelock, James: Gaia theory, 223–24

Lukács, György, 241n29

Lury, Celia: on branding, 42–43, 253n31, 254nn35–36, 268n21; on consumption and interactivity, 59; on marketing, 51; on the performativity of branding, 57

Lynch, Patrick: and actions by the Church of Stop Shopping, 241n30. See also police brutality

Maathi, Wanghari, 218

magic: and advertising, 263; and the Church of Stop Shopping, 214; and ethnography, 245; and the fashion industry, 184; and religion/science, 17, 214

Mandamin, Josephine "Water Walker," 218

mania, 203–6. See also melancholia/melancholy

Marcus, George: on fast capitalism, 2. See also capitalism

marketing, 17–18, 51, 258n10; and abstraction, 62; and AI, 287n40; and the "Americanization" of immigrants, 130; and/to children, 77, 82–83, 86; and choice, 11, 69–70, 137; and desire, 41, 69; and lifestyle, 41; and meaning, 279n13; and power, 76; and psychoanalysis, 26–27, 67–77, 81–85, 203, 249n8; and ritualization, 74–77; and social action, 40. See also advertising

Martin, Trayvon, 65, 242n37
Marx, Karl, 70, 99–100, 136, 241n29, 245n53, 270n28; on capitalism, 228
Marxism, existential, 23–24, 241n31, 245n53, 246n59, 277n113
masks: and the Church of Stop Shopping, 190–94, 197; and COVID-19, 2; manipulation of (by Talen), 105. *See also* costumes
Masuzawa, Tomoko, 16
Mata, Roberto, 276n93
materiality: and the human condition, 64–65; and religion, 99
McGinty, Derrick: and the Church of Stop Shopping, 153
McTighe, Laura, 284n18
me: time, 75; too, 164
Mead, Margaret: and cybernetics, 223; and Dichter, 74, 259n16, 286n35. *See also* cybernetics; Dichter, Ernest
mediation: and consumption, 83; and the Church of Stop Shopping, 163; and the economy, 255n39; and the human condition, 64–65; of private experience, 278n7
megachurches, 173–74
melancholia/melancholy, 27; and capitalism, 85–90; and difference, 79–80; and loss, 84; and mania, 203–6
Melquist, Heather: on "screen Christianity," 289n46
memory: and advertising, 86; and artefacts, 64; of bodily assault, 164; and the body, 36, 57; commoditized, 6; and consumerism, 66, 86, 130–31, 196–97; and consumption, 36, 203; as disruptive (to brands), 36; memorialization, 282n40, 282n44; and music, 129–31, 267n4; recovered, 197, 261n35; ritualized, 64–65; and social change, 183. *See also* nostalgia
Mickey Mouse, 95, 115; as the Antichrist (for Reverend Billy), 103, 121, 177. *See also* Disney

Mills, C. W., 277n113
Minnie Mouse: crucifixion of, 95–98, 115. *See also* Disney
misrecognition, 50, 110, 250n18, 251n19
Moeran, Brian: on the fashion industry, 184–85. *See also* fashion
monoculture, 34, 42, 54, 96, 115, 204–5
Moodie, Deonnie, 284n13
Moreton, Bethany, 17, 56, 145, 273n68; and Freedom University, 284n18; on the rational individual, 46; on the soul of neoliberalism, 20–21, 46, 240n26, 246n54
Moses, Robert, 239n18
motivation research, 43, 67–77, 83, 176. *See also* Dichter, Ernest; marketing
mourning, 79; and the Church of Stop Shopping, 24, 89, 194, 206, 208, 282n44. *See also* death
Mulvaney, Dylan, 255n42
music, 134–35, 181, 268n19; and agency, 87, 267n5, 272n61; background, 87; and the body, 135, 151; and capitalism, 263n8; commercial, 130–31, 267n4, 267n6; and community, 87–88, 129, 132–33, 138–39; as defense, 183; and desire, 131; as felt, 272n62; film, 129, 135; and intersubjectivity, 135, 138, 167; vs. language, 139, 168; and (dealing with) loss, 86–88, 167, 205; and memory, 129–31, 267n4; playlists (presidential and papal), 129–30; popular, 132–33, 136, 239n16, 268nn14–15; and rationality, 268n19; and religion, 8, 132, 134–36, 181; and remote collaboration, 270n36; and ritual, 55–56, 267n1; and the sacred, 132; and shopping, 7–8; and the Starbucks Experience, 46, 48–50, 55–56, 253n29. *See also* singing; sound
musical agency, 28, 87, 129–37, 139, 168, 181, 189, 272n61. *See also* agency; music
Musk, Elon, 279n18. *See also* space colonization
Musselman, Cody, 215

narrative: and the body, 9; and branding, 52, 269n22; and consumerism, 102, 104, 135; and ethnography, 162; and organizing, 107
Neely, Jordan, 282n40
negativity, 10, 61, 241n29
Negri, Antonio, 138
new animisms, 124–25. *See also* animisms
new management (of contemporary business), 266n48
New Sanctuary Coalition: and the Church of Stop Shopping, 63
new spirit of capitalism, 180. *See also* capitalism
New York City, 6, 10, 239nn17–18; branding of, 96, 239n17; diversity of, 167; as religious, 97; subway system, 263n2; Times Square, 96–97, 108, 281n34. *See also* gentrification; Hudson Yards
Non-Fungible Tokens (NFT), 281n31
Nooruddeen, Shaykh Abdullah. *See* Durkee, Stephen
normativity, 60–61, 79, 80, 200, 245n53, 253n32, 261n36, 263n7, 285n20; and loss, 80
norms, 61, 76, 78–79, 81–85, 200, 259n21; and change, 83–84; and consumption, 260n26; and hip-hop, 133; and the patriarchy, 240n26; and repression, 78
nostalgia, 6, 99, 101, 103, 125; and advertising, 86; and consumerism, 250n12; and music, 129, 267n4. *See also* memory
NYC (dis)Order of Sisters, 274n76. *See also* New York City

Obama, Barack, 153; musical playlist of, 129. *See also* music
objectification: of persons, 44, 100, 111, 115; self-, 126
Occupy Wall Street, 13, 121, 196, 242n37, 251n20, 260n29, 275n89
Okoumou, Patricia: monumental protest of, 5, 238n10

Oliphant, Elayne: on cultural Catholicism, 268n20; on the privilege of the unmarked, 263n7
orientation: political, 153–54; religion as, 150–51, 157
Orsi, Robert, 92, 174, 269n24, 277n113, 288n45; on class and scholarship, 51; on the "gods," 269n25; on history, 249n11; on real presence, 136; on religious subjectivity, 136; on the scientific study of religion, 243n44; on temporal "braiding," 276n98
Osteen, Joel, 173
Otto, Rudolph, 16

Packard, Vance: on Dichter's methods, 69, 72–73. *See also* Dichter, Ernest
Palestine: Israeli occupation of, 252n26
Parra, Violeta: "Los Pueblos Americanos," 196
Passion play, 9, 240n28
Paterson Silk Strike, 284n17
Pellegrini, Ann: on the leakiness of performance, 105; on secularism, 119
performativity, 11, 26, 200, 212, 218–28, 274n79, 279n20; and agency, 59; and branding, 76, 102, 134, 161–62, 252n23, 255n37; and the Church of Stop Shopping, 210; and consumption, 247n63, 253n32, 260n28; and cybernetics, 220–28, 286n37, 288n42; and difference, 80, 162, 255n39; gender, 60–61, 253n32; and history, 60–61; vs. performance, 154, 226; and psychoanalysis, 67; and queer theory, 253n32; and repetition, 57–58, 61, 80, 198; and ritualization, 56–62; and social action, 188–90; and social media, 148; and sexuality, 256n45; and visuality, 134
Perucci, Tony: on Reverend Billy's cash register exorcism, 38–39. *See also* Reverend Billy
Phelps, Fred: 153–54

Pietz, William: on the fetish, 99–100, 124. *See also* race/racism
Pine II, B. Joseph, 286n32
place: and activism, 185; public vs. private space, 182–83, 242n37; religious, 5–6
pleasure principle, 71. *See also* Freud, Sigmund
police brutality, 164, 241n30, 242n37, 242n37
Pope, Liston, 244n46
Poster, Mark: on Foucault's thought and the digital age, 262n40
posthumanism, 281n38
post-religious religious: Church of Stop Shopping as, 7, 27–28, 199, 208, 227, 275n88, 281n37, 263n4, 275n88
post-secular capitalism, 126, 135, 137, 151, 173–89, 202–4, 213–18, 246n54, 247n62, 265n33, 268n21, 269n22, 288n42; vs. the post-secular, 247n62; as reenchanted, 113. *See also* capitalism; capitalism, new spirit of; religion: and the economy; secular, the; secular capitalism
power: activist vs. scholarly ideas of, 91; of brands, 46; Butler on, 26–27, 77–85, 88, 90, 160–61, 203, 259n20; and capitalism, 3; and citation, 90; of consumers, 82; of the Earth, 122; and experience, 59; generativity of, 219; and the individual, 262n40; and language, 222; and marketing, 76; of music, 88; psychic life of, 77–85; and social theory, 91; and truth, 60
preachers' kids, 87, 171, 173
Prejean, Sister Helen, 140
privatization, 75–76
psychoanalysis, 67–85; and marketing, 26–27, 67–77, 81–85, 203, 249n8; and national identity, 68; and public relations, 185–86. *See also* Freud, Sigmund
Puar, Jasbir, 255n42
public relations, 68–69, 185–86
public vs. private space, 182–83. *See also* place

Pussy Riot: and the Church of Stop Shopping, 3

Queer Liberation March: and the Church of Stop Shopping, 13, 201, 207
Queer Nation, 255n42

Raboteau, Albert: on slave spirituals, 132
race/racism: and American democracy, 164–65, 276n93; and the Church of Stop Shopping, 144, 148, 282n40; and climate catastrophe, 195; and existential transcendence, 277n107; and the fetish, 99–100; and the First Amendment, 149–50; and the form of capitalism, 257n3, 287n2; historicity of, 284n24; and queer memorialization, 282n44; and regimes of truth, 250n13. *See also* white supremacy
Rappaport, Roy, 280n26
rationality, 46, 174–77, 179, 194, 210–11, 215, 221, 248nn64–65, 281n30; and the body, 177–78, 272n66; and the Church of Stop Shopping, 248n64; and music, 268n19. *See also* reason
Reagan, Ronald, 6, 133
reason: and abstraction, 101, 264n13, 104–5. *See also* rationality
redemptive hegemony, 52–54, 90, 113, 260n28. *See also* Bell, Catherine
refusal: of abstraction, 165; of consumer capitalism, 198, 204–5; to identify with any discourse, 226; of mediation, 103–4; of professionalism, 143, 271n44
Rehman, Jan, 274n81
religion: and activism, 120; and capitalism, 16–22, 40, 174–77, 180, 191; capitalism as, 68; and the Church of Stop Shopping, 137; and community, 137, 212; and consumerism, 45, 284n116; and consumption, 246n57; "dark green," 209–10; and the economy, 18, 111, 212; and exclusiveness, 157; fighting (with

religion), 181; and freedom, 131, 137; as hermeneutic, 224n6; as historically mediated non-essential term, 226; implicit, 134–35, 215, 285n25; and irrationality, 174; and labor, 21; and materiality, 99; and music, 8, 132, 134–36, 181; as orientation, 150–51; as performance community, 137; and political economy, 5; and place, 5–6; primitive, 124; scientific study of, 243n44; vs. the secular, 118–21; as social organization, 17, 244n47 and transformation, 213. *See also* consuming religion

religious activism, 120. *See also* activism; religion

repetition: and branding, 40, 53, 161; and capitalism, 34, 36–39, 80, 204; and Catholic Mass, 48; and choirs, 189; and consumerism, 138, 159, 198, 200; and expectation, 61; and Freudian psychoanalysis, 76, 196; and monoculture, 34; and performativity, 57–58, 61, 80, 198; personalized, 90; and ritual, 58, 61, 76, 80; and social media, 61; as teacher, 53; and work songs, 165; vs. the "zero," 198

retail therapy, 245n48

Reverend Billy, 8–12, 105–11, 163–64, 279n19, 285n22; on abstraction, 165; absurdism of, 281n34; on the academe, 213; on American exceptionalism, 21; anger of, 35, 197; arrests of, 156, 201, 208, 240n28; on Buckel, 186; on capitalism, 67–68, 180; on celebrities, 4, 12, 283n5; on chain stores, 34; as character, 27, 102–5, 117, 120, 154, 179, 215; on the Church of Stop Shopping, 238n10; on commodities, 209; on the commons, 182–83; on consumers/consumerism, 39, 44, 59, 77, 179–80, 187, 197, 202–3, 208; on COP 26, 197; on corporate songs, 162; on corporate storytelling, 264n13; on the COVID-19 pandemic, 286n28; on death, 197; on disasters (and barter economies), 286n30; on Disney, 103–4, 125; on being Earth, 86, 122, 125; and Earth Chxrch, 208, 210, 282n2; on (local) ecological destruction, 279n15; on everyday / "ghost" gestures, 10, 36, 40; exorcisms of, 38–40, 45, 104, 115, 178, 188–89; on Extinction, 165; on the "Fabulous Unknown," 264n14; on Freud, 196; on funding for the Church of Stop Shopping, 155; on gender/sexual politics, 256n44; on gifts, 280n27; on the (endangered) honeybee, 242n25; on human life (as irreducible), 64; humor of, 63; as icon, 285n24; and improvisation, 139; on iPod ads, 18–19; on liberation, 134; on life and possibility, 1; on love, 151, 203; on the marginalized/exploited, 88; mayoral run of, 13, 36, 242n36; meeting Savitri D, 170, 277n110; on the monoculture, 34, 54, 204–5; on Neely's murder, 282n40; on New York City, 96–97; on the Passion play, 240n28; performativity of, 66; on personal transformation, 12, 85–86; on police brutality, 164; on the porousness of human beings, 111, 124; on preachers' kids, 87; privilege of, 274n82; on progressive Christianity, 22; on rediscovering experience, 62; on religion and capitalism, 20, 179–80; and repair, 101; resonance of (more broadly), 215, 265n25; on saints, 243n41; on scientism, 122; on secular time, 102; on security (private vs. state), 10; on shopping and belonging, 8; sincerity of, 102–3, 108–11, 116, 118, 174, 178–79, 186, 199, 227, 281n37, 247n61, 281n37; spiritual values of, 266n43; on Starbucks, 33–34, 36–39, 43, 45, 53–56, 73–74, 252n26; and soul-saving, 33, 46, 111, 242n33; on those who stand in their way, 264n17; as wedding officiant, 111, 265n28, 273n69; on the Women's March, 225. *See also* Talen, William

Rice, Tamir, 65
Rise and Resist, 238n10
ritualization, 10, 26, 36, 39–41, 44, 47–54, 57–59, 90, 212, 224, 286n29; and branding, 15, 26, 38–40, 54–57, 90, 115, 137, 140, 250n12, 252n23, 255n37, 257n3; consumer, 4–5, 12, 18, 38, 47, 54–55, 74–77, 80, 89, 98, 100, 104, 130, 133–34, 160, 171, 200–201, 203, 205, 208, 220, 250n17, 252n25, 257n3, 261n31, 265n35, 267n1; and marketing, 74–77; and memory, 64–65; and music, 55–56, 267n1; and performativity, 56–62; and politics, 215; and social interaction, 191, 103; and societal change, 83–84; and solemnity, 191–92, 194; and the university, 144
Rivera, Sylvia: and the Stonewall riot, 282n43
Rollerina, 209
Rose, Nikolas: on governmentality, 258n7; on the "passional economy," 68
Rose, Tricia: on hip-hop, 268n15
roughness: and authenticity, 142; and beauty, 147
Rude Mechanical Orchestra, 64
Rudnyckyj, Daromir, 284n13
*RuPaul's Drag Race*, 183. *See also* drag
Rushkoff, Douglas, 219

Said, Edward, 138–39, 270n33
Samaritan's Purse: and actions by the Church of Stop Shopping, 201, 240n26
sameness: and consumerism, 53, 61, 76, 138, 165; and difference, 51–54, 58, 61, 138, 198–200, 204, 219, 255n39. *See also* convention; difference
Samuel, Lawrence: on Dichter, 73; on Freud and the American story, 68–69, 72. *See also* Dichter, Ernest
Sánchez, Abel, 132
Sartre, Jean-Paul, 144, 241n31, 246n59, 248n64, 274n77, 277n113, 279n16

Savitri D, 111–18, 248n5, 273n70, 279n19, 285n22; on abstraction, 165; on academics, 116, 140; on activism, 122, 141; on art and social justice, 64; and Black Lives Matter, 281n35; on capitalism, 3, 35, 180, 207; and Carnival 4 David, 271n48; and the Church of Stop Shopping Choir, 11, 27–28, 35, 115, 121, 138–39, 149–51, 156–57, 178, 189, 196, 206, 270n37, 272n57, 274n84; on community, 158; on consumerism, 39, 58, 77, 187, 196, 204–5; on corporate rule, 35, 207; on corporate songs, 162; on being one with the Earth, 86; on Earth Chxrch's free store for immigrants, 283n7; on (local) ecological destruction, 279n15; on ecumenicism, 274n84; on Extinction, 165; on her father's conversion, 114; feminist politics of, 271n40; on Freud, 196; on gender/sexual politics, 256n44; on gifts, 280n27; on the Israeli occupation of Palestine, 252n26; on her legacy, 123; on love, 151; on the marginalized/exploited, 88; meeting Reverend Billy, 170, 277n110; on the monoculture, 34, 42; podcasts of, 13–14, 187; and political ecology, 27, 90, 111–18, 141, 211, 261n35; privilege of, 274n82; on progressive Christianity, 22; on religious ecumenism, 274n84; on Reverend Billy, 107, 111; on Samaritan's Purse, 201; on security (private vs. state), 10; on sermons, 159; on singing/music, 129, 138–39, 146–47, 165, 211, 240n20; on social media, 142; on those who stand in their way, 264n17; and veiling, 266n37; and the voice, 145. *See also* Church of Stop Shopping
Schechner, Richard, 286n32; on performances, 279n20
Schleiermacher, Friedrich: on the Christian community, 147
Schmidt, Leigh Eric: on the commercialization of Christmas, 240n23

Schneider, Rebecca: on Butler's idea of performativity, 58–59. *See also* Butler, Judith
scholarship: and activism, 213–18, 245n51, 249n10, 287n39; and capitalism, 14–23, 212; and ecological justice, 284n15; and listening, 285n19; and organizing, 20; and politics, 267n9. *See also* ethnography
Schor, Juliet, 183; and consumer agency, 246n57
Schultz, Howard, 46–47, 252n26. *See also* Starbucks
Schwarzkopf, Stefan: on Dichter's Freudianism, 71. *See also* Dichter, Ernest
Searle, John, 253n33
secular, the: and capitalism, 245n53; and freedom, 119, 131, 136–37; vs. religion, 118–21, 250n16, 256n44; and the scientific method, 243n44. *See also* post-secular capitalism; secular capitalism
secular capitalism, 7, 104. *See also* capitalism; capitalism, new spirit of; post-secular capitalism; secular, the
September 11 attacks, 97, 110, 125, 150, 158
sexuality, 21, 201, 146; and performativity, 256n45. *See also* homophobia
Shepherd, Simon: on performance, 189, 280n24. *See also* performativity
Shiva, Vandana, 218
Shopocalypse, 13, 23, 27, 89, 121, 124–25, 174, 206, 227, 288n42
silence: and death, 196; enforced, 104; momentary, 196; vast, 114
Simon, Bryant: on brands, 251n20; on Starbucks, 52–53, 250n18, 253n27. *See also* Starbucks
Simone, Nina: "Blackbird," 147
sincerity: of the Church of Stop Shopping, 123; of Reverend Billy, 102–3, 108–11, 116, 118, 174, 178–79, 186, 199, 227, 281n37, 247n61, 281n37

Singh, Devin, 215
singing: as antidote to capitalism, 211, 240n20; and activism, 7–9, 132, 146–47, 278n10; and community, 129, 138–39, 165, 167–68; drone, 267n6; and listening, 167. *See also* Church of Stop Shopping: Choir; music
Sisters of Perpetual Indulgence, 109–10, 153, 179
Situationist International, 263n9, 264n11, 264n15
Sliwa, Curtis, 273n73
smiles: knowing (of Disney dolls), 96; as workforce requirement, 2
Smith, J. Z.: on ritual, 75. *See also* ritualization
Snyder, Gary, 218
social Christianity, 21–22
socialization, 10, 52, 68, 78–79, 145, 191, 193, 228, 241n32, 247n60, 259n21, 260n26, 262n42; consumer, 86; and gender, 82
social media, 228; academic, 148; as citational, 288n44; and context-distortion, 142; and data-collection, 51; influencers, 61, 146, 194, 255n42
social theory, 90–92, 244n47, 262n42, 284n12
Solomon, Alisa: on Reverend Billy and the Church of Stop Shopping, 117, 137
soul: vs. body, 17; consumer, 63–92; of neoliberalism, 20, 46, 67, 202, 246n54; of products, 70
soul-craft, 3–4, 9, 56, 66, 76, 85, 120, 178
sound, 267n1; and deafness, 149; and the subway, 263n2. *See also* music
space colonization, 187, 279n18
spectacle: and smell, 7–8
spirituality, 117, 167; "left," 274n80; nature, 216, 286n27; workplace, 245n50
Sprinkle, Annie, 146
Standing Rock protests, 13, 121, 242n37

Starbucks, 12, 52–53, 131, 160, 248n1, 248n5, 252nn25–26, 253nn27–30; and actions by the Church of Stop Shopping, 3, 26, 33–62, 73–74, 86, 159, 173, 178, 204–5; and control, 253n27; Experience, 45–50, 55–56, 250n18; furniture, 53; hypocrisy of, 253n28; and labor, 34, 73; logo (mermaid), 7, 35–36, 38–39, 45, 55, 257n47; and misrecognition, 250n18; and music, 46, 48–50, 55–56, 253n29; and political correctness, 47, 49; and repetition, 35–36, 39; on Reverend Billy, 33; and ritualization, 191; as "third place" (between home and work), 257n47; and unions, 55, 252n26, 257n47

Stewart, Francis: on implicit religion, 134–35, 285n25

Stoller, Paul, 263n5

Stonewall riot, 282n43

Stop Shopping Church. *See* Church of Stop Shopping

St. Ville, Susan: on performativity, 57–58. *See also* performativity

subjectivity, 219; and agency, 51; and branding/marketing, 22, 35, 41, 44, 48–49, 51–52, 75, 77, 80–85, 249n11, 252n23; and capitalism, 91, 162; economic, 176–78; and the Fourteenth Amendment, 257n3; and loss, 80, 84–85; and music, 267n5; religious, 136; and religious studies, 22. *See also* identity; intersubjectivity

subjunctive, the, 193–94, 198, 201, 205, 210

subversion, 251n20; and Freudian ideas, 89; of meaning, 278n9

suicide, 274n77; mass, 125; as protest, 186, 279n14; and the Vessel, 237n6. *See also* death

Summer, Donna: "I Feel Love," 152

Surin, Kenneth: on the Derridian system, 276n95. *See also* Derrida, Jacques

Talen, William, 3–4, 12, 27, 105, 111; on acting, 106–7; on American society, 109; on the climate crisis, 123; formative years of, 96, 103–11, 143, 164, 265n21; on Jesus, 109; on the NYC subway system, 263n2; podcasts of, 13–14, 187; radio show of, 14; and "reverse mentors," 105–6, 108, 154. *See also* Church of Stop Shopping; Reverend Billy

Tambiah, Stanley, 245n49

Target: and LGBT issues, 255n42

Taylor, Bron: on "dark green religion," 209–10. *See also* religion

Taylor, Diana: on the Church of Stop Shopping, 116

temporality: beings-in-time, 269n22; capitalist time, 76, 200; commoditized time, 104; and consumerism, 197; and logos, 254n35; "me time," 75; and morality/ethics, 288n41; and ritual, 65; secular, 102, 104; secular-Christian, 263n1

theater, 161–62: motivational (of consumption), 70; political, 107–8; and religion, 106–7; retail, 12

Thoreau, Henry David: nature spirituality of, 286n27. *See also* spirituality

Thrift, Nigel, 120

Till, Emmett, 65

Tolan, Michael, 106

transcendence, 277n107

transformation, 197; and branding, 44, 269n22; personal, 12, 85–86, 221; and religion, 213; and singing, 138

trash worship, 37

Trump, Donald, 202; as NFT hawker, 281n31; treatment of immigrants, 5, 63

Trump Tower: and actions by the Church of Stop Shopping, 34, 140–41, 145

Turner, Fred: on cybernetic discourse, 220–21. *See also* cybernetics

Turner, Mark: on creativity, 250n12

Turner, Victor, 75, 116
Tylor, E. B.: on primitive religion, 124

UBS, 12; and climate change, 188
unions, 67; and Amazon, 13; and Appalachian miners, 21; and Starbucks, 55, 252n26, 257n47. *See also* labor
USCO, 112–13

Vaca, Daniel: on American Evangelicalism as commercial religion, 20; on capitalism's commitment to efficiency, 261n36, 278n2
value: creation of (via proclamation), 184; and institutionalization, 155; "mysticism of," 40; real, 100; social (and capital), 60
Veblen, Thorstein: on consumption, 241n32. *See also* consumption
veiling, 266n37
Vessel, 4, 6, 237n6, 239n14. *See also* Hudson Yards; suicide
voice, the: and the body, 145; and the psyche, 79. *See also* singing

walking, 182; in the City, 1–2. *See also* flâneur
Walmart: and actions by the Church of Stop Shopping, 3, 12
Walsh, Marty, 185
Wanamaker, John: store/cathedral (and grandest organ) of, 238n13
Weber, Max, 28, 99, 105, 219, 245n48, 278n2, 281n30; on art and politics, 143; on capitalism, 16–17, 174–77, 180, 202, 243n44, 248n65; on the entrepreneur, 274n81; on ideal types, 224; on the institutionalization of religious energies, 155; on music, 134, 181, 268n19; on rationalization of a way of life, 156; on religion, 134, 175; and the United States, 176, 244n45

Weiner, Isaac: on sonic experience, 132
West, Cornel, 270n33; on Michel Foucault's interventions, 276n106; and the musical lens for agency, 139; on justice and pleasure, 273n72; on white supremacy, 272n64. *See also* agency; music
Westboro Baptist Church, 153–54. *See also* homophobia
Weston, Kath, 163, 261n39; on the ethnographer's notational field, 19; on Freud and consumer capitalism, 76; on indigenous cultures, 266n42; on new animisms, 124–25; on performativity, 60–61, 81, 253n32, 256n45; on the "zero," 197–98
*What Would Jesus Buy?*, 3, 109, 153–54, 173, 275n89, 277n112
white supremacy, 196, 272n64. *See also* race/racism
Whitman, Walt, 276n93; racist ideology of, 164–65, 277n107
Whyte, William H.: on the "organizational man," 265n35
Wiener, Norbert: on the American military, 223; and cybernetics, 286n31. *See also* cybernetics
Wilcox, Melissa: on "religionfuck," 119, 122; on serious parody, 179; on Sisters of Perpetual Indulgence and Reverend Billy, 109–10, 179. *See also* Sisters of Perpetual Indulgence; Reverend Billy
Williams, John, 129, 135. *See also* music
Winfrey, Oprah, 14, 269n22
Winters, Joseph, 133
Wobblies, the, 108, 264n16
Women with a Vision, 284n18
Wonder, Stevie: "Sir Duke," 151; *Songs in the Key of Life*, 162
Woolworth Building, 6, 238n13
Woolworth, Frank W., 238n13. *See also* Woolworth Building
Worth, Jess, 218

Yeats, William Butler: "The Second Coming," 65–66
Yes Men, 108
Young, Neil: and the Church of Stop Shopping, 3; and the farmworkers movement, 132

Zaretsky, Eli: on American Freudianism, 68
Zito, Angela: on the social body, 145, 250n17
Žižek, Slavoj, 140
Zwingli, Ulrich: on the Eucharist wafer, 283n9

ABOUT THE AUTHOR

GEORGE GONZÁLEZ is Assistant Professor of Sociology and Religion and Culture at the CUNY Graduate Center and Baruch College, City University of New York. His primary research and teaching interests focus on the entanglements, co-constitutions, and critiques of American religion and capitalism within empirical cases: contemporary business management, advertising, grassroots social justice activism, professional discourses, and the everyday lives of workers.

www.ingramcontent.com/pod-product-compliance
Lightning Source LLC
Chambersburg PA
CBHW031139020426
42333CB00013B/439